TOWARD RESPECTFUL UNDERSTANDING & WITNESS AMONG MUSLIMS

TOWARD RESPECTFUL UNDERSTANDING & WITNESS AMONG MUSLIMS

Essays in Honor of
J. Dudley Woodberry

Evelyne A. Reisacher
GENERAL EDITOR

Joseph L. Cumming
Dean S. Gilliland
Charles E. Van Engen
ASSOCIATE EDITORS

WILLIAM CAREY
LIBRARY

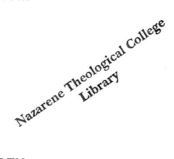

Published by William Carey Library
1605 E. Elizabeth St.
Pasadena, CA 91104 | www.missionbooks.org

Brad Koenig, copyeditor
Francesca Gacho, editor
Rose Lee-Norman, indexer
Hugh Pindur, graphic designer

William Carey Library is a ministry of the U.S. Center for World Mission
Pasadena, CA | www.uscwm.org
16 15 14 13 12 5 4 3 2 1 BP 1000
Printed in the United States of America

Library of Congress Cataloging-in-Publication Data
Toward respectful understanding and witness among Muslims: essays in honor of J. Dudley Woodberry / edited by Evelyne A. Reisacher; associate editors, Joseph L. Cumming, Dean S. Gilliland & Charles E. Van Engen.
p. cm.
Includes bibliographical references and index.
ISBN 978-0-87808-018-2 (alk. paper)
1. Missions to Muslims. 2. Christianity and other religions--Islam. 3. Islam--Relations--Christianity. I. Woodberry, John Dudley, 1934- II. Reisacher, Evelyne A.
BV2625.T69 2011
261.2'7--dc23

2011039488

DEDICATION

To a world-class scholar of Islamic Studies
for his groundbreaking research, his dedication to teaching,
his seminal contribution to Christian mission in the Muslim world,
and his profound role in fostering healthy Muslim-Christian relations.

Contents

Foreword

BY DAVID W. SHENK

"On the highway approaching Mecca, there is a barrier across the road with a sign stating: No Non Muslim Permitted Beyond this Point."

Dudley Woodberry was preaching at the concluding Communion and commissioning service of the 1976 Consultation on Muslim Evangelization in Glen Eyrie, Colorado. This was my first acquaintance with Dudley.

He continued, "In the sacrifice of Jesus the Lamb of God on the cross, the barriers are brought down. We are forgiven and all are welcome to the table of the Lord!"

I learned later that Dudley scrawled the notes for that sermon late at night on the floor of his sleeping abode with the light of a flashlight so as not to disturb his roommate, as he struggled with jet lag from his flight from Arabia. He was an activist who at that time, with his wife, Roberta, was committed to relationship building even within the Arabian heartland; he has modeled an approach and spirit that has helped to form me. In my global travels I meet people who have likewise been influenced by Dudley's Christian engagement with Muslims.

This remarkable book is an appropriate tribute to Dudley's legacy as a scholar, writer, missionary, pastor, traveler, teacher, and friend. There have been enormous transformations in the half-century since he first ventured into a Middle Eastern engagement with Muslims as a short-term agriculturalist with the American Friends Service Committee in Lebanon. This book is forward-looking, identifying these transformations while providing foundational insights into the opportunities and challenges before us as we seek to bear faithful witness to Jesus among Muslims during these opening decades of the twenty-first century. At a time when books abound that nurture un-Christian thinking about Muslims, this book refreshingly encourages a spirit of Christlike engagement with Muslims.

The introductory biography of Dudley's life provides remarkable tone and perspective to the entire book. Apostles to Muslims are men and women formed by providential circumstance and the Spirit of God for ministry. Dudley's childhood in China, separation from parents during the war, preservation of his life on several occasions, providential interventions, academic and ministry opportunities as a young man, marriage to Roberta, the open doors within the heartland of Islam, the academic engagements in North America and around the world; this journey in ministry among Muslims and on behalf of Muslims has been of God!

I like this book! I am writing this foreword during several weeks of engagements in The Gambia and Burkina Faso. I have read the manuscript en route. Much of the book is exceedingly pertinent to the church and Islam in the West African context in which I am immersed for these several weeks. The testimonies in church these past two Sundays have told about the triumph of Christ over the gods, occult, and spirits; that is what Dean Gilliland, Stephen Sesi, and Caleb Kim describe in their essays on popular Islam. As I listened to people's testimonies, I have heard further elaboration of David Greenlee's comments on ways the gospel really is good news for Muslims. In a meeting with church leaders, contextualization issues dominated the discussion, a theme that Phil Parshall so ably discusses in his chapter. Late one evening we discussed people movements with the team in The Gambia; John Travis writes about that. We sought to discern why such movements happen elsewhere but are not happening in The Gambia. This book is relevant!

The book is in three sections: Encouraging Friendly Conversation, Christian Scholarship, and Christian Witness, with five chapters in each section. These well-written chapters probe the key issues with insight and scholarly depth. I will pull this resource from my shelf again and again, for the issues addressed speak directly into my day-by-day engagement with Muslims. For example, Martin Accad's chapter urges a kerygmatic rather than a dialogical or polemical approach in bearing witness among Muslims. I find that exceedingly helpful, especially after taking the Test of Attitudes toward Muslims that Accad has developed. That is what I like about this book. It is scholarship united with practicality.

Each chapter is a trove of insights, as for example the presentation on Ishmael. Several years ago I heard Jonathan Culver teaching a seminar in Indonesia on this theme. The audience was captivated by his presentation. His chapter further elaborates the themes he has so effectively developed within the Indonesian context. Equally significant is the chapter on Allah by Rick Brown. I suppose that in every seminar I present on Islam, someone raises a hand to say, "Allah is a demon and not the God of Abraham." The editors rightfully included a chapter addressing this exceedingly significant issue. This is solid scholarship looking at the Christian influences in Arabia at the time of Muhammad, the archaeological finds, and linguistic analysis. These chapters will become foundational for me in seminars on Islam.

Space does not permit me to comment extensively on each chapter. But the key challenges and opportunities for bearing witness among Muslims are presented: an excellent chapter on ethics and Shari^{c}a with David Johnston; disturbing and intriguing insights on gender issues by Evelyne Reisacher; the ebullient hopefulness of Joseph Cumming. A book such as this would be incomplete without our elder, Bishop Kenneth Cragg, offering his insightful, scholarly, poetic tone which so many of us have come to appreciate and which has been formative to a couple generations of disciples of Jesus among Muslims.

Opportunities for sharing Christ, which current trends in Islam open before us, are identified by Warren Larson. It will surprise some to discover that Islamic jihad movements often open the doors to the gospel, for many are revolted by the activities of the militants. In dramatic contrast to the spirit of militancy, Christine Mallouhi writes about peacemaking as witness. We cannot share Jesus with Muslims if we are not living in peace with Muslims! That is Dudley and Roberta's legacy: a couple committed to living and bearing witness to the peace of Christ among Muslims.

It was in the mid-1980s that Dudley and I attended a reception by Muslim and Christian scholars at Hartford Seminary in honor of Bishop Kenneth Cragg. In his response, Bishop Cragg admonished, "It is urgently necessary within the violence and strife of our modern world that a people be present who bear witness that God is most fully revealed in the vulnerable baby born in a manger in Bethlehem, in a refugee in Egypt, in a carpenter in Nazareth, in a wandering rabbi who often had no place to lay his head, and who in his crucifixion cried out, 'Father forgive them.' That witness is healing for the nations."

After the reception, Dudley and I left for our hotel, conversing vigorously about Cragg's response. It was raining lightly, so we walked fast. Then the street became dark and ended in a dead end. We stood there laughing. I had been following Dudley, and he had been following me. Neither of us knew the way to the hotel. Then a stranger appeared. He was also on the way to the hotel, but had taken a detour. He joined us as he helped us find the way.

That event with Dudley has become a parable for me. The Christian calling that Bishop Cragg invited that evening is healing for the nations and for all who receive this good news. Yet on our own, we meet a darkened dead-end street. It is the Stranger who meets us on the Emmaus Road (to note one of the books Dudley has edited) who makes all the difference. He is the Stranger who seeks to form our thinking about Muslims and Islam in his own way.

I like this book! It urges us onward in a Christian walk with and among Muslims.

David W. Shenk
Global Consultant
Eastern Mennonite Missions

Preface

BY C. DOUG MCCONNELL

This volume is the work of a dedicated group of scholars, who like J. Dudley Woodberry, are also seasoned practitioners. We began work on the book in the months before the November 7, 2007 celebration of the life and work of senior professor and dean emeritus Dudley Woodberry by the faculty and friends of Fuller Theological Seminary, School of Intercultural Studies (formerly School of World Mission). It is fitting that this labor of love should have experienced logistical problems, since our beloved colleague has so patiently worked through the maze of logistics while teaching and embracing others in a way that so closely parallels the road Jesus walked. Now that we have completed the book, we can again celebrate by reading the work of each author who was influenced by and an influence in the life of Dudley Woodberry.

During his years as professor and dean at Fuller Seminary, Dudley has combined graciousness, humor, wisdom, and a broad knowledge of missiology. Even in his "retirement," he continues to give wise input on the expansion of our focus on Islamics and our Christian witness to the Muslim world. When asked who will replace Dudley on the faculty, as dean I answered truthfully, "We needed four scholars to cover the areas Dudley began in his tenure."

Beyond his work in establishing the study of Islam, Dudley was an outstanding leader of our school during his years as dean. He managed to build on the work of his predecessor by establishing endowed chairs and a number of programs that are major emphases in our school. Dudley contributed to the maturity of scholarship in our seminary through his knowledge of the Bible, theology, and the dynamics of global engagement. He is also the only dean who worked while standing at his desk or lying on the floor. Being unconventional is a great asset in the world of tweed jackets and messy offices. Above all, Dudley was one of the beloved leaders that have blessed Fuller Seminary.

This Festschrift is a tribute to the remarkable life and thought of our dear colleague, J. Dudley Woodberry, a truly great colleague and friend.

C. Doug McConnell
Provost and Senior Vice President
Fuller Theological Seminary

Preface and Acknowledgments

BY EVELYNE A. REISACHER

A few years ago, Doug McConnell, who was at the time Dean of the School of Intercultural Studies invited me to edit a Festschrift in honor of J. Dudley Woodberry. This project became a collaborative effort when I formed an editorial team with Dean Gilliland, Chuck Van Engen, and Joseph Cumming, all friends and colleagues of Dudley. We quickly came to the agreement that we would let the strengths of Dudley's scholarship provide the conceptual framework for this volume. The three sections of the book parallel the three main emphases of Woodberry's academic and missional life as a professor of Islamic Studies.

The first section entitled "Encouraging Friendly Conversation" focuses on resources for establishing relationships with Muslims and includes articles highlighting various ways of engaging with Muslims from a friendly perspective. This resembles very much Dudley's own approach in his ministry and interactions with Muslims. This section also provides concrete resources for those who want to engage in meaningful encounters with Muslims in the twenty-first century.

The second section entitled "Christian scholarship" provides reflections on how Christians are engaging with Muslims on an academic level. Woodberry is considered a leading Christian scholar of Islam. He has developed one of the largest Islamic study programs at an Evangelical Seminary. Many of today's deans and professors of other evangelical schools of Islamic studies have been trained by Woodberry. We therefore want this book to be a tribute to his impact on Christian leaders around the world. This section also reflects how important it is for Christians to approach the field of Islamic study with academic excellence. Dudley has mentored scores of doctoral students who are now serving in many parts of the world. He is often referred to as a contemporary Samuel Zwemer. Like him, Dudley makes a profound impact on Christian scholarship on Islam.

The third section entitled "Christian Witness" covers major issues currently researched by Christian scholars of Islam and practitioners such as conversion, contextualization, people movements, popular Islam, and peacemaking. It provides a platform for understanding how Christians currently engage in witness to Muslims in words and deeds. This section provides an overview of current trends in mission practices presented by the main theorists of these concepts.

Each section includes five essays by leading Christian scholars in the field of Islamic studies. In the foreword, David Shenk presents in a very eloquent manner the various topics covered in this volume. They are also introduced by a member of the editorial team at the beginning of each section. We have invited each contributing author to write from his/her strength and interests. This provides wonderful resources for readers who want to learn about the current trends in Christian interactions with Muslims, from the perspective of the actual scholars that developed the theories and concepts used in Christian-Muslim engagement. We also believe that this book will be a resource for those who want to know how to "Christianly think about Islam." As such, this would be a new contribution to the field.

We are aware that this Festschrift includes some topics that currently raise heated debates in the mission arena. We included them because Dudley never shied away from addressing difficult issues as long as they could be discussed and evaluated in the light of the Bible, would bring honor to God and strengthen the manifold ministries of the church. Dudley has a strong attachment to the Word of God. He is a cutting edge researcher, who likes to keep the gospel at the center of his academic explorations.

We also realize that some issues are only approached from one angle in this volume. Some readers may feel that their views are not represented. They have not intentionally been left out. The book being a Festschrift focuses on giving the opportunity to colleagues and friends of Dudley to present their appreciation rather than engage in a conversation between authors around one single issue. The value of the book lies not in the fact that it includes a review of all evangelicals' positions on Muslims and Islam but rather presents honest scholarship from researchers who are contributing significantly to the field of Islamic studies and present their latest findings. We hope that those who read the Festschrift will gain first-hand knowledge by meeting, in this volume, original authors of theories that are shaping the missiological debate. With their contributions, and the voices of proponents of differing views outside this volume, we can offer useful resources to the Christian community toward respectful understanding and witness among Muslims.

So many colleagues and friends of Dudley wanted to work on such a volume to express their affection and deep respect for Dudley who is one of the most significant evangelical thinkers of Islam. We could have added more authors from the plethora of former students, colleagues and fellow researchers whom Woodberry has influenced. But we intentionally decided to limit the number of essays so that the book can serve as a reference and perhaps a textbook for seminaries, universities, and mission-training centers. All writers are scholars with a strong connection to the field and to Christian ministries to Muslims. This is why this book is also a reference for mission leaders working in Muslim contexts. Mission organizations will be able to add this book to the list of books for training workers. We also recognize the great contribution of scholars from the Global South to this field of studies. We have included some in this Festschrift and trust that in the coming years, they will probably be the majority voices in the field of Islamic Studies.

In regards to the format of this Festschrift, there are a few matters to underline. The Arabic transliteration follows the guidelines of the *International Journal of Middle East Studies* (IJMES). I chose this journal, because it is Dudley's habit when one of his students inquires about the use of Arabic diacritics to recommend the IJMES's transliteration system. According to this system when an Arabic term is listed in the current unabridged version of the Merriam-Webster dictionary, it should be spelled as it appears there. But there are exceptions that preserve the Arabic letters "*ᶜayn*" and "*hamza*." In accordance with this rule we used for example in this volume the spelling "Qurᵓan" or "Shariᶜa" (these two terms are not italicized, as transliterated Arabic terms usually are, because they appear in the unabridged Merriam-Webster dictionary, but we have preserved the "hamza" in the first term and the "*ᶜayn*" in the second).

We have tried to keep the transliteration system consistent throughout the Festschrift except for a few articles, because we wanted to respect the choice of each author. For example, some preferred to follow the rule that says that when the Arabic definite article "*al-*" precedes a noun starting with a "solar letter" the final "*l*" of the article is dropped and the solar letter is doubled. Other authors did not. We have tried to maintain consistency within a specific chapter rather than throughout the Festschrift. Another example is the transliteration of the proper nouns. We have not adopted a standard way to transliterate them but kept the variations in the transliteration between the various chapters. There are also essays in which Arabic terms have been taken up by other languages. In this case they are rendered without diacritical symbols and we kept the transliteration system adopted by the author. The same is true for other languages like Hebrew or Greek that are used in a few places. We have not changed the system used by the author.

The suras of the Qurᵓan are identified by the transliteration of their Arabic name, followed by the number of the sura, and the verse. Authors have used a variety of different Qurᵓanic translations. We have identified the translations with the references. Likewise, Bible passages are not from the same version throughout this volume. We have given the authors the freedom to use the translation of their choice. The name of the translation is usually indicated after the quotation.

Finally, let us acknowledge a number of people without whom this Festschrift would not have been written and published. A debt of gratitude is owed to Jennifer Orona, Festschrift assistant at Fuller Theological Seminary, who was involved in the early stage of this process, collecting the articles, being in correspondence with the contributors and the publisher, formatting and managing the first round of edits.

The editors also wish to thank the contributors for their scholarship. We were hoping that this project would be completed three years ago. Many contributors had submitted their articles for a 2009 publication. The process was delayed for a number of reasons and the articles were then resubmitted to the contributors, not to be rewritten but so that a few updates could be made.

I am grateful to Doug McConnell, who has encouraged me to prepare this Festschrift. I am also thankful to my colleagues at Fuller who were so supportive during the entire process.

Dean, Chuck, Joseph and myself also want to acknowledge the wonderful, dedicated and very skillful editorial team from William Carey Library. Special thanks to Francesca Gacho, who has given excellent guidance.

This Festschrift is a gift to a treasured colleague and friend. We present it to Dudley as a token of the deep respect, gratitude, and affection with which he is considered by all of the contributors.

Evelyne A. Reisacher
General Editor

Contributing Authors

Martin Accad directs the Institute of Middle East Studies at the Arab Baptist Theological Seminary in Lebanon and teaches Islamic studies both there and at Fuller Theological Seminary in Pasadena. Having grown up in a diversity of cultures and religions in war-torn Beirut, and currently teaching and researching between two continents, his passion is to witness the transformation of relationships between diverse peoples through the model and teaching of Jesus Christ. His PhD at the University of Oxford focused on some of the complex issues of the history of Christian-Muslim relations and he has published numerous articles and chapters on the subject.

Rick Brown has served in the Muslim world since 1977, beginning in Sudan. He has a PhD in biblical studies from London School of Theology, and is a PhD candidate in linguistics at the University of Amsterdam. He has published numerous articles and is currently working on two academic books. His knowledge of Arabic, Hebrew, Aramaic, Syriac, Greek, general linguistics, and ancient church history are all brought to bear in his article on the origins and meaning of the name *Allah*.

Kenneth Cragg is an Anglican bishop noted for his work and scholarship on Christian and Islamic studies. He has worked and served in academic and ecclesiastical posts in Jerusalem, Beirut, Cairo, Nigeria, and the United States. He has also served as the Warden of St. Augustine College in Canterbury. He is retired and currently resides in England.

Jonathan E. Culver obtained his PhD in Cross-Cultural Studies under the tutelage of Dr. Dudley Woodberry and Dr. Charles Van Engen at Fuller Theological Seminary in 2001. During his thirthy years of service in Indonesia, Culver has been involved in Bible translation and the training of cross-cultural workers, as well as teaching and mentoring students in various theological institutions. Jonathan and his wife, Judith, currently reside in Southeast Asia.

Joseph L. Cumming is director of the Reconciliation Program at the Yale Center for Faith and Culture at Yale Divinity School. He also teaches courses in Islamic Studies at Fuller Theological Seminary and is completing his PhD in Islamic Studies and Christian Theology at Yale University. During his fifteen years in Mauritania, one of the poorest nations on earth, he served as director of Doulos Community, a Christian humanitarian organization working in nutrition, public health, agriculture, microcredit, and emergency relief. Joseph and his wife, Michele, a registered nurse, are parents of paternal twins born in June 1992.

Dean S. Gilliland is senior professor of Contextual Theology and African Studies at Fuller's School of Intercultural Studies. After twenty-three years as church planter and head of the Theological College of Northern Nigeria, Dean taught courses in mission theology, Islam, and African Christianity at Fuller for twenty-seven years. He is now retired and lives in Claremont, California.

David H. Greenlee has served since 1977 with Operation Mobilization (OM), and since 1998 as OM's International Research Associate. He is the author of *One Cross, One Way, Many Journeys: Thinking Again about Conversion* (Downer's Grove: InterVarsity, 2007) and editor of *Longing for Community: Church,* Ummah, *or Somewhere in Between* (Pasadena: William Carey Library, forthcoming), *From the Straight Path to the Narrow Way: Journeys of Faith* (Downer's Grove: InterVarsity Press, 2006) and *Global Passion: Marking George Verwer's Contribution to World Mission* (Waynesboro: Authentic Media, 2003). Based in Switzerland, David holds a PhD in Intercultural Studies from Trinity International University in Deerfield, Illinois.

Jared Holton managed the grant, *Conflict Transformation: Creating Collaboration and Reducing Conflict in Muslim-Christian Relations*, directed by Fuller Theological Seminary and Salam Institute, from 2005–2007. He completed Master of Arts degrees in Cross-Cultural Studies and Biblical Studies and Theology from Fuller Theological Seminary.

David L. Johnston served for sixteen years as a pastor and teacher in Algeria, Egypt, and the West Bank. After completing his PhD in Intercultural Studies from Fuller Seminary, he spent five years as a postdoctoral fellow in Islamic Studies and part-time lecturer at Yale University. He now lives with his family in Philadelphia, teaching as an adjunct at the University of Pennsylvania and St. Joseph's University. His essays on contemporary Islam have appeared in several academic journals, and his first book is *Earth, Empire and Sacred Text: Muslims and Christians as Trustees of Creation* (London: Equinox, 2010). His website, humantrustees.org, offers many resources on Islam, globalization, and Muslim-Christian dialogue.

Caleb Chul-Soo Kim has lived and researched in East Africa since 1989. He holds a ThM and PhD from Fuller Theological Seminary. Currently he is associate professor and the director of the PhD program in Intercultural Studies at Nairobi Evangelical Graduate School of Theology, Africa International University. He is also an adjunct professor at Fuller Theological Seminary. Caleb is the author of *Islam among the Swahili in East Africa* (Nairobi: Acton Publishers, 2004) and the editor of *African Missiology: Contributions of Contemporary Thought* (Nairobi: Uzima Publishing House, 2009). He lives in Nairobi with his wife, Manok, and their younger daughter Eunice.

Warren F. Larson is the former director of the Zwemer Center for Muslim Studies at Columbia International University and teaches Islamic Studies. He served as a missionary in Pakistan for twenty-three years and has written extensively about Muslims. His dissertation on how Islamism in Pakistan is paving the way for Christianity was chosen in 1998 as one of the top fifteen books in missiology in the English-speaking world. He and his wife live in South Carolina.

Christine Amal Mallouhi codirects Alkalima, an association producing books in Arabic that seek to explain Christ in culturally relevant ways to the Muslim reader. Alkalima's books are among the best-selling books at International Arab Bookfairs and their commentary, *A Sufi Reading of the Gospel of John* (Beirut: Dar Al Jil, 2004), was cited among the best books of the year in the *Arabic Publishers Journal*. They are also used as textbooks at Arab universities. Al Jazeera television featured a 30-minute program on Christine in the 2005 series, "Friends of the Arabs" for her bridge-building between Muslims and Christians focusing on her books *Waging Peace on Islam* and *Miniskirts, Mothers, and Muslims*. She has lived for thirty plus years in a number of Arab countries and currently lives in Lebanon and Australia.

C. Douglas McConnell assumed the role of provost and senior vice president of Fuller Theological Seminary on July 1, 2011. He joined Fuller in 1999 as associate professor of leadership and was then named dean of the School of Intercultural Studies in 2003, a position he held until his appointment as provost. Dr. McConnell earned his undergraduate degree and teaching credentials at California State University, San Bernardino. He completed his MA in Missiology in 1985 and PhD in Intercultural Studies in 1992 at Fuller. The McConnells spent fifteen years as missionaries in Australia and Papua New Guinea followed by five years as international director of PIONEERS. Prior to coming to Fuller, McConnell was an associate professor and chair of the Department of Missions/Intercultural Studies and Evangelism at Wheaton College. McConnell's publications include *Understanding God's Heart for Children* (editor, WorldVision, 2007) and *The Changing Face of World Missions* (coauthor, Grand Rapids: Baker Academic, 2005).

Phil Parshall and his wife Julie have lived among Muslim peoples since 1962, first with International Christian Fellowship (now SIM) in Bangladesh and then in the Philippines. Presently he is Missionary-at-Large with SIM. He holds a doctorate from Fuller Seminary and has had fellowships with Harvard and Yale Universities. He is published in a number of Christian magazines and has authored nine books on Islam.

Evelyne A. Reisacher obtained her PhD in Islamic Studies under the mentorship of J. Dudley Woodberry. She is currently associate professor of Islamic Studies and Intercultural Relations at Fuller Theological Seminary. She served twenty years as assistant director of L'Ami, a Christian organization providing care to North African immigrants in France. She also assisted in securing the *Conflict Transformation: Creating Collaboration and Reducing Conflict in Muslim-Christian Relations* grant for Fuller. Her current research involves exploring gender issues in Islam, Muslim-Christian relations, world religions and affect regulation across cultures.

Stephen Mutuku Sesi graduated from Fuller Theological Seminary with a PhD in Intercultural Studies in 2003 with a specialization in Islam in Africa and the history of Christian-Muslim Relations. Before God took him to His glory, he served at Africa

International University (earlier known as Nairobi Evangelical Graduate School of Theology) as dean and lecturer in the Mission Studies department (2004–2008) and Dean of the Africa Institute of African Realities (AISAR) until November 2011. Stephen has been involved in many forums of dialogue between Christians and Muslims in Kenya and Lebanon. His publications include three chapters in *African Missiology: Contribution of Contemporary Thought* (Nairobi: Uzima Press, 2009). He had his dissertation published under the title "African Worldview Change: The Case of the Digo of Kenya." Sesi was married to Josephine Katile Mutuku and they had three sons—James, Judah, and Jesse.

David W. Shenk grew up in East Africa and served for sixteen years with Eastern Mennonite Missions (EMM) in ministries among Muslims in Somalia and Kenya. Then for over two decades, he served in missions and academic administration (EMM and Lithuania Christian College). Currently he is global consultant with EMM, with a special focus on the world of Islam. This commitment has taken him to some one hundred countries; he has taught in a dozen academic institutions, mostly internationally; and he has authored or edited fifteen books, mostly related to the challenges of mission and witness within a world of many religions, with special focus on Islam. He is often engaged in dialogue with Muslim theologians and political leaders and is committed to peacemaking in the way of Christ. David and his wife, Grace, live in the Lancaster area of Pennsylvania.

John Jay Travis and family have had the privilege of living in Muslim communities in Asia for more than twenty years. John frequently lectures on contextualization, Jesus movements, power encounter, and Bible translation. His writings have been published in a number of books and journals and translated into a number of languages. John holds a PhD in Intercultural Studies from Fuller Theological Seminary.

Charles (Chuck) E. Van Engen is the Arthur F. Glasser Professor of Biblical Theology of Mission in the School of Intercultural Studies at Fuller Theological Seminary. Born and raised in Mexico of missionary parents, he founded a seminary and was involved in extension theological education, leadership formation, and training evangelists for the National Presbyterian Church of Mexico from 1973 to 1985. He is the founding President and CEO of Latin American Christian Ministries that seeks to form a new generation of scholars, writers and seminary professors for the churches and mission agencies of Latin America. Among his publications are *The Growth of the True Church* (Rodopi, 1981); *God's Missionary People* (Grand Rapids: Baker Book House, 1991); *Mission on the Way* (Grand Rapids: Baker Books, 1996); *God So Loves the City* with Jude Tiersma (Monrovia: MARC, 1994); *Evangelical Dictionary of World Missions* edited with A. Scott Moreau and Harold Netland (Grand Rapids: Baker Books, 2000); *Announcing the Kingdom: The Story of God's Mission in the Bible* with Arthur Glasser, Dean Gilliland, and Shawn Redford (Grand Rapids: Baker Academic, 2003); *Paradigm Shifts in Christian Witness* edited with Darrell Whiteman and Dudley Woodberry (Maryknoll: Orbis, 2008); and *You are My Witnesses* (Eugene, OR: Wipf & Stock, 2009).

Biography of J. Dudley Woodberry

BY DEAN S. GILLILAND

When you know John Dudley Woodberry well and have been asked to honor him with a dedicatory chapter, it is difficult to know how to begin. This is a many-sided man, yet all things considered, we know him first and above all as *Dudley, the missionary.* Everything else about him arises out of the life he has had in mission. He has other "lives," so to speak: scholar, teacher, pastor, administrator, mentor, humorist, and all-around friend, but these are firmly attached to what has become a lifelong purpose. The purpose of which we speak is to find the most effective, most respectful, and most appropriate ways to communicate with persons of Muslim background. Upon reviewing Dudley's life, one has to say that a confluence of events, beginning very early, put him on a divinely guided path. Taking place in the context of a unique family history, these events moved him inexorably into scholarly pursuit and enlightened ministry among Muslims. We will briefly move through his unusual family history and then attempt to show something of who Dudley is and what makes him the special person he has come to be.

I want to give special thanks to Roberta Woodberry for the great help she has given in putting this biography together.

Beginning the Story

Dudley Woodberry comes in the line of three generations of missionaries. His grandparents, John and Kitty Vanderwerp (who changed their name to Woodberry), were owners of a small chain of three stores in Muskegon, Michigan, which included a hardware store. When they were in their forties, they felt the call to missionary work. They left their business and went to Shanghai, China under the Christian and Missionary Alliance. There God used them to build a girls' school (the first in Shanghai), a boys' school and a church, the original building of which survives today. Dudley's father, Earle John Woodberry, was born in 1892. From childhood, his only world was that of the Chinese people, knowing intimately their culture and mastering their language. Ada Pierce Woodberry, an independent and talented woman, was pianist for A. B. Simpson, the founder of the Christian and Missionary Alliance. Earle and Ada were married in Old Orchard Beach, Maine. They served primarily in Shandong

Province in China, with Earle doing rural evangelism and Ada teaching. After they and the family were repatriated to the United States in a prisoner exchange during World War II, Earle returned to China under the US military as a civilian chaplain and liaison with the Chinese. Some years later during the Korean War he again served under the military, this time as a civilian chaplain of the Chinese prisoners of war where many hundreds became Christians. He was accredited with helping to stop riots among prisoners and, after the hostilities, easing their release to their choice of China or Taiwan. As a result President Eisenhower awarded him the Freedom Medal, and the Taiwanese, a similar honor.

During Earle and Ada's early ministry in Shandong Province, Dudley was born in 1934—the youngest of five children. While the family was on furlough, Dudley accepted Christ as a small child at Pinebrook, a popular Christian camp in Pennsylvania. Then going back to China, he records how at age five he fell through the ice into the harbor and came very near to death from resultant pneumonia.[1] In retrospect, he could see through this and other examples that God truly must have saved him for a purpose.

At age six, along with two brothers and one sister, he attended the China Inland Mission boarding school in Chefoo since the Presbyterian mission said that they would have to close their hospital and school in the inland city of Ichowfu (where there was no school for foreigners) if his parents do not go there. Since both cities were in Japanese-occupied China, both parents and children became prisoners of war after the Pearl Harbor attack.

The way these children were reunited with their parents was another event that Dudley has always remembered as a sign of God's providence. By living in Chefoo, the children were separated from their parents by several hundred miles, with no chance of seeing them. Providentially, God led a sympathetic Japanese officer to make arrangements for the Woodberry children to connect with their parents. The officer had arranged for Dudley and his siblings, accompanied by a teacher from Chefoo, to board a train to the city of Jinan where they would meet their parents. However, their train was, unaccountably to them, moved to a side track while another went ahead, The next morning when their train suddenly stopped and they were told to get out and walk, they saw that the train that had been moved in front of them had been wrecked by Chinese guerillas, and they knew that their lives had been spared. Another train delivered the children, still with their teacher, to Jinan, where the parents and children were reunited. The family then traveled on to Shanghai where they boarded an Italian ship to Lorenzo Marques, Portuguese East Africa. US Navy records indicate that their ship was in the cross-hairs of the American submarine *Plunger* when its radio operator rushed up and stopped them from launching the readied torpedo, since he had just decoded a message that the enemy ship contained North American civilians. In Lorenzo Marques the North Americans exchanged ships with Japanese civilians who had arrived on the Swedish ship *Gripsholm*, which returned with its new passengers to New York. Within three days

1 J. Dudley Woodberry, "My Pilgrimage in Mission," *International Bulletin of Missionary Research* 6, no. 1 (January 2002): 24–28.

of arrival in New York, the *Gripsholm* passed the burning remains of a sunken ship. Each incident gave Dudley a sense that his life had been preserved for a purpose.

Shaping of a Vision

Upon arriving, the Woodberrys stayed briefly in New York City and then moved to Ithaca, New York while the parents studied agriculture at Cornell University for a year. At this point, Earle, Dudley's father, returned to China with the military to serve as a civilian chaplain and liaison with the Chinese while Mother Ada, Dudley and his sister Grace lived on a farm near Schenectady. Then, the family moved to Nyack, New York, where Dudley continued school through the sixth grade. Subsequently, Dudley joined one of his brothers at Stony Brook School on Long Island for an important period of his life that took him through high school. The well-known headmaster of Stony Brook, Frank Gaebelien, influenced his life greatly, telling Dudley later that he had prayed for him every day.

It was at Stony Brook where Dudley first heard Samuel Zwemer, the great missionary to the Muslim world. Though at this point Dudley knew very little about Islam, Zwemer impressed upon him both how important and difficult it is to express a Christian witness among Muslim people, and Dudley wrote to his parents that he wanted—though more modestly—to follow in Zwemer's footprints. While at Stony Brook, Dudley taught a Sunday school class and handed out gospel tracts in nearby towns. Dudley speaks of attending the "Congress of Bands"[2] which was held each year in Carnegie Hall. This refers to "Bands" of Christian and Missionary Alliance missionaries who reported on the worldwide mission enterprise of the time.

After graduating from Stony Brook, Dudley enrolled at Union College in Schenectady, New York. This was a formative time in a number of ways. For one thing, he was active in the large First Presbyterian Church of Schenectady where the pastor, Herbert Mekeel, was an exemplary scholar and preacher who centered his ministry in many ways around young people. He generated programs that would challenge young people into ministry, programs that included putting them in contact with missionaries. In this way, Dudley first met Christy and Betty Wilson, the well-known missionaries from Mekeel's Church who went to Afghanistan to work among Muslims. Dudley met expenses with various jobs such as teaching horseback riding, working as a chauffeur, and writing for the local newspaper. Aptitude tests seemed to show that he should choose a scientific profession, and the chaplain indicated, ironically, in references that he wrote that public speaking was one thing he did not do well. His personal preferences, however, did not lean in the direction of the sciences and he became restless to find out what he should do.

As part of this discovery, he hitchhiked to South America one summer while in college for the purpose of visiting as many missions and missionaries as he could. This took him

2 Ibid., 24.

to schools, hospitals, and missionaries' homes, all the while conversing, asking questions, and receiving answers. This pilgrimage took him to Havana, Cuba where the small boat on which he was working his way made an unplanned stop for repairs and to sit out part of a hurricane. It was here, while visiting a local seminary, that Dudley felt the pull of God on his life to prepare by training and experience to become a teacher for indigenous church leaders somewhere in the mission world. He was nineteen years old.

Sensing the needs of Muslim peoples, along with remembrances of Zwemer's message and life, Dudley felt led to apply for a short-term ministry in an agricultural project in Lebanon through the American Friends Service Committee. The Friends sent him to Lebanon and it was there that he had firsthand engagement with Muslims as well as Christians of the ancient churches. During this very important time, he felt his calling confirmed to prepare for a life among Muslims.

With this fresh confirmation, he graduated from Union College and enrolled in Fuller Theological Seminary. A large number of Fuller students had the vision for missions, so it was not difficult to find encouragement and challenge for the world. In fact, during his second year at seminary, a number of students at both Fuller and Princeton organized what became known as the International Studies Program. This provided opportunity for taking graduate studies outside of the United States. Two students from Princeton Seminary went to India and two, including Dudley, enrolled in the American University of Beirut to pursue a master's degree in Arab Studies. Again, this was a formative time for Dudley as he encountered the complexities of relationships between Muslims and Christians. It was in Beirut that he first met Kenneth Cragg who became a model for him as one who sincerely tries to enter deeply into the world of Islam. The Beirut sojourn was very important as well because this is where he met Roberta Smith who was to become his wife and the mother of their three children. Dudley returned to graduate from Fuller while Roberta continued her studies at Beirut College for Women. He graduated from the Seminary in 1960 and in the fall of that same year he and Roberta were married.

Engaging with the Muslim World

Committed to a better understanding of the world of Islam and Muslim peoples, Dudley entered Harvard University where his professor was the well known Islamic scholar Sir Hamilton Gibb. Under H.A.R. Gibb and others, such as Wilfred Cantwell Smith, Dudley received the best of classic education in the religion of Islam. The focus of his doctoral dissertation was the theology of the founder of the Muslim Brotherhood and the Islamist tradition of which he was a significant part. Understanding the background of the Islamist movements was greater preparation than he knew at the time. As his life moved on, his interests continued to develop around Islamism and folk expressions of Islam, the latter of which turned out to be far more important in real life than his graduate studies had led him to believe. This stood him well for interpreting contemporary issues that divide Muslims and the radical events that make news today. Connections with Park Street Church, Boston, opened the way for Dudley to work as Minister to International Students. The vibrant mission program of Park Street Church added clarity and commitment to the family's future. Dudley graduated from Harvard in 1968, and that same year, Dudley and Roberta with their two young children went to Pakistan under the Presbyterian Church to work at the Christian Study Centre. This was located in Rawalpindi near Islamabad. The purpose of the Centre was to study further how Christians can relate in positive ways to Muslims and how to approach Muslims with the Christian message. Armed with the Harvard experience and all that had shaped him up to that point, Dudley was in close touch with Muslims there, producing in him sharpened perceptions and new interest. Here he encountered, as never before, local expressions of Islam and the varieties of popular Islam that would engage much of his future teaching. Here, also, were direct opportunities for working in dialogue with Muslims as a method for building relationships and understanding.

Other things were happening during their five years in Pakistan. Their son David was born, after two sons John and Robert, who were born while Dudley was still at Harvard. Dudley was also asked to become the interim pastor in Kabul, Afghanistan, filling in for Christy Wilson while he and Betty, his wife, were on furlough. As it turned out, this was to become a major transition for the Woodberrys. Subsequently, the Wilsons were unable to remain in Afghanistan, so Dudley and Roberta returned for two additional years to minister in the Community Christian Church of Kabul (1974–76). This provided the widest possible range of experiences in theological encounters and in confronting practical issues both with Muslims and with Christians in restrictive contexts.

In 1976, another major change for the Woodberry family came with a call to serve in Saudi Arabia. The invitation to Saudi Arabia came through friends that had known Dudley and Roberta in Pakistan. It was a new opportunity, as Dudley records it, for, "lessons learned in the 'closed' land of Afghanistan (to) be applied in Riyadh, the capital of Saudi Arabia, since there had not been a resident pastor in the interior since the early days of Islam."[3] Both Dudley and Roberta were involved. The Riyadh International Christian Fellowship grew to see some seven hundred persons attending both Arabic and English services. There was ministry for youth and a full music program, and daughter churches were being planted around the Kingdom.

Eventually, this success was too visible for the government, so the large meetings were closed down. This required finding a new mode for assembly which meant meeting largely in homes.

Soon, these "house churches" spread widely. To encourage and teach these churches, the Woodberrys devised a weekly guide to study and worship bearing the title, "Catacomb Contemplations." Dudley now became fully engaged in visiting and ministering to these congregations in various parts of Saudi Arabia. He was interacting with all kinds of Arab subcultures and learning continually about varieties of Islam, especially popular Muslim piety.

3 Ibid., 26.

Forming Others for Service

Returning to the United States in 1979, Dudley was appointed to teach at the Reformed Bible College (RBC) in Grand Rapids, Michigan. This was where Bob and John finished high school. Dudley's teaching at RBC drew on all the rich years of ministry among Muslims, and brought increased integration between Muslim history, Christian theology, and solid practical experiences. Also, Dudley reaped the benefits of integrating his studies in Islam with anthropology and the social sciences. In this way, a rounded view of missiology among Muslim peoples was being transferred to the classroom. This continued until 1983 when Dudley went to Pasadena, California to join the staff of the Zwemer Institute. The Institute, in addition to arousing interest and knowledge about the Muslim world in American churches, offered courses at all levels. The master's courses were accepted at Fuller because of Dudley's teaching. This was an obvious opportunity for Fuller's School of World Mission (now School of Intercultural Studies) to appropriate Dudley's expertise as an expansion of the offerings it could give in Islamics.

In 1985, Fuller offered a full-time teaching position to Dudley. The school's relationship with the Zwemer Institute brought him to Fuller in an almost seamless transition. Charles Kraft writes in his history of the School of World Mission (SWM/SIS) about this shift: "The fact that this delightful man with such scholarly credentials just kind of landed in our lap can be seen as another of God's pleasant surprises."[4] Muslim Studies became a major focus of specialization at SWM and large numbers of students enrolled in his courses, both those who were new to Islamics and those who were already active in ministry among Muslims.

A creative period in research began with Dudley's arrival at Fuller, as interest in Islam and church planting among Muslims was becoming widespread among missions and in evangelical seminaries. We recall a massive research project that was put in place to find effective models for approaching Muslims. Focused on Africa and Asia, the project was carried out under Dudley's chairmanship with funds from the Pew Charitable Trusts. The widespread interest during this period was centered primarily around one question: "How much and in what ways can religious and cultural features of Islam be retained by Muslims who desire to follow Jesus?" Or, put another way, "How can Muslims turn to Jesus as Lord with minimum disruption from their own culture and ways of faith?" Dudley brought his rich background into these innovative discussions. His years of experience fit him well for setting out principles that would guide and support believers of Muslim background without compromising the essentials of biblical Christian faith.

As a major part of this rise in consciousness about theological issues with Islam and contextual forms, major consultations were convened at Zeist (Netherlands), Stuttgart, Manila, Cyprus, and Essex (England) in the late eighties, all within a few years of each other. Dudley's role in planning for and carrying out these gatherings was always prominent.

---

4 Charles H. Kraft, *SWM/SIS at Forty: A Participant/Observer's View of Our History* (Pasadena: William Carey Library, 2005), 178.

In 1992, after consensus was reached by the SWM faculty, Dudley was asked to become the dean of SWM. After he and Roberta went through considerable thought and prayer about how this would affect their lives and whether he could do this alongside other commitments, he accepted. We remember the confluence of situations and developments in the world and in SWM at that time. His installation as dean was highlighted by a broad-based consultation that convened in Pasadena to explore these changes and the ways in which missiological education must look with fresh eyes on the world. This was a significant gathering demonstrating Fuller's unique role in facing these challenges and was witnessed by participants who came from as many branches of mission education as possible. Conceiving and carrying out this consultation signaled the way in which Dudley would conduct his deanship with respect to issues as well as demonstrating his collaborative style of leadership. Under Dudley's deanship, Kraft says, "We experienced a period of consolidation as well as further growth. Eight faculty members were added … several new programs and, perhaps most important of all, four new chairs established."[5]

Dudley's published writings are best appreciated through the many contributions he has made in books he has edited or jointly edited, chapters in books, and journal articles. Many dimensions of missionary witness and education have been enriched by chapters he has contributed to some twenty-five books. Much of what he writes deals with sensitive issues in the area of communicating to Muslims and finding appropriate ways to nurture those who are known as Believers of Muslim Background. Soon after joining us at Fuller, he headed the Muslim Track of the Lausanne Committee for World Evangelization. Many of the insights gained through this project were published under the title, *Muslims and Christians on the Emmaus Road* (MARC, 1989). His installation as Dean was commemorated by a Consultation that brought together mission educators and executives from a wide variety of denominations and mission agencies. The purpose was to hear as many perspectives as possible on the state of mission and mission education and to envision changes that could take place. These insights were gathered together in a volume which he edited with Edgar Elliston and Charles Van Engen, two other faculty colleagues. This important book, bearing the title, *Missiological Education for the 21st Century* (Orbis, 1996) was dedicated to Paul Pierson, who had preceded him as dean.

The faculty of the School of World Mission gathered weekly for sharing personal and academic issues and for giving mutual counsel on things common to faculty relationships. We have said that Dudley works in collaborative style, and this characterized his writing as well. Dudley would regularly bring a draft of his articles for the faculty to review before final editing. This was especially true during his years as dean, because he knew that whatever he published would not only represent him personally but would reflect attitudes and principles being advanced by the entire school.

5 Ibid., 198.

Knowing the Man

I want to change the order now so you can appreciate Dudley Woodberry as the human being and Christian brother that we all know and love. Besides my own commentary, I will share both directly and indirectly from some comments his colleagues have submitted when they were told about my writing this chapter.

Dudley Woodberry is a very organized person, even though one might not think so from the casual way he goes about his business. His office promises an interesting encounter. Even though he may be deep into desk-work, he always stops what he is doing when you open his door. He has a way of smiling about the interruption as though he welcomes the break. If you want quick results, there is no reason to worry. One of his closest staff members remarks that, "If you chance to ask him about where certain information might be, whether a journal or paper, even something quite inconsequential, he will say, 'Oh, I have that right here someplace.' Immediately, he begins to ruffle through several unsightly piles, and, amazingly, he will come up with the precise piece." Or, as another puts it, "The dean's office was covered with piles of papers but woe to you if you moved one. He knew exactly where everything was and could tell you down to a millimeter where a document was in any pile." A faculty friend observes that, "Dudley is very organized but perhaps due to his missionary background he does not invest in filing cabinets. The stacks on the floor are all organized in Dudley's mind, so there is no need for labels or special drawers."

One very prominent part of his office is the largest dictionary available which he keeps on a stand at arms' reach from his desk. Because I thought it rather quaint that a Harvard man would have such basic ties to a dictionary, I once asked him about this. He said, "Using the right words is a sign of the intelligent person and, besides, my professor always kept a dictionary beside him in his office." I supposed he was referring to his Harvard professor, Sir Hamilton Gibb.

The Dudley-style of humor is his and his alone. One of his associates remarks that "Dudley is always in a good mood and he can always find some humor even in the most difficult situations and then laugh at things that for others could be rather devastating." Dudley takes great pleasure in playing good jokes on his friends, especially when having fun with a colleague can entertain an audience. He is very good at this and always includes himself. I, for one, have experienced this on more than one occasion. As an example, Dudley has very little hair himself, yet once before a large student audience, he presented me with a flaming green wig to cover my baldness. Another time, at a Christmas banquet, his formal gift to me was a *Chia Pet*, the little porcelain figure that grows grass on its head when watered every day. Again, I was to be given a fine new briefcase by the Seminary as a gift for fifteen years of service. Unfortunately, the gift did not arrive and I got only a letter of regret. Dudley remembered this, and at an all-school gathering he presented me with a consolation prize, his own mother's totally worn-out suitcase which she had used in her world travels for over sixty years. In fact, Mother Ada was coming up to her one-hundredth birthday at the time. The suitcase became a standard joke, as it was passed back and forth on several occasions.

Dudley's many travels, near and far, present him with a variety of comical situations, often of his own making. Some of his travel habits tend to border on the eccentric (but no one would ever say so). On one of our trips, to Cyprus this time, we commented about his very tattered briefcase. We suggested he buy a new one at the duty-free store in Amsterdam, but he told us how attached he had become to this briefcase over the years. Then, within the hour, the handle fell off and the briefcase literally came apart, scattering his papers everywhere. But Dudley found a rope and tied it together so that it served him through the conference and back home. Another faculty colleague said that it is risky traveling with Dudley because, "With his (complicated) passport you can count on him being detained for hours when he enters any country, including the United States." As to Dudley's double life, another says, "He has a bit of Indiana Jones in him; teaching in a very controlled and methodical sort of way, then when he leaves Fuller Seminary he puts himself in harm's way at every turn, all the while sporting a devilish grin." He loves to recount his travels. One of our associates said, "How does one person travel to so many places in such short spaces of time and never look jet-lagged?" adding, "It is a marvel to behold Dr. Woodberry's ability to teach, write, run hither and thither, stay slim and smiling, and never be too busy to lend a listening ear or speak a gentle word of care."

Dudley is a classic teller of tales. As one associate said, "Dudley has a story for every occasion and once he begins you will get the *full* story, so grab a cup of coffee and be ready to listen for awhile." By the way, coffee and how to brew it, is a big subject with Dudley. One of his staff told him she would prepare the office coffee the night before then just hit the heat-up switch the next morning. With a grin Dudley said this would never do. The beans must be kept frozen then freshly ground in the morning but never reheated. His best stories are about himself which he recounts with a kind of self-effacement, always adding just enough spice to give extra delight. When he knows a story is going well he tries to control his own laughter and flashes a special kind of twinkle.

As dean, Dudley was known for the way he faced difficulties. One faculty member put it this way, "Dudley will always find a solution and then problems are just challenges." The dictum of Dudley's leadership is, "Make the right decisions then solve the problems."

The School of Intercultural Studies has had several deans, of course. Sherwood Lingenfelter, who followed Dudley as dean, had some doubts about taking on the deanship when two former deans were still very present. "Dudley promised his support and never stepped in to correct or interfere. When I wanted advice," says Lingenfelter, "he willingly gave it but did not, in any way, pressure me to follow his counsel."

Dudley also shows careful organization in the way he prepares to write or speak. He works out alliterations and provocative word pictures to make things stick in the mind. He is meticulous in getting his facts straight. This is especially important because he always speaks about issues within Islam as though Muslims are in the audiences, or when Muslims are actually present. A faculty member writes, "For a course at one university he got up at 3:00 a.m. just to make sure that he completely understood the points raised in a new book before giving the lecture on a subject that he already knew by heart."

Concluding Word

Dudley has mastered the art of speech-making to honor friends and colleagues. Very often he constructs these speeches by using the letters of the person's name in acrostic fashion to emphasize that person's characteristics. As we conclude this piece about our faculty colleague and former dean, I will presume on his style and use the letters of his first name to close our words of love and respect.

D is for *Difference*: You knew very early in your life that there needed to be a difference in the way Muslim people were understood and the way in which Islam must be presented. You have made a difference, always calling for respect and continuing to search for the deeper issues that connect rather than divide peoples of different faiths and cultures.

U is for *Understated*: Dudley, you never really get the picture as to how much your knowledge and spirit has influenced people. You understate who you are and what you have done. We call on you to accept what we have written about your knowledge and spirit which has drawn so many students into your classes and mentorship.

D for *Dialogue*: You have shown us how careful we need to be to enter into the sacred thinking of another without giving ground that would undermine our own position. Your intimacy with the Arab mind and Muslim thinking respects people of other faiths so that relationships become more important than dogma.

L is for *Largess*: You do give of yourself in large portions. This largess is the optimistic generosity with which you share your knowledge and experience. You give without reserve of what you know and without thought of yourself, whether here in the United States or among people and churches of the many countries you have touched.

E is for *Empirical*: You are someone who can be relied upon because of your experience. This leads to a deeper understanding than we knew before. It is confirmed by what you have done and where you have been, and your authority as teacher comes from a history of live connections with people of the faith.

Y is for *Yeast*: Your work of spreading insights and innovative thinking has brought about change in the bread we share with other faiths. Reforming older models of "church" among Muslims and creating new uses for old forms defines who you are. Yeast is not loud or self-assertive, but is effective from the inside, as you have been.

J. Dudley Woodberry, with this chapter and with this volume as a whole, we honor you with affection.

SECTION ONE

Encouraging Friendly Conversation

INTRODUCTION BY CHARLES E. VAN ENGEN

The first part of this work in honor of Dudley Woodberry has to do with Christian attitudes regarding Islam and Muslims. The authors of these chapters challenge Christians to self-examination. This is an essential step in the process if Christians are to begin to experience a measure of fruitful Christian-Muslim conversation. Dudley has lived out, modeled, championed, and taught us all the need for such attitude adjustment on the part of Christians. Woodberry personifies a positive, open, courteous, careful attitude of interaction with Islam and Muslims. As one of the leading evangelical Islamicists in the world, Woodberry has dedicated himself to conversing with, listening to, and learning from Muslim scholars. He has shown himself to be always careful in seeking to understand Islam. He is committed to expressing love, concern, and compassion for the followers of Islam. A reading of Dudley's writings shows a scholar who is always the gentleman in conversations with Muslims. This does not mean that he is unwilling to disagree. He remains solidly grounded on the Bible, clear in his understanding of the gospel of grace in Jesus Christ, and forthright in expressing where he disagrees with Islamic thought. Yet, his attitude toward Islam and Muslims is always grace-filled, polite, humble, and loving. The chapters in this section seek to honor Dudley in this regard.

In what is commonly known as the "Sermon on the Mount," Jesus taught his disciples about attitudes they—and we—should have with regard to our "neighbor" who may differ from us. As Christians seek to converse in Christlike ways with Muslims today, it is important for Christians to take to heart Jesus' words:

> Do not judge, so that you may not be judged. For with the judgment you make you will be judged, and the measure you give will be the measure you get. Why do you see the speck in your neighbor's eye, but do not notice the log in your own eye? Or how can you say to your neighbor, "Let me take the speck out of your eye," while the log is in your own eye? You hypocrite, first take the log out of your own eye, and then you will see clearly to take the speck out of your neighbor's eye. (Matt 7:1–5 NRSV)

How, then, may we as Christians be clear and forthright about our gospel proclamation and yet also demonstrate kindness, love, compassion, and grace in our conversations with Islam and Muslims? The following chapters offer helpful suggestions as to how we as Christians may follow Dudley's example. Martin Accad offers a typology of Christian attitudes toward Islam, ranging from syncretism to polemics. He advocates an attitude and approach he calls "*kerygmatic* interaction."

Jonathan Culver draws from his doctoral research and suggests that as Christians, we need to reexamine the way we have historically read and understood God's promises to Ishmael as recorded in the Old Testament. A change of attitude regarding Ishmael (from whom Muslims trace their lineage) could help Christians have a more positive and open attitude toward, and a more fruitful conversation with, followers of Islam. By way of example, Jonathan shares his experiences in Indonesia.

David Johnston examines the extensive discussion and controversy going on among Islamic scholars and clerics regarding Islamic law, ethics, and the possibility of contextualization and change in Muslim reading of that law. David suggests that the movements for reform within Islam on this topic may be a fruitful arena for new Christian-Muslim conversation. Johnston suggests to Christians and Muslims alike, "We must lay hold of the ethical principles contained in our sacred texts if we want to build a more just and peaceful global society in the new millennium."

Evelyne Reisacher studies the attitudes regarding women, comparing Christian views with Muslim perspectives. Reisacher suggests that as Christians, we need to reexamine our own attitudes regarding the place and role of women in the social and religious life of our faith communities and our societies in general. Such self-examination on the part of Christians could offer a positive and helpful area of conversation, learning, and mutual enrichment between Christians and Muslims.

Finally, Warren Larson reflects on Christian attitudes regarding Islamic expansion in the West. He suggests that rather than being alarmist and combative (as many have tended to be, especially after 9/11), Christians need to be aware of the deep changes that such contextual expansion is producing among Muslims themselves, including astounding numbers of Muslims becoming followers of Jesus. Quoting Samuel Zwemer, Larson calls for Christians to "'awaken sympathy, love, and prayer on behalf of the Islamic world until its bonds are burst, its wounds are healed, its sorrows removed, and its desires satisfied in

Jesus Christ.' Let this be our goal as we reflect on Muslims and their need for the gospel in the twenty-first century."

As followers of Jesus, may we all learn from Dudley Woodberry, a Christian gentleman and a scholar who is certain of what he believes and is also open, receptive, loving, and gracious in his conversation with Islam and Muslims.

1
Christian Attitudes toward Islam and Muslims: A Kerygmatic Approach

BY MARTIN ACCAD

With widespread mutual misunderstandings and misrepresentations that inform contemporary thinking between Christianity and Islam, East and West, there reigns an atmosphere of fear in many circles with regard to Christian-Muslim dialogue. Dialogue has often become a dirty word that insinuates either syncretism or polemics. But between these two extremes, are there any other viable positions on a spectrum of Christian-Muslim interaction? The purpose of this chapter is to propose a balanced, suprareligious approach to Christian-Muslim interaction, which will be called *kerygmatic* interaction.

Fear of Dialogue Today

The word dialogue today is often misunderstood, whether it is used in so-called conservative or more liberal or secular milieus. The conservative will view it as inevitably leading to syncretism, whereas the liberal will fear that it be used as a vehicle for polemics. The religious will fear to engage in dialogue, lest it forces them to compromise, whereas the secular will shun it as a platform for the assertion of exclusion. The relativist will use dialogue to flatten out differences, whereas the absolutist will use it to demonstrate the superiority of their own views.

I would like to suggest, however, that these two opposite positions stand in fact at the ends of a spectrum of potential positions and attitudes. Christian interaction with Islam need not be limited to a position of either syncretism or polemics. In fact, these two extremes hardly qualify as dialogue, since the first abolishes the distinction between two legitimate dialogical partners, and the second is too engaged in self-affirmation to be able to practice any form of listening. As such, both these extreme positions belong to the category of monologue since no dialogical partner is ever seriously engaged. Since these two positions do exist on the spectrum, I am calling the continuum a Spectrum of Christian-Muslim Interaction rather than Christian-Muslim Dialogue, in order to preserve the neutrality of the engagement. In this chapter I will describe the various positions on the spectrum, giving particular focus to the middle position, the kerygmatic interaction, in an attempt to help the reader develop a balanced attitude to the Islamic realities that are becoming more and more part of our global world, East and West.

Interaction between Christians and Muslims should no longer be viewed as one option among many. In the midst of religious and political conflicts that are continually and increasingly challenging the world we live in, the question should no longer be whether dialogue is necessary but rather what kind of dialogue needs to be carried out between the peoples of the world.[1]

The Urgency to Witness and the Challenges We Both Face

Given the sociopolitical importance of Christian-Muslim engagement, a topic in itself, the urgency of dialogue lies particularly in the fact that both religions are in essence mission-minded. Christians and Muslims cannot properly be called Christian and Muslim if they do not engage in witness to the world, including to each other. The Qurʾan defines Muhammad's message as a universal message addressed to all of creation: "Verily this is no less than a Message to (all) the Worlds: (With profit) to whoever among you wills to go straight" (at-Takwīr [81]:27, 28 Yusuf Ali).

Qurʾanic verses like the one above contain a clear summons to the Islamic *umma* (community) to spread the message of Islam to the entire world. Likewise, the Gospels are clear on this point as well, particularly in the famous passage known as the Great Commission. The message of Jesus also is to be proclaimed throughout the world:

> Then Jesus came to them and said, "All authority in heaven and on earth has been given to me. Therefore go and make disciples of all nations, baptizing them in the name of the Father and of the Son and of the Holy Spirit, and teaching them to obey everything I have commanded you. And surely I am with you always, to the very end of the age." (Matt 28:18–20 NIV)

Both Christians and Muslims need legitimately to be able to proclaim and testify to the message that they have received with neither aggressiveness nor fear of reprisal, but rather in an atmosphere of mutual respect, love, and humility. It is no secret, however, that a Muslim who would turn away from Islam and adopt Christianity as his or her religion is going to

1 Before reading any further, I recommend taking the *Test of Attitude to Islam and Muslims* (TAIM), which is found as Exhibit 1 (with its key as Exhibit 2) at the end of this chapter. The remainder of the chapter builds on the test results.

face, in most cases, some severe reprisals. Even though the Qur'an is not explicit about this, all the major legal schools of Islam down through history have been unanimous on the fate of the so-called *apostate.* They must technically face the death penalty. Although such a penalty has seldom been implemented, it must be pointed out that the legal prescription is clearly challenged by Article 18 of the United Nations Universal Declaration of Human Rights, which states:

> Everyone has the right to freedom of thought, conscience and religion; *this right includes freedom to change his religion or belief*, and freedom either alone or in community with others and in public or private, to manifest his religion or belief in teaching, practice, worship and observance.[2]

Christians are also met with a serious challenge today when attempting to witness in a Muslim context. The message that the media and leadership—political and religious—set forth is one that either demonizes or idealizes Islam. In the Christian church context, the attitude is more often one of demonization. Christians have always advocated that we are to love sinners but hate sin. This is a moral distinction that is fairly easy to maintain, as it is accompanied by the notion that we are all sinners outside the grace of God. However, there is today a parallel notion, which is spreading alarmingly fast, that we are to love Muslims but hate Islam. This notion is disturbing, for it is a very short step from the demonization of Islam and Muslims altogether. In reality, one observes that most people are unable to maintain such a theoretical separation between an ideology and its adherents. The premise of the present chapter is the following:

> Your *view* of Islam will affect your *attitude* to Muslims. Your *attitude* will, in turn, influence your *approach* to Christian-Muslim interaction, and that *approach* will affect the ultimate *outcome* of your presence as a witness among Muslims.

How then do we develop a *view*, an understanding, of Islam that will foster in us the right attitude and approach in order for our relationships to be fruitful? It is in the context of reflecting over this question that I have developed what I now call "The SEKAP Spectrum of Christian-Muslim Interaction." SEKAP is an acronym that abbreviates the five dialogical positions identified along the spectrum (D1–D5): Syncretistic, Existential, Kerygmatic, Apologetic, and Polemical. The five positions were further defined by asking ten questions: (1) What is my view of religions generally? (2) What is my understanding of Islam? (3) How do I view Muhammad? (4) What is my perception of the Qur'an? (5) How do I view Muslims? (6) What is my opinion about their eternal destiny? (7) Why do I relate to Muslims at all? (8) What approaches do I adopt? (9) What outcomes may I expect? (10) How much

2 Emphasis mine. See http://www.un.org/Overview/rights.html.

knowledge of Islam does this require on my part? The *Test of Attitude to Islam and Muslims* (TAIM) was developed based on these ten questions.[3]

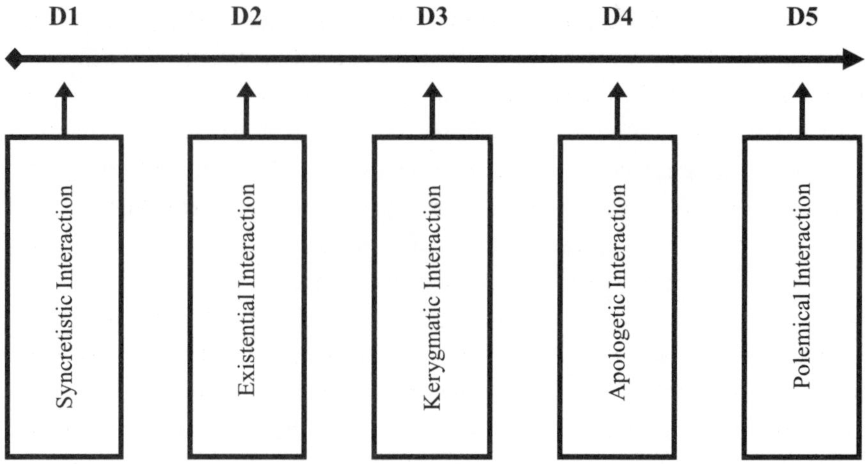

Figure 1: The SEKAP Spectrum of Christian-Muslim Interaction

The *Syncretistic* Approach to Christian-Muslim Interaction: All Roads Lead to Mecca

In his conclusion to a chapter on Christianity and other religions, theologian John Hick cites from the Hindu Bhagavad Gītā: "Let me then end with a quotation from one of the great revelatory scriptures of the world: 'Howsoever man may approach me, even so do I accept them; for, on all sides, whatever path they may choose is mine.'"[4]

The fact that Hick has to resort to a citation from outside the Christian Scripture to summarize his pluralist view begs the question as to how Christian his position actually is. Syncretism differs from pluralism. Pluralism is a category with primary concern for the question of salvation, whereas syncretism is an approach to religions that more comprehensively treats their various aspects, in addition to salvation, with a desire to reconcile their differences.[5] Syncretism relativizes differences between religions, whereas pluralism emphasizes the cultural particularity of each religious system while affirming their objective equality. As a general, all-inclusive, attitude toward other religions—and here particularly regarding the attitude of Christians and Christianity toward Muslims and Islam—I have

3 See Exhibits 1 and 2 at the end of this chapter.

4 John Hick and Brian Hebblethwaite, eds., *Christianity and Other Religions: Selected Readings* (Philadelphia: Fortress, 1980), 190.

5 The clear focus and concern for salvation inherently present in these different views is evident, for example, in the very title of Dennis L. Okholm and Timothy R. Phillips, eds., *Four Views on Salvation in a Pluralistic World* (Grand Rapids: Zondervan, 1996).

therefore chosen to call the approach to Christian-Muslim interaction at the D1 end of the spectrum syncretism rather than pluralism.

Whereas the syncretistic approach to Islam would consider all religions on an equal par, it would also be somewhat suspicious of all religions, viewing them as a potential obstacle to peace between individuals, communities, and eventually between nations. At the same time, this position would consider that the positive contribution of religions lies mainly in the moral standards that they can instill in individuals within their societies. In that view, Islam is primarily seen as a sociopolitical phenomenon like any other successful religious movement of human history. Muhammad is considered to have been a sociopolitical leader who knew how to use his contemporary economic and historical realities to the advantage of his community and personal ends. The Qurʾan is viewed as a literary achievement of Muhammad himself or some of his entourage, which the prophet of Islam used in order to impress a society that was strongly attracted to poetic literature. And in that light, Muslims would be simply considered to be adherents of a religious ideology in the same way as other religious peoples.

Syncretistic interaction is carried out with the purpose of inviting Muslims to be a positive part of a multicultural and multireligious universal humanity in all of its rich plurality. This is done by relativizing religious differences by dialoguing primarily about social, economic, and political topics, without necessarily requiring any deep knowledge of Islam. Due to the secular nature of this dialogue, it will generally take place among lay or secular scholars who may belong to various religious communities. This type of dialogue is likely to alienate religious leaders on either side.

Although this type of dialogue may offer some helpful scholarly perspectives on religion, chiefly adopting a history-of-religions approach, no deep impact into the day-to-day relationships of communities at the grass roots will be achieved. For it is generally the religious leaders that are most influential at the popular level of a culture that is religious to the core.

The *Polemical* Approach to Christian-Muslim Interaction: Seek and Destroy

Polemical interaction between Christianity and Islam stands at the other end of the spectrum. The word "polemical" comes from the Greek word *polemos*, which simply means "war." The polemical approach to Christian-Muslim interaction is precisely that approach that adopts warlike strategies in relating to the other religion, where one seeks to destroy and uproot the tenets of another in order to replace them with one's own. Many examples of this approach are found in the history of interaction between Christianity and Islam. One of the most ancient and classical ones is the treatment of Islam by John of Damascus, a Graeco-Arab Eastern church father of the eighth century (675–753), whose father was a medical doctor at the court of the Umayyad caliph. John of Damascus dealt with Islam at the end of his treatise *Against Heresies*, calling it the heresy of the Ishmaelites.

The polemical approach will generally hold a triumphalist view of Christianity in total exclusion of other religions. The ideology promoted is often a highly institutionalized form of Christianity, the religious substitute to Islam. All other worldviews are seen as simply wrong and as having nothing good to offer to Christians through dialogue. In this view, Islam is viewed as an evil and a thorn in the flesh of Christianity. Early such approaches gave rise to an apocalyptic genre of literature that considered that God had allowed the emergence of Islam as a punishment for the complacency of Christians. As bearer of that religion, Muhammad is viewed as having been possessed by demons, an Antichrist whose mission was to deceive all people. The Qurʾan was consequently inspired by the devil and is full of lies and deceit, to the point that merely reading it renders a person unclean. As a result, Muslims are the deceived followers of a religion that will lead them to hell.[6]

The chief reason why a Christian holding that view would seek to engage Islam is often to demonstrate to Muslims that Islam is false and deceitful. The message is communicated by accentuating religious differences and proclaiming that Muslims will go to hell if they do not reject Islam. A variant to this aggressive proclamation is often a loss of interest in evangelism altogether, with the consideration that Muslims are not even worthy to hear the gospel.

The most likely outcome of such a discourse is aggressive reaction. At the same time, promoters of this approach will often justify it by pointing out that many Muslims are being won to Christianity. That does seem to be the case through such TV programs as those of Coptic priest Zakaria Botros.[7] Yet the cost in terms of intercommunal conflict is high, and the converts either have to remain secret Christians or have to be extracted out of their societies to avoid being harmed, leading to the accentuation of the chasm between religious communities. Those engaged in such an approach will often be quite convincing to the listener or reader, since they will have acquired a very thorough knowledge of all the weaknesses and problems in Islam. Though the negative outcomes of this approach will probably mark religious communities in the Muslim world for decades, it can nevertheless not be dismissed altogether. The nagging reality is that numerous Muslim converts to Christianity are staunch supporters of Father Zakaria, for he undoubtedly gives a voice to their repressed frustration that has resulted quite frankly from numerous experiences of oppression and persecution by their families, community, and governments. As we consider this approach as evangelical Christians driven by God's call to mission, however, we also have to keep in mind the very serious consideration that no one openly using the polemical approach will be able to maintain a transparent presence in the Muslim world.

---

6 Two striking examples of this kind of approach are the ninth century Byzantine writers Nicetas of Byzantium and George Hamartolos. The first begins by calling the Qurʾan "abominable" and "barbarous," and Muhammad "perverse," "bestial," and possessing the "perversity of Satan" (J. P. Migne, ed., *Patrologia graeca*, vol. 105). The latter ends up referring to Muslims as "men whose slimy souls would befit pigs" (Migne, *Patrologia graeca*, vol. 110).

7 http://www.fatherzakaria.net/.

The *Existential* Approach to Christian-Muslim Interaction: Fostering Societies of Diversity

At the D2 end of the spectrum of attitudes regarding dialogue one would find the existential approach to interaction. I use the term existential here in a nontechnical and nonphilosophical sense, as it pertains to human existence. At the same time, existentialism as a philosophy, whether theistic or atheistic, arose in skeptic reaction to the affirmation of the primacy of reason.[8] In that sense, the use of the term in the present context is appropriate, since that approach to Christian-Muslim interaction has as its primary focus sociological rather than theological concerns. The concerns are existential rather than rational. The questions asked by this approach are: How can adherents of both Christianity and Islam live better side by side? How can they acquire the level of tolerance that will promote peace rather than conflict among them? How can we build a better society for the future, which respects pluralism and diversity?

In this type of Christian-Muslim interaction, religions are distinctively defined and differentiated, but Christ may be seen as not the only way to God and salvation. For those who engage in existential interaction, goodness and morality are the essence of all religions. This position will allow for a more significant divine role in the emergence of religions. In this view, Islam is a religion that originated from God, but like all religions, it underwent many human influences as well. If Muhammad did receive to some degree a divine calling to be God's Prophet to the Arabs, then the Qurʾan contains substantial elements of the divine truth and is to be respected as Scripture. Therefore, in the end, those Muslims who have been faithful Muslims will be saved.

Christians who engage in this type of interaction will do so in order to encourage mutual social and religious understanding and tolerance between Christian and Muslim communities. In order to achieve this end, they will interact at social, economic, and political levels, affirming common ground and avoiding divisive issues. It can be expected that some positive transformation of mutual perceptions and relationships will ensue from this dialogue, as well as greater tolerance and appreciation between religious communities. At least some knowledge of the broad lines of Islam is necessary at that level. An excellent example of this approach can be seen in the Second Vatican Council, where the view of other religions was primarily expounded by the Catholic theologian Karl Rahner. In its 1965 Declaration on the Relation of the Church to Non-Christian Religions, the council declared:

> If in the course of the centuries there has arisen not infrequent dissension and hostility between Christian and Muslim, this sacred Council now urges everyone to forget the past, to make sincere efforts at mutual understand-

8 For existentialism as a philosophy, see for example Mircea Eliade, ed., *The Encyclopedia of Religion* (New York: Macmillan, 1987), s.v. "Existentialism," by John Macquarrie.

> ing and to work together in protecting and promoting for the benefit of all men, social justice, good morals as well as peace and freedom.[9]

The conciliatory tone of this statement is evident. It results from the recognition of a long history of conflict between Christianity and Islam. With its focus on the promotion of social justice and good morals, peace and freedom, it typically represents this level of existential interaction.

The *Apologetic* Approach to Christian-Muslim Interaction: Drawing from the Wealth of History

There is much in the New Testament to justify adopting a fourth type of interaction that I have called apologetic interaction (D4). The Apostle Paul uses that approach numerous times in his epistles as a tool for the confirmation of the gospel, and Peter makes the famous exhortation to "always be prepared to give an answer (*apologia*) to everyone who asks you to give the reason for the hope that you have." Significantly, he adds in the same breath, "but do this with gentleness and respect" (1 Pt 3:15 NIV). That approach, then, should not so much be defensive, with the negative undertones of the English usage of the term. But rather it should be used as a tool to clarify and clear out misconceptions regarding the Christian faith. In the Gospels, the only place where a Greek form of the term is used is in Jesus' two sending discourses in Luke 12:11 and 21:14. Jesus exhorts his disciples not to linger on what defense (*apologia*) they will present to those who arrest them, for God will give them in time the words of wisdom that they need.

The main problem of this approach is the way that it has been used historically, locking up the discourse of both Christians and Muslims in generally sterile arguments that were passed along over the centuries. By the eleventh century, as I have demonstrated elsewhere,[10] what we keep coming across is a relentless repetition of the same arguments on both sides, often reflecting even a literary borrowing of age-old arguments. As I have shown, by that time the conversation based on Christian and Muslim Scriptures is taken out of any original interpretive endeavor, leading to extreme eisegesis rather than proper exegesis, to the point where the discourse emerges at best as two separate monologues.

Essentially, this position holds that there is one ultimate Truth: God. Judaism and Christianity are the only divinely established religions, and Christ who is at the center of Christianity is the only way to salvation. Islam is viewed as a human phenomenon whose

9 Hick and Hebblethwaite, *Christianity and Other Religions*, 82–83.

10 Martin Accad, "Corruption and/or Misinterpretation of the Bible: The Story of the Islamic Usage of *Taḥrīf,*" *The Near East School of Theology Theological Review* 24, no. 2 (2003); M. Accad, "The Gospels in the Muslim Discourse of the Ninth to the Fourteenth Century: An Exegetical Inventorial Table (Parts I–IV)," *Islam and Christian-Muslim Relations* 14, no. 1 (2003); and M. Accad, "The Interpretation of John 20:17 in Muslim-Christian Dialogue (8th–14th Centuries): The Ultimate Proof-Text," in *Christians at the Heart of Islamic Rule*, ed. David Thomas (Leiden, The Netherlands: Brill, 2003).

understanding of God is misleading, due to the fact that Muhammad himself was misled. The phenomenon of Qurʾanic revelation perhaps reflects that Muhammad had some psychological problems that led him to believe that he had received a prophetic calling. Hence, the Qurʾan is a plagiarism of the Bible and contains many mistakes and inaccuracies. Within that framework, Muslims are being misled by a worldly religion that drives them away from the worship of the true God.

In this type of interaction, Christians will engage with Muslims solely for the purpose of evangelism, seeking to demonstrate to them the truth of Christianity and to refute the validity of Islam. Primary methods used are public debates that make heavy use of apologetic arguments, as well as a reliance on apologetics and polemics in private attempts to convert Muslims to Christianity. Although some Muslims will be convinced to become Christians under the influence of heavy apologetic demonstrations of the truth of Christianity, circular argumentation should be expected due to the long history of learned arguments and counterarguments on both sides. Both Christians and Muslims at that level will often study and memorize standard answers to age-old questions.

The *Kerygmatic* Approach to Christian-Muslim Interaction: The Gospel as God Proclaimed It

Finally, we come to the kerygmatic level of interaction which, I believe, has the potential of being most fruitful for Christ's gospel as good news and most conducive to peace in our age of great conflicts. Without dismissing the other four approaches altogether, I believe that it is through this kerygmatic approach that we will be able to think the most Christlike about Islam and Muslims. "Kerygmatic" comes from the Greek word *kerygma* and the verb *kerysso*, more often found in the Gospels in the form of the present participle *kerysson* (proclaiming). The *kerygma* in the New Testament is both the act of proclaiming and the proclamation itself. It is connected with the proclamation of God's good news concerning repentance, the kingdom, and Jesus—first by John the Baptist (Matt 3:1; Mark 1:4; Luke 3:3), then by Jesus himself (Matt 4:23; 9:35; Mark 1:14,39; Luke 4:4; 8:1), and later by the disciples in the book of Acts (20:25; 28:31). One significant characteristic of the *kerygma* in the Apostle Paul's usage of the term is that it is not designed to be enticing through the use of wise human words, but rather relies entirely on the power of God's Spirit (1 Cor 2:4). This is why Paul entreats Timothy to proclaim (*keryxon*) the message in season and out of season (2 Tim 4:2). And when he finds himself before the tribunal in Rome, even though the session is officially supposed to be his first defense (*en te prote mou apologia*) (2 Tim 4:16), he considers it an opportunity for the proclamation (*kerygma*) to be heard fully by all the Gentiles (2 Tim 4:17).[11]

---

11 On the various meanings of the concept, both inside and outside of the biblical text, see Gerhard Kittel and Gerhard Friedrich, eds.; Geoffrey W. Bromiley, Eng. trans., *Theological Dictionary of the New Testament* (Grand Rapids: Eerdmans, 1966), s.v. "Kerygma," by Gerhard Friedrich.

I want to retain from this Pauline usage the difference between the *kerygma* and the *apologia*, the difference in attitude between an apologetic defense of one's beliefs on the one hand, and a positive proclamation of it on the other. The kerygmatic approach to Christian-Muslim interaction is thus devoid of polemical aggressiveness, apologetic defensiveness, existential adaptiveness, or syncretistic elusiveness; not because any of these other four approaches is necessarily wrong, but because that is the nature of the *kerygma*: God's gracious and positive invitation of humanity into relationship with himself through Jesus. It needs essentially no militant enforcers, no fanatic defenders, no smart adapters, and no crafty revisers.

For the kerygmatic Christ follower, religions are recognized to be an essential part of the human psychological and sociological needs. At the same time, God is seen to be above any religious system. Although God is the absolute Truth, no single religious system is infallible or completely satisfactory. I would contend that the Gospels indicate that Jesus himself, who is never seen as denying his Jewishness, had this attitude. He was at peace with his religious identity as a Jew, practiced the requirements of the law from childhood, entered the Jewish places of worship, and was trained in Jewish theology and methods. At the same time, whenever Jesus expressed frustration in the Gospels, it was generally either toward some stratified religious institutional form such as the Sabbath, or toward stubborn institutional religious leaders. His message cut through the safety of the legalistic boundaries of righteousness, and his invitation to relate to God was extended to the marginalized and outcast of his society. Further, through carefully crafted parables, Jesus proclaimed himself to be the inaugurator of God's kingdom in fulfillment of God's promise to the nations, and he established himself as the final criterion of admission into that kingdom as the way to the Father.

Therefore, in recognition that social organization is a natural human phenomenon toward which we are all inclined, the kerygmatic position and attitude does not consist in rejecting one's religious heritage, for it would soon be replaced by another form of ideology. In the kerygmatic approach it is Christ himself who is at the center of salvation rather than any religious system. The *kerygma* is never a message of condemnation, but it brings condemnation to those that are stuck within religious boundaries. The principal difference between this position and the other positions on the dialogical spectrum is that the conversation is removed entirely from the realm of institutionalized religious talk. One theologian who captured this worldview was Karl Barth. In a chapter he titled "The Revelation of God as the Abolition of Religion," he said, "We begin by stating that religion is unbelief. It is a concern, indeed, we must say that it is the one great concern, of godless man."[12]

The kerygmatic approach that we are here advocating is therefore the equivalent of this Barthian revelation of God. The *kerygma* upheld by this approach is nothing less than God's own revelation in Christ. How, then, does a kerygmatic, suprareligious approach to

12 Hick and Hebblethwaite, *Christianity and Other Religions*, 35.

the way of Christ develop a meaningful view and expression of the Islamic phenomenon? To this we now turn.

View of the Islamic Phenomenon

Whereas the kerygmatic position adopts a suprareligious approach to understanding and relating to God in Christ, it views Islam as an institutionalized religious phenomenon *par excellence*. It can adequately be said that Islamic law, Shariᶜa, is the most authentic manifestation of Islam. In a very real sense, this places it in the category of a sociopolitical phenomenon dressed up in religious clothing. This does not make the religious manifestation of Islam less real or genuine, at least from the perspective of its adherents. One could say that Islam was particularly successful because of its strong religious, ideological component.

Based on a reading of the Qurʾan itself, the kerygmatic approach considers that Islam preserved many important and positive elements from the Judeo-Christian tradition. As such, Islam contains much truth about God and his revelation. On the other hand, because the kerygmatic perspective seeks to be supremely Christ-centered, it also considers that Islam lacks many of the essential truths of God's good news as revealed and proclaimed in and by Jesus Christ in the Gospels.

Islam's prophet in the Kerygmatic approach

The kerygmatic approach would maintain that Muhammad, Islam's messenger, believed that he received a genuine divine calling to be God's prophet to the Arabs. Muhammad's personality is complex and cannot be defined entirely through one single period of his life. He was a charismatic, prophetic leader in Mecca and in the early Medinan period, but then became much more of a political, military, economic, and social leader particularly in the later Medinan period. Qurʾanic evidence seems to indicate that he saw himself very much in continuation of the Judeo-Christian prophetic line, whose mission was to turn his people away from idolatry and to the worship of the one God.

From a purely human perspective and laying aside a theological understanding of revelation and inspiration, Muhammad's personality is not unlike that of some of the Old Testament prophets and men of God. Helpful insight regarding this question can be found in an ancient dialogue between Timothy I, the patriarch of the Church of the East, and the ᶜAbbasid Caliph Al-Mahdī, a conversation that took place near the end of the eighth century. Having been asked by the caliph about his opinion concerning the prophet of Islam, Timothy draws a parallel between him and some of the Old Testament prophets. Like them, "he taught the doctrine of the unity of God," "drove his people away from bad works, and brought them nearer to the good ones," "separated his people from idolatry and polytheism, and attached them to the cult and the knowledge of one God," and "taught about God, His Word and His Spirit." Timothy compares Muhammad to Moses, as he "not only fought for God in words, but showed also his zeal for Him in the sword." Further, Timothy adds, like

Abraham, Muhammad "turned his face from idols and their worshippers, whether those idols were those of his own kinsmen or of strangers, and he honoured and worshipped only one God." Timothy ends his treatment of this subject by stating: "Who will not praise, O our victorious King, the one whom God has praised, and will not weave a crown of glory and majesty to the one whom God has glorified and exalted? These and similar things I and all God-lovers utter about Muhammad, O my sovereign."[13]

This perspective offered by Timothy I, Patriarch of the Church of the East, is helpful in our attempt to make sense of Islam's messenger. A kerygmatic approach believes in the finality of Jesus Christ, in whom the fullness of God's good news was revealed. But this needs not prevent us from admitting the greatness of Muhammad, and perceiving him, if not as a prophet, nonetheless as a *messenger*, a *rasūl*, who carried an important divine message to his people, leading them away from polytheism and drawing them to the worship of the one God.

Islam's Holy Book, the Qurʾan, as viewed in the Kerygmatic approach

> "By the Book that makes things clear, We have made it a Qurʾan in Arabic, that ye may be able to understand [and learn wisdom]" (az-Zukhruf [43]:2,3 Yusuf Ali).
>
> "So have We made the [Qurʾan] easy in thine own tongue, that with it thou mayest give Glad Tidings to the righteous, and warnings to people given to contention" (Maryam [19]:97 Yusuf Ali).
>
> "Verily, We have made this [Qurʾan] easy, in thy tongue, in order that they may give heed" (ad-Dukhān [44]:58 Yusuf Ali).
>
> "And We have indeed made the Qurʾan easy to understand and remember: then is there any that will receive admonition?" (al-Qamar [54]:17 Yusuf Ali).

Numerous verses in the Qurʾan seem to indicate that Muhammad's message was his genuine attempt to provide what he believed to be the essential elements of the Judeo-Christian Scriptures to his Arab people in a language that they could understand, namely Arabic. Some scholars have advanced that the very word "Qurʾan" is actually a borrowing

---

13 Alphonse Mingana, ed., *1. Timothy's Apology for Christianity. 2. The Lament of the Virgin. 3. The Martyrdom of Pilate*, Woodbrooke Studies 2 (Cambridge: W. Hefer & Sons, 1928), 61–62; cited from http://darkwing.uoregon.edu/~sshoemak/102/texts/timothy.html.

from Syriac "*qeryānā*," which means simply a "lectionary."[14] In that view, the Qur'an was originally largely an Arabic lectionary of the Bible, not entirely unlike a Jewish Targum.

In the first verse cited above, the wish of the Qur'an is, literally, that those who receive this Arabic book would perhaps come to a proper understanding (*laᶜallakum taᶜqilūn*) of matters about God. The next three verses are God's assertion to Muhammad that he has provided him with the Qur'an in Arabic in order to make it easy for him (*yassarnāhu*, lit. "we have made it easy) as he proclaims the message.

There are several verses in the Qur'an that seem to support the view that in the initial, Meccan and early Medinan, period, Muhammad perceived his message to be a continuation of the Judeo-Christian tradition. God encourages his messenger by telling him that if his own tribe Quraysh does not receive his message, they should ask the People of the Book (Christians and Jews), who will confirm to them that the message is authentic. There is an assumption at that stage that Christians and Jews will naturally receive his message since it does not stand in contradiction with their own Scriptures.

> "And before thee also the messengers We sent were but men, to whom We granted inspiration: if ye realise this not, ask of those who possess the Message" (an-Naḥl [16]:43 Yusuf Ali).

> "And thus [it is] that We have sent down the Book to thee. So the People of the Book believe therein, as also do some of these [pagan Arabs] and none but Unbelievers reject our signs" (al-ᶜAnkabūt [29]:47 Yusuf Ali).

Both of these passages, according to Muslim commentators, were revealed in Mecca. A third verse, cited below, is less optimistic in outlook. It is a Medinan verse that reflects Muhammad's disappointment with the way that Jews and Christians have rejected his message, as though it contained some elements that were foreign to their own Scriptures.

> "And when there came to them a messenger from Allah, confirming what was with them, a party of the People of the Book threw away the Book of Allah behind their backs, as if [it had been something] they did not know!" (al-Baqara [2]: 101 Yusuf Ali).

From that point onward, namely the later Medinan period, Muhammad begins to dissociate himself from the Judeo-Christian tradition. One of the most striking manifestations of this is the change in the direction of prayer (*qibla*) which is introduced in *Sūrat* al-Baqara [2]:143–45. Initially, the community of Muhammad had prayed in the direction of Jerusalem, as did the Jews and the oriental Christians. Al-Wāḥidī's treatise on *Asbāb an-Nuzūl*

14 For this view in recent scholarship, see Christoph Luxenberg, *The Syro-Aramaic Reading of the Koran: A Contribution to the Decoding of the Language of the Koran* (Berlin: Hans Schiler, 2007).

[The Occasions of the Revelations] mentions with regard to verse 144 that Muhammad received this new instruction sixteen months after his arrival in Medina. This was roughly the time period when Muhammad's relationship especially with the Jews of Medina had seriously deteriorated.[15]

Muslims seen through the Kerygmatic perspective

If we believe the traditional Islamic account of the development of Muhammad's early community, we may conclude that Arabs who received the initial Meccan message essentially found themselves at a similar place as the kinsmen of the biblical patriarch, Abraham, with a clear invitation to abandon polytheism and take up the worship of the one God. During the early Medinan period, however, the community surrounding Muhammad found itself in conflict with those with whom it had sought continuity, particularly the Jews of Medina. Furthermore, not unlike the Jews of Jesus' time, they had to reckon with a picture of Jesus that conflicted in many aspects with the one that was developing within Muhammad's message. Due to growing economic, social, and political conflict with the Medinan Jews, the result was a rejection of that picture and a growing distance from the Judeo-Christian tradition.

Today, a kerygmatic perception of Muslims would say that even though Muslims have as their foremost concern to please God, they lack the ability to enjoy that deep and personal relationship with God, which according to the Gospels is only possible for those who respond to Christ's invitation to approach God as Father through a brotherly sonship with himself. It is this view of the Islamic phenomenon as I have developed it here, including the understanding of where Muslims are in their search and journey toward God that motivates a follower of Christ to be a witness, to share this divine *kerygma* with Muslims. We now turn briefly to the purpose, methods, and outcomes of this endeavor.

Purpose of Relationship with Islam and Muslims

Against the background of the position developed above, those Christ followers who hold a kerygmatic understanding of Islam will engage with Muslims on two solid foundations: respect and trust. On the one hand, neither the syncretistic attitude to religions that plays down the uniqueness of a person's spiritual experience, nor the polemical attitude that seeks to emphasize the negative aspects of another person's worldview, will foster mutual respect between two people. On the other hand, both existential and apologetic approaches will shy away from true engagement, the first seeking to stay away from God talk, and the latter (in its extreme form) raising a defensive wall without ever engaging creatively and positively. These are of course somewhat generalizations, but they are helpful to identify further the middle way. Kerygmatic persons do not shy away from engagement. And because they do so based on a thoughtfully developed framework and understanding of Islam, they can do

15 An English translation of this work can be found at http://www.altafsir.com. See especially http://www.altafsir.com/AsbabAlnuzol.asp?SoraName=2&Ayah=144&search=yes&img=A.

so respectfully, with a genuine desire to learn through a mutual exchange of perceptions about God and faith. Engagement with Islam at a kerygmatic level will almost always be enriching for all involved.

In the context of this mutually-enriching relationship of respect, trust will develop, to the point where meaningful conversation can take place. Meaningful, life-transforming, conversation can hardly take place outside such respect and trust. And the kerygmatic person knows that any meaningful conversation about Christ should be life-transforming, as the uniqueness that Christ brings to our human relationship with God is shared. But it is important to emphasize that this engagement does not go merely in one direction. The relationship of trust and respect that is developed through the kerygmatic approach should precisely be mutual. Kerygmatic engagement creates an opportunity to listen to what Muslims have to say about religious issues as well, the opportunity to learn and stand corrected, rather than stick to our own perceptions of what they believe, so that misunderstandings and misperceptions may be dissipated.

Methods Used in the Kerygmatic Approach to Islam and Muslims

The practice of the kerygmatic approach in Christian-Muslim interaction knows few boundaries. Every occasion is suitable to bear witness respectfully to Christ's good news. A Christ follower using that approach will happily make use of the Qurʾan and other elements of the Islamic tradition as appropriate and acceptable bridges of communication.

This approach will not shy away from discussion forums on theological, doctrinal, social, cultural, and other issues. No topic is taboo, since a respectful exchange is prepared and assumed. At the kerygmatic level, dialogue takes place between religious and scholarly leaders that have a deeply rooted faith and are willing to share uncompromisingly with genuine people. As a result, the outcome of such exchange is deep and reaches the grass roots.

My emphasis on a middle way, the kerygmatic approach, does not negate the legitimacy of using other types of interaction found on the D1–D5 spectrum. In my experience, different settings and audiences may require different styles and approaches. I personally would in most cases avoid D1 and D5, save in some exceptional circumstances where the depth of a friendship may allow and call for the tackling of a hot and problematic issue at a D5 level. In general, I would favor a combination of D2 and D3 in a public setting, where the tackling of social issues (D2) is crucial and more likely to be fruitful. In private settings, I would favor a combination of D3 and D4, the apologetic approach often serving to clarify certain deep-rooted misunderstandings that Muslims have about Christ and the Bible. Whereas tackling such issues in public is often futile, it can be quite appropriate in conversation with a nondefensive Muslim friend who is genuinely seeking to understand. Finally I find myself leaning toward D2 in conversation with Muslim religious leaders, and more toward D4 in conversation with less prominent Muslims.

From a missional perspective, the nonaggressive and suprareligious nature of the kerygmatic attitude and discourse has the potential to avoid the immediate alienation of a Muslim who wishes to explore the implications of God's good news in Christ by other members of that person's community. This means that extraction of such a person from his or her community—whether induced or self-imposed—can be avoided, so that the community as a whole may benefit from Christ's transforming power.

Exhibit 1:
Test of Attitude to Islam and Muslims (TAIM)
For each issue, circle *one* letter that best reflects your position.

1) **My view of religions is that:**
   a) All roads lead to Rome.
   b) Goodness and morality are the essence of religions.
   c) They are an essential part of the human psychological and sociological need. Although God is the absolute Truth, no single religious system is infallible or completely satisfactory.
   d) There is only one ultimate Truth, and that is God.
   e) There is only one religion that is truly from God: Christianity.

2) **Islam was:**
   a) A religion that originated from God, but like all religions, it has undergone many human influences as well.
   b) A sociopolitical phenomenon, successful because of its strong religious ideological element, which was carried over essentially from the Judeo-Christian tradition.
   c) A human phenomenon whose understanding of God is misleading.
   d) A scheme developed and carried out by the devil.
   e) A sociopolitical phenomenon like any other successful religious movement of human history.

3) **Muhammad was:**
   a) A charismatic prophetic and political leader who genuinely believed he had received a divine prophetic calling for his people.
   b) Misled and may have had some psychological problems that led him to believe that he had received a prophetic calling.
   c) Possessed by demons, an Antichrist whose mission was to deceive all people.

d) A shrewd sociopolitical leader who knew how to use his contemporary economic and historical realities to the advantage of his community and personal ends.
e) To some degree the recipient of a divine calling to be God's Prophet to the Arabs.

4) **The Qur'an:**
   a) Was a plagiarism of the Bible and contains many mistakes and inaccuracies.
   b) Was inspired by the devil and is full of lies and deceit. Merely reading it renders a person unclean.
   c) Was a literary achievement of Muhammad himself or some of his entourage, which Muhammad used in order to impress a society that was strongly attracted to poetic literature.
   d) Contains substantial elements of the divine truth and is to be respected as Scripture.
   e) Was Muhammad's genuine attempt to provide what he believed to be the essential elements of the Judeo-Christian Scriptures in the Arabic language.

5) **Practicing Muslims are:**
   a) The deceived followers of a religion that has nothing good to offer the world.
   b) Adherents of a religious ideology that offers a viable code of ethics and makes them into good citizens.
   c) Viewed positively by God when they faithfully strive to be pious and devout.
   d) Primarily concerned to please God, but they lack the ability to enjoy a deep personal relationship with him through Christ.
   e) Being misled by a worldly religion that drives them away from the worship of the true God.

6) **In the end:**
   a) Muslims will all go to hell, because they have fallen to deception.
   b) Muslims will not be saved, because they did not come to the knowledge of Christ.
   c) Muslims who are genuine seekers may come to a knowledge of Christ even based on the Qur'an.
   d) Muslims will be saved if they are faithful to the religion of Islam.
   e) Muslims, like all other people, will be saved by the unlimited benevolence of God.

7) **My purpose in relating to Muslims is:**
   a) To evangelize them by demonstrating to them the truth of Christianity and refuting the validity of Islam.
   b) To have an opportunity to witness about the unique elements that Christ brings to enrich human beings' relationship with God.
   c) To encourage mutual social and religious understanding and tolerance between Christian and Muslim communities.
   d) To invite Muslims to be a positive part of a multicultural and multireligious universal humanity in all of its rich plurality.
   e) To demonstrate to Muslims the falsity and deceitfulness of Islam and save as many of them as possible from perdition.

8) **In interacting with Muslims, the best methods are:**
   a) The use of the Qurʾan, the Bible, and other elements of both traditions as a foundation for discussing theological, doctrinal, social, and cultural issues.
   b) The affirmation of common ground and avoidance of divisive issues.
   c) To dialogue on social, economic, and political issues.
   d) To accentuate religious differences and use polemics to discredit Islam, or not to relate to Muslims at all.
   e) Public debates that make heavy use of apologetic arguments.

9) **I believe that my interaction with Muslims should lead:**
   a) To positive transformation of mutual perceptions and relationships.
   b) To greater tolerance and appreciation between communities.
   c) To the accentuation of differences between religious communities and to the prevailing of Christianity.
   d) Muslims to convert to Christianity by being convinced of the prevailing truth of Christianity above all other religions.
   e) To deep impact into Muslim societies without creating immediate enmity between members of the community, and avoiding "extraction" for those who might take up Christ.

10) **In order to interact effectively with Muslims, I believe that:**
   a) I need to comprehend Islam as a political reality.
   b) I need to learn all the weaknesses and problems in Islam.
   c) I need to acquire a thorough knowledge of the answers to Islamic questions and challenges.
   d) I need to acquire a thorough insider's knowledge of Islam.
   e) I need to comprehend the broad lines of Islam as a religion.

Exhibit 2:

Key to the TAIM

Assign yourself the numerical value that corresponds with your answer to each question, and then calculate your total.

1) My view of religions:
a=1, b=2, c=3, d=4, e=5

2) Islam:
a=2, b=3, c=4, d=5, e=1

3) Muhammad:
a=3, b=4, c=5, d=1, e=2

4) The Qur'an:
a=4, b=5, c=1, d=2, e=3

5) Practicing Muslims:
a=5, b=1, c=2, d=3, e=4

6) In the end:
a=5, b=4, c=3, d=2, e=1

7) Purpose:
a=4, b=3, c=2, d=1, e=5

8) Best methods:
a=3, b=2, c=1, d=5, e=4

9) Outcome:
a=2, b=1, c=5, d=4, e=3

10) Extent of knowledge of Islam:
a=1, b=5, c=4, d=3, e=2

Total: _____

INTERPRETATION OF TAIM RESULTS:

10–12: Syncretistic *Attitude to Islam and Muslims*
13–22: Existential *Attitude to Islam and Muslims*
23–32: Kerygmatic *Attitude to Islam and Muslims*
33–42: Apologetic *Attitude to Islam and Muslims*
43–50: Polemical *Attitude to Islam and Muslims*

2
The Ishmael Promises and Mission Motivation

BY JONATHAN E. CULVER

Friendly conversations with Muslims seem to be in short supply these days, especially among American evangelicals. Laurie Goodstein highlights this point in her disturbing *New York Times* article on May 27, 2003, entitled "Seeing Islam as 'Evil' Faith, Evangelicals Seek Converts." Evangelicals have always believed that Islam and other religions are wrong, but what now stands out, says Goodstein, is the mean-spirited stream of anti-Islam rhetoric that is pouring forth from evangelical sources.[1] Furthermore, from the numerous examples that Goodstein cites, we find a singular absence of objective statements about Islam based on reliable academic research. Seldom do we see today a missionary passion to reach Muslims marked by respect rather than denigration. American evangelicals urgently need a more constructive attitude towards Muslims if they wish to win them for Christ. One way to do this is to reexamine the promises that God made to Abraham regarding his son Ishmael. These promises have important implications for Muslims when viewed from the perspective of God's mission.

I have been promoting the Ishmael promise theme in Indonesia, the world's largest Muslim nation, since 1994. As a result, many Christians in that country have come away with a greater desire to reach Muslims based on love and respect. I have also found that fruitful conversations often take place when I share these promises with Indonesian Muslims. Clearly, the Ishmael promise theme is a dynamic message that could also impact Christians in America and other countries. But in order to see how it could do so, I first need to explain the nature and significance of these promises and then show how they have influenced

---

1 For example, one evangelical leader describes Islam as an "evil religion." Another speaks of Muhammad, prophet of Islam, as "a demon possessed pedophile," while a well-known missionary author likens the "good verses" of the Qurʾan to "the food an assassin adds to poison to disguise a deadly taste." While these assessments might satisfy the desire of American evangelicals to "strike back" at Muslim terrorists, we should remember that they outrage moderate Muslims who might otherwise be open to the gospel. Furthermore, comments like the above suffer from serious factual distortions. See Goodstein for names and references.

Indonesian Christian thinking about mission to Muslims. At the end of this chapter, I will provide an excursus on the historicity of Arab descent from Ishmael.

The Forgotten Promises

Genesis 16–21 contains four remarkable promises that God conferred on Ishmael and his descendants. In the first instance, the angel of the Lord assured Hagar: "I will greatly multiply your descendants so that they will be too many to count … Behold, you are with child, and you shall bear a son; and you shall call his name Ishmael, because the Lord has given heed to your affliction" (16:10,11 NASB). Then in a key promise to Abraham, God pledged: "And as for Ishmael, I have heard you; behold I will bless him, I will make him fruitful … He shall become the father of twelve princes and I will make him a great nation" (17:20). Similar assurances were conveyed once again to Abraham in Genesis 21:13, and again to Hagar in Genesis 21:17,18.

A study of these Ishmael promises has helped in changing Indonesian Christian attitudes toward Muslims. When they see the angel of Yahweh speaking words of grace and promise to Hagar, it begins to tear down the walls of prejudice, fear, and resentment.

The Significance of the Promises

It is fascinating to note the striking similarity of the Ishmael promises to aspects of the Abrahamic covenant promises granting "blessing," "numerous descendants," and a "great nation" (Gen 12:2; 17:4–6). But unlike the promises for Abraham and Isaac, the Ishmaelite promises lack the essential covenant component later fulfilled in Christ: "In you all the nations will be blessed" (Gen 12:3; 18:18; 22:15; 26:4; Gal 3:14). Clearly, the promises for Ishmael do not confer any sense of missionary privilege to his line. That prerogative belongs exclusively to Abraham's promised son, Isaac, along with his lineal and spiritual descendants (Gen 26:4; Isa 42:6: 49:6; Gal 3:9,29). God makes this point very clear to Abraham when he says, "I will establish my covenant with Isaac" and not with Ishmael (Gen 17:19,21). Thus the Ishmael promises are not covenant promises.

Even though the Bible gives the primacy to Isaac's line in God's plan of salvation for the nations, we should not minimize what God does say about Abraham's other son: "And as for Ishmael … behold, I will bless him … I will make him a great nation" (Gen 17:20). This is a unique kind of promise because no other individual in the Bible outside of the covenant community is ever blessed by God in such a manner. Furthermore, God explains to Abraham that the reason he will confer such a blessing is "because he [Ishmael] is your descendant [lit., seed]" (Gen 21:13). Thus the promises for Ishmael are physically rooted in the Abrahamic family. This element distinguishes Ishmael's line from other nations.

Another aspect of Ishmael's uniqueness stands out in Genesis 21:20: "And God was with the lad [Ishmael] … in the wilderness." Ishmael is the only person outside the covenant line about whom it is said, God was "with" him. Why was God "with" Ishmael? Because Abraham prayed, "Oh that Ishmael might live before you" (Gen 18:18). For what purpose was God "with" Ishmael? To preserve him and his *descendants* for a hidden but gracious purpose,[2] a purpose that is progressively revealed in the biblical narrative.

It may surprise the reader to learn that this theme—Ishmael as the unique recipient of God's missionary purpose—recurs throughout the Old and New Testaments. For example, in Isaiah 60:6,7 it is the Arabian descendants of Abraham—the sons of Keturah and the sons of Ishmael (Gen 25:1–6,12,13)—who are the first of the nations to bring their offerings and worship God in the new Jerusalem. The passage is so striking that Samuel Zwemer referred to it as the "gem of missionary prophecy."[3] The reader should also note that the Magi, who are very likely Arabs, are the first of the Gentiles to worship Christ.[4] And if Paul was involved in missionary activity in Arabia, as argued by an increasing number of biblical scholars,[5] then the Nabataean Arabs[6] were the first of the Gentile nations to whom he preached the gospel (Gal 1:16; 2 Cor 11:32,33). These scriptural passages contain significant theological data that underscore three points: (1) God's promises for Ishmael extend beyond the Genesis narrative, (2) God's promises concerning Ishmael contain a missionary intention imbued with a sense of theological urgency (the first to come, the first to worship, the first to be reached), and (3) this divine missionary intention applies to the lineal descendants of Ishmael, most of whom are now Muslims. It could also include those who have come under the Arab Muslim religio-cultural umbrella—in other words, the worldwide Muslim community.[7]

---

2 A providential element emerges here, something that was first noticed by the Anglican priest Charles Forster in 1829. See Clinton Bennett's fascinating study on Forster's Ishmael theology in "Is Isaac Without Ishmael Complete? A Nineteenth-Century Debate Re-visited," *Islam and Christian-Muslim Relations* 2, no. 1 (1991): 42–55.

3 Isaiah 60 is open to different levels of fulfillment, but the reader should note that the imagery in the new Jerusalem passage of Revelation 21:9–27 draws extensively from Isaiah 60 according to Samuel M. Zwemer, "Hagar and Ishmael," *The Evangelical Quarterly* 22, no. 1 (1950): 35.

4 For more on the Arabian origin of the Magi, see Tony Maalouf, *Arabs in the Shadow of Israel: The Unfolding of God's Prophetic Plan for Ishmael's Line* (Grand Rapids: Kregel, 2003), 193–204.

5 For recent thinking on this subject see, Martin Hengel and Anna Maria Schwemer, *Paul Between Damascus and Antioch: The Unknown Years*, trans. John Bowden (Louisville: Westminster John Knox, 1997), 106–26; Terence L. Donaldson, *Paul and the Gentiles: Remapping the Apostle's Convictional World* (Minneapolis: Fortress, 1997), 271; Seyoon Kim, *Paul and the New Perspective: Second Thoughts on the Origin of Paul's Gospel* (Grand Rapids: Eerdmans, 2002), 103–4; Eckhard J. Schnabel, *Early Christian Mission: Paul and the Early Church*, vol. 2 (Downers Grove, IL: InterVarsity, 2004), 1031–45.

6 Paul mentions by name the Nabataean Arab king, Aretas IV, whose Damascus official tries to arrest Paul in 2 Corinthians 11:32,33, most likely because Paul had been preaching the gospel in "Arabia."

7 The link between the Ishmael promises and non-Arab Muslims is based on the phrase, "I will make him a great nation" (Gen 17:20; 21:13, 18; 25:12–18). In the Old Testament, "great nation" (Hebrew *goy gadol*) almost always refers to a multiethnic grouping. For example, the great nation promise God made to Abraham (Gen 12:2) implicitly includes much more than Isaac, Jacob, and the twelve Hebrew tribes. Indeed, Abraham's great nation embraces a grand array of "Abrahamic descendants" from many nations (Gen 17:4–6). Similarly, Jeremiah refers to Babylon as a "great nation" from the "north land" (6:22), a multiethnic entity composed of "all the families of the north" (25:9) and "all the kings of the north" (25:26; cf. Harrison 1973, 125). Similar terminology is also used for Persia (Jer 50:9,41). In accordance with these examples, the Ishmaelite "great nation" promise anticipates the gathering of various peoples under the religio-cultural umbrella such as that provided by the Arab Muslims.

As we approach the latter days, I believe that we will see a divine intervention in the strongholds of Islam that will open the hearts of millions of Muslims to the gospel. This divine visitation has already begun, attended by dreams, visions, and miracles.[8] It will move on to other amazing developments in accord with the theological urgency expressed in the Ishmael promises. In order to prepare for those days, Christian minds and hearts need to be shaped by a biblical perspective on Muslims. This kind of preparation is now taking place among some of the Christians in Indonesia.

The Ishmael Promises and Christian-Muslim Conversation in Indonesia

Motivating Christians in Indonesia to reach Muslims is no easy task. We need to recall that since 1995, Muslim radicals have destroyed or shut down hundreds of Indonesian churches. Furthermore, thousands of Indonesian Christians have been killed in recurring civil conflicts in places like Ambon and Poso. In light of these developments, it is not surprising that many Indonesian Christians believe that Ishmael and his progeny (e.g., the Muslims) are under the curse of God (Gen 16:12). A clear example of this appears in a controversial Christian tract entitled *Siapakah yang Bernama Allah Itu*? [Who Is Allah?].[9] In this work, the anonymous author argues that Ishmael is under a curse based on the following: Ishmael's mother, Hagar, was an Egyptian and thus under the curse of Ham (Gen 9:25; 10:6); and the Genesis 16:12 prophecy depicts Ishmael as a wild donkey (i.e., a barbarian perpetually in conflict with his brethren).[10]

Why does this unfortunate stereotyping occur? The reason is, if Genesis 16:12 can be interpreted as a condemnation of Muslims, it comforts Indonesian Christians who have suffered from unpleasant encounters with Muslims. This kind of interpretation reflects prejudice rather than sound exegesis. It tends to justify attitudes that condemn Muslims and close Christian hearts to reach them.

A more accurate exegesis must begin with the realization that Genesis 16:12 is given in the context of a promise to Hagar. Earlier, the angel of Yahweh had given Hagar a command to return to Abram's tent (16:9). He then gave a promise (16:10,11) to motivate her to obey. It would be strange indeed for the angel to try and motivate Hagar by pronouncing a curse on her unborn child! Accordingly, it would be better to understand the wild donkey oracle as a prophetic metaphor describing the Bedouin lifestyle of Ishmael and his descendants.

---

8 See Stan Guthrie, *Missions in the Third Millennium: 21 Key Trends for the 21st Century* (Waynesboro, GA: Paternoster, 2002).

9 *Siapakah yang Bernama Allah Itu?* [Who Is Allah?] (Jakarta: Bet Yesua Hamasiah, 1998) 1, 18.

10 Actually, the curse was directed at Ham's son, Canaan, whereas Egypt is blessed by God in Isaiah 19:25. The "wild donkey" metaphor is more adequately understood as descriptive of a Bedouin lifestyle, not a curse. Furthermore, "he will live in hostility toward all his brothers" (Gen 16:12 NIV) could also be translated "he shall dwell in the presence of all his brethren" (KJV), or "to the east of all his brothers" (NASB).

This would be in accord with Job 39:5–8 where God himself describes the wild donkey as a freedom-loving creature roaming about the wilderness in search of sustenance.[11]

The Impact of the Ishmael Promises

Since 1994 I have had many opportunities to present a more positive interpretation of these verses relating to Ishmael in sermons, seminars, and seminary classrooms throughout Indonesia. PowerPoint presentations and my book have enhanced the process. Interestingly, as Muslim-Christian conflict has increased, the receptivity of the audience has also increased. I would like to share a few examples that demonstrate how my presentation of the Ishmael theme helps tear down the walls of prejudice and provide a better theological foundation for engagement with Muslims.

During a teaching session for master's degree students at a local Bible college, I noticed a young Chinese-Indonesian pastor intently listening to my presentation on Ishmael. Afterwards he said to me, "This is a new way to look at Muslims. My entire outlook on Muslims has been changed. Please come to my church in Jakarta and preach on this subject." I accepted his invitation and was shocked to discover that this student pastored a huge five thousand-member church! A few months later, the pastor invited me to come again, along with two of my missionary colleagues. This time he asked us to present a Muslim awareness seminar for his leaders. As a result, the congregation began a serious effort to reach out to Muslims. To further the work, they allocated funds to add an experienced evangelist to their staff. This resulted in a dynamic incarnational outreach in a Muslim community in Jakarta.

Over the following years, I taught these same principles in Muslim awareness seminars in large urban centers throughout the islands of Java, Sumatra, and Kalimantan. Sometimes, my teaching produced surprising results. For example, after giving a presentation in Jakarta, the pastor asked for responses from the audience. A woman, with tears streaming down her face, confessed that she had hardened her heart toward her Muslim relatives. She explained, "The Ishmael promises showed me that God loves Muslims. My judgmental attitudes have been wrong!" In another case, at a seminary in Yogyakarta, Central Java, a young man told me that my lecture on Ishmael led him to make a commitment to give his life to reaching Muslims.

It is among Muslim converts, however, where I have found the most enthusiastic response. A case in point is that of Bambang Noorsena, a Muslim convert of Arab-Javanese descent with a master's degree in Islamic jurisprudence (*fiqh*). When I gave him an overview of the Ishmael promises he said, "*Pak* Jon, this teaching has really touched my heart. When I converted to Christianity I was told that my Muslim heritage was cursed. Thank you for lifting that burden off me!"[12]

---

11 For an extensive exegetical argument showing that Genesis 16:12 and Galatians 4:21–31 are not pronouncements of condemnation on Ishmael and the Arabs, see Tony Maalouf's *Arabs in the Shadow*, 69–79, 97–104.

12 Bambang Noorsena, interview by the author, June 30, 1994, Bandung, Indonesia.

This positive approach to Ishmael has also resonated favorably with other Muslim converts. When I asked one of them why he kept preaching on this topic, he said, "There is a great gap between Indonesian Christians and Muslims. I use the Ishmael promises to encourage Christians to care about Muslims and make friends with them." Some Christian background leaders also use the Ishmael promise theme, such as Irwan Soleman, who heads a national mission mobilization agency.

These positive responses encouraged me to publish a short book (in Indonesian) entitled *Janji-Janji yang Terlupakan: Ismael Selayang Pandang dari Alkitab* [The Forgotten Promises: Ishmael from a Biblical Perspective] (Culver 1998). As a result, the topic has spread more widely throughout Indonesia. Several Bible schools and cross-cultural training centers are now requiring their students to read this book. The chapter titles below give the reader an idea of how I present the subject:

1. The Forgotten Promises
2. Ishmael: A Name from Heaven (Genesis 16)
3. A Promise of Blessing, but not the Blessing of the Covenant (Genesis 17)
4. The Tragic Breakup of Abraham's Family (Genesis 21)
5. From Morocco to Merauke: Ishmael's Sons Become a Great Nation (Genesis 25)
6. For What Purpose Does Ishmael Become a Great Nation (Isa 60:1–7)?
7. Why Must I Love the Descendants of Ishmael?

The reader can see from this outline that I have arranged the material to promote missionary motivation to reach Muslims.

A Bridge for Friendly Conversations with Muslims

The "Ishmael promise" theme has also opened the door for friendly conversations with Muslims in Indonesia. When the opportunity arises, I ask Muslims, "Did you know that the Taurat (Torah) contains some beautiful promises that God made to Hagar and Abraham (*Siti Hajar* and *Nabi Ibrahim*) concerning Ishmael? Would you like me to recite these promises for you?" I have never had a Muslim refuse my offer.

One encounter took place during a train ride from Jakarta to Bandung. I was surprised to learn that the man seated next to me was a professor of comparative religion at an Islamic university in Bandung. How fascinating! I also was a professor, an instructor in missions and religions at a Christian theological school in Bandung. So there we were, a Muslim and a Christian, enjoying a friendly conversation together on our three-hour journey. We also had questions we wanted to ask about each other's religion, but we did our best to phrase our questions politely. But sometimes the atmosphere became a bit tense. For me, the highlight of this encounter came when I posed my last question: "Did you know that the Taurat contains some wonderful promises about Ishmael?" After I quoted the promises relating to Ishmael and narrated the background stories, this professor sat silently for a moment. Then, with a look of wonder on his face, he asked, "Does the Taurat really contain stories like that?" He could not believe that the Jewish/Christian holy book could speak so kindly about two individuals, Hagar and Ishmael, whom he deeply revered as a Muslim. The way I shared these promises indicated to him that I respected him and could speak deferentially about an important aspect of his religious traditions. Based on many other experiences like the one above, I am convinced that a sincere, heartfelt presentation of the Ishmael promises promotes friendly conversations between Muslims and Christians.[13]

Excursus: What Does Ishmael Have to Do with Islam?

The promises concerning Ishmael are beautiful, some critics have told me, but they are time-bound, basically fulfilled in Genesis 25:12–18, and thus have no ongoing force as a source of blessing for Ishmael's descendants, whoever they might be. These are some of the issues that Colin Chapman raises in a thought-provoking article entitled "Second Thoughts about the Ishmael Theme."[14] Chapman does not shut the door on the possibility of an Ishmael-Arab-Islam connection, but he avers that there is almost no exegetical or historical warrant for it.

I have already provided an exegetical foundation for this subject earlier in this chapter. For more details, I refer the reader to my doctoral dissertation and to one of my published articles[15] along with the excellent study by Maalouf.[16]

As for the historical evidence linking Ishmael with the Arabs, many Western scholars handle this problem with great skepticism. Many have maintained that descent from Ishmael was never an indigenous Arabian concept. Rather, it was a late idea that the early Muslims devised to advance the apostolic character of Islam.[17] The concept was later embellished by

13 For an example of how I presented the Ishmael promises for an international audience of Muslim readers, see Jonathan Edwin Culver, "The Ishmael Promises: A Bridge for Mutual Respect," in *Muslim and Christian Reflections on Peace: Divine and Human Dimensions*, eds. J. Dudley Woodberry, Osman Zümrüt, and Mustafa Köylü (Lanham, MD: University Press of America, 2005), 67–80.

14 Colin Chapman, "Second Thoughts about the Ishmael Theme," *Seedbed* 4, no. 4 (1989): 50–57.

15 Jonathan Culver, "The Ishmael Promises in the Light of God's Mission: Christian and Muslim Reflections" (PhD diss., Fuller Theological Seminary, 2001); Jonathan Culver, "The Ishmael Promise and Contextualization among Muslims," *International Journal of Frontier Missions* 17, no. 1 (January–March 2000): 61–70.

16 Maalouf, *Arabs in the Shadow*.

17 Cf. Alfred Guillaume, *Islam* (New York: Penguin, 1966); René Dagorn, *La geste d'Ismaël: D'après l'onomastique et la tradition arabes* (Paris: Meme, 1981).

Muslims of the second and third Islamic centuries when they forged a patriarchal pedigree for Muhammad.

The problem, it seems, lies in the fact that the Muslim sources do not successfully validate their Ishmael claims. However, if we go outside the Islamic sources, we will discover a credible line of evidence drawn from archaeology, ancient Greco-Roman authorities, and a few early church fathers that verify the broad outlines of Islam's claim of descent from Ishmael. Some of the most pertinent facts are listed below.[18]

The Historical Evidence Linking Ishmael and the Arabs/Muslims

1) The Assyrian and Babylonian inscriptions of the first millennium BC make frequent references to desert tribes bearing the names of some of the sons of Ishmael listed in Genesis 25:13–15; particularly the tribe of Kedar, Ishmael's second son.[19] Indeed, the Kedarites were the nomadic desert power par excellence through the Assyrian, Babylonian, and Persian periods. In the fifth century BC, the Kedarites and allied tribes appear to have formed some sort of confederation extending from the Nile Delta to the Persian Gulf, and from northwest Arabia to Transjordania. By the beginning of the fourth century BC, however, they gave way to the Nabataeans, and subsequently began to disappear from the historical scene.[20]

2) A fifth century BC Arabian inscription in the oasis of Dedan, two hundred miles north of Medina, mentions that a son of Jashm (Arabic *Geshem*) ruled as the governor in that vicinity. This ruler is very likely a son of "Geshem the Arab," the enemy of Nehemiah (Neh 6:1,2). This same individual is also known as "Geshem, King of Kedar" in a fifth century BC Egyptian inscription.[21] What we have here is a documented Kedarite presence close to the heartland of Islam.[22]

3) The Nabataean Arabs, whose king (Aretas) Paul mentions in 2 Corinthians 11:32, serve as an intriguing link between Ishmael and the early Muslims. Chronologically speaking, they occupy the time gap between the demise of the Ishmaelite tribe of Kedar (c. 350

18 Cf. Culver, "Ishmael Promise and Contextualization," 67–68; Culver, "Ishmael Promises in the Light," 171–230.

19 James B. Pritchard, *Ancient Near Eastern Texts Relating to the Old Testament*, Princeton, NJ: Princeton University Press, 1955), 300–310. cf. Isa 21:16; 42:11; 60:7; Jer 49:28,29; Ezek 27:21.

20 Ernst Knauf, *Ismael: Untersuchungen zur Geschichte Palästinas und Nordarabiens Im 1. Jahrtausend V. Chr* (*Ishmael: Investigations on the History of Palestine and North Arabia in the First Millennium* B. C.) (Wiesbaden, Germany: Harrassowitz, 1985), 96–108.

21 Isaac Rabinowitz, "Aramaic Inscriptions of the Fifth Century B. C. E. From a North-Arab Shrine in Egypt." *Journal of Near Eastern Studies* 15, no. 1 (1956): 1–9; William J. Dumbrell, "The Tell El-Maskhuta Bowls and the 'Kingdom' of Qedar in the Persian Period." *Bulletin of the American Schools of Oriental Research* 203 (1971): 33–44; Frank M. Cross, "Geshem the Arabian, Enemy of Nehemiah." *The Biblical Archaeologist* 18, no. 2 (1955): 46–47.

22 David Graf, "Arabia During Achaemenid Times," in *Achaemenid History IV: Centre and Periphery*, eds. H. Sancisi-Weerdenburg and A. Kuhrt (Leiden: Brill, 1990), 139–40; Frederick V. Winnett, *A Study of the Thamudic and Lihyanite Inscriptions*, Oriental Series 3 (Toronto, ON: University of Toronto Studies, 1937), 51.

BC) and the rise of Islam (AD 622). However, their precise origins are shrouded in mystery, giving rise to different theories. Thus, according to the German transjordanian scholar, Ernst Knauf, the Nabataeans are a subclan of the Kedar tribe. On the other hand, Edomite scholar John Bartlett[23] associates them with Nebaioth, Ishmael's firstborn son.[24]

4) According to early Islamic sources, Qusayy b. Kilab, a fifth-century Meccan reformer and the ancestor of Muhammad from the fifth generation, claimed to be a descendant of Kedar. Interestingly, a line of evidence indicates that Qusayy was a Nabataean.[25]

5) The Christian Arab scholar Irfan Shahid has compiled a convincing body of evidence proving that at least some of the pre-Islamic Arabs maintained an independent, self-conscious awareness of their descent from Ishmael. This information provides a context for the claim made by Qusayy above. It also seriously erodes the thesis that the idea for Arab descent from Ishmael was concocted by the earliest Muslims to establish a biblical pedigree for Muhammad and the Arabs.[26]

The outline of the above evidence clearly shows that the Muslim claim of Arab descent from Ishmael is not simply mythological. On the contrary, descent from Ishmael on the part of at least some of the Arab tribes, and perhaps Muhammad himself, is at least very feasible if not probable.

Conclusion

The Ishmael promise theme needs to be reconsidered in the light of God's missionary purposes for the worldwide Muslim community. The biblical and historical data presented in this chapter challenges the evangelical community in the West (and other countries) to humbly reconsider their negative attitudes toward Muslims. If they do so, it will surely enhance their motivation for mission. This is an urgent need as evangelicals have reached a crisis point in our post-9/11 world, as reflected in the intensity of the anti-Islam rhetoric propounded by many Christians today.

---

23 John R. Bartlett, "From Edomites to Nabataeans: A Study in Continuity," *Palestine Exploration Quarterly* 111 (1979): 53–66.

24 Knauf, *Ismael*, 96–112; Knauf, "Nabataean Origins," *Arabian Studies in Memory of Mohamed Ghul: Symposium at Yarmuk University December 8–11, 1984,* ed. Moawiyah Ibrahim (Wiesbaden, Germany: Harrassowitz, 1989), 56–61.

25 Toufic Fahd detects a Nabataean origin for Qusayy and certain members of the Meccan Quraysh clan based on a passage from the *Kitāb al-Aghānī* compiled by Abū al-Faraj al-Iṣbahānī (d. AD 967). Fahd argues that the reference refers to the Nabaṭ al-Shām, the Nabataeans of the Syro-Palestinian region, not the Nabaṭ al-Irāq, the early Muslim designation for Mesopotamia. The text says: "Where did the Quraysh come from? They are kinfolk of the Nabataeans" (*ayyi thanīyatin talafiat quraysh wa kānū mafisharan mutanabbitīnā*). I am indebted to David Johnston for assisting me in vocalizing this ancient text from Kitāb al-Aghānī, 18, 52, as quoted in Toufic Fahd, *La divination arabe: Études religieuses, sociologiques et folkloriques sur le milieu natif de l'Islam* [Arabian divination: Religious, sociological, and folklore studies of Islam's indigenous milieu] (1987), 123 n. 2; cf. al-Tabari 1988, 38; Della Vida 1986, 520).

26 Irfan Shahid, *Byzantium and the Arabs in the Fifth Century* (Washington, DC: Dumbarton Oaks, 1989), 154–58, 167–80, 332–60, 382–404.

3
Squeezing Ethics Out of Law: What Is Shari^ca Anyway?

BY DAVID L. JOHNSTON

What might the second General Guide of the Egyptian Muslim Brotherhood have in common with an Iranian intellectual, theologian, literary critic, and one of the leading lights of the first decade of the Iranian Revolution, who since 2000 has been a visiting professor in several elite universities in the West and can no longer return to his native country? Hasan al-Hudaybi and Abdolkarim Soroush both believed that past formulations of Islamic law are no longer binding, because the sacred texts (Qur^ʾan and Sunna) have to be interpreted by people and made to apply to changing sociopolitical environments. For them, sacred writ does not just implant itself onto the human mind and then act as a software program that "runs" human actions. Rather, it is people who determine its meaning and decide on its application within the changing circumstances of their societies.

What then is "Shari^{c}a"—is it synonymous with "Islamic law?" Is it the collection of theoretical and practical jurisprudence accumulated by the five surviving schools of Islamic law (four Sunni and one Shi^{c}i) as it gelled around the twelfth century? Is Shari^{c}a to be identified with the limited number of clearly legal passages in the Qur^{ʾ}an and Sunna or is it simply the ethical ideals found in that corpus? Far from being academic questions, these are burning issues at the heart of Muslim debates all over the world today—whether in the "Islamic world," in Europe, North America, or other nations where Muslims have recently migrated.

Several years of intensive polling in over forty Muslim nations by the Gallup Organization have been tabulated and analyzed in a book by John L. Esposito and Dalia Mogahed, *Who Speaks for Islam? What a Billion Muslims Really Think.*[1] In every country but Turkey, a majority favors a democratic government, but which also incorporates religious values. Specifically, while, "in only a few countries did a majority say that *Sharia* should have no

1 John L. Esposito and Dalia Mogahed, *Who Speaks For Islam? What a Billion Muslims Really Think* (New York: Gallup, 2007).

role in society; yet in most countries, only a minority want *Sharia* as 'the only source' of legislation." Only in Jordan, Egypt, Pakistan, Afghanistan, and Bangladesh, did a majority of respondents want "*Sharia* as the 'only source' of legislation."[2] Elsewhere, a majority favored Shari^ca as "a" source of legislation.

A clear indication that Shari^ca means different things to different Muslims is the fact that, according to this Gallup Poll, a great majority of those who want Shari^ca applied also want women to have equal rights. For instance, those wanting women to have the same legal rights as men: 90 percent range in Bangladesh, Indonesia, Lebanon, and Turkey; 85 percent in Iran; 77 percent in Pakistan; and 61 percent in Saudi Arabia; and rights to vote, drive, and work outside of home: 80 percent in Indonesia (right to vote), 89 percent in Iran (right to vote), and so on.[3]

Ironically, these sentiments are not very different from those expressed in the United States, where a 2006 Gallup Poll found that 46 percent wanted the Bible to be "a" source of legislation and 9 percent wanted it to be the "only" source of legislation.[4] In fact, the United States and Iran share an almost identical score in answering the following: should religious leaders have a direct role in writing a constitution? (Yes: 42 percent); should they play any role at all? (No: 55 percent).[5]

In this essay I summarize and illustrate my recent findings on the topic of Shari^ca and ethics. The above polling data show Muslim societies in effervescence, with intense debates signaling changes on the horizon. As the opening paragraph intimated, however, my focus here is on the intellectual spectrum of ideas among Muslim scholars ranging from those who see Shari^ca as essentially fixed for all times, those who see it as "a path" (Hudaybi), and those who see it as solely religious values used to inform social policy within democratic states (Soroush).

Shari^ca as Fixed in Stone: Traditionalists and Salafis

If anything, this is the position that receives wide coverage in the Western media, between the Saudi Wahhabi traditionalists and the jihadis bent on destroying the far enemy (the United States) or the close enemy (the "apostate" Muslim regime at home).[6] Yet we do well to make some important distinctions here. Swiss Islamicist, philosopher, and Muslim

2 Ibid., 48. Surprisingly, the numbers of female and male respondents are very consistent, except for Pakistan. Those who supported Shari^ca as the only source of legislation: in Jordan 54 percent of men and 55 percent of women; in Egypt it is 70 percent and 62 percent; in Indonesia 14 percent and 14 percent (ibid., 48).

3 Ibid., 51.

4 Ibid., 49.

5 Ibid., 49. This is not to minimize the differences in viewing the relationship between sacred text and law in Islam and Christianity, yet there may be less of a disparity than is usually assumed, at least in the way positions are now evolving.

6 Some of the best books on the jihadist movement are by Fawaz A. Gerges, who for the last twelve years has conducted hundreds of interviews with leaders and foot soldiers alike and keeps abreast of all the Arabic literature on the subject. See his *The Far Enemy: Why Jihad Went Global* (Cambridge: Cambridge University Press, 2005), and *Journey of the Jihadist: Inside Muslim Militancy* (Orlando: Harcourt, 2006).

activist Tariq Ramadan (b. 1962) offers us a useful typology based on the relative balance between the strict dependence on the texts and the willingness to use reason in interpreting the texts.[7] He sees three groups on the text-only side of the continuum. All three consider their literal interpretations of Qur^ɔan and Sunna as excluding any rethinking of traditional norms in order to accommodate changing circumstances. In other words, to borrow a phrase from traditional circles, "the gates of *ijtihād* remain closed"— *ijtihād* being the mechanism in Islamic jurisprudence for legal experts of the highest level to produce new rulings for new situations not covered by the texts. Muslim authorities have generally felt that the development of the four Sunni legal schools around the eleventh century signaled the end of innovation in Islamic law.[8]

Here, in brief, are the three movements Ramadan sees in the "textualist" camp:

1. The "scholastic traditionalists," that is, those who across the Muslim world hold fast either to one of the schools of law or to a more recent reform movement in a conservative direction (e.g., the Deobandis, Barelwis, Ahl-al-Sunna, the Taliban, or the Tabligh-i Jamaat).

2. The "Salafi literalists," who have nothing but scorn for the traditional schools and pride themselves in going back to the sources. Indeed, it is the *salaf* one should follow, they claim— "the Companion of the Prophet and pious Muslims of the first three generations of Islam."[9] University of California Los Angeles scholar Khaled Abou El Fadl calls them the "puritans," or the "Salafabists," resulting from the alliance between the Saudi Wahhabis and the Salafis, heirs to the nineteenth-century reform movement spearheaded by Jamal al-Din al-Afghani and Muhammad ^cAbduh.[10] Above all, they are textual literalists—no human interpretation should corrupt the pure, unadulterated message of the Qur^ɔan and Sunna.

3. The "Salafis," or, as Ramadan has put it, the "political literalist Salafis." These are the direct heirs of the chief propagandist for the

7 See Tariq Ramadan, *Western Muslims and the Future of Islam* (Oxford: Oxford University Press, 2004), 24–30.

8 A good work to consult on this is Wael B. Hallaq's *A History of Islamic Legal Theories: An Introduction to Sunni Uṣūl al-Fiqh* (Cambridge: Cambridge University Press, 1997).

9 Ramadan, *Western Muslims*, 25.

10 See Abou El Fadl's seminal chapter, "The Ugly Modern and the Modern Ugly," in *Progressive Muslims: On Gender, Justice, and Pluralism*, ed. Omid Safi (Oxford: Oneworld, 2003), 33–77, and his whole book devoted to the topic, *The Great Theft: Wrestling Islam from the Extremists* (New York: HarperCollins, 2005). It was Saudi oil wealth, flowing prodigiously in the 1970s that propelled their sectarian propaganda. But since "Wahhabism" was a derogatory word, its proponents claimed to be "Salafis" and allied themselves with the hard-liners among the heirs of salafism: Rashid Rida, Hasan al-Banna, and especially Sayyid Qutb.

> Egyptian Muslim Brotherhood of the 1950s and 1960s—Sayyid Qutb who, under the slogan of "judging according to what God has sent down" (al-Māʾida [5]:44,45,47), "imagined Islamic law to be a set of clear cut, inflexible, and rigid positive commands that covered and regulated every aspect of life" and in effect excommunicated (or declared apostate) the great majority of Muslim societies, including religious and political leaders.[11] They are "political Salafists," in that they aim to dismantle the nation-state system among Muslims and work toward restoring the caliphate. Here we think of al-Qaeda, its many offshoots and homegrown imitators, responsible for the more dramatic acts of violence (the so-called "jihadis"). Yet there are other movements that officially eschew violence, but are just as radical in their condemnation of anything Western (especially democracy), like the Hizb al-Tahrir and the al-Muhajirun.

Shariᶜa as Path: Salafi Reformism

This is by far the majority tendency in Muslim juridical and intellectual circles today. Ramadan sees himself in this category—willing to bring the tools of reason to interpret the sacred texts in the light of new political, social, and economic realities. In fact, adds Ramadan—and I agree with him—this judicious marriage of reason and revelation has always been the hallmark of Islamic tradition. To be sure, there were always heated debates in these areas, but the process of *ijtihād* was not only central to legal theory from the beginning, but it also never died out. Muhammad ᶜAbduh may have decried the intellectual stagnation of the religious leaders (ulamas) of his time, but as the Grand Mufti of Egypt he demonstrated that Islamic law had all the necessary tools to adapt the traditional system to address modern realities.

As it turns out, Tariq Ramadan is the grandson of Hasan al-Banna, founder of the twentieth century's greatest Islamic mass movement, the Society of Muslim Brothers (or the Muslim Brotherhood) in 1928. Ramadan, a lecturer in philosophy at Oxford University, the author of many books, and an esteemed advisor to legislators in the European Parliament, is indeed a worthy heir of Muhammad ᶜAbduh.[12] But before giving a closer look at his thought, we should first ponder the role of his grandfather's successor, the top-level Egyptian judge Hasan al-Hudaybi (1891–1973).

---

11 Abou El Fadl, *The Great Theft*, 82. Qutb was hanged with six other Muslim Brothers by President Gamal ᶜAbd al-Nasir in 1966, but his influence has been deeply felt among all the militant groups since, starting with the Egyptian Jihad Group, led by Mohammed ᶜAbd al-Salam Faraj, who assassinated Sadat in 1981. Faraj's pamphlet "The Absent Duty" "became the operational manual of the jihadist movement in the 1980s and remained so through the first half of the 1990s," according to Gerges, *The Far Enemy*, 44. It was Faraj who coined this key jihadi concept (the "far" and "near enemy" in "The Absent Duty").

12 Time named him one of a hundred top innovators for the new century in 2000. Sadly, though the University of Notre Dame hired him as professor in 2004, the United States refused to grant him a visa—hence his position at Oxford. In 2010 Ramadan's ban from entering the United States was lifted.

Hasan al-Banna was assassinated by government agents in 1949, but it was not until October 1951 that the Society's Guidance Council finally elected Hudaybi as his successor. This came as a surprise decision since Hudaybi was mostly unknown by the rank and file of Brotherhood members; the choice of a respected outsider likely represented the leadership's desire to bolster the movement's image among the Egyptian populace.

The following year, with the advent of the July Revolution, fomented by an alliance of the Free Officers and the Muslim Brotherhood, Hudaybi actively lobbied the new ruling junta to modify the constitution in a more "Islamic" direction. "The Qurᵓan is our constitution," went the slogan, yet Hudaybi's intentions were much different from what we imagine today as the application of Shariᶜa law. In fact, though Hudaybi did want to reform penal and family law in a more Islamic direction, he had no desire to tamper with the political freedoms and rights of the Christian Coptic minority in Egypt.

Yet Hudaybi led the Society for only three years before the advent of the "Great Persecution," triggered by an assassination attempt on Gamal ᶜAbd al-Nasir by a splinter group of the Brotherhood. Hudaybi, along with Sayyid Qutb and hundreds of other Brotherhood activists, were arrested, tortured, and imprisoned for years. Qutb spent eleven of the last twelve years of his life in prison, while Hudaybi, much older, spent seven years in prison and six years under house arrest before being released in 1971 at the age of eighty, five years after Qutb's execution.

Unbeknownst to outsiders, an ideological struggle was raging inside the walls of Egypt's prisons: Qutb and Hudaybi dueled, warring for the soul of the movement. Disciples gathered around each one while pamphlets were passed along, sparking even more acrimonious debates.[13] At the heart of the conflict was the issue of salvation: How does one become Muslim? What kind of sin causes one to revert to the status of an unbeliever (*kāfir*)?[14] A summary of Hudaybi's pamphlet, entitled "Seven Questions inside the Yemen Tur Prison,"[15] would include the following: (a) any person pronouncing the two *shahāda*[16] (*shahādatayn*) is a Muslim, (b) no Muslim can be called a *kāfir* (the act of *takfīr*—hence, Qutb's position as *takfīrī*),[17] (c) Hasan al-Banna never declared any other Muslim a *kāfir*, but (d) he did define what it took to cross the line: renouncing Islam and actively combating it.

---

13 Precious little has been written on Hudaybi. Two useful sources are David L. Johnston, "Hassan al-Hudaybi and the Muslim Brotherhood: Can Islamic Fundamentalism Eschew the Islamic State?" in *Comparative Islamic Studies* 3, 1 (June 2007): 39–56; and Barbara Zollner *The Muslim Brotherhood: Hasan al-Hudaybi and Ideology* (New York: Routledge, 2011).

14 Naturally, these were questions passionately debated in the first three centuries of the Islamic empire. Creeds developed to summarize the Sunni consensus in the fourth and fifth centuries. Hudaybi has plenty of material to draw on, and he is very adept in making his arguments on this basis.

15 This was a maximum security prison on the Red Sea which President ᶜAbd al-Nasir inherited, but which he filled beyond capacity with political prisoners during his sixteen-year rule (1954–1970).

16 "I testify that there is no God but God, and that Muhammad is God's messenger" (often considered one).

17 Amazingly, Hudaybi never mentions Qutb's name, nor does he declare that his position is that of the Kharijites (or khawārij), a sect that arose in the first generation of Muslims, known for their assassination of the fourth caliph, ᶜAli, and their withdrawing from the Muslim mainstream, calling them all "unbelievers" (*kuffār*). Many have since made this point.

Hudaybi wrote only one book, a collaborative effort of the mid-1960s. He had entrusted much of the research to seven legal and theological experts (including his brother Maʾmun, also a judge), and gave it the title "Summoners, not Judges."[18] The product is an expanded and better-researched version of the pamphlet "Seven Questions." It is also a skillful deconstruction of both Sayyid Qutb's *takfīrī* position and of the South Asian Islamist Abu al-Aʿla Mawdudi's emphasis on God's political sovereignty (*ḥākimīyyatu l-Allāh*). What is left can be seen in distilled form in another pamphlet from the same period, this time addressed to the Egyptian public as an apologetic for the Society of the Muslim Brothers. The title is "Our Constitution," an obvious play on words—first the Egyptian constitution (it was being debated at the time), and second as a reference to the Brotherhood's slogan, "The Qurʾan is our constitution."

Two things stand out here. First, the present Egyptian constitutional framework is acceptable as it stands, though the Brotherhood will continue to lobby for a greater implementation of the clear commands of the texts. In any case, they believe that political power resides with the Muslim *umma* (community), which elects its leaders by democratic means, who then are accountable both to the people and to God. And second, the constitution ensures that the moral values enshrined in both the Bible and the Qurʾan are implemented throughout Egyptian society:

> It is good for Muslims and Christians to be trained by the spiritual formation provided by their respective faiths so that they come to agreement on what is good and virtuous. It is the government's (al-hukuma) duty to provide this education with all seriousness in primary and secondary schools for both Muslims and Christians.[19]

What is Shariʿa for Hudaybi? It is any of the laws enacted by Parliament, which are in the spirit (or in harmony with the ethical values) of the Qurʾan and Sunna. No doubt, this is a weak and vague formulation, intended to assuage popular fears of a radical movement. Yet Tariq Ramadan, writing some forty years later in Europe, sets out to fill in the blanks left by Hudaybi and others.[20] The key to reform for the great majority of conservatively

18 "Summoners" translates the word *duʿa*; literally, those who do the work of *daʿwa*, or the invitation to a committed religious practice. Though *daʿwa* is often a code word for the proselytizing of non-Muslims, in this context it is the work of the Muslim Brotherhood, which from its inception was a grassroots project of leading other Muslims to a deeper faith, somewhat like the South Asian Tablighi movement (though usually more political in orientation).

19 Hasan al-Hudaybi, *Duʿat la Qudat* [Summoners, Not Judges] (Cairo: Dār al-Tabaʿa wa-l-Nashr al-Islamiyya, 1977).

20 Ibid. Likely the highest profile Muslim cleric in the world today is the charismatic Yusuf al-Qaradawi, host of the "Sharia and Life" program on the al-Jazeera satellite channel, watched by hundreds of millions of Muslims. He was a much younger member of Hudaybi's generation, who as a Muslim Brother fled Egypt in 1954 and soon settled in Qatar, where he has stayed ever since. His voluminous writings follow Hudaybi's general trend, or Ramadan's "Salafi reformism" (fighting the extremists, conservative in his approach to Shariʿa, yet seeking to implement the needed changes in the light of today's global economy).

minded Muslim thinkers, who nevertheless want to engage in bold *ijtihād*, is found in the expression "the purposes of Shariᶜa" (*maqāṣid ash-Sharīᶜah*).[21]

This trend in Islamic jurisprudence may be traced to two main sources. First, the Mālikī school (mostly in North Africa) emphasized the use of public interest (*maṣlaḥa*) as one of the sources of law. Next, as this idea began to spread, the great thinker and Shāfiᶜī jurist Abu Hamid al-Ghazali (d. 1111) laid down some safeguards, while at the same time acknowledging that attention to the Shariᶜa's objectives helped to infer new rulings for new situations. Not surprisingly, one of the scholars most cited today for this approach is the Mālikī jurist from Grenada, Abu Ishaq al-Shatibi (d. 1388). Ramadan refers to him as well in his discussion of the conditions of *ijtihād*, with a particular emphasis on the *mujtahid's* "deep understanding of the objectives of Sharia."

Starting with al-Ghazali and moving on to al-Shatibi and others, we witness the deliberate use of a quasi-rational interpretation of the texts (reason working with revelation), so as to extend the application of the divine law to new situations. This is not only a rational move; it is an ethical one as well. Three levels of *maṣlaḥa* (public interest, benefit, good) are laid out:

1. Five "essential principles": the protection of religion, life, intellect, lineage, and property.

2. The "necessary" or complementary principles: particularly that which can prevent suffering or hardship for a community.

3. The "enhancing" (or "embellishing") and "perfecting" principles: measures that make life easier for people, and in particular improve their religious practice.

To understand how these traditional juridical tools can be put to use today, consider how Ramadan analyzes the situation of Muslims living in the West. Far from being a hostile environment, North America and Europe afford them five rights: "the right to practice Islam, the right to knowledge, the right to establish organizations, the right to autonomous representation, and the right to appeal to law."[22] Muslims are called to witness (*shahāda*) before all people in word and deed to the solidarity of all people before God: "Before God, and with all men, in the West Muslims must be, with them, witnesses engaged in this resistance, for justice, for all human beings of whatever race, origin, or religion."[23]

Hence, leaving behind the binary opposition of the medieval Islamic worldview (the Abode of Islam versus the Abode of War), Ramadan urges Muslims living in the West to

---

21 For more details, see David L. Johnston, "A Turn in the Epistemology and Hermeneutics of Twentieth-Century *Uṣūl al-Fiqh*," *Islamic Law and Society* 11, no. 2 (2004): 233–82; and "*Maqāsid al-Sharīʿa*: Epistemology and Hermeneutics of Muslim Theologies of Human Rights," *Die Welt des Islams* 47, no. 2 (2007): 149–87.

22 Ramadan, *Western Muslims*, 70.

23 Ibid., 76.

consider their environment an "Islamic space," or "the Abode of Witness" (*shahāda*). The key distinction to be made, he continues, is between the faith, practice, and spirituality of Islam which is universal, and the various cultural embodiments of these foundational principles: "Let us remember that our task is to extrapolate the essence of the identity from the accident of its actualization in a particular time and place."[24] Part of the creational empowerment of the human person as God's trustee on earth is the freedom to use his or her God-given intelligence to interpret the divine sources in light of the context. This is possible, because this responsibility delegated to humans by the Creator consists in both "understanding based on knowledge and choice based on freedom," which implies that Muslims should be characterized by "an active and dynamic intelligence."[25]

This dynamic interaction between text and context results in an ethically enlightened posture for the Muslim citizen of the West. Here is but a sample of ethical values Muslims may bring to the table of Western pluralistic society:

1. A keen sense of loyalty: keeping covenant and respecting oaths are at the core of Muslim ethics (e.g., the Prophet's oath of Hudaybiyya in 629; al-Isrāʾ [17]:34; al-Muʾminūn [23]:8). Thus Muslims are bound by the laws of the state in which they reside, as long as these do not contradict the tenets of their faith. The consequences for understanding the role of Shariʿa today are far-reaching. So, in other words, Islamic law and jurisprudence command Muslim individuals to submit to the body of positive law enforced in their country of residence in the name of the tacit moral agreement that already supports their very presence. Put in yet another way, to apply the Shariʿa for Muslim citizens or residents in the West means explicitly to respect the legal and constitutional framework of the country of which they are citizens.[26]

2. The imperative of justice (al-Māʾida [5]:8 and many parallels) means a courageous stance with all people of goodwill on the side of the poor and oppressed. Shariʿa, then, is "the path to justice."[27]

3. All this implies the creational imperative of human solidarity: "there can be no religious consciousness without a social ethic … Being responsible before God for one's own person and to respect creation

24 Ibid., 78.
25 Ibid., 80–81.
26 Ibid., 95.
27 Ibid., 113.

> as a whole, one should offer to all people on the social level the means to fulfill their responsibilities and to protect their rights."[28]

Shari^c^a as Ethics through a Postmodern Lens

So far, this is the view with the least followers. People in the previous tendency often find ways around the sticky points of traditional Shari^c^a that clash with contemporary human rights norms—the death penalty for apostates, discriminatory laws for women, and the like. But in this tendency, scholars feel no need to even look at traditional formulations of Islamic *fiqh* (jurisprudence). Numerous Muslim academics in the West, for instance, would assert that Shari^c^a should only be considered a moral compass to help navigate the stormy waters of democratic, pluralistic nation-states. The authors of *Progressive Muslims* are a good example as they are mostly from North America;[29] so is Mohammed Arkoun, an Algerian-French scholar who made his career at the Sorbonne, or Chandra Muzaffar, the Malaysian academic and indefatigable human rights activist. Let us close with a short portrait of Abdolkarim Soroush, the Iranian scholar mentioned in the introduction.

Born in 1945, Soroush developed a passion for poetry while still in elementary school and studied Qur^ɔ^anic exegesis after school. During his six years at the University of Tehran, where he earned a doctorate in pharmacology, Soroush took private lessons in Islamic philosophy, studied Marxism, and deepened his knowledge of Persian poets Jalal al-Din Rumi (d. 1273) and Hafez of Shiraz (d. 1389). He then went to England for postgraduate studies in analytical chemistry. After a year, however, he switched his specialty to the philosophy of science.

The common thread in Soroush's intellectual pilgrimage is the hermeneutical question. While still at the University of Tehran, he threw himself into the study of both Shi^c^ite and Sunni commentaries and remembers being "fascinated" with "the details and intricacies of the differences in interpretation." This he combined with his passion for Rumi's *Mathnavi* and Hafez's *Divan*, and the result was a growing desire to unlock the mysteries of "the art of textual interpretation." In fact, it was the hermeneutical quest that led him to explore Western theories on the philosophy of science—a quest that could not be divorced from the epistemological issue of what we can know as human beings and how we come to know what we know.

The outcome of all of this was the theory of the contraction and expansion of the religious interpretation. Simply put, this leads us to make two very important distinctions:

1. *The distinction between religion and our human understanding of it*: Shari^c^a is God's truth, only apprehensible to human beings through their limited capacity of understanding. It follows that "religious

28 Ibid., 149.

29 Omid Safi, ed., *Progressive Muslims: On Justice, Gender, and Pluralism* (Oxford: OneWorld, 2003).

knowledge is replete with error, conjecture, and conviction," and consequently, it "changes, evolves, contracts, expands, waxes, and wanes. It is temporal and in constant commerce with other realms of human culture."[30]

2. *The distinction between personal knowledge of religion and religious knowledge*: Religious knowledge, as a human endeavor, is the product of competing paradigms, the competition between various schools of thought, and thus is shaped as much by the exchange of ideas as it is by the politics of the institutions of learning—not to mention the surrounding culture, and the socioeconomic and political conditions of the time period. Personal knowledge of religion can only grasp small, limited, and to some extent, distorted versions of that greater evolving whole.

In another passage, Soroush emphasizes the fallibility of the human quest to know after "the Fall" (which for most Muslims is the beginning of human empowerment; cf. al-Baqara [2]:30–36):

> We human beings are now expelled from heaven and deprived of revelation. We are profane and listless. Our life is blighted by Satan, and our understanding is fallible. To speak and act like prophets does not suit us. Apropos of our limited reason, we acquire a faint scent of the truth and act accordingly. We are *sharihan* [interpreters of religion], not *sahri'an* [initiators of religion].[31]

One must also keep in mind the context of Soroush's thinking. He taught for many years under the umbrella of the Islamic revolution in Iran and gradually fell into disfavor with the ruling clergy because of his consistent opposition to the cornerstone of Imam Khomeiny's ideology: *wilāyat al-faqīh* (the rulership of the jurisconsult). Opposing this is to attack the very legitimacy of the Iranian regime, and for his own protection Soroush has chosen to exile himself.

What is Shariᶜa? In the end, for Soroush and others, who hold to these epistemological assumptions, ultimate truth lies only with God; we humans can only grasp it piecemeal, through philosophy, law, and mysticism. This has at least two implications. First, it leads us to be humble and tolerant. All religions have a valid claim to the truth. Second, we must

30 Abdolkarim Soroush, *Reason, Freedom, and Democracy in Islam: Essential Writings of Abdolkarim Soroush*, trans./ed. Mahmoud Sadri (Oxford: Oxford University Press, 2000), 34.

31 Ibid., 37.

lay hold of the ethical principles contained in our sacred texts if we want to build a more just and peaceful global society in the new millennium.

Beyond the news headlines and the commentaries about whether the Arab Spring has turned to winter or not, the entire Muslim world has been and will continue to be in the throes of a comprehensive, if chaotic, reform process. The 2007 Gallup poll shows how Muslims everywhere hunger for freedom and democracy within a framework that respects religious values. Shariᶜa remains the symbol of all that is good in a society that shows respect for God—a sentiment with which we evangelicals can identify.

This yearning is nowhere more evident than in Egypt today. The Muslim Brotherhood's Freedom and Justice party won forty percent of the lower house's seats. As it turns out, its platform is a carbon copy of Hudaybi's ideas in the 1960s, complete with their membership open to Christians. Yet even the Salafi party (Al-Nour, "The Light") that won twenty percent of the votes, despite its decidedly anti-democratic and patriarchal positions, has come to recognize the equal footing of Christians and Muslims as citizens of the Egyptian state. These were the ultraconservative Muslims, who until the "January 25 Revolution" condemned any form of democracy as a tool of the devil. Now many of them have joined the political fray; this in itself is nothing short of revolutionary. Even for the diehard "textualists," it would seem God's will as read through the Qur'an and Sunna—Shariᶜa, that is—might look different as societies evolve. Theology, after all, is always worked out in particular contexts.

4
Portraying Muslim Women

BY EVELYNE A. REISACHER

"Women in Islam" is the first course I taught at Fuller Theological Seminary in summer 2001 upon the invitation of Dudley Woodberry, who had developed a state-of-the-art Islamic Study Program that drew people from all over the world to the California campus. This Festschrift in his honor provides me with an opportunity to reflect on this course, which was so fundamental to Woodberry that he made sure it was offered to students.

Woodberry was right. Views on women play a major role in Muslim-Christian relations as pointed out by Yvonne Yazbeck Haddad, Jane I. Smith, and Kathleen M. Moore: "The elaboration of the difference between Islam and the West has often centered on the status of women in the Muslim world."[1] But at the same time Asma Barlas contends, "Most people know abysmally little about Islam and what they do is usually in the form of noxious stereotypes about the hijab, the harem, and now, holy war. It's a struggle to get people to be interested in Islam or Muslims beyond the three Hs, as I call them."[2]

Thus, for the sake of developing healthy relations between people from Muslim and Christian faiths and fostering respectful Christian witness, it is of uttermost importance to portray the condition of women in Islam with less distortion as possible. Many people I meet in churches are confident that after listening to news reports or reading a bestseller on women, they have gained a crystal clear position on gender in Islam. Unfortunately this is not enough. Christians must evaluate whether their views on women is based on actual facts or not. In order to do that, I present in this chapter various lenses by which Christian and non-Christian authors attempt to interpret the condition of women in Islam.

---

1 Yvonne Yazbeck Haddad, Jane I. Smith, and Kathleen M. Moore, *Muslim Women in America: The Challenge of Islamic Identity Today* (Oxford: Oxford University Press, 2006), 23. Christians are not the only ones to use women as symbols. Muslims do it as well. Leila Ahmed writes: "They [women] are the centerpiece of the Islamist agenda at least in part because they were posed as central in the colonial discursive assault on Islam and Arab culture." *Women and Gender in Islam: Historical Roots of a Modern Debate* (New Haven: Yale University Press, 1993), 236–37.

2 Asma Barlas "Teaching about Women and Islam," AMEWS Roundtable, MESA, San Francisco, Nov. 21, 2004, accessed online at http://www.asmabarlas.com/TALKS/20041121_MESA.pdf.

Because today, it is common to hear people blame Muslims for the way they treat women, I framed this chapter around the question of women's oppression. I called the various sections of this chapter, "Is such-and-such to blame [for women's oppression]?" By doing that, I don't want to be another case of finger pointing, but instead wish to provide Christians with more data to explore this question so that when they talk to a Muslim he or she will say, "I feel you feel what I feel." From then on, one can engage in healthy relationships and a respectful witness to Muslims.

Is Islam to Blame?

It is not uncommon to hear people blame Islam, as a religious system, for the oppression of women. Those who hold this position consider that women have no other option than to leave Islam if they want to improve their life condition. For example, former Muslim[3] Ayaan Hirsi Ali finds Islam has very few things to offer to women; only subjugation. Many Christians I meet when I visit churches have adopted an anti-Islamic view as a result of reading her books. The things they remember most is how Ali has suffered in the sociocultural context where she was raised.[4]

Noted Christian authors have also propagated such views. For example, the Christian "apostle to Islam,"[5] Samuel M. Zwemer with his wife, Amy, wrote that "Under the influence and power of Islam, [the Muslim woman] has not been encouraged to develop either physically, mentally or spiritually, and during thirteen centuries her condition has grown worse rather than better."[6] Likewise, today Ergun Mehmet Caner and Emir Fethi Caner write, "Islam has deserved its reputation around the world for stifling and even enslaving women. Many Islamic women are both educated and successful, but most remain illiterate, hidden, and treated as property."[7] Christian author Colin Chapman has clearly pointed out this tendency in Christianity as he writes, "Muslims often argue that Islam has liberated women, giving them the dignity that no other religion has given them. Christians on the other hand, have often been critical of the treatment of women in Islam."[8]

---

3 Although Ali sometimes wavers between her former Muslim faith and atheism, most of the time, however, she asserts that the only way women can improve their situation is by leaving Islam. This is why I call her "former Muslim," for lack of a better term that would describe her current identity.

4 In her book *Infidel* (New York: Free Press, 2007), Ayaan Hirsi Ali recounts the story of her life: how she grew up as a Muslim Somali girl, underwent female mutilation, experienced life as a Muslim woman in countries such as Saudi Arabia and Kenya and later escaped a forced marriage that led her to live for a while in Holland and now advocate for women's rights in the United States of America.

5 "Apostle to Islam" comes from the title of a biography written by J. Christy Wilson, *Apostle to Islam: A Biography of Samuel M. Zwemer* (Grand Rapids: Baker, 1952).

6 Samuel M. Zwemer and Amy Zwemer, *Moslem Women* (West Medford, MA: The Central Committee of the United Study of Foreign Missions, 1926), 71. Despite this harsh criticism, the Zwemers also reported in their book how contemporary Muslims were attempting to advocate for the freedom and emancipation of women.

7 Ergun Mehmet Caner and Emir Fethi Caner, *Unveiling Islam: An Insider's Look at Muslim Life and Beliefs* (Grand Rapids: Kregel, 2002), 133.

8 Colin Chapman, *Cross and Crescent: Responding to the Challenge of Islam* (Leicester, UK: InterVarsity, 1995), 15.

The writings of two women, born Muslim in Syria and living today in the United States, illustrate how the analysis of the same context can be miles apart. On one hand, Wafa Sultan blames Islam for oppressing women as the title of her book *A God Who Hates* clearly reveals.[9] On the other hand, Nimat Hafez Barazangi,[10] a Muslim activist and research fellow at Cornell University, blames instead patriarchal interpretations of the Qurʾan for the same issue. These two women have in common the country of origin and the country of residence but do not blame Islam to the same degree. The last author even believes, like many Muslims, that Islam improved the status of women at the time of Muhammad and therefore contains seeds of transformation to redeem the status and role of Muslim women in every generation.

Like Barazangi, numbers of researchers have engaged in historical, anthropological, and sociological studies to prove Islam supports women's rights. One of them, Ruth Roded states, "I am aware that the role of women in traditional Islamic society has often been portrayed in extremely negative terms that are not justified by historic reality."[11] She adds, "In reading biographies of thousands of women, one is amazed at the evidence that contradicts the view of Muslim women as marginal, secluded and restricted."[12] A growing number of studies seem to support her thesis as they present historical data that has often been hidden from the larger public for centuries.[13] They are complemented with a plethora of studies from the field of social sciences.[14]

Some authors who do not blame Islam even think it is the Christians who focus too much on women's oppression in Islam as a strategy to win more converts. In a recent book, Haddad, Smith, and Moore claim:

> Western missionary strategists, who have always reasoned that "oppressed" women would be the weakest point at which they could penetrate and convert Islamic societies, continue today to identify the release of Muslim women from the yoke of male domination as one of their primary goals.[15]

Their statement is not completely inaccurate. One of the first missionary conferences on Muslim evangelism held in Cairo, Egypt, from April 5–9, 1906, issued a statement on

---

9 Wafa Sultan, *A God Who Hates: The Courageous Woman Who Inflamed the Muslim World Speaks Out Against the Evil of Islam* (New York: St. Martin's, 2009).

10 Nimat Hafez Barazangi, *Woman's Identity and the Qur'an: A New Reading* (Gainesville: University Press of Florida, 2004).

11 Ruth Roded, *Women in Islamic Biographical Collections: From Ibn Sa'd to Who's Who* (Boulder, CO: Lynne Rienner, 1994), ix.

12 Ibid., viii.

13 See Suad Joseph et al., eds., *Encyclopedia of Women and Islamic Cultures*, 6 vols. (Leiden: Brill Academic, 2003–2008).

14 See Priscilla Offenhauer, "Women in Islamic Societies: A Selected Review of Social Scientific Literature," (Washington, DC: Library of Congress, 2005), http://www.loc.gov/rr/frd/pdf-files/Women_Islamic_Societies.pdf.

15 Haddad, Smith, and Moore, *Muslim Women in America*, 26.

the oppression of Muslim women.[16] I believe missionaries are and should be concerned by the "release of Muslim women" where there is oppression because Jesus calls them to promote social justice. Haddad, Smith, and Moore's critical comments should not prevent Christians to continue advocating for women's rights. But on the other hand, they should also encourage Christians to evaluate the real motivations that lie behind their desire to reach out to Muslims. Is it fair to use oppression as a "mantra" to motivate crowds to witness to Muslims or should this mantra instead be used for its intended purpose, which is advocacy for women whether the end result is their turning to Christ or not?

As we have seen in this section, not everyone lays the blame on Islam for the oppression of women. Some authors even make a strong case that Islam is good for women. If we want to engage in respectful witness among Muslims we must be aware of these contrasting views. There may be other causes of women's oppression in Muslim societies that are not directly linked to Islam as a whole. It requires a lot of listening and researching to find the exact roots of women's suffering. It is further important to warn Christians who give women no other option than to leave Islam in order to be free. In effect, the choice of Muslim women is often limited to three options: condoning the system and staying, fighting the system and staying under immense pressure, or rejecting the system and leaving Muslim societies. For those women who do not have the resources to challenge the system from within, the only option left is to leave the sociocultural context that has adopted Islam as a way of life. The warning to these Christians from outside the Muslim world who encourage women to leave Islam thus is: Are you ready to provide the emotional support and become the family and social basis for these women if they are ostracized from the family and society when they leave the system?

Is Muhammad to Blame?

Instead of blaming Islam, some Christians choose to blame Muhammad, whom Muslims consider to be the last prophet. This attitude is as ancient as the Muslim-Christian encounter. In effect, in one of the earliest documents dealing with a Christian's analysis of Islam, apologist John of Damascus questions Muhammad's views on marriage and divorce.[17]

Since John of Damascus, the list of accusations made by Christians toward Muhammad has grown longer: he had too many wives; he forcefully wed his captives; ᶜAʾisha was far too young when he married her; he should not have married Zaynab, the ex-wife of his adoptive son Zayd; his sex life was inappropriate for a prophet; why did he depict huris in heaven who are meant to satisfy the sexual desires of men?; etc.[18] One of the staunchest

16 Samuel Marinus Zwemer, *The Moslem World* (New York: Board of Foreign Missions of the Presbyterian Church in the U. S. A., 1908), 203–5.

17 Daniel J. Sahas, *John of Damascus on Islam: The "Heresy of the Ishmaelites"* (Leiden: Brill, 1972).

18 For such lists used in polemics or apologetics, see http://www.answering-islam.org/Women/index.html, or Phil Parshall and Julie Parshall, *Lifting the Veil: The World of Muslim Women* (Waynesboro, GA: Gabriel, 2002).

critics of Muhammad's lifestyle and moral decadence is Christian writer Don Richardson. He says, "Mohammad could not even reach up to touch the underside of the moral standards of an average rogue."[19] Addressing the issue of the marriage with the young girl ᶜAʾisha, Richardson writes, "Mohammad left himself open to suspicion of pedophilia,"[20] and "Any time Mohammad wanted to add spice to his sex life, all he had to do was raid another town or caravan for female slaves, or buy some, and his God would approve."[21] Richardson does not blame the "God of Mohammad," as he calls him, for the oppression of women as much as he blames Muhammad. Van Sommer and Zwemer also express very harsh criticism of Muhammad when they wrote, "Mohammedan law, custom, and the example of their founder place woman on a level with beasts of burden and no nation rises above the level of its women."[22]

There are other Christians who do not express such harsh condemnation of Muhammad. Most of them have mixed feelings about him. Parshall and Parshall, for example, don't say only negative things about Muhammad's views of women. They are inclined to interpret his behaviors in the context of the time, which made some of his practices more understandable.[23] But at other times, they use a condemning tone when they talk about the "sexual prowess of Muhammad."[24]

Christians are not the only ones divided about Muhammad's stance on gender. One can find a variety of views amongst Muslims, although they would often be more supportive of Muhammad's views on women. This is easily explained by the fact that Muhammad is a role model for most Muslims, although he is not considered sinless.[25] Due to the high respect Muslims have for their prophet, it is often difficult for them to see any wrongdoings in his life. If there are critiques of Muhammad in Islamic literature, they are usually softer than the ones Christians make. Fatima Mernissi, for example, calls Muhammad's passion for Zaynab "scandalous, by his own people's standards,"[26] and Riffat Hassan writes, "According to the Prophet, women are deficient both in prayer (due to menstruation) and in intellect (due to their legal witness counting for less than a man's)."[27]

---

19 Don Richardson, *Secrets of the Koran: Revealing Insights into Islam's Holy Book* (Ventura, CA: Regal, 2003), 82.

20 Ibid., 76.

21 Ibid., 77.

22 Van Sommer and Zwemer, *Our Moslem Sisters*, 15.

23 They sometimes adopt a listening and favorable attitude toward the Muslim commentaries and do not directly blame Muhammad, although at the same time they do not excuse a number of decisions of Muhammad, especially the marriage with Zaynab and with ᶜAʾisha, and express their surprise toward Western authors like Annemarie Schimmel who is a "defender" of Muhammad. They write, "Schimmel appears to have a blind spot in her mostly unconditional praise of the Prophet." See Parshall and Parshall, *Lifting the Veil*, 24.

24 Ibid., 27.

25 See Ghāfir [40]:55; al-Qalam [68]:4.

26 Fatima Mernissi, *Beyond the Veil: Male-Female Dynamics in Modern Muslim Society* (Cambridge, MA: Shenkman, 1975), 56.

27 Riffat Hassan, "Challenging the Stereotypes of Fundamentalism: An Islamic Feminist Perspective," *The Muslim World* 91 (Spring 2001): 59.

Christians who choose to blame Muhammad in polemical encounters with Muslims should be aware that their arguments might not necessarily reach the goal intended. First, many in Islam will affirm that Muhammad was only a man and that his life was not flawless. In this, he is different from Jesus Christ who "committed no sin" (1 Pt 2:22 NSRV). Second, it is quasi-impossible to interpret Muhammad's behaviors from a modern standpoint. When one looks at his reforms, he is more like a forerunner than an oppressor. Many of the laws that he supported would be considered valid in premodern contexts. In this regard he would be akin to Old Testament prophets or kings who followed other social norms than contemporary Western societies by having, for example, numerous wives and concubines.[28] Third, Muslims can show a long list of positive texts about Muhammad in the Qurʾan and the Hadith. Even detractors of Muhammad must admit there were good practices in his life. Blaming Muhammad is not so simple.

However, there is still an important contribution that Christians can make to this conversation. They can highlight the teaching and attitudes of Jesus in regards to women from the biblical texts. Of course some Muslims may wonder why Jesus in the Bible was not married, compared to Muhammad who expressed his piety in the context of a family. They may have many questions in regards to Jesus' lifestyle. However, there are numerous lessons from Jesus' encounter with women and his teaching on family and society that address the deepest longings a heart can have and can become an eye-opener for Muslims.

Is the Post-Muhammadan Era to Blame?

Among Christian authors, some believe that Islam brought positive changes during the lifetime of Muhammad. Zwemer admitted with Annie Van Sommer that Islam is to thank for banning the custom of burying female girls alive.[29] Caner and Caner affirm that early Islam elevated the status of women.[30] W. Montgomery Watt wrote, "The position of women was improved at various points by Muhammad and the new religion he proclaimed."[31] However, many authors contend that the positive reforms of early Islam were short-lived. Muslim writer Fariba Zarinebaf-Shahr explains this phenomenon by the familiar academic concept of "rise and decline paradigm."[32]

There are diverse interpretations of the reasons for this decline. Zarinebaf-Shahr, for example, blames it on the ᶜAbbasid caliphate (AD 750–1258), which closed the golden age

---

28 One difference I see, however, in comparing Old Testament characters and Muhammad is that when the former do something blamable, their actions are strongly condemned by God (see 2 Samuel 12). Their wrong behaviors become examples of things followers of God should not do.

29 Annie Van Sommer and Samuel M. Zwemer, eds., *Our Moslem Sisters: A Cry of Need from Lands of Darkness Interpreted by Those Who Heard It*, 4th ed. (New York: Revell, 1907), 6.

30 Caner and Caner, *Unveiling Islam*, 133.

31 W. Montgomery Watt, "Women in the Earliest Islam," *Studia Missionalia* 40 (1991): 161.

32 Fariba Zarinebaf-Shahr, "Women, Law, and Imperial Justice in Ottoman Istanbul in the Late Seventeenth Century," in *Women, the Family, and Divorce Laws in Islamic History*, ed. Amira El Azhary Sonbol (Syracuse, NY: Syracuse University Press, 1996), 81.

of improving the status of women and ushered in the deterioration of women's condition.[33] Asma Barlas blames, on the other hand, the patriarchal customs of the societies that embraced Islam,[34] just as Iranian lawyer Shirin Ebadi did when she said, "The discriminatory plight of women in Islamic States ... whether in the sphere of civil law or in the realm of social, political and cultural justice, has its roots in the patriarchal and male-oriented culture prevailing in these societies, not in Islam."[35] Still, others contend that it is when Islam encountered more oppressive customs resistant to Islam that the situation of women worsened.[36] Finally, some blame it on patriarchal leadership practices, claiming that Muslim religious texts "have been interpreted only by Muslim men who have abrogated to themselves the task of defining the ontological, theological, sociological and eschatological status of Muslim women."[37]

Whatever the reasons may be those who believe in the rise and decline paradigm explicitly or implicitly admit that Islam has brought positive changes and consequently may still provide resources for improving the life of women today. It may thus be possible for outsiders to partner with Muslims to advocate for women's rights. But some authors go even further and openly challenge the rise and decline paradigm. An example comes from a recent book by John L. Esposito and Dalia Mogahed, who question the missionary statement on mission to Muslim women released at the Cairo Conference in 1906. A century after this conference, Esposito and Mogahed are disappointed by the following statement of the conference proceedings: "They [Muslim women] will never cry for themselves, for they are down under the yoke of centuries of oppression." They comment: "In sharp contrast to the popular image of silent submissiveness, Gallup findings on women in countries that are predominantly Muslim or have sizable Muslim populations hardly show that they have

33 Ibid. Some authors trace this deterioration even earlier in time. Reza Aslan believes that it started under the second caliph Umar. He explains, "Umar's misogynist tendencies were apparent from the moment he ascended to the leadership of the Muslim community. He tried (unsuccessfully) to confine women to their homes and wanted to prevent them from attending worship at the mosque." *No god but God: The Origins, Evolution, and Future of Islam* (New York: Random House, 2005), 71. Fatima Mernissi thinks that the deterioration started as soon as Muhammad died. *The Veil and the Male Elite: A Feminist Interpretation of Women's Rights in Islam*, trans. Mary Jo Lakeland (Jackson, TN: Perseus, 1991).

34 The preface of Asma Barlas' book, *"Believing Women" in Islam: Unreading Patriarchal Interpretations of the Qur'an* (Austin: University of Texas Press, 2002), xi, reads, "Since the Qurʾan was revealed in/to an existing patriarchy and has been interpreted by adherents of patriarchies ever since, Muslim women have a stake in challenging its patriarchal exegesis." For Barlas it is not the Qurʾanic text itself that is patriarchal but rather its interpretations. Unlike Barlas, Ayaan Hirsi Ali affirms that patriarchal ideas are woven into the Qurʾan that also erased forms of pre-Islamic matriarchy. Ali shows that "Islam is strongly dominated by a sexual morality derived from tribal Arab values dating from the time the Prophet received the instructions from Allah, a culture in which women were the property of their fathers, brothers, uncles, grand-fathers, or guardians." *The Caged Virgin: An Emancipation Proclamation for Women and Islam* (New York: Free Press, 2006), xi.

35 Shirin Ebadi, "Shirin Ebadi's Nobel Peace Prize Speech," Oslo, December 10, 2003, http://www.mwlusa.org/news/shirin_ebadi_acceptance_speech.htm.

36 S. Akbar Ahmed, "Women and the Household in Baluchistan and Frontier Society," in *Family and Gender in Pakistan: Domestic Organization in a Muslim Society*, eds. Hastings Donnan and Frits Selier (New Delhi: Hindustan, 1997), 64–87.

37 Riffat Hassan, "Equal before Allah: Woman-Man Equality in the Islamic Tradition," *Harvard Divinity Bulletin* 17 (January–May 1987): 2.

been conditioned to accept second-class status."[38] Their findings contradict the views that the condition of women has worsened after an early reformation during the time of Muhammad.

Christians must exercise caution in this debate about the role of the post-Muhammadan period in the lives of Muslim women. They should not make a hasty judgment, but instead grab history books to understand the past and the present. Just as some issues related to women in the Christian community can only be evaluated by studying church and mission history, the condition of Muslim women after Muhammad cannot be dissociated from sociological, cultural, economical, and political factors that have helped shape the contours of Islamic history.

Is Antireformism to Blame?

Despite the encouraging reports of the Gallup findings mentioned earlier, there are still numerous voices in the Muslim community that call for greater reforms of the status and role of women in the Muslim world. A vocal proponent of such view is Irshad Manji, whose perspective is expressed in the title of her widely read book *The Trouble with Islam Today: A Muslim's Call for Reform in Her Faith.*[39]

But can reform flow from Islam? A number of noted authors believe it does. Esposito, for example, writes, "Muslims have a rich legacy of traditions that call upon them to reform their societies in every age."[40] Watt several times pointed out that the message of Muhammad called for social reforms.[41] And today, scores of books contain the voice of vocal Muslim and non-Muslim authors who argue for social transformation from within Islam.[42] Even Irshad Manji believes it can be done!

How does this quest for reform from within Islam impact Christians' view of Islam? It should be encouraging to see there are Muslims striving for the welfare of women in their midst. I have already mentioned above that some authors find in early Islam accounts of positive change. Other authors contend that the Qur᾽an was not just an instrument of reform in early times but that it contains seeds of transformation for every generation. Muslim author Khaled M. Abou El Fadl writes, "In studying the Qur᾽an it becomes clear that the

---

38 John L. Esposito and Dalia Mogahed, *Who Speaks for Islam? What a Billion Muslims Really Think* (New York: Gallup, 2007), 101.

39 Irshad Manji, *The Trouble with Islam Today: A Muslim's Call for Reform in Her Faith* (New York: St. Martin's Griffin, 2003). Manji is a Uganda-born Muslim woman from Pakistani descent who now works in Canada as a journalist. In her book she directly confronts Muslims about the rigidity of Islam and its inclination toward blaming others rather than dealing with injustices and oppression within its own context. She critiques the way Muslims today deal with minorities, women, homosexuality, and Israel.

40 John L. Esposito, *Unholy War: Terror in the Name of Islam* (New York: Oxford University Press, 2002), 84.

41 W. Montgomery Watt, *Muhammad: Prophet and Statesman* (New York: Oxford University Press, 1974).

42 See for example: Charles Kurzman, *Modernist Islam, 1840–1940: A Source-Book* (New York: Oxford University Press, 2002); Khaled M. Abou El Fadl, *The Great Theft: Wrestling Islam from the Extremists* (New York: HarperSanFrancisco, 2005); and Tariq Ramadan, *Radical Reform: Islamic Ethics and Liberation* (New York: Oxford University Press, 2008).

Qur'an is educating Muslims on how to make incremental but lasting improvements in the condition of women that can only be described as progressive for their time and place."[43]

But this widely publicized quest for reform should not overshadow or belittle in the eyes of outsiders the following problems: First, some existing legal systems in place in Muslim countries may kill reforms in the bud.[44] Second, some advocates for change are forced to migrate because their call for reform is contested in their home country. Third, Muslims sometimes resist reform presented by the West because they leave God out of the equation or they do not correspond to their values. Fourth, when Muslims long to live as the early companions of Muhammad, they sometimes force upon women customs from the seventh or eighth century of Arabia that are not compatible with modernity or postmodernity.[45]

Does this mean that one should underestimate the reforms that are taking place in many parts of the Muslim world? Instead of blaming Islam for "not enough reforms," it may be better to say, "not enough reforms in certain parts of the Muslim world." At the same time, one may continue to advocate for change, recognizing however that changes have sometimes been slow in other contexts and other faiths.

This quest for reform further raises an important question for Christians: do they feel comfortable with defending women's rights from within Islam, or do they claim that only Christianity can defend womens' rights? According to Barazangi, Christian missionaries in the past have neglected the insider's voice. She says, "Missionaries did not want Muslim women to be liberated from within the Islamic worldview."[46] Her comment is valid. Are mission agencies willing to acknowledge resources from inside Islam, or do they want to impose their own standards and criteria that sometimes are at odds with the context and alienate women from the rest of the society? Christians should provide access to the biblical principles. But they don't have to indiscriminately impose their own cultural and social norms unless it is for the good of Muslim societies and if these changes don't contradict the teachings of Jesus Christ.

Is the Qur'an to Blame?

When Islam or Muhammad is not blamed, it is sometimes the Qur'an that becomes the culprit. Christian authors Caner and Caner write, "The Qur'an is so clear that those who regularly

---

43 Abou El Fadl, *The Great Theft*, 262.

44 As an example, Zoya Hasan explains, "Although those engaging in the current debate over personal law cite the Qur'an in their arguments for and against reform—whether state induced or community based—what gets ignored is the fact that Islamic jurisprudence is a separate entity from the Qur'an, and is so not only because of its own relations with the state, but also because its historical development has actually made it such. Furthermore, when combined with the power of the modern nation-state, the degree of change is limited because the moral and legal framework on which it is based is itself immutable." "Shah Bano Affair," in *Encyclopedia of Women and Islamic Cultures: Family, Law, and Politics*, vol. 2, eds. Suad Joseph et al. (Leiden: Brill, 2005), 742.

45 This is especially true for some forms of literal salafism.

46 Barazangi, *Woman's Identity*, 13.

abuse their wives are more faithful to their sacred text than those who would rationalize away its teachings. If a woman is honored and respected in an Islamic home, it is in spite of the teachings of Muhammad, rather than because of them."[47] Let us look therefore more closely to that question of whether the Qur᾿an is actually to blame for the oppression of women.

Most Muslims believing that the Qur᾿an is the revelation of God would affirm that the Qur᾿an is not to be blamed for injustices against women. Abou El Fadl shows how the Qur᾿an "reformed social conditions that were oppressive and exploitative toward women."[48] Likewise Hassan clearly states that the Qur᾿an "does not discriminate against women."[49] She explains further, "The Qur᾿an, as God's Word, cannot be made the source of human injustice, and the injustice to which Muslim women have been subjected cannot be regarded as God-derived."[50] She then concludes, "Indeed, not only does the Qur᾿an address women, but it frequently does so in a manner that should leave little room for doubt that it considers them equal to men."[51]

If it is not the Qur᾿an that is to be blamed, how must one read its stories and practices that seem to infringe on the liberty of women from today's perspective? First, a number of Muslim authors believe it is not the text itself but the people who interpret it that are misleading. "The existing inequality between men and women cannot be seen as having been mandated by God but must be seen as a subversion of God's original plan for humanity."[52]

Second, the problem may not come from the Qur᾿an but from the many "silences" the text contains in regards to women's issues. For example, on the issue of veiling, the Qur᾿anic text is not specific about the part of the body the woman must cover and therefore leaves the door open for interpretations.[53] Likewise, it does not mention female mutilation, which nonetheless is practiced in some Muslim countries but condemned in others. It does not say either that women should be stoned to death in case of adultery.[54] Muslim feminists and reformers point to these gaps to argue that interpreters who define oppressive laws have read too much into the Qur᾿anic texts.

Third, there are texts about a same issue in the Qur᾿an that seem to contradict each other. For example, on gender equality, some Qur᾿anic texts can be read as emphasizing gender equality and/or gender subjugation.[55] Depending on the interpreters, these texts are either seen as contradictory or complementary. Non-Muslims often have a hard time

47 Caner and Caner, *Unveiling Islam*, 140.

48 Abou El Fadl, *The Great Theft*, 272.

49 Hassan, "Challenging the Stereotypes," 62.

50 Ibid., 63.

51 Riffat Hassan, "Religious Conservatism: Feminist Theology as a Means of Combatting Injustice toward Women in Muslim Communities/Culture," http://www.oozebap.org/biblio/RELIGIOUS_CONSERVATISM.rtf.

52 Hassan, "Challenging the Stereotypes," 62.

53 *Sūrat* an-Nūr [24]:31; al-Aḥzāb [33]:53,59.

54 *Sūrat* an-Nūr [24]:2,3.

55 Compare and contrast al-Baqara [2]:228 and at-Tawba [9:]71,72; 51:49.

knowing what to do with these passages. Parshall and Parshall attempt to explain this matter by talking about two contradictory realities.[56]

Fourth, many discussions focus on the actual interpretations of gender texts in the Qurʾan. Some affirm that all texts must be interpreted literally, which makes the contextualization of certain Qurʾanic practices nearly impossible. Others believe there can be no monolithic interpretation of these texts.[57] The discussion on domestic violence in Islam provides a good example of such an issue. I have commonly heard Christians quote *Sūrat* an-Nisāʾ [4]:34 to argue that the Qurʾan encourages wife beating. In response to such criticism, Muslims have defended the Qurʾan by providing a variety of interpretations, some in favor of wife beating and others against it.[58]

Fifth, many argue the Qurʾan needs new interpretations. Esposito writes about the contemporary situation that, "Reformers have argued that Quranic verses favoring men need reinterpretation in light of the new social, cultural, and economic realities of the twentieth and twenty-first centuries."[59] Consequently a number of Muslims have proposed not only new interpretations but also new ways to interpret the Qurʾan. Mohammed Arkoun has been a fervent advocate for new analytical tools to contextualize the Qurʾan.[60] Barazangi has formed Qurʾanic study circles for women who read the text from a female perspective to find resources for women's rights.[61]

Sixth, instead of the Qurʾan, there are Muslims who blame the Hadith, second source of authority in Islam, which may promote gender inequality. Abou El Fadl writes, "By picking and choosing the traditions that appear demeaning to women, puritans are able to impose limitations on women that can only be described as suffocating."[62] While the majority of Muslims, as I said earlier in the text, hesitate to directly blame the Qurʾan for

---

56 Parshall and Parshall, *Lifting the Veil.*

57 For more information on the interpretation of legal texts, see John Esposito and Natana J. Delong-Bas, *Women in Muslim Family Law* (New York: Syracuse University Press, 1982); and Joseph Schacht, *An Introduction to Islamic Law* (Oxford: Oxford University Press, 1982). See also the research of Professor Abdullahi Ahmed An-Naʿim at http://www.law.emory.edu/aannaim.

58 *Sūrat* an-Nisāʾ [4]:34, traditionally referring to wife beating, receives diverse interpretations. The discussion centers on the meaning of the verb *ḍaraba* (to strike), used in this verse toward women. Traditionally this verb is read as "to beat." This can encourage men to domestic violence. Other interpreters translate the same verb by "beating slightly." Abdullah Yusuf Ali, *The Qurʾan: Text, Translation and Commentary* (Elmhurst, NY: Tahriqe Tarsile, 1987). It is thus important to read a variety of interpretations before making up one's opinion. Asma Barlas challenges the traditional interpretations of this verse and contends its meaning is ambiguous. She presents evidence for the following ways to read the verb *ḍaraba* (to strike): (1) symbolic gesture, (2) restriction rather than a prescription, (3) an obsolete restriction, (4) other meanings than "to beat." *"Believing Women" in Islam: Unreading Patriarchal Interpretations of the Qurʾan* (Austin: University of Texas Press, 2002), 188–89. Amina Wadud emphasizes that the verse "should be taken as prohibiting unchecked violence against females." *Qur'an and Women: Rereading the Sacred Text from a Woman's Perspective* (New York: Oxford University Press, 1999). Despite the disagreements about the interpretation of this verse, it is still important to remember that it has led to much abuse of women and thus should be seriously challenged.

59 Esposito, *Unholy War,* 90.

60 Mohammed Arkoun, *Rethinking Islam: Common Questions, Uncommon Answers*, trans./ed. Robert D. Lee (Boulder, CO: Westview, 1994).

61 Barazangi, *Woman's Identity*.

62 Abou El Fadl, *The Great Theft*, 258.

sexual inequality, they are less afraid to blame the Hadith. For example, Fatima Mernissi quotes a customer of her Moroccan grocer who used an "obscure" text from the Hadith to claim women should not be leaders.[63] Likewise Hassan is not afraid to reject all the hadiths claiming that women were created from a rib. She believes they are in opposition with the Qur'anic account that they are weak with reference to their *isnad*, or chain of transmitters. She claims, "The rib story has no place in the Qur'an."[64] Christians also often rely on the Hadith to argue that Islam is oppressive to women. If they do, they must however take the following into consideration. The hadiths on women's issues are not as authoritative as the Qur'anic texts.[65] One must be an expert on the Hadith to engage in authoritative interpretations. And one cannot just quote hadiths that appear negative and leave out the positive. I have noticed a difference between Muslim feminists and Christian writers. The former try to emphasize the primacy of the Qur'an against the debatable hadiths in order to argue for reform from within Islam, and the latter use the Hadith and the Qur'an as proof texts to find evidence that Islam subjugates women. The risk is that Muslims who deeply respect their sacred texts will disregard the argumentation of Christians if they do not approach the texts with academic integrity. Finally, although it is rare, there are some Muslim authors who directly attack the Qur'an. Most Muslim feminists would not go as far as blaming the Qur'an itself for gender inequalities.

I have started this section by a quote of Christians criticizing the Qur'an for its ill treatment of women. We have then looked at some Muslim approaches. I could have quoted a number of Christians who have a more open approach to the Qur'an. But I wanted to underline here a major difference between Muslims and Christians who combat oppression. Very few Muslims are directly blaming the Qur'an for the abuse of women but provide other reasons as shown above. Christians who directly attack the Qur'an on the question of gender may therefore stumble on defensive responses and even strong resistance from Muslims. I suggest therefore that unless one has a good mastery of the Qur'an, the Hadith, and their interpretations, it is safer to use first the biblical texts that Christians already know and study as basis for discussion and engaging with Muslims. As Christians use this approach, they will find that Muslims are open to share their knowledge about the Islamic texts with them, and it will be a good learning experience for everyone. Furthermore, Christians will soon realize that Muslims are not the only ones to wrestle with their texts on gender. Biblical texts have also created challenges for Christian commentators over the centuries. One should discuss this with Muslims. Then there are texts in the Bible that highlight, from a unique perspective, God's view on gender relations. It is the responsibility of Christians to share these views with Muslims if they want to share with the latter the nature of the God who revealed himself in Jesus Christ.

---

63 Fatima Mernissi, *The Veil and the Male Elite*, 1.

64 Hassan, "Challenging the Stereotypes," 62.

65 The Hadith is only the second source of authority and not considered by Muslims as the actual words of God, although it still has a lot of influence in their interpretations of the Qur'an and the elaboration of their legal system because it reports what Muhammad did, recommended, or tacitly approved.

Is Shari^ca to Blame?

Shari^{c}a is a concept that nowadays has probably become one of the most controversial.[66] It is central to most discussions on women in Muslim-majority countries, where family laws often fall under the Shari^{c}a.[67] But it is difficult to come to a consensus on this issue. Even amongst Muslims, the views can be very diverse. On one hand, Fatima Mernissi claims, "Sexual inequality is rooted in Shari^{c}a."[68] But on the other hand, there is evidence that "Working for women's progress by drawing upon the Sharia instead of by eliminating it is a reemerging theme among Muslim societies."[69]

How should Christians then stand on this issue? Is the Shari^{c}a to blame for the subjugation of women? Before answering, the following points are essential to consider. First, Muslims do not all have a negative view of Shari^{c}a like most outsiders have. In Islam, Shari^{c}a means "God's path,"[70] and the concept resonates to Muslim ears like the Old Testament passages on the law of God do to Christians.[71] Many Muslims rely on Shari^{c}a, God's law, to implement social justice in the world and stay connected to God. As a result, Muslims may often dismiss the critics of the Shari^{c}a.

Second, the Shari^{c}a is not static, and therefore its content may change depending on which legal experts are in leadership at the time. One day it can be in favor of women, and the other day it can subjugate them. Family laws in Muslim countries have a tendency to swing like a pendulum between modernity and tradition, or puritanism and liberalism. In Afghanistan, for example, there were times when women could wear the burqa in a traditional manner, then were being allowed to take it off under King Mohammad Zahir Shah, then were forced to wear it again under the Taliban, and now are allowed to legally take

66 Shari^{c}a can diversely mean the way, the spring, the religious law, or the holy law, depending on who is speaking. See also the chapter on Shari^{c}a by David L. Johnston in this Festschrift.

67 In Islam, many family laws are inspired by the Qur$^{\circ}$an and its interpretations and are more resistant to change than other societal laws. Leila Ahmed acknowledged that Islamic family law has not seen the amelioration that other parts of women's issues have. *Women and Gender in Islam*, 241. In many countries, this fact creates frustration amongst women who want to embrace modernity and postmodernity.

68 Fatema Mernissi, *Scheherazade Goes West: Different Cultures, Different Harems* (New York: Washington Square, 2001), 23. She explains further, "No one contests the principle of equality, which is considered to be a divine precept. What is debated is whether Shari'a, the law inspired by the Koran, can or cannot be changed" (ibid., 22).

69 Esposito and Mogahed, *Who Speaks for Islam?* 115.

70 See the meaning of Shari^{c}a in Tariq Ramadan, *Western Muslims and the Future of Islam* (New York: Oxford University Press, 2003).

71 A few examples of biblical passages referring to the law are: "You must obey my laws and be careful to follow my decrees. I am the Lord your God. Keep my decrees and laws, for the man who obeys them will live by them. I am the Lord" (Lev 18:4,5 NIV); "Keep all my decrees and laws and follow them, so that the land where I am bringing you to live may not vomit you out. You must not live according to the customs of the nations I am going to drive out before you" (Lev 20:22,23 NIV); "Blessed are they whose ways are blameless, who walk according to the law of the Lord. Blessed are they who keep his statutes and seek him with all their heart. They do nothing wrong; they walk in his ways" (Ps 119:1–3 NIV); "I have not departed from your laws, for you yourself have taught me. How sweet are your words to my taste, sweeter than honey to my mouth!" (Ps 119:102,103 NIV).

it off again. Due to these fluctuations, it is best not to make generalizations. It is better to examine each case and country individually.

Third, legal reforms about family and society in the Muslim world should not be overlooked. For example, in 2004 the status of Muslim women in Morocco improved through revisions done to the *Mudawwana* (Personal Status Code), although not to the satisfaction of all. Why is it important to acknowledge these changes? For the sake of fairness, those who press Muslims for reform should applaud any positive changes that occur. If not, news about reforms may be sidetracked by the far too common overload of critics of the status of Muslim women in Islam.

Fourth, what I just said does not mean Christians should keep silent if they see abuse or neglect of women's right in Muslim laws. There are several places in the Muslim world where the laws on divorce or child custody, for example, need reform. But in order to challenge such laws, one must not just be a theologian but also a legal expert. Very few Christian seminaries prepare their students to deal with legal matters in Islam by offering a course on the interpretation of the Hadith and on jurisprudence. This is unfortunate.[72]

Finally, I do not think Christians can comment on the Shariᶜa without looking at their own context and address the way the Christian community deals with legal issues. They face similar challenges to interpret laws in their own sacred texts. In every generation, the church wrestles with whether to interpret legal passages from the Bible literally or not. There are times when churches even had their own legal courts to deal with family issues such as marriage or adultery. And today Christians who live in secular systems sometimes fiercely debate over accepting or rejecting legal decisions from their governments that contradict biblical teaching.

Conclusion

There are a few other lenses that I could have described in this chapter. I have essentially looked at the question from a religious and theological perspective. But one could also have addressed this question from a purely sociological and cultural perspective, and looked at how cultures, social organizations, or history shape Islam. Christian anthropologist Miriam Adeney points out that nationality, ethnicity, personality, economical, and religious contexts shape the status and role of women.[73] Likewise, Ida Glaser, director of the Oxford Study Center for Muslim-Christian Relations, and coauthor Napoleon John wrote in the prologue

72 While Christian seminaries teach the Qurʾan, I do not know many (or any) that teach the science of Hadith, as it is taught in Muslim universities, and as a result, very few Christians are equipped to evaluate the weakness and the strength of each individual hadith. Furthermore, many hadiths are still not translated into other languages, and therefore only accessible to those who have a good mastery of Arabic. Having said that, Christians are not the only ones prone to use hadiths without serious scholarship. many Muslims do it as well. Take as proof what Mernissi said above about her grocer.

73 Miriam Adeney, *Daughters of Islam: Building Bridges with Muslim Women* (Downers Grove, IL: InterVarsity, 2002). Secular and Muslim authors similarly have dealt with this diversity. See Herbert L. Bodman and Nayereh Esfahlani Tohidi, eds, *Muslim Societies: Diversity Within Unity* (Boulder, CO: Lynne Rienner, 1998).

of their book, "For many Westerners, the images that immediately spring to mind are of silent, submissive creatures covered with black tents. Yet there are many different Muslim women, from many countries, with different cultures, different personalities, and different experiences in life."[74]

At the end of this chapter, I must reiterate my initial question: Who or what are we blaming? Is it Islam, the post-Muhammad era, antireformism in Islam, Muhammad, the Qurʾan, the Shariʿa, or none of those? As we have seen above, the situation is much more complex than it first appears. In order to continue to engage with the various voices heard in this chapter, I make a few recommendations.

There is a growing awareness of the kaleidoscopic views on women in Islam. There must be therefore no room for oversimplification[75] or stereotyping.[76] To gain a better knowledge on this topic, it is necessary, as was done in this chapter, to listen to a variety of sources (Muslim, Christian, traditional, secular, etc). And even among these categories there are different views.[77]

As traditionally the view of Christians was rather negative, they must show to non-Christians that if their views change or do not change, their position at least is based on valid research. There is an encouraging comment made by Haddad, Smith, and Moore on Miriam Adeney's book *Daughters of Islam: Building Bridges with Muslim Women*: "Many of these writings on contextualization as a strategy for conversion do provide a more balanced picture of Muslim women than is reflected in traditional stereotypes."[78]

The situation in the world has drastically changed. There are now more opportunities than ever to meet Muslim women face-to-face. In order to develop a better understanding of women, one has to meet them. Christian Iranian-American author Shirin Taber makes the core of her book a plea for Christians to let go of the fear of meeting Muslim women.[79]

---

74 Ida Glaser and Napoleon John, *Partners or Prisoners: Christian Thinking about Women and Islam* (Solway Gallery, 1998), xi.

75 In some Christian circles the status and role of Muslim women is summarized as a list of ten controversial issues: illiteracy, female mutilation, divorce, polygamy, honor killing, domestic violence, forced marriage, stoning for adultery, the burqa, and purdah (women's seclusion from public observation among Muslims). Unfortunately such a list is often reductive and should be used with great caution. I hope this chapter has shown why.

76 Stereotyping of Muslim women is very common. Asma Barlas from Ithaca College shared about students in general, "It really is a struggle to get my students to develop some empathy for a group of people from whom they feel existentially distanced and politically alienated largely as a result of having imbibed damaging stereotypes about them over a life-time." "Teaching about Women and Islam," AMEWS Roundtable, MESA, San Francisco, November 21, 2004. Is it a surprise that Haddad, Smith, and Moore (*Muslim Women in America*, 21–40) include Christian mission and evangelism in "the various factors that generate stereotypes of Muslim women in the West"? Telling stories of women's individual journeys helpfully balances the use of symbols. Miriam Adeney (*Daughters of Islam*, 23), illustrating "every woman is an exception," writes, "When mission executives are not aware of this, they sometimes lump Muslim women into narrow categories."

77 For example, you have different approaches to women in literal salafism, reformist salafism, Sufism, and traditional or liberal Islam.

78 Haddad, Smith, and Moore, *Muslim Women in America*, 26–27.

79 Shirin Taber, *Muslims Next Door: Uncovering Myths and Creating Friendships* (Grand Rapids: Zondervan, 2004).

Similarly, when they write on gender, Parshall and Parshall[80] do not just present data but introduce their female friends to the readers. In her book, Joy Loewen learns to "feel at home with Muslims," thanks to personal encounters of women and especially her friend Zarina.[81] All these Christian authors have found the value of developing relationships with women instead of just writing about them.

We have come a long way from the situation in the 1970s when one of the rare biographies of a Muslim woman available on the evangelical book market was the story of how the Muslim Pakistani woman Bilquis Sheikh became a follower of Jesus.[82] Today scores of stories are told in books, television programs, or on the Internet. The Christian community has produced a plethora of resources for those who want to witness to Muslim women or relate to them in a healthy way.[83]

Finally, it is clear from this chapter that Muslims are not unique in how they wrestle with gender issues. Their texts on gender may not be exactly the same as biblical passages, and their way of dealing with legal issues may differ from what is done in the Christian community, but they still ask similar questions (what to do in cases of marriage, adultery, divorce, child custody, female leadership, male-female relations, etc.). Christians have therefore plenty of opportunities to engage with Muslims on these issues and share their own journey with them. In doing that, they may reach the same conclusion as Ida Glaser and Napoleon John when they wrote, "Islam as it has been practiced has often encouraged the dominance of men over women, but it is not alone in that. Every analysis of the oppression of women through Islam could be matched with an analysis of the oppression of women in the West or in the name of Christianity. Which system has had the worst record is debatable."[84] And after that assessment, Christians may want to revisit the biblical texts to find what is really unique to their faith, what they are still trying to figure out and interpret in the present context, and what they can share with Muslims as good news for women; not in a spirit of superiority or pride, but in genuine desire to lead them to find the life Jesus Christ has intended for them.

---

80 Parshall and Parshall, *Lifting the Veil*. They start their book by introducing their "first Muslim female buddies."

81 Joy Loewen, *Woman to Woman: Sharing Jesus with a Muslim Friend* (Grand Rapids: Chosen, 2010). The entire theme of the book is about feeling at home between Muslims and Christians. The preface reads, "May you be encouraged and inspired to move from fear to love and compassion, so that you, too can say without hesitancy, 'I am at home with Muslims.' It is possible." She shows the differences of values and obstacles but also joy of Muslim-Christian relations by telling her own experience interacting with Muslim women in the United States. She tells her own mistakes in the relations and shows how Muslim women react to our own misperception of them.

82 Bilquis Sheikh, *I Dared to Call Him Father: The Miraculous Story of a Muslim Woman's Encounter with God*, with Richard H. Schneider (Grand Rapids: Chosen, 2005).

83 See for example: Fran Love and Jeleta Eckheart, eds., *Longing to Call Them Sisters: Ministry to Muslim Women* (Pasadena: William Carey Library, 2004); Christine Mallouhi, *Miniskirts, Mothers, and Muslims: A Christian Woman in a Muslim Land* (Oxford: Monarch, 2004); Cynthia A. Strong and Meg Page, *A Worldview Approach to Ministry among Muslim Women* (Pasadena: William Carey Library, 2007); and Mary Ann Cate and Karol Downey, *From Fear to Faith: Muslim and Christian Women* (Pasadena: William Carey Library, 2002).

84 Glaser and John, *Partners or Prisoners*, 2.

5
Current Trends in Islam and Christian Mission

BY WARREN F. LARSON

September 11, 2001, was not the day when everything changed, but the day that revealed how much had changed. It therefore behooves us to question common perceptions. For example, what most Westerners know about Muslims comes from television, and since Islamists[1] are in the press, a common perception is that all Muslims are extremists.[2] As for Muslims, a common self-perception is that they are under economic, cultural, and military siege by the West.[3]

This chapter will begin by looking at Muslim expansion in the West. Next, it will focus on Islamists and note positive responses to Christian witness, not in spite of extremism and violence but because Islam is at war with itself.[4] Finally, it will turn the spotlight on Christians, encouraging right attitudes and calling for a deeper study of the historical, theological, and ideological levels of both faiths.

---

1 In order to illustrate the diversity and define select terms, "Islamism"—another word for extremism, radicalism, fundamentalism, or militancy—is a belief that the Qur'an and Hadith (traditions of the Prophet's life) should be followed completely on how to live, govern, and relate to others. Contrary to what many Westerners think, it is the most powerful ideological force that Muslims have. Moderate Muslims adapt to Western ways and education.

2 Admittedly, there are reasons for such perceptions: *The Sunday Telegraph* of February 19, 2006, reported that radical elements in England went from 15 percent in 2001 to 43 percent in 2006. Undoubtedly, the war on terror had something to do with the rise. And, sadly, there are indications that Christians are beginning to hate Muslims. Warren Larson found that American evangelical attitudes toward Muslims since September 11, 2001, have hardened in "Unveiling the Truth about Islam: Too Many Christian Books Miss the Mark," *Christianity Today*, June 2006, http://www.christianitytoday.com/ct/2006/june/29.38.html.

3 Meic Pearse, *Why the Rest Hate the West: Understanding the Roots of Global Rage* (Downers Grove, IL: InterVarsity Press, 2004). The author exaggerates, but Muslims do have a feeling of being held by a huge cultural and economic juggernaut, and the problem is that Westerners are not even aware they are doing it.

4 Bernard Lewis finds historical roots for Islam's current confusion and violent confrontations in *The Crisis of Islam: Holy War and Unholy Terror* (New York: Random House, 2004). His perspective is much preferred to Samuel P. Huntington's view that Islam's struggle with the West is simply the clash of civilizations in *The Clash of Civilizations and the Remaking of World Order* (New York: Touchstone, 1996).

Understanding Muslims in the Twenty-first Century

Given the fact that this chapter was written three years ago much has changed in the Muslim world. The best example is the so-called Arab Spring and ongoing revolutions in several Middle Eastern contexts. Nevertheless, the material is relevant, particularly in reference to evangelical Christian understanding of Muslims.

The context

The study of Muslim people groups uncovers significant contrasts. Besides linguistic, religious, political, and cultural differences, Muslims may be pious or profane, fundamentalist or secular, impoverished or rich, unethical or honorable, angry or passive, dominating or submissive, demanding or mild-mannered. Yet despite differences, a recurring theme, fueled by wealth and rapid growth, is that "Islam will triumph." In fact, some Muslims are openly saying that the twenty-first century belongs to Islam.

In America, Islam is getting into schools, gaining positions of power, and winning converts, particularly in black communities.[5] For African-American men, often the context in which they are first exposed to Islam is prison. For African-American women, modesty, chastity, and economic rights in Islam attract them. Prior to conversion, their perception was that they had been abandoned by a spouse, left to fend for themselves and their children. For them, Islam is an alternative to neglect and indiscipline. It is a neat package with rigid prayer rituals, precise rules for relationships, male leadership roles, and family values—even a new name. Where Christianity lacks power to effect social change, Islam provides laws, controls moral behavior, and brings reform.

Turning to Europe, there is a stark contrast between the growth and vitality of Islam[6] vis-à-vis the stagnation and dwindling numbers of indigenous people. The fertility rate in the continent is only 1.4 children per woman. The reality is that Europe is demographically dying and desperately needs immigrants to survive. Muslims are ready and willing to fill the empty spaces, but often repulsed by pornography, filth, sexual immorality, divorce, and homosexuality. Even worse, many are not integrating into society, and some are facing discrimination. Capitalizing on these negatives, Islamists are preaching that the West is a religious and moral vacuum and that Islam can sweep the West and fill the void. Too many

---

5 Audrey Parks Shabbas, leader of Arab World and Islamic Resources and School Services in Berkeley, California, is quoted in "Taking the Mystery Out of the Middle East," *Aramco World* 53, no. 1 (2002): "A decade ago" the average seventh to twelfth-grade social studies class spent "three or four days" on Islam and the Middle East "and now it's three or four weeks, maybe six." Keith Ellison, African-American convert to Islam, is the first Muslim elected to the US House of Representatives. Upon taking office, he shocked the nation by swearing on the Qurʾan, not the Bible.

6 Tracing Islam's growth on six continents over the last hundred years, Patrick Johnstone (2001) projects for the next fifty years: Europe from 1900–2050: from 1.42 to 11 percent; North America: .01 to 5 percent; Latin America: .10 to 5.8 percent; Pacific Rim: .22 to 3 percent; Asia: 17 to 31 percent; Africa: 32 to 40 percent. Globally, Muslim numbers increase from 12 percent in 1900 to 27 percent in 2050. Remember, this is a projection, and only God knows. Patrick Johnstone, *Projected Growth of Islam* (London: Paternoster Press, 2001).

Europeans, however, refuse to admit that religion has a significant role to play, as if deaf to Islamist rhetoric that appeals to Islam.[7]

The context for Islamic expansion in Europe, therefore, could not be better. The continent is increasingly post-Christian with a diminishing connection to traditional values. Even Prince Charles, previously "Defender of the Faith," is now "Defender of Faiths," with no apparent loyalty to his religious heritage. Europeans have forgotten that freedom, democracy, human rights, and liberty are primarily the result of Christianity. In the midst of these mounting tensions, the somber predictions are that the European-Muslim relationship will continue to deteriorate and that Islam will continue to gain ground.[8] Perhaps these have prompted right-wing conservatives in the United States to warn that America may be headed in the same direction.[9]

Nowhere is the progress and strength of Islam seen more clearly than in London, where Islamists are asserting their power, wealth, and influence.[10] With 700 mosques, 1,200 schools, 10,000 converts, and 1 million Muslims, it has been called the "Capital of Islam."[11]

A closer look

John Esposito, probably the most influential and erudite Islamic scholar in North America, sounds prophetic at times. In *The Islamic Threat: Myth or Reality*? he says that Islam is a threat to the West, particularly the United States, but not because Islam is inherently violent. *Unholy War: Terror in the Name of Islam* might have been entitled "I Told You So."[12] The thesis of one of his latest books is that a war conducted militarily, rather than diplomatically and through social change, will lead to increased anti-Americanism, greater global instability, and bloodshed.

American foreign policy, including uncritical support for Israel and military action in the Middle East, has enraged Muslims. Moreover, the stated goal of the Bush administration

---

7 Bat Ye'or, who borrowed the term "Eurabia" for her book *Eurabia: The Euro-Arab Axis* (Cranbury, NJ: Fairleigh Dickinson University Press, 2005), says only 21 percent of Europeans think religion is important. See also *The Dhimmi: Jews and Christians under Islam* (Cranbury, NJ: Fairleigh Dickinson University Press, 1985).

8 See Walter Laqueur, *The Last Days of Europe: Epitaph for an Old Continent* (New York: St. Martin's, 2007); Bruce Bawer, *While Europe Slept: How Radical Islam Is Destroying the West From Within* (New York: Random House, 2006); Claire Berlinski, *Menace in Europe: Why the Continent's Crisis Is America's Too* (New York: Three Rivers, 2006); Bat Ye'or, *Eurabia*.

9 Some publications seem to be alarmist because religion is of importance to many Americans. Nevertheless, Americans should take the warnings seriously. In *America Alone: The End of the World as We Know It* (Washington, DC: Regnery, 2006), Mark Steyn may hold an alarmist view, but it is possible.

10 In *Londonistan: How Britain is Creating a Terror State Within* (New York: Encounter, 2006), Melanie Phillips accuses British officials of scandalous appeasement. Groups like al-Muhajiroun, under the fiery preaching of exiled Sheikh Omar Bakri Muhammad, were permitted to say what they wanted for years.

11 Plans for Europe's largest mosque in Newham (part of London) were shelved due to opposition (some from their own community), but Muslims do not lack the motivation and the money to press forward. This massive undertaking for a building to seat 40,000 Muslim worshipers is being pushed by Tablighi Jamaat. Moreover, the Saudi-based Muslim World League spends vast amounts of money building mosques, sending missionaries, and printing Islamic literature, much of it destined for the West.

12 John L. Esposito, *The Islamic Threat: Myth or Reality?* (Oxford: Oxford University Press, 1992); and *Unholy War: Terror in the Name of Islam* (Oxford: Oxford University Press, 2002).

was widely interpreted in the Muslim world that Muslims face a Christian crusade aimed at destroying Islam. Furthermore, Esposito would probably agree that there are other reasons behind Islamist rage. Among them, globalization, years of unhappy Muslim-Christian relationships, "Westophobia" in the Muslim media, and even conspiracy theories—like the one that makes Jews responsible for 9/11—thrive in Islamic circles.[13]

Yet the question must be asked why any society would react so angrily to rumors and perceived threats or be so gullible as to believe such unfounded theories. In response, Khaled M. Abou El Fadl, a prominent (Western) Muslim scholar, gives the less-than-satisfactory theory that the problem with Islam is that it lacks a final authority. As a result, self-proclaimed "experts" pronounce judgments at will—and get away with it. He goes on to say that since 1998 *fatwās* (formal, legal opinions by Islamic scholars) have increased dramatically, and there is no shortage of people to act on them. His plea to assuage such an abuse of religious authority is that the "silent majority" wages a counterjihad and rescues the soul of Islam from a "militant and fanatic minority."[14]

Another moderate Muslim, Tawfik Hamid, goes much further in his analysis and outspoken denunciation of current trends. He says that something is seriously wrong with Islam and the best thing Muslims can do is admit it and take steps to fix it.[15] For example, women are stoned, female circumcisions are permitted, homosexuals are hung from the gallows, and Palestinian mothers teach their sons to glorify martyrdom. In some contexts it is perfectly acceptable to persecute Christians.

Muslims, he says, are not being honest when they avoid critical self-inspection. They must diagnose their own diseases, prescribe their own treatments, and take their own medicine—be it ever so bitter. He, too, pleads with the silent majority to stand up and be counted. His sharp rebuke extends to secularist Westerners who loudly demonstrate against the war in Iraq but not against those who kidnap others and either cut their throats or behead them. By remaining silent about such unspeakable atrocities, they themselves become obstacles to Islamic reform.[16] Frankly, the openness, honesty, and courage of such moderates as Abou El Fadl, Hamid, and others is indeed refreshing and must not escape the attention of those who fall into the trap of criticizing others but failing to critique their own societies. Perhaps a new day is dawning as other moderates come forward and boldly speak the truth.[17]

---

13 Peter G. Riddell and Peter Cotterell, *Islam in Context: Past, Present, and Future* (Grand Rapids: Baker Academic, 2003), 152–60. My own book, *Islamic Ideology and Fundamentalism in Pakistan* (Lanham, MD: University Press of America, 1998), suggests several causes of fundamentalism: history, local conditions, trauma, successes, failures, and the West.

14 Khaled M. Abou El Fadl, *The Great Theft: Wrestling Islam from the Extremists* (New York: HarperCollins, 2006), 15. Cf. Irshad Manji, *The Trouble with Islam Today: A Muslim's Call for Reform in Her Faith* (New York: St. Martin's, 2003); and others.

15 Tawfik Hamid, "The Development of a Jihadi's Mind," in *Current Trends in Islamic Ideology*, vol. 5, eds. Hillel Fradkin, Husain Haqqani, and Eric Brown (Washington, DC: Hudson Institute, 2007). See also Tawfik Hamid, *The Roots of Jihad* (Newton, PA: Top Executive Media, 2006).

16 Ibid.

17 It is most heartening to see moderate Muslim women eloquently publishing material. See Manji, *The Trouble with Islam*; Asra Nomani, *Standing Alone: An American Woman's Struggle for the Soul of Islam* (New York:

Recognizing the Hand of God

Several years ago Dudley Woodberry spoke of the hand of God in the glove of human circumstances to illustrate one way God is drawing Muslims to himself. The phrase seems more appropriate today than ever.

Case studies and growing receptivity

On my bookshelf are two texts with titles that clearly quantify how Muslims used to become Christians, even as recent as forty years ago: The first, *Seven Muslims Make their Greatest Discovery*, and the second, *Ten Muslims Meet Christ.*[18] Today the good news is that some Muslim people groups are responding in far greater numbers than before. For example, more Iranian Muslims have come to Christ since the 1979 revolution than in the hundreds of years preceding it.

Turning to other traditionally resistant areas in Muslim contexts, Patrick Johnstone's 1995 estimates of MBBs (Muslim background believers)[19] are almost incredible: Algeria 50,000; Bangladesh 500,000; Benin 40,000; Burkina Faso 200,000; Cameroon 80,000; Egypt 10,000; Ethiopia 400,000; Ghana 50,000; Indonesia 6 million; Iran 50,000; Kazakhstan 25,000; Kyrgyzstan 15,000; Malaysia 6,000; Nigeria 500,000; Tanzania 150,000; USA 300,000; and Uzbekistan 8,000.

It is difficult to say precisely why more Muslims are responding than at any other time in history, and surely not wise to dogmatize, but the following appear to be some of the reasons. First, there is a political element. In reference to Pakistan, it is not conversion figures but an apparent openness to the gospel. During the late 1970s, in the midst of Islamic resurgence, the sale of Bibles through the Pakistan Bible Society and the number of Bible correspondence students throughout the country increased dramatically. At that time General Muhammad Zia ul-Haqq imposed the rigid rules of Islamic law. And in 1995, when I interviewed thirty-two Pakistani MBBs, almost without exception they said that "Islam's harshness is driving Muslims to Christ."[20]

Similarly, and much more significantly, Iranian converts said in 1981: "Khomeini has become the biggest blessing because he revealed Islam for what it is." Despite the euphoria in 1979 when the Ayatollah Khomeini took over from the shah, Iranians quickly became

---

HarperOne, 2005).

18 Mark Hanna, *The True Path: Seven Muslims Make Their Greatest Discovery* (Colorado Springs: International Doorways, 1975); William McElwee Miller, *Ten Muslims Meet Christ* (Grand Rapids: Eerdmans, 1976).

19 These figures were received through private conversations with the author, and it must be remembered that they are only estimates. Only God knows how many converts there are since it is often difficult, if not impossible, to collect solid research. Though it is impossible to vouch for their accuracy, these numbers do indicate a growing openness.

20 Warren Fredrick Larson, *Islamic Ideology and Fundamentalism in Pakistan: Climate for Conversion to Christianity* (Lanham, MD: University Press of America, 1998), 152.

disillusioned by the cruelty and harshness of the new Islamist regime, and as noted above, thousands have turned to the Messiah.[21]

Second, Muslims are suffering. In most cases where Muslims are turning to Christ, it has had something to do with suffering. Bangladesh (formerly East Pakistan) suffered unspeakable cruelty at the hands of fellow Muslims in 1971. Kurds experienced genocide at the hand of Saddam Hussein and are now more open to the gospel. A similar case can be made for the growing receptivity in Algeria, where horrendous acts were carried out in the name of Islam, again through Muslim-on-Muslim violence.

Third, God is using supernatural means. In certain areas where folk Islam is strong, Muslims convert because of their desire for *baraka* (blessing) and need for power over evil spirits. They usually point to at least one dream, but when facing persecution for their testimony, some attest to successive dreams of Jesus. He is invariably the one who brings comfort, assurance, and strength to persevere.

Fourth, when Muslims come to Christ, it is always the sovereign work of God.[22] Workers bear witness to the truth that prayer is the answer to Muslim receptivity and urge their supporters to pray diligently for responsive hearts. What is encouraging is that God is not hindered by circumstances, however difficult they might be.

Fifth, theological reasons also play a role. Former Muslims often say that it was the unconditional love and forgiveness of God that touched their hearts. Others, in contrast to what they see in Muhammad, say it was the moral beauty of Christ, as well as his power to intercede, deliver, and save from sin.

Sixth, contextualization must be included. In some contexts, like Bangladesh, the Camel Method (building on the Qurʾanic Jesus) has been successful, but not always in other places.[23] It certainly is not the panacea.

In summary, amidst opposition, persecution, and intense suffering, there are indications that Muslims are becoming more receptive to the gospel. Though most areas are still resistant, there is increasing openness, and sometimes there are remarkable people movements to Christ. All this adds weight to the theory that conversion may be a way of "getting even" with society.[24] Though Islam claims absoluteness in all religio-socio-political matters, many Muslims lack meaning and identity. Indeed, Islam fails to give complete fulfillment, even though it seems to function more as an ideology than as religion. The truth is that when

---

21 This information was gleaned through reports from Brother Andrew, who wrote *God's Smuggler*, with John and Elizabeth Sherrill (Grand Rapids: Chosen, 1967), about his experiences of smuggling Bibles in communist areas. After the fall of communism in Europe, Brother Andrew shifted his focus to the Middle East in order to strengthen the church in the Islamic world.

22 Avery Willis, *Indonesian Revival: Why Two Million Came to Christ* (Pasadena: William Carey Library, 1977). He points out that an overemphasis on the importance of miracles by some writers must give way to a more accurate picture of the sovereign work of God as a possible paradigm for church growth in other countries. The so-called Indonesian Revival was really a movement set in motion by God decades before.

23 Kevin Greeson, *The Camel: How Muslims Are Coming to Faith in Christ!* (Bangalore: WIGTake Resources, 2007).

24 This is the theory presented in Seppo Syrjänen, *In Search of Meaning and Identity: Conversion to Christianity in Pakistani Muslim Culture* (Helsinki: Finnish Society for Missiology and Ecumenics, 1984).

Muslims have lost their moorings, Jesus Christ gives personal value and identity to all who trust in him.

Reflecting the Spirit and Mind of Christ in the Face of Islamism

The author attended a conference recently where a speaker made the keen observation that people in the West react to Islam in one of three ways: Fear, fury or fascination. Too many evangelical Christians seem to fall into the first category when they should be engaging in bold and loving witness.

Christian scholarship

Ever since September 11, 2001, there has been a sharp increase of books on Islam by evangelical Christians in the United States.[25] Having read nearly a dozen of them that came out soon after the tragic events of September 11, 2001, a dominant theme was noted: even if the titles did not include the word "unveil," most attempted to expose Islam for its theological, historical, and moral shortcomings.[26]

This "unveiling," however, will not succeed unless evangelicals get their act together. One reason is that their polemic is often historically inaccurate, theologically misinformed, and simply bad mission strategy. Another reason is that it seems too many evangelicals have negative attitudes toward Muslims. Perhaps they reflect such attitudes because they take their cue from the media, listen to simplistic solutions, and paint all Muslims with the same brush. "Islamophobia," by definition, is the fear that every Muslim hates Christians, and every Muslim is out to kill Christians.[27]

Therefore, when evangelicals critique Islam, they must do it in a way that is fair and accurate; when they make Muslim-Christian comparisons, they must do so from a position of "informed engagement" as those who have learned to love Muslims by living among them; when they relate historical tensions between the two faiths, they need to apply a rigorous historical analysis; and when they write about Islam, they ought to bear in mind that love is the greatest apologetic.

It seems fair to say that, generally, evangelicals who live and work in Islamic contexts see Muslims first as human beings who need to be redeemed. They do not judge Muslims by the violence and hatred of a minority, because they have developed positive relationships with some Muslims. They have learned by experience that the majority of Muslims

25 This is not to deny that non-Christians have also written many books, some quite excellent.

26 Larson, "Unveiling the Truth about Islam."

27 Melanie Phillips' definition of "Islamophobia" is "the thought-crime that seeks to suppress legitimate criticism of Islam and demonize those who would tell the truth about Islamist aggression" *Londonistan* (New York: Encounter Books, 2006), xvii. The author has a point, but it sounds like she is denying that Islamophobia exists. In an excerpt from *America Alone*, Mark Steyn says that the West will lose out to Islam for three reasons: demographics, decline of democracy (Shari^{c}a law), and death of civilization. CAIR (Council on American-Islamic Relations) calls this article inflammatory, Islamophobic, and offensive.

in our world are in fact peaceful. Neither do they presume that Islam (and Muslims) can be understood solely by looking at the Qur'an or Islamic ideology. Islam is much broader than that, and Muslims are not so easily defined.

Practical steps

In light of the above analysis, two suggestions are offered, including a quote by Samuel Zwemer, referred to as the "Apostle to Islam." First, Christians could use a good dose of evangelical optimism as they consider the task of reaching Muslims with the gospel. In light of case studies mentioned above and numerous other credible sources of information, there is every reason to anticipate greater Muslim receptivity in the days ahead. Christians have been praying for centuries that Muslims would respond, but often there has been little lasting fruit. Now, it would seem, we are embarking on a new day.

Second, Christians must devote themselves to a serious study of Islam, and diligent research needs to be carried out in reference to each Muslim people group. Serious scholarship must be conducted by Christians and material (electronic and in print) produced in order to understand Islam, encourage proper attitudes, and promote mission to Muslims. This is what Samuel Zwemer, perhaps the greatest missionary the United States has ever sent to the Muslim world, had to say one hundred years ago:

> If the churches of Christendom are to reach the Moslem world with the Gospel, they must know of it and know it. The Cairo Conference (1906) marked a new era in the attitude of Christian missions toward the subject. This Conference, through its reports and the other missionary literature resulting from it, made clear the unity, the opportunity, and the importunity of the task of evangelizing Moslems everywhere. Missionary leaders felt that the church was called to a deeper study of the problem, as well as to a more thorough preparation of its missionaries and a bolder faith in God, in order to solve it. To this end there is need for a common platform, a common forum of thought; a common organ for investigation and study.[28]

In this first edition of what was then called *The Moslem World*, Zwemer's plea for "a deeper study of the problem [Islam]," as well as a more thorough preparation of missionaries, must be taken seriously. He wanted to avoid stereotyping Muslims as he stressed their varied aspects and deep needs. He desired to be of practical help to Christians in order to, as he put it, "awaken sympathy, love, and prayer on behalf of the Islamic world until its bonds are burst, its wounds are healed, its sorrows removed, and its desires satisfied in Jesus Christ."[29] Let this be our goal as we reflect on Muslims and their need for the gospel in the twenty-first century.

28 Samuel M. Zwemer, *The Moslem World: A Quarterly Review*, Vol. 1, 1911 (New York: Krause Reprint, 1966), 2–3.

29 Ibid.

SECTION 2

Christian Scholarship

INTRODUCTION BY JOSEPH L. CUMMING

In view of Dudley Woodberry's outstanding scholarship on Islam—both on its historic and sacred texts and on the "lived Islam" of contemporary Muslim-majority cultures—the second section of this Festschrift is appropriately dedicated to highlighting innovative scholarship on various aspects of Islamic practice, theology, and civilization. While it is true that basic to our Christian presence among Muslims is simple witness to the good news with reliance on the Holy Spirit and humble, godly character, and while we would be remiss to forget that the Lord Jesus was born in simplicity as a carpenter's son, one cannot read the Bible without also noting that God has called certain people throughout history to dedicate themselves to excellence in scholarship, particularly scholarship on the thought systems of great world civilizations.

In considering Islam, we are engaging not just a religion but one of the greatest civilizations in human history—one that has profoundly developed systems of thought and a rich intellectual, theological, and ethical history which, from a human and academic standpoint, is fully the equal of our own intellectual traditions. In such a context we do well to consider how the Lord's servants in the Bible dealt with the major world civilizations and empires of their times. The examples of Moses (with ancient Egyptian civilization), of Daniel (with Babylonian/Persian civilization), and of Paul (with Greco-Roman civilization) illustrate God's intentional appointment of educated intellectuals during critical points of history.

We read the following in Acts 7:20–22 (NIV) regarding God's servant Moses:

> At that time Moses was born, and he was no ordinary child. For three months he was cared for in his father's house. When he was placed outside, Pharaoh's daughter took him and brought him up as her own son.

> Moses was educated in all the wisdom of the Egyptians and was powerful in speech and action.

During that generation, Egypt was the most powerful and sophisticated civilization in the greater region. God providentially positioned a certain man so that he would become well trained in the educational, philosophical, literary, and cultural heritage of that civilization. God arranged for Moses to be "educated in all the wisdom of the Egyptians." Similarly, in our generation Providence raises up men and women of God like Dudley Woodberry who dedicate themselves to serious scholarship and learning about Islamic civilization—a civilization which has had a profound influence on world history and intellectual development during the past fourteen centuries and continuing today.

During the time of the prophet Daniel, the most powerful and influential civilization was that of the Babylonians. And similarly, God providentially positioned Daniel to master the scholarship of Babylonian civilization. In Daniel 1:3–20 (NIV) we read:

> Then the king ordered Ashpenaz, chief of his court officials, to bring in some of the Israelites from the royal family and the nobility—young men without any physical defect, handsome, showing aptitude for every kind of learning, well informed, quick to understand, and qualified to serve in the king's palace. He was to teach them the language and literature of the Babylonians … To these four young men God gave knowledge and understanding of all kinds of literature and learning … At the end of the time set by the king to bring them in, the chief official presented them to Nebuchadnezzar. The king talked with them, and he found none equal to Daniel, Hananiah, Mishael and Azariah; so they entered the king's service. In every matter of wisdom and understanding about which the king questioned them, he found them ten times better than all the magicians and enchanters in his whole kingdom.

Thus, in the case of Daniel and his three companions, Scripture attests not only that they became learned in Babylonian literature and thought, but that their scholarship on Babylonian civilization was "ten times better" than that of the elite scholars of that kingdom. Similarly, in our generation, God seeks godly followers of Christ like Dudley Woodberry who dedicate themselves to becoming not merely "good" scholars of Islamic thought and civilization, but "ten times" better-informed scholars than even their Muslim colleagues in areas of Islamic philosophy, literature, theology, law, and practice.

In the time following the Lord Jesus' ministry on this earth, the Apostle Paul provides an example of a follower of Jesus who was also well educated in the religion, philosophy, and literature of the great thought system of his world—that of Greco-Roman civilization. Athens was the place of higher education in that society, much as we might think of the Ivy

League or Oxford and Cambridge today. In Acts 17:27,28 (NIrV) we read the following in Paul's words to the scholars at the Areopagus in Athens: "God did this so that people would seek him. Then perhaps they would reach out for him and find him. They would find him even though he is not far from any of us. 'In him we live and move and exist.' As some of your own poets have also said, 'We are his children.'"

In this passage Paul quotes two different writers known to Athenian scholars, probably the philosopher Epimenides of Crete (or words attributed to him) and the poet Aratus in his hexameter work "Phainomena." What is particularly striking is that Paul was apparently prepared to cite such quotations impromptu in an interactive situation. In order to do so, he would have to have spent substantial time on earlier occasions poring over Greek philosophical and poetic texts, taking careful note of points of common ground that might constitute a basis for dialogue and a starting point for making the good news intelligible to the Athenians. Similarly, in our generation, God raises up men and women who make the effort to become familiar with the writers and poets and philosophers commonly known to Muslims around the world. Sometimes Christians look for "magic keys" to communicate with Muslims. But God is looking for people who will do their homework, who love Muslims enough to devote long hours to learning and understanding what Muslims believe and how Muslims think and feel, in order to speak with them in a way that will be meaningful.

Dudley Woodberry embodies the intellectual commitment we see in the prophets Moses and Daniel and the Apostle Paul. He earned his PhD at Harvard under Sir Hamilton A. R. Gibb, who was perhaps the greatest Western scholar of Islam of his time. In that context Dudley studied the same Arabic texts that Muslim scholars study when they train at the elite Al-Azhar University in Cairo, and thus Dudley became "learned in the wisdom of the Egyptians." Then, in addition to keeping up his textual scholarship, Dr. Woodberry took up an additional scholarly interest in the popular piety found in the contemporary "lived Islam" of Muslim-majority cultures around the world, including what Dean Gilliland refers to in his chapter as "folk Islam." Dudley blended the best of text-based scholarship with the anthropological and sociological study of Islam as it is lived by ordinary Muslims day to day. And he did this at a time when very few evangelicals engaged in either kind of scholarship. Then, through his leadership, those who studied directly under him or who were influenced by his writings and public speaking produced a generation of excellent Christian scholars in both areas. This section then represents a very small sample of the many scholars who have been influenced by Dudley, and whose scholarship contributes significantly to Muslim-Christian relations and to faithful representation of the Lord Jesus among Muslims.

The section begins with a chapter by the highly respected scholar, Bishop Kenneth Cragg, who likewise has contributed significantly to the body of credible and constructive Christian scholarship on Islam. Then, as someone who has been personally influenced by Dudley Woodberry's approach to scholarship, I present a chapter exploring possible parallels between an important Muslim theologian's doctrine of God and the Christian concept of the Trinity. Dudley's example inspires me to avoid jumping to oversimplified conclusions, but instead to engage in a study of the relevant primary texts themselves to understand in a nuanced way the extent to which the drawing of this parallel is or is not accurate.

Rick Brown then contributes an important chapter reflecting serious linguistic research and scholarship. He explores the evidence for the use of the term *Allah* for God among Jews and Christians prior to the birth of Islam. He then presents significant research to address a number of common misconceptions about the name *Allah*. This chapter does much to make it possible for Christians and Muslims to speak about faith matters with respect and with greater potential for accurate and effective communication.

Dean Gilliland, one of Dudley Woodberry's esteemed colleagues at Fuller, presents a chapter that illustrates and amplifies much of Dudley's own research. In this chapter, the elements of popular piety present in everday "lived Islam" in the African context are examined.

Following this essay, Stephen Mutuku Sesi, further illustrates this point in his chapter on the Kaya 'Shrine' and the mosque in which he shares with us his observations on the daily experiences and religious worldview of the Digo population in Kenya.

One of the central principles of interfaith relations is that when we talk about the beliefs of another person or group, we must strive to represent them so accurately that those who hold those beliefs would agree, "Yes, you have accurately described what I believe." Otherwise, the other person or group feels misrepresented or tendentiously distorted, and the opportunity for mutual understanding is lost. Unfortunately, a significant amount of Christian scholarship on Islam has not followed this principle, and has presented Islam and Muslim beliefs in a way that Muslims themselves feel misrepresented and misunderstood.

By contrast, Dudley Woodberry has embodied this principle of accurately representing the beliefs of Muslims and the tenets of Islam in his own scholarship, while also faithfully bearing witness to his own Christian faith in a manner that is winsome and truthful. In this way, he has provided us with an active and excellent example of scholarship that does not bear false witness, but presents truth with respect and love. And through his influence he has left a legacy of Christian scholars of Islam who are committed both to excellent scholarship on Islam and Christianity and to respectful witness of their faith in Christ.

6
The Christian Scholar with Islam: "Go, Take, Learn"

BY KENNETH CRAGG

How readily the verbs in the great invitation of Matthew 11 translate into the great commission of Mark 16. The sequence to "come" belongs with the order to "go." For the "yoke" is known as a task, and the task, likewise, is a learning story. The very term "scholar" entails becoming—and staying—a learner. In a strangely wonderful way, the truth about the apostolic church is that their going was their knowing. Their "educating the world" concerning Jesus as the Christ, "the Christ of God," was indeed the education of themselves into Christ. In the telling was the finding.

How this might still be so fits well as Festschrift meant in salutation to a practitioner in this double school through decades of recent Christian-Muslim relations. When somewhat enigmatically *Sūrat* al-Baqara [2]:79 reproaches "those who write the Scripture with their own hands and then say: 'This is from God,'" it notes what is true about the New Testament text but not in terms of inventing the contents which is what the mind of the Qur᾿an assumes. Indeed, the alleged distorted untrustworthiness of the Christian text has long been a grievous issue of controversy.[1] Never in a way has the sura assumed did the first-generation Christians or their close successors indeed "write" their defining text.

The Word Enshrined in the Text

The phrase "the New Testament" plainly means two things, and it is wise to keep both in perspective. There is the new "covenant of open" grace, and there is its documentation in Gospels and Letters (likewise with "the Gospel" and the "Gospels of Matthew," and so on).

1 The books are endless and issues ramify, for example, around a "Gospel of Barnabas," or "the Paraclete" as Muhammad, or the presence of four Gospels and not only one—verbatim (like the Qur᾿an) from ᶜIsa "the messenger."

First in the order of time was the history—as event, the drama of "God in Christ" enacted in the ministry and theme of Jesus Messiah. Second was the cumulative formation of that drama as a text via its outreach into the world. This necessarily followed, yet owed itself utterly to the first which had left no writings but pursued its way ever verbally and manually, by hand and touch, by voice and deed, by things ever oral and eventual. If these were ever to take in the world, beyond their original time and place, they would need to betake themselves to script and find their documentation through the community they brought to pass.

It was precisely this which happened. The record and the narrative of that "who" and "how" critically waited for their telling the loyal community of fellowship and memory and discipleship to which they had given being. It was "the Word" he had been that kindled the necessity for—and the means to—the text that would enshrine him. So, in a very essential way, the faith had to write itself as a result of the impulse within it to take the event of Jesus crucified into the world at large. This had to mean a further Scripture in heritage with, but distinguished from, the antecedent texts of story, psalm, and prophet, about Jewry.

The World-seeking Instinct of the Church

That documentary text, however, only supervened because the apostolic church had a compelling sense of the world. It saw its destiny as meant for the nations at large. The word in action was the word in travel. It required diaspora—not as of old with Jewry—because of forced exile, but by will and mind. It also reversed the old introverted, local, centripetal concern of the Hebrew mind. For this, as in exilic prophets and many psalms, meant the nations gathering to Jerusalem to learn "the name of the Lord" in the temple precincts where, as Solomon long before had prayed, the Lord had set it there. Now all was centrifugal, the center seeking out the circumference. "From Jerusalem to the uttermost parts" was the new mandate.

It is well to realize that "the great commission" was being obeyed well before it was formalized in the Gospels of Mark and Matthew. Indeed the directive sprang from the direction already taken, and taken in part by "lay" initiative of "men of Cyprus and Cyrene." The faith community takes a geographical spread. Galilee and Capernaum are in a transition to Antioch, Galatia, Corinth, and Thessalonica. To be sure, the direction is all westward and northward. We have no letters to Edessa or Alexandria because the New Testament narrative stays with Paul, but a world-seeking instinct moves also elsewhere. It is explicitly transcending the old Jew-Gentile distinction, "making both one." And that one, this way, is becoming place-wise and race-wise the many. Hence the need for an apostolic correspondence to bind the many into one by a discipline of moral and spiritual education and ministry to a sense of unity which monitors diversity. This is, in part, to reassure wayfaring Jewry that even "Gentile" admission poses no threat to the ethics of a right Judaism. It also comes to grips with the brutal and the licentious in the Greco-Roman milieu in which these newborn communities must fulfill themselves.

Such is the logic which explains why half of the New Testament is "Letters" which guide, direct, cherish, and nurture this implicit "worldwideness" of a nascent and continuing Christianity. It does not come by empire or dominance. Indeed, it arrives only in the teeth of sustained and often malignant hostility as what is "to Greeks foolishness and to Jewry scandal." It grows and holds despite adversity and suffers persecution with a ready mind. While we must not idealize the church of these first generations but concede how frail and hazardous its progress and "how partial the narratives we possess," there is no discounting of "the word in the action" nor of "the action in the word."

Another symbol of "one-many-ness in many-one-ness" is that historic council in Jerusalem. Its verdict after due cognizance in Antioch for "Gentile" inclusion coined a telling phrase: "It seemed good to the Holy Spirit and to us" (Acts 15:28 NIV). That "and" might give us pause. Surely what is "good to the Holy Spirit" is good. What can "and us" add? Yet there lies the whole incarnational principle of "word and action." There is no "thus says the Lord" without some Amos thrust out of Tekoa and crying in Samaria. How bewildered, even terrified, Mary must have been at her annunciation, before she could respond: "Be it to me according to thy word" (Luke 1:38 KJV). What logic made "the handmaid" such unless learning how? "It is his love's prerogative to come by need of you. In every enterprise of Good some human part is due. Emmanuel here seeks nativity, the travail of your low estate his own necessity."[2]

"And us" is always the rubric of the Holy Spirit. Of course, the council was concerned for its own authority and a due discipline of oneness for the many. But they did not write: "It seemed good to us and to the Holy Spirit," nor was there a dissentient who said: "It seemed good to the Holy Spirit and to me." The Holy Spirit is the Spirit of fellowship, of a will to common mind and single purpose.

Doubtless there is danger in this formula. It could become the banner of the fanatic and the bigot riding roughshod over unity and despising the will to it. But Acts 15:28 gives us the clear precedent for a will to unity we must endeavor to keep as a genuinely strenuous vocation in which we do not preen ourselves on being liberated pioneers over against benighted victims of scruple and taboo who ought to grow up into a right maturity. Paul had a longer patience with those with deep reservations about idol meats, saying: "I will eat no flesh while the world standeth," (1 Cor 8:13 KJV) yet reserving his liberty for due time. For he knew how pervasive and pernicious idolatry can be, far beyond a ritual of diet and invocation.

Patiently questing for the common mind is no small part of the yearning towards the outer world: "That ye also may have fellowship with us" (1 John 1:3 KJV). When interior controversy becomes polemical, impatient, and crude, there creeps into it an element of *lex talionis*—it is me and mine, or ours, which must prevail here: it is we who have to win and "they" who must concede defeat. Here the "and us" of Acts 15:28 yields the great principle of Romans 14:4–23, how "To his own master he stands or falls: Who am I to judge another

---

2 Kenneth Cragg, *Poetry of the Word at Christmas* (London: Churchman Publishing Ltd, 1997), 3.

man's servant?" (paraphrased). It is thus that the specific world of the Epistles illuminates our contemporary path.

The imperative for the twenty-first century returns to the first. A theology relational to Islam will heed the learning significance of the fact that the New Testament Scripture comprises "letters to dispersed churches" composing one church, betokening a faith that has intended the world as its parish, has obeyed a will to embrace all humankind, and done so in definitive terms which could then share its defining text.

Under the Impulse of the Love of Christ

Holding fast to *how* they had done so, we have now to turn to *why*. Paul, a great architect of that "building of God," had argued: "The love of Christ leaves us no option," or "The love of Christ makes up our mind" (*sunechei*, 2 Cor 5:14). The reason was the Christhood of Jesus they had come wonderingly to recognize and identify in "him crucified." It is this recognition, this discovery, we have here to understand, discerning how it essentially consisted in and followed from the theme of "Messiah" which is the crowning clue to the four New Testament Gospels.

For that theme and its realization by the disciples (and so making them apostles) is plainly the very matrix of the Gospels, but only because there was the "going" church. Do we not have to see that had there been no going there would have been no Scripture knowing? It was the epistle-taught churches which evoked the Christ-telling narratives by their demanding need for the Galilean-Palestinian measure of their own founding story. How else were Ephesus, Thessalonica, and Rome to know "whence they were hewn"? In the fabric of the New Testament, letters must perforce precede Gospels, while Gospels latent in memories perforce preceded the origin of the church. It is this "unity of time" incidence we have to interpret for Islam.

The salient fact is that, to our knowledge, Jesus never wrote, except perhaps unintelligibly in sand, soon to be erased by scuffling feet (John 8). At the Ascension, all that was left was a group of men and women—and they were all that was required. Yet crucially on them turned the whole trust of the Christic reality of divine history. The catalyst which precipitated their memory, and that of their successors in immediate access to it, into textual record was the existence—and the appetite—of the churches they had founded. The process, we must concede, was fraught with many hazards, was frail in the extreme so that we must always come with a scholarly, critical mind to the evangelists, a mind nonetheless with a sober confidence, while all is highly selective.

The material point is that the diaspora we have studied land- and place-wise occurred in lapsing time. The generation that had companied with Jesus was passing away. Note the reference in Acts 21:16 to "one Mnason … an old disciple with whom we should lodge" (KJV). Such "original" figures were a diminishing breed so that it became vital to distill all that they knew into a script that might outlast the centuries. It was this double inducement of a yearning diaspora and a passing scene that brought into being what might satisfy the one and ensure the meaning for the other. Otherwise, who shall say that the parables of Jesus, the riches of Jesus the teacher and healer, the Jesus of Nazareth and Gethsemane, might have remained unperpetuated and forgotten? For that Sermon on the Mount—and all else—had lived only in the open air of Galilee and lingered on the wind and the echo of embracing hills. It was Jesus who gave perennial, credal mention to the brief duration (ten years?) of Pontius Pilate's posting to the East. Otherwise, what would history know of him? Could an unforgettable Jesus have been likewise elided from all human story? Roman and Jewish notice is minimal. Only the Gospels narrated and portrayed him: they only arrived to do so via the discipleship/apostolate his Christhood had generated inside the learning—and so writing—experience of their faith community.[3]

Relational Islam-related Christian Theology

Linking the defining learning of the faith and its documenting in its Scripture this way may serve to illuminate the way into an Islam-related Christian theology. For Islam's puzzlement and "denial posture" vis-à-vis a Christian textuality made up of Gospels (plural) and letters are a major initial obstacle to the heeding they deserve. For Christian textuality this way is in such contrast to the *Tanzīl* of the Qur'an, as a heaven-sent verbal text mediated to Muhammad in "pure Arabic"—and he a nonparticipating "reciter."[4] Having our Scripture appreciated by how and why it came to pass will be no small part of an intelligent ministry with its meanings.

But lurking throughout will be the daunting matter of the authority they and the Qur'an purport to carry. What of its temper, its openness to query, its need for an honest, internal scholarship from its "people"?

There are certainly large issues interior to Islam, concerning the traditional view of a passive Muhammad, and concerning the strange process of the Qur'an's arrival in the form it now presents.[5] Some Western academics have ventured into these fields and, by their criteria, with legitimacy. The view here is that these labors are best left to Muslim academ-

3 The interaction between "knowing and going" was crucial. The world would never have had Beatitudes or parables and no "Sermon on the Mount" had there been no "preaching of the Cross." It is not suggested that "going now" into all that contemporary "learning" means brings about a new Scripture. It certainly evokes and requires a responding exegesis which lets questioning situations educate sufficient answers.

4 This "orthodox" view of Muhammad's total "passivity" does not tally with the actual content of the Qur'an which is replete with direct address to him, and interengaging situations, and what it calls asbāb an-nuzūl (occasions of revelation). For my part, I tried to make the case in *Muhammad in the Qur'an: The Task and the Text* (Sawbridgeworth, UK: Fox Communications & Publications, 2001). His evidently active role does not make him "author." On the contrary, he is "recipient of *Waḥy*." The idea that he "has to be out of the way" derives from the principle that "the more this is from God the less it must be from humans." The Bible, and supremely the New Testament, proceeds on the opposite—the divine readily engages and employs the human.

5 I.e., how its "fragments" by "piecemeal givenness" (al-Isrā' [17]:106) were gathered in suras, and suras into the single *Kitāb* as the authoritative canon.

ics. No Christian scholarship can be merely academic in the sense of "neutral" and "aloof," as if dissecting a dead thing. Such do not sense the "imperialism" others identify in their ventures. Nor do they concede that they may be treading on "confidences" they have made no effort to understand.

By contrast, the Christian scholar wills to be relational, ready to meet what is contrary, to discern where it might be recruited for what might mediate, or retrieved from that which it has missed through its own assertion. It matters more that we should be the risk takers than that we be risk free. Communication matters more than self-conservation, venture more than security. We can well, relationally, take the Qur'an as Muslims take it but with no compromise to our own entrustment in Christ, since we are learning this way—and perhaps only this way—how to tell him.

The alternative is to incur an unwinnable conflict of sheer rival authorities which allows no bridge across them. We are left with heat without light, if—unlike Ezekiel in a different context—we do not "sit where they sit." Avoiding to set up an argument, we are set with a plea which learns the "gentleness" of the Christ of whom it speaks. "Jesus, being wearied with his journey, sat thus on the well" and said: "Give me to drink." There is a learning for theologians to come this way.

Some will interject, "But Christianity is inherently controversial, 'foolishness to the Greeks and a stumbling block to Jews.'" We ought to relish this contrariety; it is its "cutting edge." Was Jesus polite to Nicodemus as "a ruler of the Jews"?[6] Do not Muslims need to be confronted with how violent they are? Some indeed are, and what in their origin conduced to their being so?[7] And what of the others? What of the ongoing issue of rescinding the violence by Islamic light? Will the world ever have the Islam it needs to have—coexistent, peaceable, tolerant—unless by dint of Islamic factors via the Islamic mind? Such constraints are there: it is urgent to help Muslims to realize them in their own Qur'an by the quality of relationship that serves to give them rein.

Can the "taking, learning" Christian, then, not relate respective Scriptures as either party, *de facto*, does their own, leaving aside the *de jure* question of how legitimate their status is? Then, beyond all the vexing status issues, we go expectantly for actual content. Where that content is identical with ours we welcome it. The "them-and-us" syndrome of instinctive antipathy is broken. An expectancy prevails against antagonism. We bring a better humility

---

6 "You must be born again" was surely near offensive to anyone prizing Jewish birth as *per se* membership already in "the people of Yahweh."

7 It is this point which is so often ignored when Islam is lauded as "the religion of peace," and even of "ecumenism." This happily *can* be true, and the Qur'an can be cited in evidence. While in Mecca, Islam was only and always a *balāgh*, a faith-message pleading—under adversity—for a hearing. After the Hijrah and the adoption of a power complex in Medina, a marked change of temper ensued. A *lex talionis* via conflict came into play—whence the will to violence here and now by the rubric, "Fight till there be no more *fitna*" (hostility). In Mecca, *fitna* had been "persecution." The burning question now is, therefore, whether Islam can return to its Meccan self, having no truck with a "law of retaliation." Will Western politics deserve that it should?

to the complexity of truth. We shoulder the "learning yoke" of what incomprehension can arise, what affinities emerge to be saluted.

Welcoming Common Scenarios

Immediately, such relational theology finds a Qurʾan that is deep in the parable of the vineyard and the husbandmen. "How so?" the skeptical will say, seeing that the Muslim Scripture contains no parable of Jesus. Indeed, its only verbal echo of any words of Jesus is *ighfir lanā dhunūbanā* (forgive us our sins); just that—despite its strong tribute to Jesus (ᶜIsa) as the penultimate "Prophet."[8] Yet a human creaturehood in charge of the good earth is emphatic in the Qurʾan's doctrine of *khilāfa*. Each of us, a *khalīqa* (creature), is a *khilāfa* (custodian/tenant). *Sūrat* al-Baqara [2]:30 and several other passages record this divine intention for our humanity and the angelic protest against its trustful policy with us, foreseeing how we will "corrupt and shed blood" in our perverse discharge of so large a "vicegerency" as Allah's submanagers. Thus creation has taken a known and deliberate "gamble with history." There is a divine seriousness behind all that is. What, then, might this imply concerning fixed views of "omnipotence"? Here is one that actually inquires, musing on our perversity: "Am I not your Lord?" (al-Aᶜrāf [7]:172).

This Qurʾanic theme of creaturely entrustment undergirds the whole enterprise of science and technology. When carried also, as the Qurʾan carries it, into the realm of human sexuality, it comes close to the Christian theme of the "sacramental." Islam does not take to the term. Yet it is explicit in the constant accent on the *āyāt* (signs).These in the natural order have a dual role. They alert the scientist to experiment, uncover, invent, and deploy these means-toward-ends which the natural order affords us so liberally and invitingly by dint of its "sign" quality suited for our "reading." But more, the same "signs" are there to promote gratitude, wonder, reverence, and awe at their presence; these are there to require a due "consecration" in right ordering the economic, social, and material realm to which they lead. All is reinforced by the Qurʾan in its reiteration (more than a hundred times) of the particle *laᶜalla* (perhaps) followed by sundry verbs about being alert, thoughtful, thankful, minded of Allah as Giver of "data," and the like. Humans are meant to be discreet, perceptive, liable, and responsible in farm, market, laboratory, factory, hospital, or wherever. The case has often been made, and the evidence is ample.[9] Its bearing on the present global, environmental situation is crucial.

As for the "messengers" requiring the fruits of the vineyard, does not Islam have a whole long sequence of them from Enoch to Muhammad? Prophethood is for it the supreme confirmation of the human dignity so privileged, the risk in its donation so precarious because of our evil-mindedness. The Lord would not be known sending "messengers" either to perfectly

8 *Sūrat* Āl ᶜImrān [3]:16, reporting on Christians but with the words incomplete.

9 In Muslim and Christian writing. It is clear that the skills of the sciences do not discriminate between religions. The Internet, the laboratory, the aircraft, the process will function indifferently for all alike—and the atheist.

obedient selves or entirely "puppet" ones. The entire Qur'anic scheme—creation, creaturehood in trust, prophethood—is plain for all to see and, in its own idiom, completely biblical.[10]

Is it not with this common scenario that a Christian relational theology is wise—and bound—to begin? Moreover, despite Islam's rejection of redemption (the Shiʿah apart), and an impression of optimism about human amenability to law, guidance, and exhortation (its main prescripts), the Qur'an tells a deep awareness of sin and wrong in the soul and society. Yusuf (Joseph) in his hour of crisis knew how "bent towards evil" is the will (Yūsuf [12]:53).[11]

The ruling term and concept here is that of *ẓulm* (wrongdoing) in all its devious, criminal forms. The verb *ẓalama* (to wrong) and its derivatives run throughout the Qur'an with *fasād* (that "corruption" the angels feared), with *ḍalāl* (deviance) and the *nifāq* (hypocrisy), which became so heinous after the Hijra inaugurated Islam's "success" criterion.[12] Only *ikhlāṣ* (sincerity) suffices to counter and disown these perversities to be almost a synonym for *Islam*.[13] "Conscience" may not be a factor the Qur'an has in mind—thanks to its deeply "given" theme of divine Shariʿa (for which human conscience might figure as pretentious or superfluous)—nevertheless it knows of *an-nafs al-lawwāma* (the self-reproaching soul) (al-Qiyāma [75]:2). The very need for Islam to exist, to urge incessantly that "there is no deity but Allah," and to cry in its stentorian tones, "*Allāhu akbar*," (God is most great) is proof enough of how real idolatry is, how possible blasphemy, how prevalent false worships—of money, lust, nation, power, profit, religion itself. Surely Islam witnesses by its very mission that "God has to be *let be*" and that—by us humans who have the option to do otherwise, an Allah who admits *de facto* (but never *de jure*) of human denial and defiance, but in wisdom knew what he was doing in having it so and never failing to care for his divine intent with us.

Parting of the Ways

It is here that the Christian scholar with Islam finds a parting of the ways, but only because thus far they have converged. The dual case takes more exposition than there is space for. Perhaps it can be identified, in both parts, in a pivotal verse in *Sūrat* an-Nisā' [4]:165, a

10 The great divergence being that the one theme of creation and humans in creaturehood so quickly becomes particular and specific around one tribal people, one story, one territory. The Qur'an's particularity is not ethnic but linguistic—its being sent as "an Arabic Book."

11 *Ammāratun bi'-s-sū'i*—from the root *amara* with *amr* (command)—(prone to, or enjoins itself to), so that wrong is deliberately chosen and the self finds in its wake a self-accusation.

12 See the point regarding the change in meaning from "persecution" to "sedition" of fitna as, by first definition, "that which tries or tests you." During armed conflict it meant a reluctance to fight. "Sedition" only challenges successful power; only unarmed faith incurs "persecution."

13 *Ikhlāṣ* comes into action as "integrity" wherever there is guile, contumely, dissembling, or hypocrisy such as characterized the Medinan period in Islam (see *Sūrat* al-Ḥujurāt [49]:14,15). It is important to realize that Arabic has no capital letters. We need to distinguish between *islām* (small *i* and italics) and Islam, the one being the inward piety and practice, the other the institutional shape it took into history as creed and liturgy and caliphate. There is the same difference *between muslims* and Muslims. Abraham and Moses were "*muslims*." There were no "Muslims" until "the final Prophet" gave them final form and *Fawz* (victory).

verse which has the very precious Christian "feel" for God as "liable for us and with us," in no way "incarnational" yet entailed in action for us in—as it were—an obligation. *Sūrat* an-Nisā᾿ [4]:165 runs:

> These [i.e., "messengers"] were all bearers of good tidings, of warning, thanks to whose coming humankind could have no possible case against Allah, the God of infinite power and wisdom.

The "case, or argument, against God (*ḥujjah ᶜalā*)" is very daring. Had the envoys not been sent, Allah would have been in default and accusable as divinely delinquent. Why? Because without these "apostles" we would have been left in *jāhilīya* (hapless ignorance), lacking all guidance, reminder, counsel, and hope in the discharge of our earth tenancy.

But what, a Christian realism has to ask, if and when all these, as directional hortatory, advisory, and legally moral, do not answer our need, our situation, our rebellious condition? Can, will, may this clear principle of God's "undertaking us" go further when the "messenger strategy" fails to suffice? Can our Christian "taking/learning" here read—and tell—this liability principle in terms of "God in Christ" and of redemption by the love that suffers, by a majesty of thorns that tells an adequate sovereignty divine? Doing so would be consistent with what history demonstrates of our perversity and all that, for example, Paul meant by "The good that I would I do not, but the evil which I would not, that I do. Who shall deliver me?" (Romans 7:19 KJV, paraphrased). Could it not also be consistent with that "power and wisdom" in *Sūrat* an-Nisā᾿ [4]:165—just the twain the New Testament links to the "God of our salvation"?

The Christian mind has no will to stay in a world where these dimensions of the divine in grace and the human in need cease to be articulated down the years. Rather we learn their commendation by serving how distinctive from all else in religions they remain. The reach of their realism, their sanity, their longsuffering, their patience informs a right theology and equips its scholarship. The early church could learn to write its own Scripture and order its own ministry as a community "knowing in going." What they then bequeathed in both realms of text and task we take up now by letting the worlds we encounter educate us in the art an Isaiah called "the word in season," the "season" of its own—by the other's—mind. There are other aspects here we ought to note.

How Do We Value God Right?

One of the most vital is the use of metaphor and analogy, of which Islam has been wary, because of the "incomparability" of Allah. Yet language *per se* is full of often hidden imagery and *Sūrat* Āl ᶜImrān [3]:7 concedes that the Qur᾿an has *mutashābihāt* (similitudes). The Christian scholar needs to realize how opaque, even revolting to the unfamiliar, language usages can be. That "blood cleanses" must be puzzling to those who know that blood only stains and that it is well it should, so that crime may be requited. How can "washing" apply effectively to wrongdoing? "Sacrifice" is a darkly sinister as well as a vastly trivialized word. Can it ever relate to the things of God?

Allah as "Shepherd" is utterly incongruous to the Muslim mind. There is record of a Turkish girl who, on first hearing Psalm 23, thought of it as almost blasphemous. Should the psalmist not be saying, "The Lord is my *Amir*, my King"? "Shepherd" is derogatory, a minimizing word. Shepherds are likely to be poor and illiterate, and certainly no candidates for marriage with "a girl like me." Why is the language of these Christians so careless about "the majesty on high"?

The difficulty here, if only it is allowed to come to light and have its say, is the very opportunity. *Importune, opportune.* The clue lies in the whole psalm. By a poet's art, it is inside "sheepness" as every clause proves. The shepherd is indeed in entire, sovereign control but in terms appropriate to sheep. He tempers power, charge, discipline, authority, to patience and solicitude. He submits entirely to the kind of burden he carries, and that burden is sheep. He makes himself the subject of his cares, yet in those cares he rules and reigns.

Once rightly read, the point of perplexity becomes the point of the luminous. Exegesis fulfills its role but only by engaging with its duty as dictated by its audience. There are endless situations of this order for the Christian scholar with Islam and its instinctive prejudgments against what it sees as unworthy or impossible, crude or unintelligible, concerning God. The "Son," "begotten" language—unless handled the way the "shepherd" was—is sadly mired in confusion.

All exegesis passes finally into a theology concerning the nature, character, and integrity of God. The honest theologian has to be an honest historian, a realist about the human drama, the spectacle of human centuries. We might bring the "taking/learning" task—"the yoke of Christ"—into line with three places where the Qurʾan has Muhammad tell his Meccan folk that they did not "think of Allah worthily" (al-Anʿām [6]:91; al-Ḥajj [22]:74; az-Zumar [39]:67). *Mā qadarū Allāha haqqa qadrihi* (noun from cognate verb) has the rich meaning of "worth," "esteem," "measure," "reckoning." We might paraphrase the import by "Their theology was not adequate to the adequacy of Allah." It did not fully match the reality it had to tell.

But how do we "value," "weigh," God aright? Failing to do so makes us, in effect, idolaters, worshiping less, or other, than we should. How is theological faith to be verified as God-warranted? Where are the credentials worthy of our assurance? May there be a case for deep trust that fails in downright dogma?

The questions multiply. How well, how far, how long, can we pursue them? Our task is only to "commend" what we have learned, have loved, have known, and been "persuaded." It has to do with "valuing," "esteeming," "weighing," and so embracing in mind and heart the God whose insignia could be the womb and the thorns of the love that comes, and coming suffers, and suffering redeems and saves.

A recent Muslim review of a Christian "scholarship" dismisses "metaphysical constructs" as "language games" and adds: "God simply does not share His divinity with any created being, and no Muslim believes that Allah is *present* in the Qur᾿an." If not "present," Allah is certainly "engaged" there, occupied in an enterprise of which we are the crux, pledged to a purpose for which this "vineyard" is the scene and we humans the "husbandmen." Perhaps we should let the "dialogue" between faiths take into a hopeful silence how the difference between us concerns the costliness to him because of us in that creating, life-endowing enterprise.

7

Ṣifāt al-Dhāt in al-Ashᶜarī's Doctrine of God and Possible Christian Parallels

BY JOSEPH L. CUMMING

It scarcely needs to be stated that Abū al-Ḥasan ᶜAlī ibn Ismāᶜīl al-Ashᶜarī (d. 324/935) is one of the three or four most influential and orthodox thinkers in the history of Islam since the generation of the Prophet and Companions.[1] Ignaz Goldziher refers to him as "this greatest theological authority in orthodox Islam."[2] His doctrine (which he saw simply as a systematic statement of the teachings of the Qurᵓan and the Sunna as understood by the earliest Muslim community) gradually overcame rival doctrines like Muᶜtazilism until, by the end of the fifth/eleventh century, Ashᶜarite doctrine became recognized as the official orthodoxy of Sunni Islam. His teaching is generally seen as the embodiment of Islamic orthodoxy—so much so that modern English-language writers on Islam frequently use the term "orthodox" as though it were synonymous with "Ashᶜarite."

On the other hand, much of the content of his teaching is relatively unknown to many ordinary Muslims today. Daniel Gimaret has rightly pointed out: "Of all of the Muslim theologians of the classical era, al-Ashᶜarī (d. 935) was, beyond any doubt, the most important. Nevertheless, paradoxically, his doctrine remained very poorly known."[3,4]

---

1 Abū Ḥāmid al-Ghazālī, Aḥmad ibn Ḥanbal and al-Imām al-Shāfiᶜī also come to mind.

2 Ignaz Goldziher, *Introduction to Islamic Theology and Law*, trans. Andras Hamori and Ruth Hamori (Princeton: Princeton University Press, 1981 [1910]), 104.

3 Daniel Gimaret, *La doctrine d'al-Ashᶜarī* (Paris: Cerf, 1990), cover. "De tous les théologiens musulmans d'époque classique, al-Ashᶜarī (m. 935) a été, sans nul doute, le plus important. Or, paradoxalement, sa doctrine restait encore très mal connue."

4 All translations from French, German, and Arabic works in this paper are my own, unless otherwise indicated.

Of course Gimaret's own books[5] have contributed greatly to making the content of al-Ashᶜarī's doctrine better known (particularly to the French-speaking world). But it is still true that much work remains to be done.

One of the central issues at stake in al-Ashᶜarī's teaching, and in his refutation of Muᶜtazilism, was the question of the divine *ṣifāt* (often translated "attributes")[6] which are derived from God's "beautiful names" in the Qurᵓan, and the relation of these *ṣifāt* to God's attributes. If God is Powerful, Knowing, and Living, does this mean God has power, knowledge, and life? Has God acquired these *ṣifāt* in time, or has God eternally been characterized by them? And if God's power, knowledge, and life are eternal, then is God synonymous with that power, knowledge, and life, or are they something other than God's essence?

The sixth/twelfth-century historian of religious doctrines Muḥammad ibn ᶜAbd al-Karīm al-Shahrastānī wrote a pithy summary of al-Ashᶜarī's answer to these questions, as follows:

> Abū al-Ḥasan [al-Ashᶜarī] said: "The Creator (exalted is He) is Knowing by virtue of [His] knowledge, Powerful by virtue of [His] power, Living by virtue of [His] life[7] … These *ṣifāt* are eternal, subsisting in His essence (exalted is He) (*qāᵓima bi-dhātihī*). One should not say that they are He, nor other than He, nor not He, nor not other than He.[8]

Since the Middle Ages, these ideas (formulated in various ways) have been understood to be the orthodox Islamic statement of who God eternally is. Particularly significant has been the formula that God's *ṣifāt* are "not His essence, nor are they other than He" (*lā dhātuhū wa-lā ghayruhū*), and the idea that they are "eternal realities[9] subsisting in His essence" (*mafiānī azaliyya qāᵓima bi-dhātihī*). The pages which follow below in this chapter will examine in depth al-Ashᶜarī's own words on these questions, and what he meant by those words, and the exegetical reasons in the Qurᵓan and Sunna that led him to these conclusions.

Any reader who is familiar with the writings of Christian thinkers from the pre-Islamic patristic period and from the medieval scholastic period will readily see remarkable parallels between al-Ashᶜarī's doctrine on this point and the Christian doctrine of the Trinity.

---

5 Ibid.; Daniel Gimaret, *Les noms divins en Islam* (Paris: Cerf, 1988); Abū Bakr Muḥammad ibn al-Ḥasan ibn Fūrak, *Mujarrad Maqālāt al-Shaykh Abī al-Ḥasan al-Ashᶜarī*, ed. Daniel Gimaret (Beirut: Dar al-Mashriq, 1987); among other publications of Gimaret.

6 Cf. discussion below on how best to understand the technical meaning of *ṣifa*.

7 Al-Shahrastānī's list does not stop at knowledge, power, and life. He rightly says that al-Ashᶜarī spoke specifically of seven such "*ṣifāt* of God's essence"—knowledge, power, life, word, will, hearing, and sight—and that al-Ashᶜarī's view on God's permanence (*baqāᵓ*), as a possible eighth *ṣifa* of essence, was ambiguous. Nonetheless al-Ashᶜarī's discussion often focuses on the three *ṣifāt* of knowledge, power, and life (e.g., chapter 1 of *Kitāb al-Lumaᶜ*, as will be seen below), and then mentions God's word, will, hearing, and sight almost as an afterthought.

8 Muḥammad ibn ᶜAbd al-Karīm al-Shahrastānī, *Kitāb al-Milal wa-l-Niḥal*, vol. 1, ed. William Cureton (London: Society for the Publication of Oriental Texts, 1842–1846), 68, lines 8ff.

9 Cf. discussion below on how best to understand al-Ashᶜarī's technical use of the term *maᶜānī*. For now, the translation "realities" should be taken as provisional.

Al-Ashᶜarī's technical use of the terms *ṣifa* and *dhāt* (essence) bears remarkable resemblance to the Cappadocian tradition's distinction between *hypostasis* (ὑπόστᾰσις) and *ousia* (οὐσία). Indeed, as I will show below, a variety of medieval writers—Muslim, Christian, and Jewish alike—noticed this resemblance and commented on it. This is not to say that there is no difference between the Muslim doctrine of *ṣifāt* and the Christian doctrine of the Trinity (though some medieval Muslim writers suggested precisely that), nor that either doctrine can be understood entirely in terms of the other. What this chapter seeks to do primarily is to examine in detail what al-Ashᶜarī taught about *ṣifāt* and why. Only after this effort to understand al-Ashᶜarī's thought in terms of its own, internal, Islamic logic—rooted in the Qurʾan and the Sunna—will it be appropriate to consider the possible relationship of that doctrine to the Christian doctrine of the Trinity.

Defining Terms

Al-Ashᶜarī uses a number of technical Arabic terms in discussing these issues. Before attempting to translate his writings into English, one must first consider what he means by these terms. The terms *dhāt*, *nafs*, *ṣifa*, and *maᶜnā* are particularly crucial to understanding his thought.

Dhāt and *Nafs*

The first two of these terms are fairly straightforward. The term *dhāt*, as used in Islamic theological writing, is usually translated "essence." This is indeed the sense in which al-Ashᶜarī usually uses the term. It should be noted, however, that unlike "essence," the Arabic word *dhāt* does not have the verb "to be" in its etymology, and it can mean simply "self" or "same." Al-Ashᶜarī does sometimes use the word *dhāt* to mean simply "self," but usually he uses it with the more technical sense of "essence."

The word *nafs* also means "self" or "same." Al-Ashᶜarī sometimes uses *nafs* virtually interchangeably with *dhāt*, as a term for God's "self." The word *nafs* can also mean "soul," of course, but al-Ashᶜarī does not use it in that sense in the texts which this chapter will consider. In the material below which I quote from al-Ashᶜarī's writings, I will normally translate *dhāt* as "essence," and *nafs* as "self."

Ṣifa

It is not so simple to choose an adequate English equivalent for what al-Ashᶜarī means by the term *ṣifa*. *Ṣifa* is often translated in secondary literature as "attribute." It is not unreasonable to use the term "attribute" to refer to God's knowledge, power, will, etc., especially in the sense in which the Muᶜtazila used the term *ṣifa*. Nonetheless, al-Ashᶜarī (as will be shown below) intended something quite different from the Muᶜtazila in his use of the word. In the writings of al-Ashᶜarī the term *ṣifa* took on more substantive metaphysical weight than is normally understood by the English word "attribute." And in the context of the issues which are in focus in this chapter, I believe that the term "attribute" may be downright misleading because of the very different history of technical usage of the term "attribute" in Latin Christian theological writing.

Richard Frank has insightfully explained this problem:

> The term *ṣifa* or "attribute," as it is normally and often quite exactly rendered, is of so common occurrence in the sources and is so manifestly natural an expression to most contexts in which it occurs that the peculiarly Islamic character of the term, and the concept may easily escape notice as one's attention is more forcibly drawn to other idiosyncracies of the texts. One tends to forget that Greek and Latin have no equivalent term that holds a corresponding position of central importance and prominence in the Patristic and Scholastic traditions.[10]

Gimaret, in his book *La doctrine d'al-Ashᶜarī*,[11] demonstrates that Ashᶜarite use of the term *ṣifa* intends a very different meaning from Muᶜtazilite use of the same term. For the Muᶜtazila, he says *ṣifa* = *qawl* (word); it is merely a verbal way of predicating something about God or describing God. For Ashᶜarites, he says *ṣifa* = *maᶜnā* = "an entity residing in the divine essence."[12] Gimaret continues:

> When a Sunnite (i.e., Ashᶜarite) theologian speaks of the *ṣifāt Allāh* … the nouns (*qudra, ᶜilm, ḥayāt*) … are not mere words for him; they represent real entities—maᶜānī joined with the divine essence, existing like that essence, eternal like that essence … For A(shᶜarī) only positive realities, existent things, may be truly called *ṣifāt Allāh.*[13]

So for Gimaret "entity" or "reality" or "existent thing" might be more accurate translations of *ṣifa* in al-Ashᶜarī's writings, even if "attribute" might be accurate in Muᶜtazilite writings. However, neither Gimaret nor al-Ashᶜarī intends *ṣifa* to mean "separate being," as one might misinterpret a translation like "entity."

One other point should be mentioned as background to understanding the meaning of *ṣifa* in Islamic theological writing. Fairly early in Islamic history Muslim thinkers noted a distinction between the "*ṣifāt* of [God's] essence" (*ṣifāt al-dhāt*) and the "*ṣifāt* of act" (*ṣifāt*

10 Richard Frank, *Beings and Their Attributes: The Teaching of the Basrian School of the Muᶜtazila in the Classical Period* (Albany: State University of New York Press, 1978), 8.

11 Gimaret, *Doctrine*, 235–37.

12 Ibid., 236, 243. "Une entité résidant dans l'essence divine."

13 "Quand un théologien sunnite [i.e., Ashᶜarite] parle des *ṣifāt Allāh* … les substantifs (*qudra, ᶜilm, ḥayāt*) … ne sont pas pour lui de simple mots, ils représentent des entités réelles, des *maᶜānī* conjointes à l'essence divine, existantes comme elle, éternelles comme elle … Pour A[shᶜarī] ne sont véritablement *ṣifāt Allāh* que des réalités positives, des existants."

al-fiᶜl). The same distinction appears also in Christian and Jewish theological writing in Semitic languages.

The "*ṣifāt* of essence" are those *ṣifāt* which may be eternally predicated of God, without reference to the temporally created order. The "*ṣifāt* of act" are those *ṣifāt* which may be predicated of God only in reference to God's interaction with creatures. For example, God can be properly called "Forgiving" (*ghafūr*) only in relation to some created person who has sinned and needs forgiveness. God's forgiveness is manifest only in time, in relation to creation. So forgiveness is a "*ṣifa* of act." By contrast, God has eternally been "Knowing." Even apart from the creation, God knew God's own self, and God foreknew what would be created. Knowledge is therefore a "*ṣifa* of essence," in that it has eternally existed in God's essence.

Al-Ashᶜarī often uses the unspecified term *ṣifāt* as shorthand for *ṣifāt* of essence. When he speaks of God's *ṣifāt* without specifying which he means, he is virtually always referring specifically to the *ṣifāt* of essence. He repeatedly mentions a list of seven *ṣifāt* of essence: knowledge, power, life, word, will, sight, and hearing. When Gimaret says that for al-Ashᶜarī the *ṣifāt* are "real entities," "positive realities," "existent things,"[14] Gimaret is also referring specifically to the *ṣifāt* of essence, not to the *ṣifāt* of act.

Joseph Van Ess, in his book *Theologie und gesellschaft*, makes an interesting observation about this distinction between *ṣifāt* of essence and of act. He comments that the distinction appeared in Islamic theology and Arab Christian theology during the same time period. He adds: "The distinction was important to the Christians because, in contrast to Greek-Western theology, they also considered the hypostases as attributes and in this way could separate these from the remaining divine attributes."[15]

I do not think that it would be accurate to imply that eastern Christians disagreed on this point with their Greek- and Latin-speaking coreligionists (certainly they were not *aware* of any disagreement on it), or that they thought that hypostases were synonymous with what the English theological term "attribute" denotes. Van Ess means simply that Arab Christians thought that the *aqānīm* (hypostases) could rightly be called *ṣifāt*. This only underlines my point that the word "attribute," as understood in Latin Christian theology, does not adequately convey the metaphysical significance intended by the Arabic word *ṣifa*, especially as used by al-Ashᶜarī.

To conclude, we have reviewed options for translating *ṣifāt* which include "attributes," "entities," "realities," "existent things," and "hypostases." I think that the word "attributes" does not adequately reflect what al-Ashᶜarī intends, and that it could be actually misleading in the context of this chapter. "Entities," "realities," and "existent things" risk being misunderstood as implying multiple eternal beings, which al-Ashᶜarī would reject as polytheism.

14 Ibid. "des entités réelles, des réalités positives, des existants."

15 Joseph Van Ess, *Theologie und gesellschaft im 2. und 3. jahrhundert Hidschra*, vol. 4 (Berlin: Walter de Gruyter, 1991–1997), 437. "Den Christen war die Unterscheidung wichtig, weil sie—im Gegensatz zur griechisch-westlichen Theologie—auch die Hypostasen als Attribute betrachteten und jene auf diese Weise von den übrigen Eigenschaften trennen konnten."

And "hypostases" improperly imposes a Christian category onto al-Ashᶜarī's thought. Thus I think it best to leave the word *ṣifa* untranslated as a technical term, and to trust that its meaning will be clear enough from the foregoing discussion and from the context of its use in al-Ashᶜarī's writing (see below).

Maᶜnā

The word *maᶜnā*, which al-Ashᶜarī uses in asserting that the *ṣifāt* are *maᶜānī*, is a notoriously slippery term in Islamic theological writing. Its basic meaning is "meaning" (i.e., the referent to which a word refers), but it is used as a technical term in various senses. It can refer to the "underlying reality" or "actual meaning" which underlies a "form." M. Horten proposed translating it as "geistige Realität [spiritual/intellectual/metaphysical reality—perhaps *ḥaqīqa rūḥāniyya*]."[16] J. W. Sweetman defined it as "the reality of a thing, or its entity."[17] Watt proposed that in some places in Islamic theological writing it "might be rendered 'hypostatic quality.'"[18]

Richard Frank has written two articles treating this subject in depth. In 1967[19] he argued (contra Wolfson) that *maᶜnā* must be understood (especially in Muᶜtazilite writings) as referring to an "intrinsic, determinant cause of some real aspect of the being of the subject … a distinct and separate cause of the thing's being-so."[20] I understand him to mean by this that a *maᶜnā* is, for example, that causal reality intrinsic in a knower and which causes the knower to be knowing.

But writing more recently (thirty-two years later),[21] Frank argues the following:

> *Maᶜnā*, which most commonly occurs in the sense of meaning or intention, is frequently employed by the Ashᶜarites and Muᶜtazilites alike in the sense of 'something' that one has in mind or refers to explicitly or implicitly … It occurs very frequently in the expression '*maᶜnā zāidun ᶜalā al-ḍāt*' (something distinct from the subject described) … It is thus that '*maᶜnā*' is frequently employed as a term for entitative attributes … The basic sense or connotation of '*maᶜnā*' here … is that of referent or, if

16 M. Horten, "Was bedeutet Maᶜnā als philosophischer Terminus," ZDMG 64 (1910): 392–96; cited in H. A. Wolfson, "The Muslim Attributes and the Christian Trinity," in *The Philosophy of the Kalām* (Cambridge: Cambridge University Press, 1976), 115 n. 10.

17 J. Windrow Sweetman, *Islam and Christian Theology*, part 1, vol. 2 (London: Lutterworth, 1945–1967), 232.

18 W. Montgomery Watt, *The Formative Period of Islamic Thought* (Edinburgh: Edinburgh University Press, 1973), 287.

19 Richard M. Frank, "*Al-Maᶜnā*: Some Reflections on the Technical Meanings of the Term in the Kalām and Its Use in the Physics of Muᶜammar," in *Journal of the American Oriental Society* 87 (1967), 248ff.

20 Ibid., 252.

21 Richard Frank, "The Ashᶜarite Ontology: I Primary Entities," in *Arabic Sciences and Philosophy*, vol. 9 (Cambridge: Cambridge University Press, 1999), 163–231. I am indebted to Tariq Jaffer for bringing to my attention both of Frank's articles on this subject.

> you will, of a 'something' understood as the referent of one of the terms, whether explicit or implicit, of the proposition in question.[22]

Here Frank comes closer to Wolfson's view that *maᶜnā* should be translated as "thing."[23]

In light of the foregoing, it seems best in the context of al-Ashᶜarī's writings to translate *maᶜnā* as either "underlying reality" or "thing" or "something." In order to avoid retaining another untranslated technical term like *ṣifa*, while still wishing to retain some of the ambiguity inherent in the term, and in order to reflect the ordinary sense of "meaning" (*maᶜnā*) as the underlying reality which is the referent of a word, I will translate *maᶜnā* as "underlying reality." When the reader sees "underlying reality" in the pages which follow below, this can be readily understood as translating *maᶜnā*, with reference to the discussion above. Of course al-Ashᶜarī does sometimes also use the word *maᶜnā* in a nontechnical sense to mean simply "meaning." In places where he does, so I have translated accordingly.

Historical Context

The other background material which must be reviewed before looking at al-Ashᶜarī's teaching in his own words is the historical context in which he wrote. This is essential to understanding the significance of what he wrote. One of our best historical sources for the doctrines of various Muslim thinkers who preceded al-Ashᶜarī is his own book *Maqālāt al-Islāmiyyīn*,[24] which is an encyclopedic review of the various sects and teachers present in the Islamic community up to and including his time.

Al-Ashᶜarī's doctrine must be seen as a conservative reaction against the sect of the Muᶜtazila, who eventually came to be regarded as heretical. Scholars occasionally refer to the Muᶜtazila as "liberals," because of the relatively high importance which they attached to reason (in relation to revelation) and because of their metaphorical interpretation of verses in the Qurᵓan whose literal interpretation seemed to them to be contrary to reason (e.g., God's having "hands," "taking His seat upon a throne," "descending nightly to the lowest heaven," "weighing our deeds in a scale," etc.). They also insisted that the Qurᵓan was created in time, despite a substantial body of hadiths (attributed to the Companions) which suggested that it was not. However, the Muᶜtazila were scarcely "liberal" in the way in which they used the apparatus of the state to persecute those who disagreed with their views. It was they who were responsible for the *Miḥna*, the so-called "Inquisition" of the first half of the third/ninth century under the caliph al-Maᵓmūn, in which they imprisoned and executed opponents.

22 Ibid., 182, 214.

23 Wolfson, "Muslim Attributes," 115–16.

24 Abū al-Ḥasan ᶜAlī ibn Ismāᶜīl al-Ashᶜarī, *Maqālāt al-Islāmiyyīn wa-Ikhtilāf al-Muṣallīn*, ed. Helmut Ritter, published under the name *Die dogmatischen lehren der anhänger des Islam*, in *Biblioteca Islamica*, vol. 1 (Istanbul: Devlet Matbaasi, 1929).

Despite the support of the caliphal state, the Muᶜtazila did not succeed in carrying popular opinion with them. They were courageously opposed by Aḥmad ibn Ḥanbal (d. 241/855), whose rallying cry was "Back to the Qur'an and the Sunna!" He became a popular hero after his imprisonment under the *Miḥna*. Ibn Ḥanbal insisted that God does really have hands, does take His seat upon a throne, etc., though we do not ask "how" these things are so. He also insisted on the uncreatedness of the Qur'an. Whereas the Muᶜtazilites rejected the idea that God had *ṣifāt* such as knowledge and power in any sense other than a verbal one, Ibn Ḥanbal insisted that these *ṣifāt* are real in God because the Qur'an speaks of God's "knowledge" and "power," and not just of God as "Knowing" and "Powerful." Ibn Ḥanbal was seen as embodying a conservative popular reaction, driven by loyalty to the Qur'an and the Sunna, against the "innovating" Muᶜtazila.

Al-Ashᶜarī was himself a Muᶜtazilite until the age of 40, and he was one of the leading disciples of the most important Muᶜtazilite thinker of his day (al-Jubbā'ī). Then, at the age of 40, he underwent a dramatic conversion to the teaching of Ibn Ḥanbal. Unlike Ibn Ḥanbal before him, al-Ashᶜarī used the method of dialectical theological discourse (*kalām*) which he had learned from the Muᶜtazila, but he turned this method on them to refute their doctrines and to defend the doctrines of Ibn Ḥanbal.

Some scholars have described al-Ashᶜarī as representing a "middle ground" between Muᶜtazilism and Ḥanbalism. However, I believe that even a cursory reading of al-Ashᶜarī's book *Al-Ibāna ᶜan Uṣūl ad-Diyāna*[25] clearly shows this to be untrue. More recent scholarship[26] agrees that al-Ashᶜarī was fully loyal to Ḥanbalism, and that he was totally opposed to the Muᶜtazila. His reasons for believing as he did were exegetical—rooted in the Qur'an and Sunna—not rationalist. Though he used the rational methods of the Muᶜtazila, he did so only to refute what he saw as their pernicious doctrines.

In this context we can trace the historical development of the doctrine of the divine *ṣifāt al-dhāt* and their relation to the divine essence. The main line of development on this question moves from Abū al-Hudhayl through al-Naẓẓām through Ibn Kullāb to al-Ashᶜarī.

Abū al-Hudhayl

Abū al-Hudhayl al-ᶜAllāf (d. between 226/840 and 235/850 in extreme old age) was the first speculative theologian of the Muᶜtazila. In tracing the historical process of reflection on the *ṣifāt*, Joseph Van Ess begins with Abū al-Hudhayl's exegetical study of the Qur'an:

> With Abū al-Hudhayl, namely, a major shift takes place. He seems to be the first person to have addressed the problem through a systematic analysis of the Qur'anic data. The Scripture contains ... not only "names"

---

25 Abū al-Ḥasan ᶜAlī ibn Ismāᶜīl al-Ashᶜarī, *Ad-Ibānah ᶜan Uṣūl ad-Diyānah* [The Elucidation of Islam's Foundation], translation with introduction and notes by Walter C. Klein (New Haven: American Oriental Society, 1940).

26 E.g., Gimaret's books, cited previously.

of God, but also attributes: In addition to statements like *inna llāh$^{a c}$ālim^{u} ġaib^{i} s-samawāt^{i} wal-arḍ* ... stood others like *qul: innamā l-ʿilm^{u} ʿinda llāh* or *wasiʿa rabbunā kull^{a} šai$^{\prime in}$ ʿilm^{an}*. So one was justified in deriving nouns, i.e., the attributes, from the adjectival names. God is "Knowing" could be understood as "God has knowledge."[27]

However, in Abū al-Hudhayl's view these *ṣifāt* were identical with God's essence. God has knowledge and power, but God's knowledge and power are the same as God's essence—the same as God's own self. Al-Ashʿarī, in his description of Muʿtazilite doctrine in *Maqālāt al-Islāmiyyīn*, says the following:

> Their sheikh Abū al-Hudhayl al-ʿAllāf said, "The knowledge of the Creator (exalted is He) is Himself (*huwa huwa*). And the same is true of His power, His hearing, His sight, His wisdom. He says the same about the rest of the *ṣifāt* of His essence. He used to assert that when one asserts that the Creator is Knowing, one affirms a knowledge which is God, and one denies ignorance of God, and this indicates something known, regardless of whether it exists or will exist. And when one says that the Creator is Powerful, one affirms a power which is God, and one denies powerlessness of God, and this indicates something over which power is exercised, whether or not it exists. He says the same about the rest of the *ṣifāt* of essence.[28]

Elsewhere in the same book al-Ashʿarī writes: "Abū al-Hudhayl said, 'He is Knowing by virtue of knowledge which is He. He is Powerful by virtue of power which is He. He is Living by virtue of life which is He ... If I say that God is Knowing, I affirm that He has knowledge which is God.'"[29]

Al-Ashʿarī also makes the intriguing remark that "Abū al-Hudhayl took this doctrine from Aristotle."[30] Whether or not Abū al-Hudhayl's doctrine really was influenced by Aristotelianism, it is clear that al-Ashʿarī *thought* that the Muʿtazilite doctrine on this point (which al-Ashʿarī rejected) had been influenced by what he considered to be pagan, non-Islamic sources, and not just by the Qurʾan and the Sunna.

---

27 Van Ess, *Theologie und gesellschaft*, vol. 4, 441–42. "Mit Abū l-Hudhail nämlich vollzieht sich eine Wende. Er scheint als erster das Problem durch eine systematische Analyse des koranischen Befundes angegangen zu haben. Die Schrift enthielt ... nicht nur „Namen" Gottes, sondern auch Attribute: Neben Aussage wie inna *llāh$^{a c}$ālim^{u} ġaib^{i} s-samawāt^{i} wal-arḍ* ... standen andere wie *qul: innamā l-ʿilm^{u} ʿinda llāh oder wasiʿa rabbunā kull^{a} šai$^{\prime in}$ ʿilm^{an}*. Man war also berechtigt, aus den „Namen," den Adjektiven, die Nomina, d.h. die Attribute, herauszuholen; „Gott ist wissend" ließ sich verstehen als „Gott hat ein Wissen."

28 Al-Ashʿarī, *Maqālāt al-Islāmiyyīn*, 484, lines 5ff.

29 Ibid., 165, lines 5–8.

30 Ibid., 485, line 7.

Al-Naẓẓām

The Muᶜtazilite theologian Abū Isḥāq Ibrāhīm al-Naẓẓām (d. between 220/835 and 230/845), who was a nephew of Abū al-Hudhayl, generally accepted the basic outline of his uncle's system, but he made one important modification which, in al-Ashᶜarī's opinion, moved the Muᶜtazila even further away from the traditional doctrine of the Qurᵓan and the Sunna.

Van Ess describes as follows al-Naẓẓām's critique of Abū al-Hudhayl's doctrine and the solution which al-Naẓẓām proposed: "But now, when one postulates in God not only an act of knowledge, but also an act of will (parallel to *Allāh murīd*), and an act of creation (parallel to *Allāh khāliq*), etc., doesn't this introduce plurality into God?"[31]

The Muᶜtazila saw themselves as champions of the divine unity. They described themselves as *ahl al-ᶜadl wa-l-tawḥīd*—the People of Justice and of Divine Unity. If God possesses knowledge which is eternal, and will which is eternal, etc., that would seem to mean multiple eternal things. And that would seem to compromise the divine unity. Not all Muᶜtazilites were persuaded by al-Naẓẓām's argument, but most did follow him on this point. Thus Van Ess writes:

> (Al-Naẓẓām) modified Abū al-Hudhayl's model in a way which became the standard for the Muᶜtazilites in Baṣra and Baghdād: he replaced the statement "God is Knowing by virtue of knowledge which is identical with Himself" with "God is Knowing through Himself." He retained the remainder of Abū al-Hudhayl's framework.[32]

Al-Ashᶜarī describes post-Naẓẓām Muᶜtazilite doctrine as follows: "Most of the Muᶜtazila and the Khārijites, and many of the Murjiᵓa, and some of the Zaydites say that God is Knowing and Powerful and Living by virtue of Himself, not by virtue of knowledge or power or life. They say that God has knowledge only in the sense that He is Knowing."[33]

Al-Ashᶜarī further describe's al-Naẓẓām's doctrine as follows:

> As for al-Naẓẓām, he denies knowledge, power, life, hearing, sight and the *ṣifāt* of essence, and he says that God is eternally knowing, living, powerful, hearing, seeing, and permanent by virtue of Himself, not by virtue of knowledge or power or life or hearing or sight or permanence.

31 Van Ess, *Theologie und gesellschaft*, vol. 4, 442. "Bringt man nicht, wenn man nunmehr nicht nur einen Wissensakt, sondern auch einen Willensakt (parallel zu *Allāh*[u] *murīd*), einen Schöpfungsakt (parallel zu *Allāh*[u] *ḫāliq*) usw. bei Gott postuliert, doch eine Vielheit in ihn hinein? Naẓẓām formulierte darum anders: Gott is nicht wissend durch einen Wissensakt, den er hat, sondern er ist wissend durch sich selber (*bi-nafsihī*)."

32 Joseph Van Ess, *Theologie und gesellschaft im 2. und 3. jahrhundert Hidschra,* vol. 3 (Berlin: Walter de Gruyter, 1991–1997), 399. "An dem Modell Abū l-Hudhail's nahm [al-Naẓẓām] jene wichtige Änderung vor, die für die Mehrzahl der Muᶜtaziliten in Baṣra und in Baġdād maßgeblich wurde: er ersetzte die Aussage „Gott ist wissend aufgrund eines Wissenaktes, der mit ihm identisch ist" durch „Gott ist wissend durch sich selber" … Das übrige Gerippe von Abū l-Hudhail's Theorie behielt er bei."

33 Al-Ashᶜarī, *Maqālāt al-Islāmiyyīn*, 164, lines 14ff.

> He says the same about the rest of the *ṣifāt* of essence. He used to say, "When I affirm that the Creator is Knowing, Powerful, Living, Hearing, Seeing, and Permanent, I affirm His essence, and I deny of Him ignorance, powerlessness, death, deafness, and blindness." He says the same about the rest of the *ṣifāt* of essence.[34]

Thus God's knowledge and power, of which the Qurᵓan speaks, do not have any real existence. To say "God has knowledge" is simply a circumlocution for "God is Knowing." God's knowledge and power, then, are nothing more than verbal terms used as a way of speaking. They have no underlying reality. To traditionalists like Aḥmad ibn Ḥanbal this sounded shockingly like "explaining away" (*taᵓwīl*) difficult-to-understand statements in the Qurᵓan, rather than accepting at face value what God's word has said.

Ibn Kullāb

The theory of al-Naẓẓām had at least two serious problems. The first, noted above, is exegetical. The Qurᵓan seems to most readers to speak of God's knowledge, power, word/command, etc., as real things that God has. And, in al-Ashᶜarī's opinion (as will be seen below) it even ascribes to God's knowledge and word some kind of agency in creation, when it says that God creates things by the agency of God's word (*qawl*), "Be!," and when it says that the mountains are established by God's command, and when it says that God "sends things down by His knowledge." The Muᶜtazila had to explain away these kinds of verses by treating them as metaphorical, just as they treated as metaphorical other verses which speak of God's hands, God's sitting on a throne, God's descending to the lowest heaven, God's weighing of our deeds in a scale, etc.

The second problem with the theories of both Abū al-Hudhayl and al-Naẓẓām is logical. If God's knowledge, power, and life are all identical with God's essence, then they are identical with each other. They are simply three different ways of speaking about the same thing. Thus, as al-Ashᶜarī points out, the Muᶜtazila are forced to claim that God's knowledge is alive, that God's power knows things, that God's life exercises power, etc. This seems logically absurd.[35]

One of the more prominent thinkers who argued publicly against the Muᶜtazilite doctrine on this point was ᶜAbdallāh ibn-Saᶜīd ibn Kullāb (d. shortly after 240/854). He was a contemporary of Aḥmad ibn Ḥanbal and is said to have argued against the Muᶜtazila at the court of the caliph al-Maᵓmūn.[36] This would mean that he risked his life or freedom in doing so, and it would also make him an ally of Ibn Ḥanbal.

W. Montgomery Watt says the following about Ibn Kullāb:

---

34 Ibid., 486, lines 10ff.

35 Though perhaps on this point John of Damascus' concept of perichoresis (2nd/8th century) might be seen as a way of defending the Muᶜtazilite view.

36 Watt, *Formative Period*, 287.

> There were also Mutakallimūn [theologians] during the ninth century whose doctrinal position was not far removed from that of the Ḥanbalites and Ḥanafites. The most influential seems to have been Ibn Kullāb, who died shortly after 854, and who was remembered for his elaboration of the doctrine of the attributes (*ṣifāt*) of God. For a time there was a group of Sunnite[37] Mutakallimūn known as the Kullābiyya, and it was apparently to this group that al-Ashᶜarī attached himself when he abandoned the Muᶜtazilites.[38]

> It is now realized that there were forms of Sunnite Kalām before al-Ashᶜarī, notably among the Kullābiyya … and it is probable that on his "conversion" al-Ashᶜarī attached himself to the Kullābiyya … It was possibly nearly a century later before this group of theologians began to think of themselves as Ashᶜarites, and to be so regarded by others.[39]

Richard Frank goes further, describing al-Ashᶜarī and his school as "descended from" Ibn Kullāb and as "tracing its origins to" Ibn Kullāb.

It seems to me that Watt and Frank may be overstating somewhat the degree of al-Ashᶜarī's dependence on Ibn Kullāb. In al-Ashᶜari's writings which remain extant today, it is to Ibn Ḥanbal, not Ibn Kullāb, that al-Ashᶜarī eagerly professes his loyalty. True, he speaks of Ibn Kullāb's ideas in positive terms, but the evidence of al-Ashᶜarī's extant writings suggest to me that he would have preferred the label "Ḥanbalī" over the label "Kullābī."

Nevertheless Ibn Kullāb did influence al-Ashᶜarī and his intellectual descendants in their view of the *ṣifāt* by providing the verbal formula which expressed in one pithy phrase the idea that al-Ashᶜarī saw as being implicit in Ibn Ḥanbal's thought. Watt writes: "Ibn-Kullāb's chief contribution to Kalām, however, was his elaboration of the doctrine of the attributes (*ṣifāt*) of God … These attributes were 'not God and not other than God.'"[40]

Most Muᶜtazila, it will be recalled, under the influence of al-Naẓẓām, asserted that God does not have knowledge, power, word, etc., except in a strictly verbal sense. In this view, the Qurᵓan's references to God's knowledge, power, word, etc., did not refer to underlying realities, but were nothing more than circumlocutions for speaking of God as the Knowing One, the Powerful One, the Speaking One. For if these *ṣifāt* were realities other than God's essence, the Muᶜtazila reasoned, and if they were eternal, then there would have to be multiple eternal beings, which would be polytheism. The problem with this theory was that

---

37 By "Sunnite" Watt means loyal to the kind of traditionalist, anti-Muᶜtazilite beliefs championed by Aḥmad ibn Ḥanbal and others like him.

38 W. Montgomery Watt, *Islamic Philosophy and Theology*, 2nd edition (Edinburgh: Edinburgh University Press, 1985), 58–59.

39 Ibid., 64.

40 Watt, *Formative Period*, 287.

it seemed to most people to be exegetically unfaithful to the Qur'an, and that it seemed to contain logical inconsistencies.

Van Ess describes as follows Ibn Kullāb's role in the reaction against this theory:

> The countermodel first takes shape with Ibn Kullāb; later the determining spokesperson is al-Ashᶜarī. For Ibn Kullāb the attributes were no longer identical with God, but rather were "moments" (*maᶜānī*) in his essence, which could lay claim to an existence of their own … Thus Ibn Kullāb landed on the formula that they were "neither identical with God nor not-identical with him."[41]

To say that God's knowledge, power, life, etc., are "not His essence, nor are they other than He," but that they are "underlying realities eternally subsisting in His essence"[42] is to embrace the paradox that seems inherent in the Qur'anic texts on the subject. This paradox may be beyond the finite capacity of the human mind to fully understand. But, then, Ibn Ḥanbal and other traditionalists did not hesitate to say that there are certain things (like God's hands, God's sitting on the throne, etc.) which we affirm to be true because the Qur'an asserts them, even though we do not know "how" they are true, nor do we ask. God is infinite, and we are finite. It is not given to us to understand about God everything that God understands about God's own self. The principle of *tawqīf* asserts that we must not presume to know about God anything more than exactly what has been revealed about God in the Qur'an and the Sunna.

Van Ess makes an interesting observation at this point:

> Thus Ibn Kullāb landed on the formula that they were "neither identical with God nor not-identical with him." This was the way in which Christians for ages had described the relationship between the divine essence and the hypostases. Ibn Kullāb opened himself up thereby to the suspicion of having been influenced by Christians. Nonetheless, even if this was at all true, it was a polemical oversimplification. The formula was quite at home in Islamic theology.[43]

---

41 Van Ess, *Theologie und gesellschaft*, vol. 4, 443–44. "Das Gegenmodell nimmt zum erstenmal Gestalt an bei Ibn Kullāb, der entscheidende Wortführer ist später al-Ašᶜarī. Für Ibn Kullāb waren die Attribute nich mehr identisch mit Gott, sondern „Momente" (*maᶜānī*) in seinem Wesen, die ein eigenes Sein beanspruchen können … Ibn Kullāb landete darum bei der Formel, daß sie „weder identisch mit Gott noch nicht-identisch mit ihm" seien.„"

42 See below for where Ibn Kullāb said this and al-Ashᶜarī agreed.

43 Van Ess, *Theologie und gesellschaft*, vol. 4, 444. "Ibn Kullāb landete darum bei der Formel, daß sie „weder identisch mit Gott noch nicht-identisch mit ihm" seien. Auf diese Weise hatten die Christen seit je das Verhältnis zwischen dem göttlichen Wesen und den Hypostasen umschrieben; Ibn Kullāb setzte sich darum dem Verdacht aus, von ihnen beeinflußt zu sein. Jedoch war dies, wenn es überhaupt stimmte, eine polemische Verkürzung. Die Formel war in der islamischen Theologie längst heimisch."

I agree with Van Ess here. Ibn Kullāb's formula, "not His essence, nor other than He," was deeply rooted in Islamic thought and in Qurʾanic exegesis, as I believe is evident from the material I have reviewed above. In the review below of al-Ashᶜarī's own writings this should become even clearer. One need not resort to non-Islamic influences to explain this statement.

Al-Ashᶜarī himself summarized Ibn Kullāb's teaching as follows:

> He used to say, "The underlying reality of 'God is Knowing' is that He has knowledge. And the underlying reality of 'He is Powerful' is that He has power. And the underlying reality of 'He is Living' is that He has life. The same is true of statements about the rest of His names and *ṣifāt*." He used to say that the names of God and His *ṣifāt* of His essence are not God, nor are they other than He (*lā hiya Allāh wa-lā hiya ghayruhū*), but that they are subsistent in God (*qāʾima bi-Allāh*).[44]

> The *ṣifāt* of essence … do not subsist in themselves (*lā taqūmu bi-anfusihā*): rather they are subsistent in God (*qāʾima bi-Allāh*). [Ibn Kullāb] asserted … that His *ṣifāt* are not He and not other than He. The same is true of the statement about the *ṣifāt* … that [God's] knowledge is not [God's] power, nor is the former something other than the latter. The same is true of the rest of the *ṣifāt*.[45]

It was in the context of this discussion that al-Ashᶜarī underwent his conversion from Muᶜtazilism to the traditionalism of Aḥmad ibn Ḥanbal. This is the historical background and debate that provide the context for understanding al-Ashᶜarī's own statements about God's *ṣifāt* and their relation to the divine essence.

Al-Ashᶜarī's Doctrine in His Own Words

After al-Ashᶜarī's death, his "school of thought" gradually became the dominant orthodoxy of Sunni Islam. In the process, many of his ideas were developed and modified by his successors. As a result, ideas are sometimes associated with his name which he himself may have never formulated. A good example of this would be his doctrine of the uncreatedness of the Qurʾan. He certainly did teach this. But in succeeding centuries the discussion of this doctrine became much more detailed, with debate focused on whether the paper and ink in the physical book are created, and whether the sounds brought forth by the human tongue in reciting it are created. Al-Ashᶜarī was cited in support of one or another position on questions which he himself may have never even considered.

---

44 Al-Ashᶜarī, *Maqālāt al-Islāmiyyīn*, 169, lines 10ff.

45 Ibid., 546, lines 8ff.

In what follows below I hope, by giving the reader direct access to al-Ashᶜarī's own words, to minimize the danger of falling into the same trap myself. In particular, since the next section of the chapter after this one will consider the sensitive question of possible parallels between al-Ashᶜarī's doctrine and the Christian doctrine of the Trinity, I think it is especially important to give the reader substantial undiluted material from the primary sources.

The chief primary sources available today on al-Ashᶜarī's thought are five books/treatises from his pen:

1. Maqālāt al-Islāmiyyīn wa-Ikhtilāf al-Muṣallīn

2. Al-Ibāna ᶜan Uṣūl al-Diyāna

3. Kitāb al-Lumaᶜ fī al-Radd ᶜalā Ahl al-Zaygh wa-l-Bidaᶜ

4. Risāla ilā Ahl al-Thaghr fī Bāb al-Abwāb

5. Risālat Istiḥsān al-Khawḍ fī ᶜIlm al-Kalām

In addition to these, Daniel Gimaret has argued persuasively (see below) that Ibn Fūrak's book *Mujarrad Maqālāt al-Shaykh Abī al-Ḥasan al-Ashᶜarī* should be viewed as an excellent primary source on al-Ashᶜarī's thought.

I have read through each of these six books/treatises and have sought to cull from them all that al-Ashᶜarī says in them on the questions of interest in this chapter. In only one of the six (*Risālat Istiḥsān al-Khawḍ fī ᶜIlm al-Kalām*) did I find nothing directly relevant to the issues of the divine *ṣifāt* and their relation to the divine essence.

Rather than analyzing al-Ashᶜarī's ideas in my own words, and running the risk of falling into the trap mentioned above, I will provide the reader with lengthy verbatim quotations from al-Ashᶜarī in his own words, with only minimal analysis. The main exceptions are those places where there is need to summarize a long argument for reasons of space, or where I omit an argument that he has already made elsewhere. Then at the end I will try to summarize what I understand to be the main points of al-Ashᶜarī's teaching, and the reader can judge whether I have summarized accurately. All translations from Arabic works in this chapter are my own. In some cases, where published English or French translations exist, I have consulted those translations. However, the translation decisions in this chapter, and the responsibility for any errors that result, remain my own.

Maqālāt al-Islāmiyyīn wa-Ikhtilāf al-Muṣallīn

This book, as noted above, is primarily al-Ashᶜarī's encyclopedic analysis of the views of other Muslim sects and teachers, not those of al-Ashᶜarī himself. We have already seen his analysis of the doctrines of Abū al-Hudhayl and al-Naẓẓām. In his analysis of Ibn Kullāb we saw a clue to al-Ashᶜarī's own views. The main clue, though, to al-Ashᶜarī's own views in *Maqālāt al-Islāmiyyīn* is found in the chapter which he titles "The Teaching of the People of the Hadith and the Sunna."[46] Here he is essentially summarizing the teaching of Aḥmad ibn Ḥanbal, and he shows his own agreement by concluding this chapter with the words, "This is our teaching."[47] This chapter is sometimes referred to as al-Ashᶜarī's "Credo." It is parallel to a similar "Credo" chapter in *Al-Ibāna ᶜan Uṣūl al-Diyāna.*

Among the affirmations of the "People of the Hadith and the Sunna" are the following:

> [They confess] that the names of God should not be said to be something other than God, as the Muᶜtazila and the Khawārij say. They confess that God (lofty is He) has knowledge, as He says, "He sent it down by His knowledge (Q 4:164)," and as He says, "No female becomes pregnant nor gives birth except by His knowledge (Q 35:12)." They affirm hearing and sight, and they do not deny them of God as do the Muᶜtazila. They affirm that God has strength *(quwwa)*, as He says, "Do they not see that God, who created them, is mightier than they in strength? (Q 41:14)."

Al-Ibāna ᶜan Uṣūl al-Diyāna[48]

This book contains a similar "Credo" titled "Chapter on Making Clear the Teaching of the People of Truth and of the Sunna." The chapter explicitly expresses loyalty to Aḥmad ibn Ḥanbal by name. At the beginning of this chapter[49] he says that this is "our teaching, which we teach, and our religion, which we profess." He goes on to say:

> [We hold] that whoever claims that "God's names are other than He" is in error. [We hold] that God has knowledge, as He says [Q 4:166], "He sent it down by His knowledge," just as He says [Q 35:11], "No female becomes pregnant or gives birth except by His knowledge." We affirm that God has hearing and sight, and we do not deny this as the Muᶜtazila and the Jahmiyya and the Khawārij have done. And we affirm that God has strength *(quwwa)*, as He says [Q 41:15], "Did they not see that God, who created them, is mightier than they in strength?" And we say that God's word *(kalām)* is uncreated, and that He has not created anything without saying to it, "Be!" as He says [Q 16:40], "Rather Our saying *(qawl)* to a thing, if we want it, is to say, 'Be!' and it is."[50]

46 Al-Ashᶜarī, *Maqālāt al-Islāmiyyīn*, 290–97. There are a few other places in the book which he labels as "teaching of the people of truth" and other similar labels, but the material which directly addresses the questions in which this paper is interested are in the chapter in 290–97.

47 Ibid., 297, line 8.

48 Abū al-Ḥasan ᶜAlī ibn Ismāᶜīl al-Ashᶜarī, "Kitāb al-Ibāna," in *Al-Rasāʾil al-Sabᶜa fī al-ᶜAqāʾid* (Hyderabad, India: Maṭbaᶜat Jamᶜiyyat Dāʾirat al-Maᶜārif al-ᶜUthmāniyya, 1948).

49 Ibid., 5.

50 Ibid., 6, lines 11ff.

Later in the book al-Ashʿarī has a chapter on the uncreatedness of the Qurʾan as God's word. This also contains material relevant to the questions with which this chapter is concerned:

> If someone asks for proof that the Qurʾan is God's uncreated word (*kalām*), we say to him that the proof of that is His saying (mighty and glorious is He) [Q 30:25], "Among His signs is that the heavens and the earth are established by His command." The command (*amr*) of God is His word (*kalām*) and His utterance (*qawl*). Since He commanded them to be established, and they were established and do not fall, their being established is by His command. And He says [Q 7:54], "Do not the creation and the command belong to Him?" Everything He has created is included in "the creation." So when He says, "Does not the creation belong to Him?" this is referring to all of creation. And when He says, "and the command," He is referring to a command which is something other than all of creation. So what we have described proves that God's command is not created.[51]

> Another proof: Among the proofs from God's Book that His word is uncreated is His saying (mighty and glorious is He) [Q 16:40], "Rather Our saying to a thing, if we want it, is to say, 'Be!' and it is." So if the Qurʾan were created, then "Be!" would have to be said to it, and it would be. But if God (mighty and glorious is He) were saying "Be!" to His utterance (*qawl*), then the utterance would have an utterance. And this would necessitate one of two things: 1) either that the matter be interpreted to mean that God's utterance is uncreated, or 2) every utterance would occur by virtue of another utterance *ad infinitum*, and this is absurd. Since this is absurd, it is solid and firmly established that God (mighty and glorious is He) has an uncreated utterance.[52]

Pages 27–33 are an entire chapter which simply lists one hadith after another in support of the uncreatedness of the Qurʾan.

Kitāb al-Lumaʿ fī al-Radd ʿalā Ahl al-Zaygh wa-l-Bida[53]

Kitāb al-Lumaʿ affirms the same doctrines as the *Ibāna*, but its style is very different. The *Ibāna* was very likely written for a traditionalist audience, which might have been suspi-

---

51 Ibid., 19.
52 Ibid., 20, lines 2ff.
53 Abū al-Ḥasan ʿAlī ibn Ismāʿīl al-Ashʿarī, *The Theology of al-Ashʿarī: The Arabic Texts of al-Ashʿarī's Kitāb al-Lumaʿ and Risālat Istiḥsān al-Khawḍ fī ʿIlm al-Kalām, with briefly annotated translations, and appendices containing material pertinent to the study of al-Ashʿarī*, ed. Richard McCarthy (Beirut: Imprimerie Catholique, 1953).

cious of al-Ashᶜarī's Muᶜtazilite background. The argumentation in the *Ibāna* is therefore primarily exegetical—from the Qurᵓan and Hadith—rather than emphasizing dialectical reasoning. By contrast, *Kitāb al-Lumaᶜ* may have been written for a Muᶜtazilite audience (or at least an audience of *mutakallimīn*). He uses their method of dialectical reasoning to refute Muᶜtazilite doctrines. Nonetheless the exegetical/Qurᵓanic element is also prominent in *Kitāb al-Lumaᶜ*. Gimaret writes, "Of al-Ashᶜarī's own works, which were considerable, alas very few have survived. Of the few that do remain, indisputably the most precious is the *Kitāb al-Lumaᶜ*."[54]

In the opening paragraphs of the book al-Ashᶜarī seeks to prove the existence of God and the unity of God. Then in paragraphs 13–14[55] he argues that the wise works which order the universe show that God is Knowing, and that they must have been produced by a being who is also Powerful and Living. Then he continues:

> If someone says, "Do you say that God (exalted is He) has eternally been Knowing, Powerful, Hearing, Seeing?" we say, "That is what we say." If someone then says, "What is the proof of that?" we say, "The proof of that is that the Living One, if He were not Knowing, would be characterized by the opposite of knowledge, such as ignorance or doubt or other defects. If the Creator (exalted is He) were eternally Living but not Knowing, He would be characterized by the opposite of knowledge, such as ignorance or doubt or other defects. If He were eternally characterized by the opposite of knowledge, then it would be impossible for Him to know [anything]; for this opposite of knowledge, if it is eternal, could not cease to exist. And if that could not cease to exist, then it would not be possible for Him to perform wise works. Since He has performed such works, this proves that He is Knowing. It is solid and firmly established that He has eternally been Knowing, since it is impossible that He should have been eternally characterized by the opposite of knowledge.[56]
>
> In the same way, if He were eternally Living but not Powerful, He would have to have been eternally powerless, characterized by the opposite of power. If His powerlessness were eternal, it would be impossible that He should exercise power or that acts should originate from him. In the same way, if He were eternally Living but not Hearing and not Seeing, He would have eternally been characterized by the opposite of hearing (such as deafness and other defects) and by the opposite of sight (such as

---

54 Gimaret, *Doctrine*, 9. "De l'oeuvre même d'A[shᶜarī], qui fut considérable, très peu, hélas, a survécu. Du peu qui subsiste, la pièce la plus précieuse est incontestablement le K[itāb] al-Lumaᶜ."

55 Al-Ashᶜarī, *Theology of al-Ashᶜarī*, 10.

56 Ibid., 11, paragraph 16.

blindness and other defects). But it is inconceivable to speak of defects in the Creator, since they are marks of temporality. So what we have said proves that God (exalted is He) has eternally been Knowing, Powerful, Hearing and Seeing.[57]

If someone says, "Why do you say that the Creator (exalted is He) has knowledge by virtue of which He knows?" we say, "Because wise works, just as they come only from someone knowing among us, likewise occur among us only from someone who has knowledge. If the works do not prove the knowledge of the person among us from whom they come, then neither do they prove that the person among us from whom they come is knowing. If they were to prove that the Creator (exalted is He) is Knowing (by analogy with their proving that we are knowing), but if they were to fail to prove that He has knowledge (by analogy with their proving that we have knowledge), then one could say that they prove our knowledge but do not prove that we are knowing. And if this cannot be said, then neither can the statement of our questioner."[58]

If someone says, "You do not deny, do you, that a wise act proves that a human being has knowledge which is something other than he, just as you said that it proves [the existence of] knowledge?" we say, "If a wise act proves that a human being has knowledge, that does not prove that it is other than he, just as, if it proves that he is knowing, that does not prove that he is other than himself (*mutaghāyir*) in any sense at all. And furthermore, the meaning of 'otherness' (*al-ghayriyya*) is that it is possible for one of two things to be separated from the other in some sense. So since we have already proved the eternity of the Creator (exalted is He) and of His knowledge, it is impossible that they should be something other than each other (*ghayrayn*)."[59]

The proof that God (exalted is He) has power and life is like the proof that God (exalted is He) has knowledge.[60]

Among the things which prove that God (exalted is He) is Knowing by virtue of knowledge is the fact that God must be Knowing either by virtue

57 Ibid., paragraph 17.

58 Ibid., 12, paragraph 18.

59 Ibid., paragraph 20. The implication is that if God and His knowledge were two different beings, and if they were both eternal, then this would violate the unity of God. Al-Ashᶜarī is here affirming the *lā ghayruhū* (not other than He) part of Ibn Kullāb's formula.

60 Ibid., 13, paragraph 23.

> of Himself or by virtue of knowledge which cannot be Himself. If He were Knowing by virtue of Himself, then His self would be knowledge. For if someone were to say, "God (exalted is He) is Knowing by virtue of an underlying reality which is other than He, then he would be compelled to admit that that underlying reality is knowledge." It is impossible for knowledge to be knowing, or for the knower to be knowledge, or that God (exalted is He) be synonymous with His *ṣifāt*. Do you not see that the way by which it is known that knowledge is knowledge is that the knower knows by virtue of it? For a human being's power (by which he does not know) cannot be knowledge. Since it is absurd to say that the Creator (exalted is He) is knowledge, it is absurd to say that He is Knowing by virtue of Himself. And if that is absurd, then it is true that he is Knowing by virtue of a knowledge which cannot be Himself. This proof proves the affirmation of all of God's *ṣifāt* of His essence (exalted is He), such as life, power, hearing, sight, and the rest of the *ṣifāt* of the essence.[61]
>
> If someone says, "Why do you say that God (exalted is He) has eternally been Speaking, and that the word (*kalām*) of God (exalted is He) is uncreated?" we say, "We say that because God (exalted is He) says, 'Rather, our utterance (*qawl*) to a thing, if We want it, is to say to it, "Be!" and it is.' (Q 16:40). So if the Qurʾan were created, then God (exalted is He) would be saying to it 'Be!' But the Qurʾan is His utterance, and it is absurd that His utterance should be spoken to. For this would necessitate a second utterance, and one would have to say about the second utterance and its relation to a third utterance the same thing that was said about the first utterance and its relation to a second utterance. This would result in an endless process of utterances, and that is senseless. If that is senseless, then it is senseless to say that the Qurʾan is created. If one could say that He speaks to His utterance, then one could say that He wills His will, and that is senseless both in our opinion and in theirs."[62]

In chapter 2, paragraphs 34–35,[63] he argues for the eternity of God's word by a process of dialectical reasoning, in which he shows the close relationship between God's knowledge and God's word, and shows that the proof of the eternity of one of them proves the eternity of the other. Then in chapter 36[64] he applies the same proof to the eternity of God's will.

---

61 Ibid., 14, paragraphs 25–26. In this paragraph al-Ashʿarī affirms the *lā dhātuhū* (not His essence) part of Ibn Kullāb's formula.

62 Ibid., 15, paragraph 27. "And in theirs," i.e., in the opinion of his Muʿtazilite opponents.

63 Ibid., 17–18.

64 Ibid., 18.

The rest of the chapter[65] argues that this proof does not apply to other things by which God is described, such as God's acts.

Risāla ilā Ahl al-Thaghr fī Bāb al-Abwāb[66]

This treatise is a letter which al-Ashᶜarī wrote to a group of Muslims living in a frontier town (Bāb al-Abwāb) on the outskirts of the Muslim empire. Its purpose is to provide them with accurate information about what constitutes sound doctrine, about the basis for asserting that doctrine, and about how to refute opposing doctrines.

Robert Caspar suggests that this treatise is "of discussible authenticity."[67] The chief authenticity problem is that its preamble ascribes to it an erroneous date. Nonetheless, ᶜAbdallāh Shākir al-Junaydī offers a vigorous defense of its authenticity,[68] and I find his argument persuasive. He points out, among other things, that Ibn ᶜAsākir viewed it as authentic, that Ibn Taymiyya quoted it repeatedly, that Fuat Sezgin does not question its authenticity, and that its contents agree in doctrine and in language with al-Ashᶜarī's other writings which are undisputed.

The book contains two parts. The structure of the second (larger) part is a list of fundamental principles (*uṣūl*), i.e., doctrinal affirmations, on which the early Muslim community (*salaf*) were unanimous (*ajmaᶜū*). The following affirmations relate to the concerns of this essay:

> The fourth unanimous affirmation: They were unanimous in affirming God's life (mighty and glorious is He), by virtue of which He has eternally been Living, and [God's] knowledge, by virtue of which He has eternally been Knowing, and [God's] power, by virtue of which He has eternally been Powerful, and [God's] word, by virtue of which He has eternally been Speaking, and [God's] will, by virtue of which He has eternally been Willing, and [God's] hearing and sight by virtue of which He has eternally been Hearing and Seeing.
>
> Nevertheless none of these *ṣifāt* can possibly be temporal (*muḥdath*), for if any of them were temporal, then before its creation in time He (exalted is He) would have been characterized (*mawṣūf*) by its opposite. And if that were the case, then He would have departed from divinity.[69]

65 Ibid., 19–23.

66 Abū al-Ḥasan ᶜAlī ibn Ismāᶜīl al-Ashᶜarī, *Risāla ilā Ahl al-Thaghr fī Bāb al-Abwāb*, ed. ᶜAbdallāh Shākir Muḥammad al-Junaydī (Medina, Saudi Arabia: Maktabat al-ᶜUlūm wa-l-Ḥikam, 1988).

67 Robert Caspar, *Traité de théologie musulmane* (Rome: Pontificio Istituto di Studi Arabi e d'Islamistica, 1987), 177. "d'une authenticité discutable"

68 Al-Ashᶜarī, *Risāla ilā Ahl al-Thaghr*, 103ff.

69 Ibid., 214–15. Note the formula *lā dhātuhū wa-lā ghayruhū* (not His essence, nor other than He).

> These *ṣifāt* must be affirmed … [God] has made that clear by His saying (mighty and glorious is He) "Possessor of strength, the Firm" [Q 51:58], and He has said, "He sent it down by His knowledge" [Q 4:166], and He has said "And they do not comprehend anything of His knowledge except what He wills" [Q 2:255].[70]

> Though these *ṣifāt* are not other than He, they cannot be Himself, because of the impossibility of His being life or knowledge or power; for an act does not originate in one who is thus. That is, an act originates in the Living, Powerful, Knowing One, rather than in life and knowledge and power.[71]

> The sixth unanimous affirmation: They were unanimous that His command (*amrahū*) (mighty and glorious is He) and His utterance (*qawlahū*) are not temporal and not created. God (exalted is He) has proved the truth of this in His saying (*bi-qawlihī*), "Do not the creation and the command belong to Him?" [Q 7:54]. So He distinguished (exalted is He) between His creation and His command. He also said, "Rather His command, if He wills a thing, is to say to it, 'Be!' and it is." [Q 36:82]. By this He made it clear (exalted is He) that by His utterance and His will the created things become things after having not existed.[72]

> So His utterance is not the created things, since His command (exalted is He) to these things and His utterance to them is existential. If it were created, He would have had to create it by another command. And that utterance, if it were created, would have been created by another utterance. This would impose upon the One who uttered it one of two possibilities: either (1) that every utterance is created and preceded by a created utterance *ad infinitum* (this is precisely the teaching of the Dahriyya), or (2) that utterance occurs without His (mighty and glorious is He) giving a command to it, but then His being praised for that would cease to have any meaning.[73]

Mujarrad Maqālāt al-Shaykh Abī al-Ḥasan al-Ashᶜarī[74]

As noted above, Daniel Gimaret[75] argues convincingly that Ibn Fūrak's book *Mujarrad Maqālāt al-Ashᶜarī* should be viewed as an excellent primary source on the teachings of

---

70 Ibid., 217.
71 Ibid., 219.
72 Note the agential role of God's word in creation.
73 Ibid., 221–23.
74 Ibn Fūrak, *Mujarrad Maqālāt al-Ashᶜarī.*
75 Ibid., introduction, 11–20; Gimaret, *Doctrine*, 16–20.

al-Ashᶜarī. Abū Bakr Muḥammad ibn al-Ḥasan ibn Fūrak al-Anṣārī al-Iṣbahānī (d. 406/1015) was one of the leading Ashᶜarite theologians of his time, and only one generation stood between him and al-Ashᶜarī. The stated purpose of his book *Mujarrad Maqālāt al-Ashᶜarī*, as the title implies, is to set forth al-Ashᶜarī's own words on various theological issues, without additional comment or redaction by Ibn Fūrak.

Gimaret is convinced that Ibn Fūrak was reliably successful:

> I need not repeat here the considerable interest of this text: everyone will now be able to judge for themselves. To be sure, the thought of al-Ashᶜarī was not completely unknown to us, at least in its essentials, thanks in particular to the *Kitāb al-Lumaᶜ*, edited by McCarthy. Nonetheless, that was relatively little in comparison with the profusion of information which the *Mujarrad* brings us, and the word resurrection in this connection is perhaps not too strong. This is because, for those who might still have doubts—given how often al-Ashᶜarī has been the victim of false ideas—this is indeed the authentic thought of al-Ashᶜarī which here is restored to us in its fulness. This is attested not only by the authority of Ibn Fūrak, as well as by the abundant references to the works of the master (thirty titles cited, of which some are cited more than ten times), but also the perfect agreement between the arguments advanced here and those in *Kitāb al-Lumaᶜ* or those reported by Baghdādī, Juwaynī, Abū al-Qāsim al-Anṣārī, etc.[76]

Al-Ashᶜarī can be found in various parts of the book to have addressed the issues which are the focus of this essay. Some of his remarks are as follows:

> [Al-Ashᶜarī] says, "The underlying reality (*maᶜnā*) of knowledge—its reality (*ḥaqīqa*)—is that by which the Knower knows what is known." He relied on this in his proof that God (exalted is He) is Knowing by virtue of knowledge, for if He were Knowing by virtue of Himself, His self would be knowledge. For the reality of the underlying reality (*maᶜnā*) of knowledge is that by virtue of which the Knower knows what is known.

---

76 Gimaret, introduction to Ibn Fūrak, *Mujarrad Maqālāt al-Ashᶜarī*, 11–12. "Je n'ai pas besoin de redire l'intérêt considérable de ce texte: chacun désormais pourra en juger par lui-même. La pensée d'Ašᶜarī, certes, ne nous était pas complètement inconnue, du moins pour l'essentiel, grâce en particulier au *K. al-Lumaᶜ* édité par McCarthy. C'était cependant bien peu de chose par rapport à la profusion d'information que nous apporte le *Muğarrad*, et le mot de *résurrection*, en l'occurrence, n'est peut-être pas trop fort. Car, pour ceux qui pourraient encore en douter—tellement le personnage a été victime d'idées fausses—c'est bien l'authentique pensée d'Ašᶜarī qui nous est ici restituée dans son intégralité: l'attestent non seulement l'autorité d'Ibn Fūrak, ainsi que les abondantes références aux œuvres du maître (trente titres cités, dont certains plus de dix fois), mais aussi la parfaite conformité des thèses énoncées avec celles du *K. al-Lumaᶜ* ou avec celles rapportées par Bağdādī, Ğuwaynī, Abū l-Qāsim al-Anṣārī, etc."

If the self of the Preeternal One (*al-qadīm*) (lofty is He) were a self by virtue of which He knew the things which are known, it would have to be knowledge, even in its underlying reality (*maᶜnā*).[77]

He said in his book *Naqḍ Uṣūl al-Jubbāʾī*, "The names of God (exalted is He) are His *ṣifāt*, and it cannot be said of His *ṣifāt* that they are He, nor that they are other than He."[78]

He said, "The *ṣifāt* of God (exalted is He) fall into two categories: (1) those which cannot be said to be other than He (these are subsistent in His essence [*qāʾima bi-dhātihī*]), and (2) those which must be other than He because of their subsisting in something other than Him (*li-qiyāmihā bi-ghayrihī*).[79]

He used to say, "The underlying reality of Powerful (*qādir*) and Strong (*qawiyy*) is the same, and power (*qudra*) and (*quwwa*) are the same." And he said that power (*qudra*) and ability (*istiṭāᶜa*) are the same.

Likewise he did not distinguish among knowledge (*ᶜilm*) and awareness (*dirāya*) and understanding (*fiqh*) and comprehension (*fahm*) and sagacity (*fiṭna*) and reason (*ᶜaql*) and sense (*ḥiss*) and cognition (*maᶜrifa*).[80]

As for what is predicated by saying that He is Loving and Pleased, or Displeased or Hostile, for [al-Ashᶜarī] that was a reference to His will. He used to say that God's pleasure (exalted is He) over believers is His will to reward them and to praise them, and His displeasure over unbelievers is His will to punish them and to censure them. The same is true of His love and His enmity.[81]

He used to say, "The word of God (exalted is He) is a preeternal *ṣifa* belonging to Him, eternally subsisting in his essence (*inna kalām Allāh taᶜālā ṣifa lahū qadīma lam yazal qā'im bi-dhātihī*)."[82]

---

77 Ibn Fūrak, *Mujarrad Maqālāt al-Ashᶜarī*, 10, line 12.
78 Ibid., 38, line 19.
79 Ibid., 40, line 4.
80 Ibid., 44, lines 10–12, 14–15.
81 Ibid., 45, lines 11–13.
82 Ibid., 59, line 11.

> [Al-Ashʿarī said in reference to both divine and human speech] "The Word is the underlying reality (*maʿnā*) subsisting in the self, apart from the sounds and letters."[83]

Summary of al-Ashʿarī's Doctrine on the *Ṣifāt*

As promised earlier, I will attempt here to summarize the main points of al-Ashʿarī's teaching about the *ṣifāt* and their relation to the divine essence. I see the following as the major points in summary:

1. God has seven *ṣifāt* of essence—knowledge, power, life, word, will, sight, hearing. This is not necessarily a closed list, but God does have other *ṣifāt* which are not on this list.

2. These are not merely ways of speaking; they are underlying realities. God is Knowing by virtue of His knowledge, Powerful by virtue of His power, Living by virtue of his life.

3. These *ṣifāt* have existed eternally. They are not temporally originated or created.

4. They are not His essence, nor are they other than He.

5. Rather, they are underlying realities eternally subsisting in His essence.

6. The Qurʾan describes God's knowledge and word as having some kind of agency in creation. That is, God creates by them.

The reader can judge whether these points accurately and adequately reflect al-Ashʿarī's ideas as seen in his writings reviewed above.

Possible Parallels in Christian Doctrine

So God's power, God's knowledge and God's life are eternal realities which have always been present in God. They are not God's essence, nor are they other than He; rather they are underlying realities eternally subsisting in His essence.

This description of God is remarkably similar to the Christian doctrine of the Trinity as expounded by Patristic and Scholastic Christian writers. Indeed at first glance the two doctrines seem nearly identical. As I will show below, a variety of Muslim, Christian, and Jewish writers through the centuries have noticed this similarity and have commented on it.

83 Ibid., 68, line 6.

Some Christians have simply suggested that God's "power" is precisely what is meant by the first hypostasis of the Trinity, and that God's "knowledge" is what is meant by the second hypostasis of the Trinity, and that God's "life" is what is meant by the third hypostasis of the Trinity. Ibn Ḥazm, the fifth/eleventh-century Muslim historian of religious ideas, met Christians who asserted precisely this.[84]

However, this is not how all Christians would state the doctrine. Virtually all writers from the Patristic period would take as a starting point that God's knowledge, God's wisdom, God's understanding, and God's word are all different ways of referring to the same thing, which in Greek is called the *Logos* (λόγος).[85] And all see the Logos as being the second hypostasis of the Trinity. The third hypostasis—the Spirit—is variously described as being God's life,[86] God's power, and God's love.[87]

An interesting example from the Scholastic period, with remarkable parallels to al-Ashᶜarī's teaching, comes from the pen of Thomas Aquinas in the seventh/thirteenth century.[88] He describes the second hypostasis of the Trinity (the Logos) as being God's understanding/word, and the third hypostasis (the Spirit) as being God's love.[89] Aquinas says:

> God's word is coeternal with God Himself.[90] But in God, understanding is not something other than His being, and consequently neither is the Word which is conceived in His intellect some accident or something foreign to His nature.[91] That divine Word is not any accident, nor any part of God, who is simple, nor is it something foreign to the divine nature; rather it is something complete subsisting in the divine nature.[92]
>
> We do not say that these three hypostases or Persons are different by essence … Whatever is said about God absolutely is not something other than God's essence. For God is not Great or Powerful or Good acciden-

84 Abū Muḥammad ᶜAlī ibn Ḥazm al-Andalusī al-Ẓāhirī, *Kitāb al-Faṣl fī al-Milal wa-l-Ahwāʾ wa-l-Niḥal* (Baghdad: Maktabat al-Muthannā, [1964?]), 50, lines 18ff.

85 As has been seen above in Ibn Fūrak, *Mujarrad Maqālāt al-Ashᶜarī*, 44, al-Ashᶜarī would agree that God's knowledge, wisdom and understanding are different ways of saying the same thing. But he did not think that knowledge and word were the same thing, though in chapter 2 of *Kitāb al-Lumaᶜ* he described them as being closely intertwined.

86 Note the term ζωοποιόν (zōopoion, meaning "life-giver") in the Nicene-Constantinopolitan Creed.

87 The suggestion that the Spirit is God's love is found particularly in the Western, Augustinian tradition.

88 Thomas Aquinas, "De Rationibus Fidei ad Cantorem Antiochenum," in *Sancti Thomae de Aquino Opera Omnia* (Rome: Leonine Commission, 1969), 58ff.

89 Recall that in Ibn Fūrak, *Mujarrad Maqālāt al-Ashᶜarī*, 45 (quoted above), al-Ashᶜarī says that God's love is a reference to God's will.

90 Aquinas, "De Rationibus Fidei," chapter 3, lines 105–6. Here and below the translation from Aquinas' Latin is mine.

91 Ibid., chapter 3, lines 55ff.

92 Ibid., chapter 3, lines 62ff.

> tally, but by His essence.[93] The essence of the Word and Love in God is not other than the essence of God.[94]

The primary concern of this essay is al-Ashʿarī's doctrine, not Christian doctrine, so I will not go into further detail on the doctrine of the Trinity as expounded in various Christian writers of the Patristic and Scholastic periods. However, the one example given above should at least provide a small indication of the kinds of parallel ideas and language that can be found between al-Ashʿarī and these writers. When one moves to medieval Christian writers who wrote in Arabic, the parallels become more explicit.

This is not to imply that there are *only* parallels and no differences between Muslim *ṣifāt* and Christian hypostases. In another section below I will examine some possible points of difference. But first I would like to review some of the other writers in history who have noticed how much the Muslim and Christian doctrines have in common.

Others Who Have Noticed This Connection

The observation of striking similarities between al-Ashʿarī's doctrine of *ṣifāt* and the Christian doctrine of the Trinity is far from being original with me.[95] A long and diverse list of scholars, both medieval and modern, and including Muslims, Christians, and Jews, have noticed these similarities and have commented on them. Some have gone so far as to say that there is no difference between the Muslim and Christian doctrines—that they are essentially identical.

An example of this in the modern period is H. A. Wolfson, who wrote an essay on the subject of "The Muslim Attributes and the Christian Trinity."[96] He concludes that "Muslims [were led] to adopt a Christian doctrine which is explicitly rejected in the Koran,[97] and transform it into a Muslim doctrine … [They were] led to the substitution in Muslim theology of divine attributes for the Christian Trinity."[98]

I would argue that Wolfson does not give sufficient credit to the indigenously Islamic reasons, rooted in the Qurʾan and the Sunna, for orthodox Islamic doctrine to make the choices it did. The analysis in this present paper, and al-Ashʿarī's own words, should make clear that al-Ashʿarī was most certainly not simply adopting a Christian doctrine. And I think Wolfson oversimplifies both the Ashʿarite and Christian doctrines on some points.

93 Ibid., chapter 4, lines 74ff.

94 Ibid., chapter 4, lines 109–11.

95 My attention was first drawn to these similarities by J. N. D. Anderson, *Islam in the Modern World* (Leicester, UK: Apollos, 1990). However, I am not aware of any book or article which has analyzed the similarities between the two doctrines in the kind of depth I have attempted in this present chapter.

96 Harry Austryn Wolfson, *The Philosophy of the Kalam* (Cambridge, MA: Harvard University Press, 1976), 113–32. This is a revision of an earlier, freestanding article in *The Harvard Theological Review* 49 (1956):1–18. I am indebted to Tariq Jaffer for calling my attention to this essay.

97 I would question whether the Qurʾran does explicitly reject the Trinity. Certainly it rejects a triad of God, Jesus, and Mary as three gods, but it is not at all clear that it addresses the concept of one God in whom three hypostases or *ṣifāt* of essence subsist.

98 Ibid., 128.

Nevertheless the forcefulness of Wolfson's comment (perhaps deliberately hyperbolic) shows just how similar (identical?) he thought the two doctrines were.

I think that Joseph Van Ess is closer to the truth in his remarks, noted earlier, about the formula that the divine *ṣifāt* are not God's essence, nor are they other than He:

> Thus Ibn Kullāb landed on the formula that they were "neither identical with God nor not-identical with Him." This was the way in which Christians for ages had described the relationship between the divine essence and the hypostases. Ibn Kullāb opened himself up thereby to the suspicion of having been influenced by Christians. Nonetheless, even if this was at all true, it was a polemical oversimplification. The formula was quite at home in Islamic theology.[99]

Some of the strongest examples of medieval texts which compare the Ashᶜarite doctrine of *ṣifāt* with the Christian Trinity come from Muslim members of anti-Ashᶜarite groups (no longer extant today) who rejected *both* al-Ashᶜarī's doctrine *and* Christianity on the grounds that both taught the same thing. One example of this is Ibn Ḥazm, mentioned above. He writes:

> One of [the Christians] has said, "Since it must be the case that the Creator (exalted is He) is living and knowing, it must be the case that He has life and knowledge. His life is what is called the Holy Spirit, and His knowledge is what is called the Son."
>
> But this is the feeblest kind of argumentation there is, since we have previously shown that the Creator (exalted is He) should not have anything like this predicated of Him based on deductive reasoning, but rather specifically based on divine revelation (*al-samᶜ*).
>
> If they [the Christians] say that he [the Son] is not he [the Father] nor is he other than he, then they have become insane in the same way as those[100] who claim the *ṣifāt* are not the same as the One of whom they are predicated (*al-mawṣūf*) nor are they other than He.[101]

99 Van Ess, *Theologie und gesellschaft*, vol. 4, 444. "Auf diese Weise hatten die Christen seit je das Verhältnis zwischen dem göttlichen Wesen und den Hypostasen umschrieben; Ibn Kullāb setzte sich darum dem Verdacht aus, von ihnen beeinflußt zu sein. Jedoch war dies, wenn es überhaupt stimmte, eine polemische Verkürzung. Die Formel war in der islamischen Theologie längst heimisch."

100 Miguel Asín Palacios, in his Spanish translation of Ibn Ḥazm, has a footnote here: "Alude a los axaríes," i.e., the Ashᶜarites. Miguel Asín Palacios, *Abenházam de Córdoba y su historia crítica de las ideas religiosas*, vol. 2 (Madrid: Real Academia de la Historia, 1928), 156.

101 Abū Muḥammad ᶜAlī Ibn Ḥazm al-Andalusī al-Ẓāhirī, *Kitāb al-Faṣl fī al-Milal wa-l-Ahwāʾ wa-l-Niḥal*, vol. 1, part 1 (Baghdad: Maktabat al-Muthannā, [1964?]), 50, lines 18ff.; 55, lines 24ff.

Michel Allard points out examples of Muᶜtazilites who accused the traditionalists of being closet Christians because they affirmed the uncreatedness of God's word and the reality of the divine *ṣifāt*:

> This state of mind appears clearly, for example, in the letters (reported by Ṭabarī) which the caliph al-Maᵓmūn is reported to have written to demand an examination of his *qāḍīs* [judge] on the question of the nature of the Qurᵓan In the second of these letters, in reference to those who hold that the Qurᵓan is uncreated, we read in effect: "By this affirmation they become like the Christians, who say that Jesus son of Mary (according to their claims) is uncreated because he is the Word of God."[102]

Allard says that Ibn al-Nadīm reports that Ibn Kullāb was accused of being a Christian because he affirmed that the word of God is God:

> Subkī, who in his *Ṭabaqāt* takes up the information given by Ibn al-Nadīm, declares that the accusation is unfounded. As an argument he states that this accusation is nothing but a particular form of the accusation "of all of the Muᶜtazilites against the partisans of the *ṣifāt*: the Christians are infidels because they affirm three (divine entities), and you because you affirm seven."[103]

Al-Shahrastānī makes the following interesting comment on the Muᶜtazilite Abū al-Hudhayl: "Abū al-Hudhayl affirmed these *ṣifāt* [specifically: knowledge, power, life] as aspects (*wujūh*) of the [divine] essence. These are precisely the same as the hypostases of the Christians (*hiya bi-ᶜaynihā aqānīm al-naṣāra*) or the 'modes' (*aḥwāl*) of Abū Hāshim."[104]

Wolfson cites similar examples of several medieval Muslim and Jewish writers:

> Abulfaraj, also known as Bar Hebraeus, speaking of the Muᶜtazilites, who denied the reality of divine attributes, says that thereby they steered clear

102 Michel Allard, *Le problème des attributs divins dans la doctrine d'al-Ashᶜarī et de ses premiers grands disciples* (Beirut: Imprimerie Catholique, 1965), 154–55. "Cet état d'esprit apparaît clairement par exemple dans les lettres rapportées par Ṭabarī, que le calife al-Maᵓmūn aurait écrites pour réclamer l'examen de ses *qāḍī* sur la question de la nature du Coran. Dans la deuxième de ces lettres on peut lire en effet, à propos de ceux qui soutiennent que le Coran est incréé: "Par cette affirmation, ils deviennent semblable aux chrétiens qui disent que Jésus fils de Marie, selon leurs prétentions, n'est pas créé, puisqu'il est le Verbe de Dieu."

103 Ibid. "Subkī, qui reprend dans ses Ṭabaqāt les informations données par Ibn Nadīm, déclare que l'accusation … est sans fondement. Il donne comme argument que cette accusation n'est qu'une forme particulière de celle … de tous les muᶜtazilites à l'égard des partisans des *ṣifāt*: les chrétiens sont infidèles en affirmant trois (entités divines), et vous en affirmant sept."

104 Al-Shahrastānī, *Kitāb al-Milal wa-l-Niḥal*, 34. The relevance of Al-Shahrastānī's comments to the question of this chapter is pointed out in Watt, *Formative Period*, 246; Sweetman, *Islam and Christian Theology*, 26; and ibid., 92–93. It was Frank Griffel who called my attention to this passage in Watt.

> of "the persons (*aqānīm*) of the Christians," the implication being that the belief in the reality of the divine attributes indirectly steers one into the belief of the Christian Trinity. ᶜAḍad al-Dīn al-Ījī similarly reports that the Muᶜtazilites accused those who believed in the reality of divine attributes of having fallen into the error of the Christian belief in the Trinity. And prior to both of them, among the Jews, David al-Muḳammaṣ, Saadia, Joseph al-Bāṣir, and Maimonides, evidently reflecting still earlier Muslim sources, whenever they happen to mention the Muslim doctrine of the reality of divine attributes, compare it to the Christian doctrine of the Trinity.[105]

McCarthy notes that "Averroes found this doctrine [i.e., that God's *ṣifāt* are not God's essence, nor are they other than He] as distasteful as that of the Trinity."[106]

But the witnesses on this are not only hostile witnesses who reject both Ashᶜarism (or Sunni traditionalism) and Christianity. Examples can also be found of Muslims and Christians who tentatively explored this theological territory to seek whether there might really be common ground between the two religions on this point.

Thus, in the famous Hāshimī-Kindī[107] dialogue (originally held at the court of the caliph al-Maʾmūn in the early third/ninth century, but the text was substantially redacted later) we see an exchange between a Muslim and a Christian who (according to the text) are personally good friends. The Christian tries to explain the Trinity as follows:

> We know that the *ṣifāt* in God (blessed and exalted is His name) are of two kinds:
>
> - An essential (*dhātiyyah*), natural *ṣifa*, by which He is eternally described
> - A *ṣifa* which He has by acquisition, and this is the *ṣifa* of act (*ṣifat al-fiᶜl*)
>
> As for the *ṣifāt* which He has by acquisition by virtue of His act, they are for example: Merciful, Forgiving, Compassionate. As for the eternal *ṣifāt*, which are natural and essential, and which are eternally predicated of Him (majestic and mighty is He), they are Life and Knowledge. For indeed God is eternally Living and Knowing. So Life and Knowledge are both eternal; there is no way around this.

105 Wolfson, "Muslim Attributes," 112–13. Wolfson provides footnotes here for the reader who wishes to trace these Jewish and Muslim writers in the primary source literature.

106 In al-Ashᶜarī, *Theology of al-Ashᶜarī*, 17 n. 16.

107 *Risālat ᶜAbdallāh ibn Ismāᶜīl al-Hāshimī ilā ᶜAbd al-Masīḥ ibn Isḥāq al-Kindī* … (London: Rivington, 1880), 32–35.

> The conclusion that we can draw from the foregoing is that God is One, having Word and Spirit, in three hypostases (*aqānīm*) subsisting in their essence, encompassed in the single divine substance (*jawhar*). This is the manner of description of the One—triple in hypostases—whom we worship; and this is the manner of description which He has been pleased to choose for Himself.

J. N. D. Anderson, a modern Christian scholar of Islamic law at the University of London, was more tentative and cautious in suggesting that the parallels between the Ashʿarite doctrine of *ṣifāt* and the Christian Trinity might serve as a bridge of understanding for dialogue. He wrote:

> So is there, perhaps, some controversy in the history of Islamic theology which might help Muslims to understand this mystery [i.e., the Trinity]? I think that a "stepping stone"—no more—can be found in the debate about the relationship between God's divine essence (*dhāt*) and his divine qualities (*ṣifāt*) … The orthodox insisted that God's eternal qualities are "not He nor are they any other than He" (lā dhātuhū wa lā ghayruhū). This last statement is certainly not the doctrine of the Trinity, but provides a stepping stone for Muslim understanding.[108]

For an example of a Muslim scholar who is similarly open but similarly cautious, I would suggest the case of Fakhr al-Dīn al-Rāzī (d. 606/1210), the great Qurʾan commentator and theologian. In his comments on *Sūrat* an-Nisāʾ [4]:171,172, he lists multiple different possible interpretations of the meaning of "And do not say 'Three.' Cease!" One option is the following:

> The doctrine of the Christians is very little known. What emerges from it is that they affirm an essence (*dhāt*) characterized (*mawṣūfa*) by three *ṣifāt*. However, even if they call them *ṣifāt*, in reality they are essences (*dhuwāt*). Even if they call them *ṣifāt*, nevertheless in reality they are affirming a multiplicity of essences subsisting in themselves (*qāʾima bi-anfusihā*). And that is downright unbelief. So it is in this sense that He said (exalted is He), "And do not say 'Three." Cease!"
>
> But if we take the word "three" as referring to their affirming three *ṣifāt*, then this is something that cannot be denied. How could we not say that? We ourselves say: "He is God—there is no god but He—the Ruler, the Holy One, the Faultless, the Knowing, the Living, the Powerful, the

108 Anderson, epilogue to *Islam in the Modern World.*

> Willing," and we understand by each of these terms something other than what we understand by the other terms. The multiplicity of *ṣifāt* has no meaning other than that. And if speaking of a multiplicity of *ṣifāt* were unbelief, then we would have to reject the entire Qur'an, and we would have to reject reason, since we know of necessity that what is understood from His (exalted is He) being Knowing is [something] other than what is understood from His (exalted is He) being Powerful or Living.[109]

Al-Rāzī here does not think the Christian use of the term *ṣifa* can be consistently maintained. He thinks the Christian concept of hypostases (just before the passage above, he notes the term *uqnūm*) is really equivalent to essences, not to *ṣifāt*—i.e., that the Christians really *mean* three essences, regardless of what they *say*. But *if* (and this is a big "if") the Christians *really do mean* three *ṣifāt* subsisting in a single essence, then he thinks that the Christians and Muslims actually do not have to disagree on this point. He notes that Muslims, following the Qur'an, also believe in certain essential *ṣifāt* which subsist eternally in the single divine essence.

Possible Differences between the Two Doctrines

I have argued above that al-Ashᶜarī was certainly not copying or "adopting" (Wolfson's term) the Christian doctrine of the Trinity, whether wittingly or unwittingly. The reasons for his views were thoroughly rooted in the Islamic tradition. Indeed, as will be seen below, he accused his Muᶜtazilite *opponents* of being improperly influenced by Christianity.

Furthermore, al-Ashᶜarī was sufficiently familiar with Christian doctrines that he is unlikely to have *accidentally* slipped and imitated Christian doctrine which he did not recognize as such. Ibn Fūrak tells us that al-Ashᶜarī wrote an entire book "containing an exposition of the doctrine of the Christians."[110] Al-Ashᶜarī certainly could judge better than anyone else the extent to which he agreed or disagreed with Christians. If there is common ground between his doctrine and Christian doctrine, he was very likely aware of it.

I have found four specific points on which al-Ashᶜarī *distanced* himself from the Christian doctrine of the Trinity as he understood it. Nonetheless, I would suggest that these points of difference are not on the core issues at stake, either in his doctrine of *ṣifāt* or in the Christian doctrine of the Trinity.

The first point is, of course, that al-Ashᶜarī has a list of seven *ṣifāt* of essence which eternally subsist in God's essence, and this is not necessarily a closed list, whereas the Christians insist on speaking of three and only three subsistences in God. In the *Ibāna* he writes:

109 Muḥammad Al-Rāzī Fakhr al-Dīn et al., *Tafsīr al-Fakhr al-Rāzī, al-Mushtahir bi-l-Tafsīr al-Kābir wa-Mafātīḥ al-Ghayb.* Khalīl Muḥyī al-Dīn al-Mays, ed., vol. 6 (Beirut: Dar al-Fikr, 1990), 118.

110 In Al-Ashᶜarī, *Theology of al-Ashᶜarī*, 227.

> The Muᶜtazila deny the *ṣifāt* of the Lord of the Worlds, and they claim that the meaning of "Hearing, Seeing (*samīᶜ baṣīr*)" is "Seeing (*rāʾin*)," in the sense of Knowing, just as the Christians claim that [God's] hearing is His sight (*baṣruhū*), and is His vision (*ruʾyatuhū*), and is His word, and is His knowledge.[111]

> [Those such as the Jahmiyya who deny that God has hearing or sight] agree with the Christians, for the Christians do not affirm that God is hearing or seeing except in the sense that God is Knowing.[112]

In effect he is accusing the Muᶜtazila and Jahmiyya of being unduly influenced by Christians. In his opinion their effort to collapse the various *ṣifāt* into a single thing is just like what he perceives to be the Christians' effort to collapse seven *ṣifāt* into three. He implicitly accuses Christians of acknowledging too *few* hypostases in God, not too *many*!

On the other hand, he himself does see God's word and God's knowledge as being very closely linked. From the Christian point of view, both "word" and "knowledge" translate the Greek word *Logos* in the New Testament.[113] Christian writers often suggest that a word is simply the outward expression of inward thought/understanding.

In the *Ibāna* al-Ashᶜarī also says that some of the Muᶜtazilites "distinguish between [God's] knowledge and [God's] word,"[114] so that they affirm that God has a word, but deny that God has knowledge. In response al-Ashᶜarī argues that the proof of one proves the other. He does not say or imply that God's word and God's knowledge are the same thing, but he does see them as closely linked concepts.[115]

The second point of apparent difference between al-Ashᶜarī and the Christian Trinity is that Ibn Fūrak says that al-Ashᶜarī explicitly rejected equating God's life with God's spirit, on the grounds that life is an "accident" (*ᶜaraḍ*) in created beings and a *ṣifa* in God, but spirit is a substance (*jism*) which can have life subsisting in it but which cannot *be* life.[116] On the other hand this seems to be more of a difference in definition of the term "spirit" rather than an unbridgeable difference on the core issues at stake in the Muslim and Christian doctrines. And since it comes from Ibn Fūrak, not from any surviving writings

---

111 Al-Ashᶜarī, "Kitāb al-Ibāna," 49, lines 8–10 (in the "Chapter on refuting the Jahmiyya in their denial of God's knowledge and power, etc.").

112 Ibid., 39, lines 20ff.

113 John 1:1—"In the beginning [i.e., εν αρχή] was the Logos, and the Logos was with God, and the Logos was God. It was in the beginning (εν αρχή) with God. All things came into being through it, and apart from it nothing came into being which came into being. In it was life, and that life was light for humankind" (translation mine).

114 Ibid., 46, lines 2ff. (in the "Chapter on refuting the Jahmiyya in their denial of God's knowledge and power, etc.").

115 Ibid.

116 Ibn Fūrak, *Mujarrad Maqālāt al-Ashᶜarī*, 44, lines 20–21; 257, lines 1–18.

from al-Ashʿarī's own hand, one may question whether al-Ashʿarī was as unequivocal on this point as Ibn Fūrak implies.

The third point of difference is that al-Ashʿarī explicitly rejects the idea that God's word could become incarnate or have *ḥulūl* (taking up residence, or descent) in any particular place (*maḥall*), since God's *ṣifāt* do not have location in space, but only subsistence in God's essence. Thus he writes in the *Ibāna*: "The Jahmiyya claim the same thing as the Christians. For the Christians claim that Mary's womb contained the word of God, and the Jahmiyya go beyond them and say that God's word is created and descended (*ḥalla*) into a bush, and that the bush contained it."[117]

This is a more serious point of difference than the previous two. But it is, strictly speaking, a problem related to the Christian doctrine of incarnation, not to the Trinity as such. Furthermore, one wonders whether al-Ashʿarī does not, after all, imply elsewhere that God's word *does* have *ḥulūl* in the Qurʾan. The relation of the Qurʾan as uncreated *kalām Allāh* [God's speech] to the Qurʾan as physical book is a question that often preoccupied al-Ashʿarī's successors.[118]

The fourth (and last) point of difference is the one which prompts al-Ashʿarī's most vehement objection to Christianity. Christians argue that since God's thought or word is something God conceives or generates within God's being, one may legitimately speak of the word thus conceived or generated in God as metaphorically God's "offspring" or "Son." Thomas Aquinas, in the treatise cited above, makes use of the fact that the Latin word *conceptus* means both "concept" and "offspring." Al-Ashʿarī thinks this is anathema. Thus he writes: "The Christians claim that [God's] hearing is His sight (*baṣruhū*), and is His vision (*ruʾyatuhū*), and is His word, and is His knowledge, and is His Son. Mighty and glorious is God and exalted highly above that!"[119]

This is also a very serious objection, but like the third objection above, it is, strictly speaking, a Christological issue, not a Trinitarian issue. It is worth remembering in this context that al-Ashʿarī (like Ibn Ḥanbal before him) rejects *all* use of metaphor (*majāz*) in describing God. So when the Qurʾan speaks of God's hands and God's sitting on a throne and God's nightly descent to the lowest heaven, these must be understood as literal realities, though we do not ask "how."[120] Summarizing al-Ashʿarī's views on God's sitting on a throne, Gimaret concludes, "As elsewhere, all metaphorical interpretation is excluded."[121]

If one rejects all metaphorical language in reference to God, then the only way to understand the word "Son" is as implying that God literally took a wife and carnally begot a son. Such a suggestion is seen by both Muslims and Christians alike as blasphemous and

117 Al-Ashʿarī, "Kitāb al-Ibāna," 21, lines 7–9. The "bush" is an allusion to Moses' encounter with the burning bush.

118 Their conclusions on this point sound, in some ways, very similar to the Chalcedonian Christian doctrine of incarnation, but it would be beyond the scope of this chapter to explore that further.

119 Ibid., 49, lines 8–10 (in the the "Chapter on refuting the Jahmiyya in their denial of God's knowledge and power, etc.").

120 Ibid., 6, lines 8ff., 40ff.

121 Gimaret, *Doctrine*, 328. "Comme par ailleurs toute interpretation métaphorique est exclue."

offensive. Christians would agree with al-Ashᶜarī in reacting to such a suggestion by saying, "Mighty and glorious is God and exalted highly above that."

Conclusion

The average Christian today has a relatively superficial understanding of the Trinity, just as the average Muslim knows little about al-Ashᶜarī's doctrine of *ṣifāt*. But what both would probably agree on is that they *disagree* about their doctrine of God in this area, and that the differences are too profound and too wide to be bridged.

I think, though, that a deeper analysis of both doctrines shows that they are much closer to one another than is commonly supposed. The differences which al-Ashᶜarī has noted about *ḥulūl*/incarnation and about the use of the word "Son" are important, but they are, properly speaking, related to Christological doctrine, not to the Trinity as such.

The issues he raises which relate specifically to the Trinity itself—namely: (1) equating of "word" and "knowledge" and insisting on only three hypostases, and (2) al-Ashᶜarī's apparent insistence that God's life cannot be called Spirit—are both bridgeable differences, in my opinion. Furthermore, apart from these differences, there is a huge amount of common ground between Muslims and Christians on the fundamental issues at stake in the *ṣifāt* and in the Trinity—far more common ground than is generally supposed by either Muslims or Christians. I hope that this essay has made a small contribution to taking up the challenge proposed by Fakhr al-Dīn al-Rāzī and by J. N. D. Anderson—a challenge to cautious exploration of this common ground.

8
Who Was "Allah" before Islam? Evidence that the Term "Allah" Originated with Jewish and Christian Arabs

BY RICK BROWN[1]

In talking with Muslims, it is essential to understand their names for God. In most languages spoken by Muslims, the term *allâh* is at least one of their names for God. Dudley Woodberry[2] has pointed out that the name *allâh* "is of Christian Syriac origin and was in use long before Muhammad's time." Syriac-speaking Christians have always believed this, and scholars like Arthur Jeffery[3] have noted this as well. But violent acts perpetrated by some militant Islamists in the name of *allâh* have led some people in the West to conclude that *allâh* must be someone besides God.

For example, I was recently at an academic conference where one of the speakers was noting that each of the languages of Africa has an indigenous name for the Supreme Being, the Lord and Creator of the universe, and that this local name is used by the Christians in their worship and in their translations of the Bible.[4] Suddenly, however, he was struck with some doubt, so he qualified his remark by saying, "Well, at least everyone south of the Sahara has a name for God." He was uncertain whether the Muslims and Christians of northern Africa had a name for God! This doubt stemmed from claims he had read that

---

1 The author acknowledges with gratitude the helpful feedback received from a great many reviewers. A note on transliterations: All transliterations of foreign words are in lowercase, even if they are names, but when names are cited as borrowed into English, they are capitalized, as with "Allah."

2 J. Dudley Woodberry, "Contextualization among Muslims: Reusing Common Pillars," *International Journal of Frontier Missions* 13, no. 4 (1996): 173.

3 Arthur Jeffery, *The Foreign Vocabulary of the Qur'an* (Baroda, India: Oriental Institute, 1938), 66.

4 In point of fact, as Lamin Sanneh in *Translating the Message: The Missionary Impact on Culture* (Maryknoll, NY: Orbis, 1989), 181, points out, long-time Islamized language communities like Hausa and Fulani have "allowed *Allāh* to displace the god or gods of pre-Islamic times," with the result that some groups no longer even remember the name by which their ancestors invoked the Most High God.

allâh, the Arabic word for God, does not refer to the Lord and Creator of the universe but to some demon or idol, such as the ancient Semitic moon god *sīn*. Their poorly substantiated claims have left many Western Christians fearful of the term *allâh* and opposed to its use.[5] Some Western Christians have even removed the term *allâh* from translations of the Arabic Bible and from other materials.[6]

Dudley Woodberry, however, has long warned us about the dangers of such rejectionism. In an article entitled "When Failure Is Our Teacher: Lessons from Mission to Muslims," he made this observation:

> Many missionaries branded so-called Muslim forms of worship and religious vocabulary as wrong, without knowing that virtually all qur'anic religious vocabulary, including the name "Allah," and virtually all the forms of worship, except those specifically related to Muhammad, were used by Jews and/or Christians before they were used by Muslims.[7]

But when Muslims encounter Christian religious materials that have carefully avoided all mention of the name *allâh*, they often fear the materials are intended to lead them away from God. And if Western Christians "explain" to their Muslim friends that Muslims use the name *allâh* to invoke a demon or moon god, then the Christians lose all credibility. Besides these fears and follies, there is the simple fact that if we are speaking to people in their own language and yet reject the names they use to refer to God and the prophets, then we convey rejection of them personally. Such insults often prompt their rejection of our testimony before they have even considered it.[8] Consequently, those who believe these myths regarding the term *allâh* are doomed to failure as witnesses to Muslims. Of course, people who have lived closely with Muslims understand that Allah is their most cherished name for God, and a name that Christians use as well from Senegal to Indonesia. But some of them encounter opposition to its use from people in their supporting churches or in their home offices, people who have misconceptions about the term.

Christians who are unaccustomed to religious diversity are often confused by the fact that different monotheistic religions teach different conceptualizations of God, and some Christians even suppose that adherents of different religions are referring to different gods,

---

5 Opposition to use of this term in translations of the Bible is discussed and addressed in Kenneth J. Thomas, "Allah in the Translation of the Bible," *International Journal of Frontier Missions* 23, no. 4 (2006): 171–74.

6 An example is ArabBible, http://www.arabbible.com, which has published the Van Dyck Arabic Bible online with all mentions of *allâh* removed.

7 J. Dudley Woodberry, "When Failure Is Our Teacher: Lessons from Mission to Muslims," *International Journal of Frontier Missions* 13, no. 3 (July–September 1996): 122.

8 Rejection of the audience's language is just one part of a wider phenomenon of cultural denigration that characterizes polemical approaches. Unfortunately, such approaches tend to antagonize people and to harden them in their positions rather than to open them up to the love of God in Christ (see Heather J. Sharkey, "Arabic Anti-Missionary Treatises: Muslim Responses to Christian Evangelism in the Modern Middle East," *International Bulletin of Missionary Research* 28, no. 3 (2004): 98–104.

as if there were a pantheon to choose from. In the technical language of semantics, these people are confusing different "senses" (or "conceptions") with different "referents." The referent is the person or entity to which one is referring, who in this case is God. The sense encompasses the characteristics that are attributed to God in their conception of him. People can have different conceptions of the same referent. Even Christians differ among themselves in their conception of God.[9] A person's concept of God can change, but this does not happen simply by calling God a different name; it happens by grace when a person ponders the characteristics of God as he is presented in the Bible, and especially as he is revealed in the person of Jesus Christ. It happens when people hear the testimonies of believers, when they experience God's grace in their lives, when they apprehend God in their inner life, and when they receive illumination from the Holy Spirit.

There have been many articles that falsified erroneous claims about the Arabic name *allâh*. In one I showed the mistakenness of claims that *allâh* was ever the name of a moon god, and showed that the crescent symbol used in modern Islam does not come from an ancient moon-god religion but was a medieval symbol of Ottoman political domination.[10] Kenneth Thomas[11] followed up with an article showing that Arabic-speaking Jews, Christians, and Muslims have always referred to the one true God as *allâh*. Bob Cox[12] emphasized that Arab Christians call God *allâh*, and that the term is related linguistically to Hebrew terms for God. Imad Shehadeh,[13] director of an Arab Christian seminary, noted that the oldest extant Arab Christian translations of Scripture use *allâh*, and that this practice is documented from ancient times until the present. This fact was exemplified in the essays in David Thomas,[14] especially the one by Hikmat Kachouh.[15] Shehadeh noted the total lack of evidence that anyone ever used the term *allâh* as the name of a moon god. Quoting Montgomery Watt, he says the claim that "Christians worship God and Muslims worship Allah" is as sensible as saying "Englishmen worship God and Frenchmen worship Dieu." He goes on to say that "Muslims and Christians … believe in the same God as subject [but] the nature of God as conceived by Islam is not at all identical to the nature of God within the Judeo-Christian

---

9 See Baylor Institute for Studies of Religion, *American Piety in the 21st Century: New Insights to the Depths and Complexity of Religion in the U.S.* (Waco, TX: Baylor University, 2006), http://www.baylor.edu/content/services/document.php/33304.pdf. For a description of the main features of the biblical concept of God compared to features of Muslim concepts of God, see Rick Brown, "Muslim Worldviews and the Bible: Bridges and Barriers; Part 1: God and Mankind," *International Journal of Frontier Missions* 23, no. 1 (2006): 5–12.

10 Rick Brown, "Who Is 'Allah'?" *International Journal of Frontier Missions* 23, no. 2 (2006): 79–82.

11 Thomas, "Allah," 2006.

12 Bob Cox, "The Etymology of the Word 'Allah,'" *Seedbed* 20, no. 2 (2006): 14–17.

13 Imad Shehadeh, "Do Muslims and Christians Believe in the Same God?" *Bibliotheca sacra* 161, no. 641 (2004): 14–26.

14 David Thomas, ed., *The Bible in Arab Christianity* (Leiden: Brill, 2006).

15 Hikmat Kachouh, "The Arabic Versions of the Gospels: A Case Study of John 1.1 and 1.18," in Thomas, *The Bible,* 19–36. Kachouh reviews over fourteen independent traditions of Bible translation into Arabic, from the ninth century to the eighteenth, from Greek, Syriac, Coptic, and Latin source texts, and all of them use Allah as the name of God, as do all the modern translations.

faith."[16] The need, then, is for Muslims to encounter the nature of *allâh* as presented in the Bible.

These articles, however, have not assuaged the concerns of some who think that the term *allâh* has its origin as an Islamic invention or as a pre-Islamic demon or idol, and some people remain worried by the apparent similarity of the name *allâh* with that of the pagan goddess *allāt*.[17] So following Luke's example, it seemed good to me to investigate these things carefully, and to present in this essay detailed evidence relevant to what Dudley Woodberry wrote, namely that *allâh* was the term used by Arab Christians for the God of the Bible before the rise of Islam, and that it has its origin in the Aramaic term for God, which Jesus himself would have used. If so, then the term *allâh* is freer of pagan history than is the Hebrew word *ᵓel*, which was used by the Canaanites as the name of the chief deity of their pantheon,[18] or the English word "God," which comes from a generic term for middle-rank Teutonic deities.[19]

In what follows I present evidence that Christianity pervaded all parts of Arabia prior to the rise of Islam, that most Christian Arabs used Aramaic Scripture and liturgy in which God was called *alâh(â)*, that they borrowed this term into Arabic as *allâh*, and that even non-Christian Arabs identified *allâh* as the God of the Bible, the Supreme Being, who is Creator and Lord of all and above any other gods. I argue that in languages like Arabic where *allâh* is the normal term for God, its avoidance by Western Christians is unjustified. Similarly there is no reason to avoid calling our Lord Jesus Christ by his well-known Arabic epithet, *kalimat allâh*, the eternal "Word of God," incarnate as a man, the visible image of the invisible God, and the Lord and Savior of humankind.

---

16 Shehadeh, "Muslims and Christians," 26.

17 Except for geographical names and the word *ałłâh*, Arabic words have been transliterated in accord with DIN31635, which is identical to ISO 233 except for the long vowels. The exception in *ałłâh* is that the velarized "el" sound, which occurs uniquely in this word in Arabic, is represented on occasion with the "dark el" symbol *ł*, and the velarized (low-back) vowel sound that follows it is represented with the symbol *â*. The symbol *ā* is used in accord with convention to represent the normal long /a:/ vowel in Arabic, as in *ᵓilāh* "god." Thus the name of the supposed goddess is transliterated as *al-lāt*, which rhymes with "cat," whereas the name of God is transliterated as *al-łâh*, which rhymes with "law." Transliterations of Hebrew, Aramaic, and Syriac consonants are in accord with ISO 259, which is followed by the Society of Biblical Literature. The seven vowel qualities represented in the Tiberian system have been represented here as *i, ê, e, a, â, o, u,* and similarly for Syriac. Thus a low-back vowel sound has been represented in the same way in all of these languages, i.e., as *â* rather than as *ā*, to maintain uniformity of representation for this sound.

18 See Jack B. Scott, "אלה (*ᵓlh*) god, God," in *Theological Wordbook of the Old Testament*," vol. 1, eds. R. L. Harris, G. L. Archer, Jr., and B. K. Waltke (Chicago: Moody, 1980), 41–45. He notes that the word *ᵓēl* is used across the Semitic languages both as a generic term for a god and as an epithet for the most high God. The latter meaning is sometimes made explicit in Hebrew by use of the phrase *ᵓēl ᶜelyôn*.

19 See the entry for *gheu(ə)-* in Calvert Watkins, ed., *The American Heritage Dictionary of Indo-European Roots*, 2nd ed. (Boston: Houghton Mifflin, 2000). Some historical linguists think the English word "god" originates in the name of a Teutonic king named Gaut who was deified after his death.

1. Pre-Islamic Arab Christians Referred to God as *allâh*

In what follows I show first of all that Arabic-speaking Jews and Christians lived throughout Arabia for centuries before Islam. Therefore they would have had a term for referring to God. I then note the existence of pre-Islamic Christian names that incorporated the term *allâh*. I also show that ancient Arabic Bible translations and the Qur'an itself reflect pre-Islamic Jewish and Christian usage of *allâh* to refer to God. The conclusion is that pre-Islamic Jews and Christians referred to God as *allâh*.

Arabic-speaking Christians lived throughout Arabia for centuries before Islam

Although Muslim historians tend to emphasize the paganism and depravity of pre-Islamic Arabia, a more accurate description is that Judaism had been in Arabia from ancient times, with several Arab tribes having converted. This had been followed by a wave of conversions that made Christianity the dominant religion in much of Arabia. The town of Yathrib (later called "Medina") had long been settled and dominated by Jews.[20] In the south of the Arabian Peninsula, the populations of Najran and Yemen included large numbers of Jews and proselytes.[21] The witnesses of Pentecost included Arabic-speaking Jews and proselytes (Acts 2:11), and they would have taken the gospel back to their homelands. Paul made a trip to Arabia as well (Gal 1:17), probably the kingdom of Nabataea, meaning "the peoples of the towns and villages that existed throughout the whole region east of a line from Aleppo to the Dead Sea" and including Sinai.[22] So Judaism was present in Arabia before Christ was born, and the gospel entered Arabia soon after his resurrection.

The number of Christians quickly grew. Origen, the third-century theologian and commentator, gave theological lectures in Petra in 213 or 214 at the invitation of the governor.[23] Origen returned again to "Arabia" to correct Beryllus, bishop of Bostra,[24] and returned again in 246 to settle theological disputes in the Arab church synod, which was "of no small dimensions."[25] In the introduction to his Hexapla edition of the Old Testament, Origen wrote

---

20 R. B. Winder, "Al-Madina," in *The Encyclopaedia of Islam*, vol. 5, ed. P. J. Bearman (Leiden: Brill, 1999), 999–1007.

21 Irfan Shahid, *The Martyrs of Najrân: New Documents*, vol. 49 (Brussels: Société des Bollandistes, 1971).

22 J. Spencer Trimingham, *Christianity among the Arabs in Pre-Islamic Times* (New York: Longman, 1979), 72.

23 Erwin Preuschen, "Origen," in *New Schaff-Herzog Encyclopedia of Religious Knowledge*, vol. 8, ed. P. Schaff (Grand Rapids: Baker, 1953 [1908]), 268–73.

24 According to Eusebius, Beryllus had been teaching that Jesus was not preexistent. Eusebius, "Historia Ecclesiastica," in *The Ecclesiastical History*, vol. 2, Books 6–10, trans. J. E. L. Oulton (London: William Heinemann, 1932), 326. This was also a doctrine of the Ebionites, a Jewish Christian sect that might have influenced some of the Arab Christians.

25 According to ibid., 6:37, Origen sought to correct an unorthodox doctrine that had developed in Arabia, namely that the soul died with the body and was restored with it at the resurrection. It might be noted that a form of this doctrine survives in Islam, as does the view of Beryllus regarding the mere humanity of Jesus Christ.

that he consulted Bible translations in several languages, including Arabic.[26] This suggests that at least portions of the Old Testament had been translated into Nabataean Arabic by the third century, presumably using Nabataean script, although it is possible that it was a translation into Nabataean Aramaic. In AD 244, an Arab Christian, Philip the Arab, became emperor of Rome, indicating the degree to which Arab Christians were involved in the Roman Empire.[27] Their status in the church is indicated by the presence of Arab bishops at the Council of Nicaea in 325 and at the later councils as well.[28]

By the early fourth century, northern Arabia and the Arabian Gulf were ruled by the Christian Arab King Imrul Qays (AD 288–328), whose capital was the town of Hira in Mesopotamia and who ventured as far south as Najran. His Lakhmid dynasty of Christian Arab kings continued until 602, when their kingdom was destroyed by the Persians. According to Bellamy,[29] it was this Christian Lakhmid kingdom that fostered the development of the Arabic alphabet and the writing of classical Arabic poetry, some of which survives. He notes that according to Arab traditions, three Christian Arabs—Muramir, Aslam, and ᶜAmir—developed the Arabic alphabet from the Syriac alphabet and taught it to the people of the Lakhmid kingdom. It is said that the alphabet was brought from there to Mecca by Bishr ibn ᶜAbd al-Malik. Prior to this, the Meccans and South Arabians had used the Musnad alphabet, which was very different from the Syriac script, to which people in the rest of Arabia had become accustomed.

As for northwestern Arabia (modern-day Syria and Jordan), it was ruled by the Arab Nabataean kingdom. In 106 it was annexed to the Roman Empire and became the province of "Arabia." Then from 363 this whole region was ruled by a succession of Orthodox Christian Arab monarchs who were outside the empire but were federated with it. Māwīya, Queen of the Saracens, ruled AD 363–378, and she lobbied successfully for the appointment of Moses of Sinai as bishop of the Saracens.[30] Moses was famous for the miracles that attended his ministry. He evangelized the Bedouin and was later recognized as a saint. Māwīya was eventually succeeded by King Zokomos (Dhujᵓum), who converted to Christianity in

26 Alfred F. Beeston, "Background Topics," in *Arabic Literature to the End of the Ummayad Period*, eds. A. F. Beeston, T. M. Johnstone, R. B. Serjeant, and G. R. Smith (Cambridge: Cambridge University Press, 1983), 22.

27 See Eusebius, "Historia Ecclesiastica," 326, 6:34. This would make Philip the first Christian emperor. It is also recorded that Origen corresponded with him. Philip stopped the persecution of Christians, but he did not give favored status to Christianity, and he maintained certain imperial Roman religious traditions (Michael Grant, *The Roman Emperors: A Biographical Guide to the Rulers of Imperial Rome*, 31 BC–AD 476 (New York: Scribner's 1985), 155.

28 See "Arabia" in Charles Herbermann, ed., *Catholic Encyclopedia* (New York: Robert Appleton, 1913), 668, where it is reported that six bishops participated in the Council of Nicaea from the Roman province of "Arabia." There were also bishops from Mesopotamia, which was outside of the Roman Empire, and which would have included the Christian Arab Lakhmid kingdom.

29 James A. Bellamy, "The Arabic Alphabet," in *The Origins of Writing*, ed. W. M. Senner (Lincoln: University of Nebraska Press, 1990), 91–102.

30 John A. Langfeldt, "Recently Discovered Early Christian Monuments in Northeastern Arabia," *Arabian Archaelogy and Epigraphy* 5, no. 1 (1994): 53. The word "Saracen" is from the Arabic word *šarqiyīn* "Easterners." See the extensive footnotes in Langfeldt's article for his sources.

response to an answered prayer. Zokomos began a dynasty of Christian Arab kings,[31] with the result that, according to Langfeldt,[32] "The indigenization of Christianity among Arabian tribes proceeded rapidly from the late fourth and early fifth centuries." By the sixth century, the Christian Arab Ghassanid kingdom covered most of Syria, Palestine, and Jordan, and extended south almost to Yathrib (Medina). It competed with the Christian Arab Lakhmid kingdom in Mesopotamia and the Gulf.

As for the people in southern Arabia and Yemen, which the Romans called "Arabia Felix," they had converted to Judaism in the fourth century, but by the sixth century large numbers of them had become Christians. The church building in Najran was so large that their Jewish persecutors were able to force two thousand people inside before burning it down.[33] In Sanaa (Yemen), there was an even larger cathedral, built by King Abraha,[34] the site of which remains to this day.

Langfeldt provides further detail on the extent of Christianity:

> A brief summary of the 4th–7th centuries shows a great many of the tribal groupings in the areas now called Jordan, Syria and Iraq becoming Christian, including the Tanukhids, the Kalb confederation of tribes, the Tamim, the Taghlib, Banu Ayyub, and the majority of the tribes in the Hijaz, Nafud, Najd, Yamama and Bahrain sections of present day Saudi Arabia. A large portion of the Kinda tribe, having left the Yemeni Hadramawt in the 4th C and migrating to the Najd, by the 5th C, had forged alliances with the Maʾadd; this "federation" stretched from a point two day's journey east of Mecca, north and east to include the entire heart of central Arabia. As part of an alliance with the Byzantine Empire in the opening years of the 6th century the Kinda federation adopted Christianity. Many of the Yamama centering in the area of modern Riyadh were Christian (since the middle of the fourth century), as was the great tribal grouping of the Bakr ibn Waʾil in the central and eastern regions.
>
> South west Arabia had a strong Christian enclave in Najran where some 2,000 believers were massacred in AD 523. There was also a Christian presence in the Hijaz. In the process of hurling invectives at the Umayyad poet Jamil (ca. 701), a Christian of the ʿUdra tribe, Jaʾfar ibn Suraqa testified to Christian monks living in the Wadi al-Quara near Medina. The

31 Irfan Shahid, *Byzantium and the Arabs in the Fifth Century* (Cambridge, MA: Harvard University Press, 1989), 3–8.

32 Langfeldt, "Early Christian Monuments," 53.

33 Shahid, *Martyrs of Najrân;* René Tardy, *Najrân: Chrétiens d'Arabie avant l'Islam* (Beirut: Dar el-Mashriq, 1999); and Sebastian P. Brock and Susan Ashbrook Harvey, *Holy Women of the Syrian Orient*, updated ed., vol. 13 (Los Angeles: University of California Press, 1998), chapter 4, esp. 105.

34 Alfred Guillaume and Muhammad Ibn Ishaq, *The Life of Muhammad: A Translation of Isḥaq's* "Sīrat Rasūl Allāh" with Introduction and Notes (New York: Oxford University Press, 2002 [1955]), 21.

> ᶜUdra were Christianized, probably by the 5th century, and maintained that faith well into the Islamic period. There is evidence of Christian monasteries located at strategic locations on the caravan routes and functioning as caravanserai. The writings of al-Muqaddasi, al-Azraqi and other Islamic sources record a) a Christian cemetery (Maqbarat al-Nasara) and Christian stopping place (Mawqif al-Nasrani) in or very near Mecca, and b) the mosques or praying places of Maryam (Masajid Maryam) outside of Mecca on the road to Medina—quite likely a church turned mosque since the Qurᵓan accepts the Virgin Mary. In the Kaᶜba itself in 630 when Muhammad captured the city, paintings of the Virgin Mary and Jesus occupied positions on the pillars along with Abraham and the prophets. [35]

So as Langfeldt observes, Christianity dominated the Arab religious scene in most of pre-Islamic Arabia and was "the primary religious allegiance of the vast majority of the population," even after the rise of Islam.[36]

Daniel Potts concludes his two-volume history of *The Arabian Gulf in Antiquity* with a similar observation:

> As we have seen, Christianity was widespread both amongst the tribes of northern Arabia and in the settled communities along the coast.
>
> It is not incorrect to say that, in one sense, the Nestorian Church, for the space of over three centuries, united a region which secular rulers from Sargon to Šapur had never mastered so completely. [37]

So by the time Islam appeared Christianity was present throughout Arabia, and Christians dominated the major kingdoms into which Arabia was divided: Ghassanid, Lakhmid, Himyarite (Yemen), and Kindite (Southern Arabia). Christians had the weakest presence in the towns that fell outside these kingdoms, notably Mecca and Yathrib (Medina), the very places that gave birth to Islam. Yet the ᶜUdra tribe in Mecca was Christian, and in Yathrib (Medina) there were three or more Jewish tribes. Since Christianity was widespread across the various Arab tribes and Judaism was present as well, their name for the God of the Bible,

35 Langfeldt, "Early Christian Monuments," 53.

36 Ibid. It should not be thought, however, that Arab Christianity was uniform or even orthodox. Many of the Jews converted to Jewish Christianity of the Ebionite or Nazarene kind. Origen went there in 214 and 246 to correct theological abberations, such as a doctrine that the dead remain in the grave until the judgment. According to Epiphanious, writing in 375, some Christians in Arabia worshiped Mary as a goddess and made offerings to her (*Panarion* 79). In 381, after the ecumenical Council of Constantinople, the Roman emperor Theodosius expelled from all churches anyone who did not subscribe to the "Nicene faith," and many "heretics" moved to the Arabian kingdoms. The Qurᵓan agrees with most doctrines of Jewish Christianity and rejects doctrines of other Christian sects, but the distinct doctrines of Nicene Christianity are not even mentioned.

37 Daniel T. Potts, *The Arabian Gulf in Antiquity*, vol. II (Oxford: Clarendon, 1990), 353.

the Creator of the universe, would have been well known to all of the Arabs. In what follows we will discover what name they were using for God.

Pre-Islamic Christian names incorporated the term *allâh* in reference to God

There has been speculation that some of the pre-Islamic Arab churches would have developed an Arabic-language liturgy and lectionary in the fourth or fifth century. Irfan Shahid[38] entertains this as a likelihood. He affirms with confidence, however, that there was pre-Islamic Christian Arabic poetry, as does Kenneth Cragg.[39] Trimingham lists five of the poets by name.[40] These pre-Islamic Arab Christians would have had a name for God that they used when speaking Arabic; the poetry that survives from Nābigha al-Dhubyānī shows that he used the term *allâh*.

The hardest pre-Islamic evidence comes in the form of stone inscriptions that bear theophoric Arab names, i.e., Arabic names that incorporate a word for deity. The word one finds most often in the surviving inscriptions is *ʾlh*, pronounced [ałłâh][41] and sometimes the shortened or Hebraic form, *ʾl*.[42] There is no evidence for a significantly different term for God used in place of this, such as Greek *theos* or Hebrew *ʾadonai* or *elohîm*, although

---

38 Shahid, *Byzantium and the Arabs*, 528f.

39 Kenneth Cragg, *The Arab Christian: A History in the Middle East* (Louisville: Westminster John Knox, 1991).

40 Nābigha al-Dhubyānī (died AD 604), Jarīr ibn ʿAbd al-Masīḥ (died AD 580), Abu Duʾād al-Iyādī, Aws ibn Ḥajar, and Maimūn ibn Qais (a.k.a. al-ʾAʿshā, died AD 625). Trimingham, *Christianity among the Arabs*, 177, 201, notes that the poetry which survives does not focus on Christian themes.

41 Since doubled consonants were not usually marked in ancient Syriac and Arabic inscriptions, *ʾlh* could be pronounced with one el or two. Gonzague Ryckmans, *Les noms propres sud-sémitiques* (Leuven, Belgium: Universitaires, 1934–1935), vocalized them as *ilāh*, evidently under the influence of Wellhausen's thesis that henotheism developed later in history. Frederick V. Winnett in "Allah before Islam," *The Moslem World* 28 (1938), 247, objects to this view, presenting linguistic evidence for the pronunciation *allāh*: "Against this theory it may be urged that when we meet names like *W-h-b-ʾ-l-h* and *W-h-b-ʾ-l-h-y* in Nabataean no one doubts that the theophorous element is Allah. It cannot very well be *ilāh*, because the Nabataean word for God is *allāhā* which would require a final *alif* after the *ha* in the inscriptions. The Greek transliterations of these Semitic names are a further proof that the theophorous element should be read as Allah. If we admit that these names are Allah names when they appear in Nabataean, on what ground shall we deny them the same interpretation when they appear in Lihyanite or Thamudic?" When Arabic names are found in Greek texts and inscriptions, the letter *lambda* is doubled. This means the Arabic *lām* must have been pronounced with doubling, as *allâh*. For example, the common Arabic name وهب الله '*wahab allâh*' "Gift of God" is found written, as in Ancient Arabic, as *whbʾlh*, but in Greek as Ουαβαλλας *ouaballas*, showing that the *lām* was pronounced doubled at an early time. See also Antonin Jaussen and Raphaël Savignac, *Mission archéologique en Arabie*, vol. 4 (Paris: Leroux, 1914), 264, cited in Michael A. C. Macdonald, "Personal Names in the Nabataean Realm," *Journal of Semitic Studies* 44, no. 2 (1999): 275.

42 There is literary evidence for the pre-Islamic use of the phrase *al-ʾilāh* "the god" to designate the Supreme Being, but this does not appear in the pre-Islamic epigraphic evidence or in pre-Islamic names. Later, one does find the name *ʿabd al-ʾilāh* عبد الاله "servant of the god," meaning servant of the one who is truly God.

YHWH is found on occasion, probably as part of an Arab Jewish name.[43] Harding's[44] *Index and Concordance of Pre-Islamic Names and Inscriptions* includes the following observation: "A feature which emerges very clearly from these lists [of theophoric names] is the overwhelming popularity of ʾl, ʾlh." So while many inscriptions bore theophoric names that incorporated the names of pagan deities, there was an "overwhelming" number of theophoric names that incorporated *ʾlh* [ałłâh] and the shortened form *ʾl*. The widespread usage of these terms in the two centuries before Islam correlates with the well-documented spread of Christianity throughout most of Arabia that occurred during that same period.[45]

The Arabs used a number of scripts, but what we now call "Arabic" script was not developed until the fifth or sixth century. The earliest dated Arabic-language inscription in this "Arabic" script is the Zebed inscription. It was inscribed onto a shrine honoring a Christian martyr in AD 512, where the inscribed texts are in Greek, Syriac, and Arabic.[46] The Arabic text includes a name or statement in which God is referred to as *alâh*.[47] This

43 Jane Taylor in *Petra and the Lost Kingdom of the Nabataeans* (London: Tauris, 2001), 168, notes that among the seven thousand Nabataean inscriptions in the Sinai (mostly from the first and second centuries AD), none of the theophoric names mention traditional Nabataean deities. There are names incorporating *allâh*, as well as names with *ʾel* and even names with *baʿal* (which might mean the Canaanite god "Baal" but more likely has its normal meaning of "Lord" or "husband"). But she also notes the names *šmʾyw*, *ʿbdyw*, and *ʿabdʾhyw*, which appear to "relate to the worship of YHWH." In addition to Nabataea, in review of "Les religions arabes préislamiques," *Journal of the American Oriental Society* 72, no. 4 (1952): 178, Frederick V. Winnett (1952) cites epigraphic evidence in North Arabia for theophoric names that end with *-yah* (i.e., YHWH) as well as *allâh*. See "Review of *Les religions arabes préislamiques* by G. Ryckmans," *Journal of the American Oriental Society* 72, no. 4 (1952): 178. One notes that any or all of these names could be Jewish, including those with *baʿal*, and so they might belong to Jewish, Christian, or Jewish Christian Arabs.

44 G. Lankester Harding, *An Index and Concordance of Pre-Islamic Names and Inscriptions* (Toronto: University of Toronto Press, 1971), 907.

45 See Guillaume and Ibn Ishaq, *Life of Muhammad*, 18. It would be useful for someone to make a map of pre-Islamic Arab sites, correlating what is known of the distribution of Christians with the epigraphic evidence of theophoric names using *allâh*. This is complicated, however, by the fact that the documentation on inscriptions is spread over a large corpus, such that the list of relevant books and articles—K. A. Kitchen, *Documentation for Ancient Arabia, Part I: Chronological Framework and Historical Sources* (Liverpool: Liverpool University Press, 1994)—runs to 821 pages, and the index of names—Harding, *Index and Concordance*—runs to 943 pages.

46 For dates and literature, see Beatrice Gruendler, *The Development of the Arabic Scripts: From the Nabatean Era to the First Islamic Century according to Dated Texts* (Atlanta: Scholars, 1993). There is also an inscription on a church in Jabal Ramm which is thought to be from the fourth or fifth century, but it is not dated and does not include a word for God. There are two earlier Arabic inscriptions written in the Nabataean alphabet, namely the ʿEn ʿAvdat inscription of the second century AD and the Namarah funerary inscription of the Christian Arab King Imrul Qais of Hira, dated AD 328, but neither inscription includes a reference to deity. Earlier Arabic inscriptions exist, such as a first-century BC inscription in Musnad script at Faw, in southern Arabia, but they do not include the term *allâh* or any other reference to God. For a catalogue of early Arabic inscriptions and dialects, see Michael C. A. Macdonald, "Reflections on the Linguistic Map of Pre-Islamic Arabia," *Arabian Archaelogy and Epigraphy* 11, no. 1 (2000): 28–79.

47 Photographic plates are found in Adolf Grohmann, *Arabische paläographie II: Das schriftwesen und die lapidarschrift* (Vienna: Hermann Böhlaus Nochfolger, 1971), 6–8. The letter 'l' may have been pronounced doubled. The term *allâh* is found at the beginning of a list of names of Christian martyrs, but it is not clear if it is part of a name meaning "Help of God," or is a statement, "By the help of God." The spelling of *allâh* is phonetic, with the long second vowel indicated by an *alif*: *ʾlʾh* (Arabic script: الاه), which is normal for long vowels in Arabic. But elsewhere the term is spelled without marking the long vowel, probably because it is not marked in Jewish Aramaic and Christian Syriac.

shows that pre-Islamic Christians were using this term in reference to God in Arabic, just as they used *alâh(â)* to refer to God in Syriac.

This archaeological evidence is corroborated by historical sources as well. For example, a leader of the Christians who was martyred in Najran in AD 523 is said to have been ᶜAbdullah ibn Abu Bakr ibn Muhammad. Not only does he bear a theophoric name that means "servant of *allâh*," he is also said to have worn a ring that said "*allâh* is my Lord."[48] Similarly, when four of the leading pre-Islamic men of Mecca pledged to renounce idolatry, worship God alone, and seek the true religion, it was *allâh* whom they acknowledged, and three of them found *allâh* in Christianity.[49]

There is also evidence that henotheism had become widespread among the pagan Arabs, i.e., that they acknowledged that the God of the Bible was the Lord and Creator of the universe, while continuing to fear and appease lesser beings instead of God alone. This is reflected in the Qurʾan in verses like al-ᶜAnkabūt [29]:61,63, which speaks of pagan Arabs who refused the message of Muhammad:

> If indeed thou ask them who has created the heavens and the earth and subjected the sun and the moon (to his Law), they will certainly reply, "Allah." How are they then deluded away (from the truth)? … And if indeed thou ask them who it is that sends down rain from the sky, and gives life therewith to the earth after its death, they will certainly reply, "Allah!" Say, "Praise be to Allah!" But most of them understand not (Yusuf Ali).

For example, Muhammad's father was named ᶜAbdullah "servant of Allah," yet it seems that the one who named him, his father ᶜAbdul Muttalib, was a henotheist rather than a monotheist.[50]

In summary, there is epigraphic evidence that the pre-Islamic Arab Christians were using *allâh* as the name of God, and there is no evidence that they were avoiding this name and using some other name instead. As Cox[51] has noted, *allâh* is the only word in Arabic for God, it is cognate with the Hebrew and Aramaic terms used in the Bible, and it has been used by Arabic-speaking Jews and Christians to refer to God for as long as we have records.[52]

---

48 Guillaume and Ibn Ishaq, *Life of Muhammad*, 18.

49 Ibid., 98–103.

50 See ibid., 66–68.

51 Cox, "Etymology."

52 It might be noted that in proto-Hebrew, the word for a deity would also have been *ʾilāh* or *ʾelāh*, but long /ā/ vowels shifted to /o/ vowels in stressed syllables, resulting in the form *ʾeloh*. This is a common word for "god" in biblical Hebrew, as in Psalm 18:32 ("Who is god besides Yhwh"), although in Job and Proverbs 30 it is used as a name for God. In Aramaic the vowel shift was less pervasive and less pronounced, from a long low-front /ā/ vowel to a low-back /a/ vowel, written here as /â/. In some dialects this was pronounced [ɔ] as in British "ought" and later [o] as in "coda." In Arabic the word for "god" remained *ʾilāh*. To refer to the one true God in Arabic, the Aramaic word *ałâh* was used. At an early stage the "el" sound was doubled, resulting in the word *ałłâh*, but with either pronunciation the word was written as *ʾlh*, at least until the seventh century.

Arabic Bible translations reflect pre-Islamic Christian usage of *allâh* to refer to God

Bruno Violet[53] published a bilingual fragment of Psalm 78 [77 in LXX], discovered in Damascus, in which the Greek text is in one column and the parallel column contains an Arabic translation in Greek characters. Michael Macdonald,[54] a paleographer and an expert on Ancient Arabic, makes the following evaluation of this text:

> Following a detailed study of this text I am convinced that it is pre-Islamic. This is the most valuable text in Old Arabic so far discovered since the Greek transliteration seems to have been made with great care and consistency from an oral source, and thus is uncomplicated by the orthographic conventions of another script.[55]

In this fragment, the Greek term for God, *ho theos*, is found in verses 22, 31, and 59. It is translated there into Arabic as αλλαυ (= Arabic *allâh*) (where the Arabic /h/ has been transliterated with a Greek *upsilon*, as is the custom in this manuscript). This provides further evidence that pre-Islamic Arab Christians were using *allâh* to refer to God. One also notes that the Greek letter *lambda* is doubled; this demonstrates that the Arabic letter *lām* must have been pronounced double by this time as well. Given the practice in Ancient Arabic of not writing doubled letters twice or an internal /ā/ vowel at all,[56] this Greek evidence provides further support for Winnett's claim[57] that *ʾlh* in the epigraphic evidence was pronounced as *allâh*.

The New Testament or parts of it were translated many times into Arabic. Kachouh[58] has compared 210 different ancient and medieval translations of the Gospels, and he discerns among them 22 different translation traditions. The extant manuscripts date from the post-Islamic period, but there is evidence for pre-Islamic translations of the Gospel, although scholars disagree on the matter.[59] It is said that Waraqah ibn Nawfal translated a Gospel and

53 Bruno Violet, "Ein zweisprachiges Psalmfragment aus Damascus [A Bilingual Psalm Fragment from Damascus]," *Orientalistische litteratur zeitung* 4, no. 10 (1901): 384–403.

54 Michael C. A. Macdonald, "Ancient North Arabian," in *The Cambridge Encyclopedia of the World's Ancient Languages*, ed. R. D. Woodward (Cambridge: Cambridge University Press, 2004), 50.

55 In line with his general thesis, Sydney H. Griffith, in "The Gospel in Arabic," *Oriens Cristianus* 69 (1985): 134, had suggested an eighth century date.

56 Macdonald, "Personal Names," 271.

57 Winnett, "Allah before Islam," 247.

58 Hikmat Kachouh, personal correspondence, 2006. See Kachouh, *Arabic Gospels: A Classification, Description, and Textual Examination of the Arabic Gospel MSS of a Continuous Text* (Birmingham: University of Birmingham, 2007) http://syneidon.org.uk/Hikmat.htm.

59 Orientalist Anton Baumstark in "Der älteste erhaltene griechisch-arabische text von Psalm 110 (109) [The Oldest Preserved Greek-Arabic Text of Psalm 110 (109)]," *Oriens Christianus* 31 (1934), argued that the Gospel and Psalter were translated into Arabic prior to Islam. But Griffith in "The Gospel in Arabic," 166, disagreed, noting that since no dated Arabic manuscripts survive from the pre-Islamic period, "All one can say about the possibility of a pre-Islamic, Christian version of the Gospel in Arabic is that no sure sign of its actual existence has yet emerged." Griffith's judgment seems a bit too dismissive, however, because few

other portions of the Bible into Arabic in Mecca in the sixth century. Ibn Ishaq (died 761) wrote that in AD 570 one of the stones of the Kaᶜba was found to have writing on it, and the words he quotes are clearly taken from Matthew 7:16.[60] Irfan Shahid[61] presents evidence that before AD 520 the Christians of Najran had the Gospel in their language, meaning their dialect of Arabic, written in Musnad script. Trimingham[62] cites Michael the Syrian's twelfth-century *Chronicle* to the effect that John of Sedra, patriarch of Antioch, arranged in the early seventh century for "the first translation of the four Gospels" into Arabic for use by Muslim scholars. The patriarch's translation does not survive, except perhaps, for a passage from John that is "quoted" by Ibn Ishaq.[63]

Many translations were lost, largely due to the destruction of monasteries, but copies of many translations have survived and can be viewed in various libraries and museums. The following chart lists the principal ancient and medieval Arabic translations that I have examined,[64] showing the dates of the surviving manuscripts and the evident origin and source language of each translation.[65] The translations that appear to be earliest in origin are presented first.

---

manuscripts were dated in that period in any language, and in later manuscripts that do have a date, it is usually the date of copy that is noted rather than the date of the original translation.

60 Guillaume and Ibn Ishaq, *Life of Muhammad*, 86.

61 Shahid, *Martyrs of Najrân*, 249–50.

62 Trimingham, *Christianity among the Arabs*, 225.

63 For discussion of the quote in Ibn Ishaq, its relation to the Palestinian Syriac Lectionary, and its possible relation to the translation sponsored by John of Sedra, see Griffith, "The Gospel in Arabic," 137; Guillaume and Ibn Ishaq, *Life of Muhammad*, 104; and Alfred Guillaume, "The Version of the Gospels Used in Medina c. A.D. 700," *Al-Andalus* 15 (1950): 289–96. According to Michael, the Muslim scholars asked John of Sedra to use terminology in the translation that was acceptable to them; Michael says that John resisted, but the passage cited in Ibn Ishaq is clearly contextualized, in that "Father" is translated as *Rabb*, which then meant "Sustainer, Patriarch, Paterfamilias," whereas the extant Christian Arabic manuscripts use *Rabb* to translate κύριος, "Lord." Although Trimingham cites Michael's note as part of his argument that Arab churches used Aramaic liturgy and Scripture rather than Arabic, it is not clear what lies at the origin of this tradition. It could represent the first translation of the four Gospels into the Arabic language, or the first that used the new Arabic script, or the first authorized by the Syrian Orthodox Church, or the first for Muslim scholars, or the first that included the "Four Separated Gospels," in contrast with the *Diatessaron*. (The *Diatessaron* Gospel harmony had been the standard form of the Gospel in Syriac until the fifth century. The Arabic *Diatessaron* that survives today was translated or revised by Abdullah ibn al-Tayyib in the tenth century.)

64 I am grateful to Kenneth Bailey for loaning me photocopies and microfilms of many of these manuscripts so that I could duplicate them, and to Berend-Jan Dikken as well, for providing digital versions of some manuscripts. Microfilms of some manuscripts were ordered from libraries.

65 For discussions of provenance see Georg Graf, *Die Christlich-arabische literatur bis zur fränkischen zeit (ende des 11. jahrhunderts): Eine literarhistorische skizz* (Freiburg im Breisgau, Germany: Hercer, 1905); Bruce Metzger, "Early Arabic Versions of the New Testament," in *On Language, Culture, and Religion; in honor of Eugene A. Nida*, eds. M. Black and W. A. Smalley (The Hague: Mouton, 1974), 157–68; Kenneth E. Bailey, *Finding the Lost: Cultural Keys to Luke 15* (St. Louis: Concordia, 1989); and Griffith, "The Gospel in Arabic."

Name of Arabic Version	Source Language	Place of Origin	Date of Origin	Date of ms
The Palestinian Gospels[66]	Greek	Palestine	probably pre-Islamic	9th to 11th
The Elegant Gospels[67]	Syriac	uncertain	possibly pre-Islamic	10th
Vatican Arabic 13 Gospels[68]	Syriac	uncertain	possibly pre-Islamic	8th or 9th
Vatican Arabic 13 Epistles	Greek	uncertain	probably post-Islamic	9th
Treatise on the Triune God[69]		Palestine	776	9th
Mt. Sinai 151[70]	Syriac	Damascus	867	867
Vatican 71[71]	Greek & Syriac	Damascus	10th	11th
Abdullah ibn al-Tayyib[72]	Syriac	Baghdad	980	many

66 The Palestinian Gospels are also called "Mt. Sinai Family A." This family of manuscripts includes Sinai 72 (copied 897 AD), Sinai 16, Sinai 74, Vatican Borgia 95, and Berlin 1108 (copied 1046 AD). This version is quoted in some patristic quotations. A study of this version is presented in Anton Baumstark, "Die sonntägliche Evangelienlesung im vor-byzantinischen Jerusalem," *Byzantinische zeitschrift* 30 (1929–1930), 350–59. According to Griffith, "The Gospel in Arabic," 153–54, Baumstark shows that all of these manuscripts are marked for the Sunday lectionary readings according to a liturgy that was used in Palestine *prior* to the rise of Islam but *not afterwards*. He reasons, therefore, that this translation was made prior to the rise of Islam.

67 The Elegant Gospels survive in Leiden 2378 (OR 561), Vatican Arabic 17, and Vatican Arabic 18. The translation uses rhyming prose, with names and terms similar to those in the Qur'an. It translates both the Greek epithet *(ho) theos* "God" and the proper noun Kurios "LORD" as *al-lâh*. For a critical edition with textual commentary see Joséphine Ibrahim Nasr, تقديم مخطوط إنجيل لوقا وتحقيقه وفهرسته [Edition critique et étude de l'Evangile rimé de Saint Luc d'après les Manuscrits Vatican 17, 18 et Leiden Or. 2378 (=561), avec Index, etc.] (Beirut: Université Saint Joseph, 2000). She writes that Vatican 18 was copied in Cairo in AD 993, while Vatican 17 was copied in AD 1009. The date of the Leiden 2378 manuscript is unknown.

68 Kenneth E. Bailey and Harvey Staal in "The Arabic Versions of the Bible: Reflections on Their History and Significance," *Reformed Review* 36 (1982), 3–11, date Vatican Arabic 13 to the eighth or ninth centuries but say the translation itself is earlier. It is not a single work but a collection of works from five different scribes. The Gospel of Matthew appears to be the oldest. Bailey and Staal think it was translated from Greek, in part at least, but Syriac influence is evident as well. For example, it uses the Aramaic loanword *salīḥ* for "apostle" (as well as the term *ḥawārī* for "disciple"), and this is a characteristic of Syriac-based translations. Kachouh has compared Vatican Arabic 13 diligently with other versions and is convinced that the Gospels were translated from Syriac and the Epistles from Greek.

69 The so-called "Treatise on the Triune Nature of God" is not a Bible translation, but it contains many biblical quotations in Arabic. The terminology resembles the usage in the Qur'an and in the Elegant Gospels, but the wording is different from the Elegant Gospels. Part of the Treatise is found as part of Mt. Sinai 154 and was published in Margaret Dunlop Gibson, *An Arabic Version of the Acts of the Apostles and the Seven Catholic Epistles: With a Treatise on the Triune Nature of God* (London: Clay and Sons, 1899). Additional fragments of this treatise exist in other locations but have not been published.

70 Mt. Sinai Arabic 151 consists of the Acts and Epistles. It was written in Damascus at different stages. The Epistles of Paul are dated 867, and the dates of the Acts and other Epistles are assumed to be near that.

71 Other manuscripts similar to Vatican 71 include Vatican Arabic 467, Leiden 2376, Leiden 2377, and St. Petersburg AsiaticMuseum D226.

72 Ibn al-Tayyib translated Tatian's *Diatessaron* using the text of the Syriac Peshitta, and he produced a translation of the four Gospels with a running commentary that is still used today. Manuscripts can be found in many libraries.

Name of Arabic Version	Source Language	Place of Origin	Date of Origin	Date of ms
Alexandrian Vulgate[73]	Coptic	Alexandria	uncertain	1202
Mt. Sinai 76 (Sinai Family B)	Greek?	uncertain	uncertain	13th
Lectionary of Abdishu[74]	Syriac	Levant	1299	many

Figure 2: Surviving Arabic Translations of the New Testament or Portions Thereof

Years ago I tabulated the key terms used in these translations in a comparative fashion. They exhibit such a diversity of wording that one is forced to conclude that they represent several independent traditions of translation. In other words, the earliest ones seem to have been translated independently of one another by different churches in diverse locations from different source texts. One of the things they have in common, however, is that they all use the word *allâh* to refer to God. Since the Arab Christians were spread over a vast region and belonged to diverse and warring churches long before the rise of Islam, the fact that all of them used *allâh* to refer to God in the earliest surviving translations is an indication that the term *allâh* must have been in widespread use by Arab Christians in pre-Islamic times.[75]

More recently, Hikmat Kachouh has studied a newly discovered Arabic manuscript of the Gospels. He shows that it represents a translation made from a Greek text whose unique text type lies between Sinaiticus and Beza.[76] Since it is highly unlikely that a translator would base his work on a source text that was no longer in use, and since by the sixth century the Byzantine/Syrian text type of the Gospels had become the standard in the Middle East and had replaced the previous text types, this Arabic translation must almost certainly have been made before then, at a time prior to Islam. Since the translation uses *allâh* for the name of God, it is another witness to the usage of that term by Arabic-speaking Christians.

The Qur'an reflects pre-Islamic Christian usage of *allâh* to refer to God

Prior to his mission, Muhammad interacted with a number of Arabic-speaking Christians and Jews, notably the Jordanian monk Bahira[77] and later Waraqah ibn Nawfal, who was an

73 The Alexandrian Vulgate is represented in Vatican Coptic 9 (Coptic and Arabic). It became the normative Arabic translation of the New Testament in Egypt. A later version was printed in Rome in 1591, and afterwards in the Paris and London Polyglots.

74 This Lectionary of Abdishu ("servant of Jesus") is translated in rhyme. It was widely used in the Levant.

75 It is not known when the first Jewish translations of the Bible were made into Arabic, but ancient fragments survive that use the pre-Islamic spelling of *allâh* with one el letter, as אלה. The principal medieval Arabic Jewish versions were made in the tenth century by Saadia Gaon and by the Karaites. They used *al-lâh*, sometimes written in Hebrew script as אללה, to translate both *(hâ-)elohîm* "God" and YHWH. Meira Polliack, *The Karaite Tradition of Arabic Bible Translation: A Linguistic and Exegetical Study of Karaite Translations of the Pentateuch from the Tenth and Eleventh Centuries C.E.* (Leiden: Brill, 1997).

76 Hikmat Kachouh, "Sinai Ar. N.F. Parchment 8 and 28: Its Contribution to Textual Criticism of the Gospel of Luke," *Novum Testamentum*, 50/1 (2008), 28–57.

77 Guillaume and Ibn Ishaq, *Life of Muhammad*, 89–91.

older cousin of Muhammad's wife Khadija and lived in Mecca.[78] According to Fr. Joseph Qazzi, Waraqah was an Ebionite cleric who groomed Muhammad for his mission, including instruction in the Torah and the Gospel of the Hebrews.[79] Muhammad also attended lectures by an unnamed Christian teacher near Mecca.[80] So he would have been immersed in the religious terminology of Christian Arabs of that region. After the commencement of his mission, Muhammad often debated with Jews and Christians, including a delegation of Christians from Najran. The participants in such discussions must have used mutually intelligible names for God. Some of the Qurʾanic prophecies are addressed to Christians, repeatedly declaring the Qurʾan to be a "confirmation" in Arabic of the previously revealed Book, in which there is "no doubt."[81] In other words, the Qurʾan says it is reiterating what the Bible says about God and the prophets. It does not present itself in opposition to God or the Bible but as the final part of a heavenly book that includes the Jewish and Christian Scriptures. Such a claim would not have been possible if the Qurʾan had been proclaiming in *allâh* a different god or if he had been using radically different terminology from that used in the Arab Christian tradition of that region.

Some Western scholars argue that many of the Meccan suras are based on hymns and poetry of the pre-Islamic Arab Christian tradition. This is based in part on the presence of Syriac words that were used by Christians but were not used or understood by non-Christian Arabs. Luxenberg[82] and Lüling[83] show that when the words are interpreted in accord with their meaning in Syriac, it is possible, with some further editing, to recover fragments of Christian hymns and poetry. It is also based on similarities between pre-Islamic poetry

---

78 The Hadith (*Sahih al-Bukhari*, volume 9, book 87, number 111) and *Kitab al-Aghani* state that Waraqah ibn Nawfal, the cousin of Muhammad's wife Khadijah, was a Christian who studied the Bible and who translated a Gospel into Arabic. Such an activity would suggest that Muhammad had access to Christian Arabic terms for God.

79 See Joseph Qazzi, *The Priest and the Prophet: The Christian Priest, Waraqa ibn Nawfal's Profound Influence upon Muhammad, The Prophet of Islam*, ed. David Bentley, trans. Maurice Saliba (Los Angeles: Pen Publishers, 2005). Ebionite Christians derived from early Jewish Christianity. They rejected Paul, obeyed the Torah, and used a single Gospel, based on Matthew, as their only New Testament Scripture. They rejected the Trinity and regarded Jesus as human rather than the incarnation of God. Muhammad's teachings continued this doctrinal tradition. For a discussion of Jewish Christianity in Arabia, see Shlomo Pines, *The Jewish Christians of the Early Centuries* (Jerusalem: Central Press, 1966).

80 The usual speculation is that this teacher was Bahira, as noted in Thomas Patrick Hughes, *A Dictionary of Islam* (New Delhi: Asian Eductional Services, 2001 [1885]), 30:

> Sprenger thinks that Baḥīrā remained with Muhammad, and it has been suggested that there is an allusion to this monk in the Qurʾan, Surah xvi. 105 [103]: "We know that they say, 'It is only a man who teacheth him.'" Ḥusain the commentator says on this passage that the Prophet was in the habit of going every evening to a Christian to hear the *Taurāt* and *Injīl*.

81 Sura Yunus [10]:37.

82 Christoph Luxenberg, *Die syro-aramäische lesart des Koran: Ein beitrag zur entschlüsselung der Koransprache*, 2nd ed. (Berlin: Verlag Hans Schiler, 2004).

83 Günter Lüling, *A Challenge to Islam for Reformation: The Rediscovery and Reliable Reconstruction of a Comprehensive Pre-Islamic Christian Hymnal Hidden in the Koran under Earliest Islamic Reinterpretations* (Delhi: Motilal Banarsidass, 2003).

and verses of the Qurʾan, as shown by Abul Kasem.[84] Lüling[85] states the thesis of his book quite forcefully: "The text of the Koran as transmitted by Muslim Orthodoxy contains, hidden behind it as a ground layer and considerably scattered throughout it (together about one-third of the whole Koran text), an originally pre-Islamic Christian Text." It might be noted that medieval Christian sources claim that parts of the Qurʾan were written by the Nestorian monk Bahira.[86] If many of the Meccan suras were indeed drawn from Christian poetry, then their terminology, including the name *allâh*, would seem to have its origin in Christian Arab sources. A more likely explanation, however, is that the apparent Aramaic loanwords and other biblical terms were simply the normal Arabic religious terminology as used by Waraqah ibn Nawfal and other Christians and Jews in Mecca. They are found, for example, in poetry quoted from Jews and Christians in Ibn Ishaq's *Life of Muhammad*.

In later stages of his mission, the Prophet of Islam was engaged in disputation with Christians of diverse views. There are a number of passages in the Qurʾan that cite these disputes. Some of these passages quote statements made by the Christians, and the Christians are quoted as using the term *allâh*. Examples include their claim that "*allâh* is Jesus" (al-Māʾida [5]:17), that Christians are "sons of *allâh*" (al-Māʾida [5]:18), and that Jesus is a "son of *allâh*" (at-Tawba [9]:30). Nowhere in the Qurʾan is there any indication that Arab Christians and Jews referred to God by a name different from those used in the Qurʾan. All of the disputation passages reflect situations in which the same God is in view and is referred to in the same basic ways.

In light of this evidence from inscriptions, historical documents, and Arabic translations of the Bible, we can conclude that *allâh* was the term used by pre-Islamic Jewish and Christian Arabs to refer to God.[87] In the next section I will argue that Jews and Christians introduced this term themselves into Arabic from Aramaic.

---

84 Abul Kasem, "Who Authored the Qurʾan?" (Sydney, 2005), http://www.islam-watch.org/AbulKasem/WhoAuthoredQuran/who_authored_the_quran.htm.

85 Lüling, *Challenge to Islam*, 1.

86 A. Abel, "Baḥīrā," in *The Encyclopaedia of Islam*, vol. 1, ed. P. J. Bearman (Leiden: Brill, 1999), 921–23.

87 Christians in Yemen and other parts of southern Arabia also called God *raḥmān-an*, which equals northern Arabic *al-raḥmān*, but this was in reference to God as the Father. In AD 541, King Abraha, the Christian ruler of Yemen and southern Arabia, placed an inscription on the dam at Marib (in Musnad script) that began with an expression of the Trinity: "By the power and grace of the *Raḥmān* and his Christ and the Holy Spirit." Académie des Inscriptions et Belles-lettres, *Corpus Inscriptionum Semiticarum; Pars Quarta: Inscriptiones Himyariticas Et Sabœas Continens* (Paris: Académie des Inscriptions et Belles-Lettres, 1911), fig. 541, 278. Abraha also placed an inscription on a cliff at Mureighan that begins "by the power of the *Raḥmān* and his Christ" (Wickens et al. 1954). See A. G. M. Wickens, Alfred F. Beeston, and J. Daniels, "Notes on the Mureighan Inscription," *Bulletin of the School of Oriental and African Studies,* 16/2 (1954), 389–394.
The Jewish Aramaic term *raḥmân-â*, רחמנא, was a common epithet for God among Jews, and one finds Jewish Arabic inscriptions in South Arabia that use this term (Abdallah 1987), so this is the evident source of the Arabic term. See Y. M. Abdallah, "The Inscription CIH 543: A New Reading Based On The Newly-Found Original," in Christian Robin and Mohammad Bafaqih (eds.), *Sayhadica: Recherches Sur Les Inscriptions De l'Arabie Préislamiques Offertes Par Ses Collègues Au Professeur A.F.L. Beeston* (Paris: Geuthner, 1987), 4–5. The root *rḥm* means "womb," and *raḥmān* describes a male who is compassionate like a father.
The Aramaic term *raḥīm-â* means "beloved one." It is possible that the term *raḥīm* was used by Christians in Southern Arabia to refer to Jesus as God's Beloved and the bearer of his love. In that case the *basmala* might

2. The Term *allâh* Is Most Likely Derived from the Aramaic Word for God, *alâh*

Dudley Woodberry stated that the term *allâh* is derived from Syriac, which was the form of Aramaic commonly used in literature and Scripture in the Middle East from the fourth to the ninth centuries. (Forms of Aramaic had been the lingua franca for centuries, but Syriac took on the role of a literary language.) Kenneth Thomas[88] supports Woodberry's claim with the observation that "Western scholars are fairly unanimous that the source of the word Allah probably is through Aramaic from the Syriac *alâhâ*." Arthur Jeffery[89] wrote that "there can be little doubt" about this, and F. V. Winnett,[90] an expert in Ancient Arabic, came to the same conclusion. Syriac-speaking Christians, most of whom speak Arabic as well, have had the same opinion, namely that the Arabic term *allâh* is a loanword from Syriac, and Imad Shehadeh[91] has supported the argument from the perspective of an Arab Christian scholar. But since this statement runs contrary to the claims of both Muslim tradition and anti-Muslim polemicists, it seemed worthwhile to see if there was compelling evidence for it, and that is what follows.

Aramaic was the language of scripture and liturgy for most Arab Christians

For most of Arabia, the principal literary language was Aramaic, whether in Syriac script, Nabataean script, or others. From what we know of Jewish practice in the sixth century, the Scriptures would have been read aloud in Hebrew, followed by recitation of an Aramaic translation of the passage and perhaps one into Arabic. (This practice was later codified into written triglot versions of the Jewish Bible.) As for the Arab Christians, although some of those in northwestern Arabia were Greek Orthodox, the historical records indicate that many or most of the Arab Christians used Scriptures in Syriac, a variety of Aramaic.

Most of the common-era pre-Islamic inscriptions found in Arabia were written in varieties of Aramaic, although there are also inscriptions in Greek, Arabic, and South Arabic. When the Kaᶜba was being demolished and rebuilt in AD 605, five years prior to the beginning of Muhammad's mission, an Aramaic inscription was found on the foundation cornerstone of

be derived from an originally Christian formula that meant "in the name of God, the Compassionate One and the Beloved One and the Holy Spirit." No evidence, however, survives to verify or falsify this speculation.

88 Thomas, "Allah," 171.

89 Jeffery, *Foreign Vocabulary*, 66.

90 Winnett, "Allah before Islam," 247.

91 Shehadeh, "Muslims and Christians."

the Kaᶜba.[92] (In AD 570 the words of Matthew 7:16 had been found on another stone, but it is not recorded whether it was in Aramaic or Arabic.)[93]

A great many pre-Islamic Aramaic (and Greek) inscriptions survive until today in Arabia, and many of them include names that are Arabic in form although written in Greek or Syriac scripts. So the Arabs were obviously using these languages for literary purposes. One of the Syriac scripts, Nabataean, was used by the Arabs of northwestern Arabia in their Aramaic inscriptions, and it is thought that this script contributed to the later development of the Arabic script by Christians in Mesopotamia.[94]

In Aramaic, God is called *alâh-â*, where the final *-â* is removable. It is the same word that our Lord Jesus would have used when speaking Aramaic. It is found in the Aramaic portions of Daniel and Ezra, in the Jewish Aramaic translations of the Old Testament (Targums), and in the Syriac Aramaic translation of the whole Bible. It is cognate with the corresponding Hebrew term *elōh*.

Many Aramaic names and terms were borrowed into Arabic in the pre-Islamic period

As one would expect, when speakers of Arabic wanted to refer to biblical concepts and names of biblical personages, they often borrowed them from the language in which they were hearing them, meaning Aramaic, Greek, and in some places Ethiopic. Woodberry[95] cites a number of key religious terms that were borrowed into Islam from Christian usage, and the work of Jeffery[96] on this topic is well known. As with loanwords in general, these words were made to conform to the sound patterns of Arabic, which used triconsonantal roots and had only three vowel qualities. For example, Greek *diabol-os* "devil" became *iblīs*, Greek and Aramaic *euangeli-on* "Gospel" became *ingīl* (and later pronounced *injīl*), and Aramaic *sâtân-â* "Satan" became *saytān*, later pronounced *šaytān* and *šētān*. Note that when words were borrowed from Aramaic into Arabic, the word-final suffix *-â* was regularly dropped. This suffix had originally been a definite article in Aramaic, but by the fourth century it had lost this function in most varieties and had become redundant. So Aramaic words like *alâh-â* were usually borrowed into Arabic without the suffix, i.e., as *alâh*. Given the prevalence of Judaism and Christianity in Arabia, the term *alâh-â* would have been well-known, and one

92 According to Ibn Ishaq's biography of the Apostle of Islam (Guillaume and Ibn Ishaq, *Life of Muhammad*, 85–86), when the walls of the Kaᶜba were demolished in preparation for rebuilding it and roofing it, the builders found a Syriac inscription on the cornerstone. A literate Jew read it to them as follows: "I am Allah the Lord of Bakka [an earlier name for Mecca]. I created it on the day that I created heaven and earth and formed the sun and moon, and I surrounded it with seven pious angels."

93 Guillaume and Ibn Ishaq, *Life of Muhammad*, 86.

94 See Bellamy, "Arabic Alphabet." While it is widely held that the Nabataeans spoke Arabic as their mother tongue, Macdonald in "Reflections," 47, suggests that only those of northern Arabia (modern-day Syria) spoke Arabic, while those of Petra and the Sinai might have spoken Aramaic.

95 Woodberry, "Contextualization among Muslims," 173–74.

96 Jeffery, *Foreign Vocabulary*.

would expect them to have Arabicized it by dropping the final -*â* vowel. Further evidence for this can be found in its pronunciation, which is unusual for Arabic.

The Arabic name for God has the low-back vowel and darkened "el" sound of its Aramaic counterpart

Standard British and American pronunciations of English include both clear els and dark els, [l] and [ɫ], the choice depending on their position in the syllable or on the vowel that follows. (Irish, Welsh, and Minnesotan varieties of English have only clear els, and Australian English has only dark els.) The difference is that the dark el is "velarized," meaning it is pronounced with the center of the tongue depressed and the back of the tongue raised towards the velum. The dark el can be heard in "pill," which contrasts with the clear el in "lip." Usually the clear el occurs at the beginning of a syllable and the dark el at the end. In American pronunciation either el can be found between two vowels, such that "elicit" has a clear el and "illegal" has dark els. More importantly for our purposes, the el is dark if it is followed by a low-back vowel, as in the American pronunciation of "ought" [ɒt] (British [ɔt]). This vowel depresses the center of the tongue and moves the back of the tongue towards the velum, with the result that the el in "law" is darkened and the word is pronounced [ɫɒ], with a dark el.

The el sound in Aramaic, written with the letter *lâmad*, is normally clear, but it is velarized to a dark el if it is followed by the vowel *zqâpâ*.[97] This is a slightly rounded, low-back vowel that was pronounced [ɒt] or [ɔt], depending on the dialect. Thus the Syriac word for God is pronounced as [aɫâhâ], where [ɫ] represents the dark el sound and [â] equals the low-back vowel sound [ɒ]. The first vowel in this word is called *ptâḥâ* in Syriac. It sounds something like the vowel in English "map."[98]

Classical Arabic has only three distinctive vowel qualities, although it distinguishes two vowel lengths. It has the *ptâḥâ* vowel, which it calls *fatḥa*, but it does not have the *zqâpâ* vowel.[99] The el sound in Classical Arabic, written with the letter *lām*, is always clear, never dark. The one exception is the word for God, which is pronounced [aɫɫâh]. This one word has both the dark el and the low-back vowel sound that is found in the Syriac pronunciation [aɫâh(â)]. This contrasts with the Arabic word *ʾilāh* "god," which has a clear el and a low-front vowel. As Shehadeh[100] points out, Arabic does not have a vowel with the "ought" sound of the Syriac *ptâḥâ* in *alâh(â)*, and the only reasonable explanation for its presence

97 This velarization of *lâmad* is confirmed in personal correspondence from Dr. Abdul-Massih Saadi, professor of Syriac and Arabic at the University of Notre Dame. This vowel is called *qâmets* in the Tiberian system, but since then it has split and merged with *pataḥ* and *ḥolem*.

98 In Syriac script *alâhâ* is written as ܐܠܗܐ. In the Western Syriac system of vowel diacritics, the *ptâḥâ* is represented by a Greek alpha and the *zqâpâ* by a Greek omicron. It seems that Western Syriac *zqâpâ*, Hebrew/Aramaic *qâmets*, and Greek *omicron* had a pronunciation at that time like the rounded low-back vowel sound in the British pronunciation of "law," while in Eastern Syriac, the *zqâpâ* was unrounded, like the American pronunciation of "law."

99 Although Arabic has only one low vowel, the *fatḥa*, it can sound somewhat like the Syriac *zqâphâ* vowel if it follows a velar or pharyngeal consonant. So once the dark el has been learned, it is quite natural to follow it with a back-low variety of *fatḥa*.

100 Shehadeh, "Muslims and Christians," 19.

in *ałłâh* is that the vowel was borrowed from Syriac along with the word *alâh(â)*, "making the second vowel in 'Allah' unique." Since the Syriac word *ałâhâ* would have been well-known to the Arabs and used by them when speaking Syriac, it would have been natural for them to use it in Arabic as well, in an Arabicized fashion. The presence of this Syriac vowel sound in the second syllable of the Arabic word *ałłâh* is compelling evidence that the Syriac word *ałâhâ* was borrowed into Arabic as *ałłâh*.

It is normal for words to undergo some alteration when they are borrowed into another language. An obvious alteration in this case is that the el sound in *ałłâh* is doubled, whereas it is not doubled in Syriac. This suggests that when monolingual Arabs heard the dark el that had been borrowed into Arabic, they perceived it as longer than their own clear el and pronounced it as doubled. This lengthening of dark el happens in British and American English as well, although this is due in part to the position of the el relative to the syllable. For example, the dark el sound in "Bill" and "Phil" is longer in duration than the clear el sound in "billet" and "Philip."

There is historical evidence for the doubling of the letter *lām* in *allâh*

In Arabic, as in other Semitic dialects, if a consonant in a word is pronounced doubled, it is still written just once. In manuscripts the doubling is sometimes marked with a diacritic called the *shadda*, but not in inscriptions, especially ancient inscriptions. In the Zebed inscription there is a single letter *lām* in the word for God, but this does not reveal to us whether it was pronounced doubled at that time or not. Evidence for doubling can be found, however, in ancient Greek transliterations in which the Greek letter *lamda* is written twice. In the Greek-script Arabic translation of Psalm 78 [77 in LXX], the Greek term for God, ο θεός, is translated into Arabic as αλλαυ, showing that the el sound was pronounced long. In contrast the Arabic phrase *al-ʾilāh* "the god" is written without doubling the *lamda*, as ελ ιλευ (Ps 78:56). Note that this spelling indicates the difference in vowel quality as well, ε versus α. The doubled el sound is also indicated in some pre-Islamic Arabic theophoric names written in Greek characters, such as ουαβαλλας, which equals *wahab ałłâh*, "Gift of God."

With time, the doubled el sound on the *lām* was reinterpreted as two distinct letters, the first one belonging to a definite article, *al-*. Thus *ałłâh* was reinterpreted as consisting of two parts: *al-łâh*. As Shehadeh[101] points out, in dialogue with Christoph Heger, this reinterpretation of *lām* happened with other loanwords as well, such as the name Alexander, which was reinterpreted as *al-iskander*.

Since the *l* of the definite article *al-* is always written separately in Arabic, this resulted in the letter *lām* in *ałłâh* being written twice, with the first *lām* belonging to the definite article. In other words, the spelling of the term changed from اله to الله both pronounced [ałłâh]. This process of reinterpreting and respelling the *lām* as a definite article can be seen in some of the early inscriptions. In the Zebed inscription of AD 512 the word *ałłâh* is written with a single *lām*. In a post-Islamic inscription on a tomb in Cyprus, dated AH 29 (AD 649), *ałłâh*

101 Ibid., 19–20.

is still being spelled with one written *lām*, as found in the word بسمله "in the name of God."[102] In a slightly later inscription, a prayer dated AH 46 (AD 666), the text begins by addressing God in the vocative as *ał-łâhumma*, "O God," spelled with two *lāms* (اللهم), yet when the supplicant writes his own name, *ᶜabdułłâh*, which means "servant of God," he spells it the old way, with one *lām*: عبد اله.[103] Later inscriptions use a doubled *lām*.

This same process is seen in manuscripts of Jewish Arabic Bible translations. In fragments of an ancient Hebrew-Aramaic-Arabic triglot that were preserved in the Cairo Genizah, the name of God was translated with one *lamed* as אלה *ałłâh*, but in the Bible translations done by Saadia Gaon and others in the tenth century the *lamed* was written twice, as אללה *ał-łâh*.[104] So we can see a progression in Jewish sources from Aramaic אלהא *ałâhâ* to early Judeo-Arabic אלה *ałłâh* to classical Judeo-Arabic אללה *al-łâh*.

This reinterpretation of *ałłâh* as *ał-łâh* was most likely prompted by an analogy with the Arabic tradition of using epithets to refer to deities, since these epithets usually begin with the definite article, *al-*.[105] For example, the so-called "ninety-nine beautiful names of God" are all epithets; each of them begins with the definite article *al-* and continues with a noun that indicates some characteristic of God. Examples are *al-quddūs* "the Holy One" and *al-khāliq* "the Creator." Some of the traditional pagan deities had names that were epithets rather than proper nouns. The goddesses *al-lāt* and *al-ᵓuzzā*, for example, are named with epithets meaning "the kneader" and "the powerful (female)," respectively. This tradition of using epithets for divine names would naturally incline people to reinterpret *ałłâh* as *ał-łâh*, i.e., as the definite article *al-* plus a noun *łâh*.

This resegmentation of *ałłâh* into *ał-łâh* made *łâh* a noun and the source of further lexical derivations. It also raised the question of what *łâh* meant. On this matter the Arab philologists were perplexed. According to D. B. MacDonald[106] and Arthur Jeffery,[107] some ten different derivations were suggested, most notably a derivation from the root *LYH*, meaning "to be lofty." A few scholars said the term *ałłâh* was actually a loanword from Syriac, but this was rejected by most Muslim clerics. They preferred the theory that *ałłâh* has always been God's name and that this is why it was used in Aramaic as well. In the end, the explanation that was adopted by many was that *łâh* was a special word that denotes the very essence of God, his unique and eternal, divine nature, whereas the other ninety-nine epithets denote

---

102 Grohmann, *Arabische paläographie* II, 71.

103 Ibid., 124.

104 See for example, the translation of Exodus 29:39 in the Cairo Geniza manuscript Taylor Schechter B1.17, in which YHWH is translated as אלה.

105 By "epithet" I mean a common-noun phrase that functions like a name, i.e., it is conventionally used for referring to a unique referent, even though it is not a proper noun. In the Greek New Testament, for example, *ho kurios* "the Lord" and *(ho) christos* "Christ/ the Messiah" are common epithets for Jesus. In the Hebrew Old Testament, *adonâi* "my lord," which is translated into English as "the Lord," is an epithet for God, as is *qdosh yisrâᵓēl* "the Holy One of Israel." In Arabic, *kalimat ałłâh* "the word of God" is a well-known epithet for Jesus.

106 D. B. MacDonald, "Ilāh," in *The Encyclopaedia of Islam*, vol. 3, ed. P. J. Bearman (Leiden: Brill, 1999), 1093–94.

107 Jeffery, *Foreign Vocabulary*, 66.

mere characteristics of God. And *łâh* did indeed gain this meaning. Christian theologians then derived from *łâh* the term *lāhūt* "the divine nature, the Godhead" and the term *lāhūtiyya* "theology." But unlike the definite article, the *al* in *ałłâh* is inseparable. Normally the definite article is omitted after *yā*, but this does not happen with *ałłâh*. One says *yā ałłâh*, not *yā łâh*. This shows that *ałłâh* functions as a single word rather than an epithet, just as it does in Aramaic, and is basically the same word. Nestorian Christians spread the Aramaic form of the name eastwards as far as India and China, and with the spread of Islam, the Arabic form was disseminated even wider.

3. The Term *ałłâh* Is Not a Contraction of *al-ʾilāh* as Some Authors Have Suggested

It is often claimed that Arabic *ałłâh* is simply a contraction of *al-ʾilāh*, "the god." The evidence given for this is that both words begin with the definite article *al-*, and both have the letters *lām* and *hāʾ*, with a long vowel between them. In the previous section, however, I explained that the el sounds are not the same; they are different, as are the two vowels. In addition, the word *ʾilāh* begins with an initial radical consonant, the glottal stop *alif muhammaza*, whereas the word *łâh* does not. Since the meaning and identification of an Arabic word depend on the radicals of its root, such a deletion is problematic. As Shehadeh[108] notes, "This popular view [of contraction] does not explain the elimination of the second syllable *ʾel* (or *ʾil*), which is the most important in *al-ʾilah*, where *ʾel* or *ʾil* is the Semitic word for God since time immemorial." If this were a common process, then the root might be recoverable, but to my knowledge there is no evidence of such a process in classical Arabic, one in which an initial glottal stop radical of a noun is deleted, along with its vowel, following the definite article *al-*. So although these two phrases seem similar in English transcription, they are significantly different in Arabic.

One of the reasons polemicists make this claim is so they can then make the additional claims that (1) *al-ʾilāh* could designate any particular "god," including pagan gods, and that (2) *ałłâh* was a contraction of *al-ʾilāh* and therefore *ałłâh* could designate a pagan god.[109] These claims, however, have never been substantiated. For the first, there is a lack of clear evidence that *ałłâh* was ever used as a substitute for *al-ʾilāh* "the god." If *ałłâh* were simply a contraction *al-ʾilāh*, then one would expect to find the contraction in contexts where *al-ʾilāh* is used in its normal, common-noun functions, such as anaphora or as a classifier or as part of a restrictively modified noun phrase. An example of anaphoric usage is Jonah 1:6: "What do you mean, you sleeper? Arise, call out to your god! Perhaps the god will give a thought

108 Shehadeh, "Muslims and Christians," 18.

109 To my knowledge, these views were first promulgated by Julius Wellhausen in *Reste Arabischen heidentums* (Berlin: Reimer, 1897), 218ff. They are consistent with his general academic goal of interpreting religious history such that henotheism and monotheism are seen as late developments in the evolution of religion. This view has been refuted by extensive anthropological research around the world, which has found that henotheism is quite common, even in cultures that Wellhausen would have regarded as evolutionarily "primitive."

to us, that we may not perish" (ESV). Here "the god" is anaphoric because it means "the god who was previously mentioned," in this case the one served by Jonah. In other words, it simply means "the same god as was previously mentioned." We do not find *ałłâh* occurring with such a usage, only *al-ʾilāh*. An example of a classifier usage is Acts 7:43: "You also took along the tabernacle of Moloch and the star of the god Rompha, the images which you made to worship" (NASB). Here the phrase "the god" serves to identify "Rompha" as one of a class of entities called "gods." We do not find *ałłâh* occurring as a classifier, only *al-ʾilāh*. An example of restrictive modification is Elijah's semantic reference to "the god who responds with fire" in 1 Kings 18:24. In Elijah's case the restrictive modification refers to *either* of two supposed "gods," depending on the outcome. Such phrases exist in Arabic texts as well, but they are expressed as *al-ʾilāh*, not as *ałłâh*.[110]

A definite noun phrase can also be used to present its referent as unique or superlative, as in "the sun" and "the lord," respectively. It is unique because it belongs to a singular class (i.e., a category with only one member). The story of Elijah goes on to use the Hebrew definite noun phrase *hâ-ʾelohîm* "the god" in a unique or superlative sense:

> Then you will invoke the name of your god, and I will invoke the name of YHWH. The god who responds with fire will demonstrate that he is the [true] god (1 Kings 18:24).[111]

It is the second instance of *hâ-ʾelohîm* "the god" in this verse that has a unique or superlative meaning, "the one true god," whether *YHWH* or Baal. This usage can be found in Arabic as well, in texts and dictionaries that say *ałłâhu smu l-ʾilāh* "Allah is the name of the [one true] god." Such statements would make no sense if *ałłâh* were merely a contraction of *al-ʾilāh*. It would be like saying "The god is the name of the god" or "God is the name of God." D. B. MacDonald,[112] however, cites two passages in the Qurʾan, 6:3 and 28:70, where he says *ałłâh* might be a contraction of *al-ʾilāh*, i.e., in the superlative sense of "the only true god." These verses are shown below in Yusuf Ali's translation:

---

110 An example from a nonbiblical text: أطلس هو الإله اليوناني الذي يحمل الأرض "Atlas is the god the Greek [i.e., the Greek god] who carries the earth." This is written as *al-ʾilāh al-yūnānī*, never as *allâh al-yūnānī*, but if *allâh* really were a contraction of *al-ʾilāh*, then one would expect to find the latter usage as well.

111 This is quoted from the New English Translation, except that (1) I have bracketed "true" to show that it was added by the translators, (2) I used "YHWH" instead of "Lord," and (3) I put the second instance of "god" in lowercase, since it is used here as a noun rather than a name. Note that the word "true" is needed in English to bring out the sense of uniqueness implied by the article in this context. Most English translations omit the article of uniqueness and use the name "God," which makes little sense in this context, since the English name "God" is coreferential with the name "YHWH."

112 D. B. MacDonald, "Ilāh," in Peri J. Bearman (ed.), *The Encyclopaedia of Islam* (Vol. III; Leiden: Brill, 1999), 1093–94.

> Āl ᶜImrān [6]:3: And He is Allah in the heavens and on earth. He knoweth what ye hide, and what ye reveal, and He knoweth the (recompense) which ye earn (by your deeds).
>
> Al-Qasas [28]:70: And He is Allah: There is no god but He. To Him be praise, at the first and at the last: for Him is the Command, and to Him shall ye (all) be brought back.

If *al-ʾilāh* had been used in these passages, one could argue that it must mean "the supreme god" or "the one true god," or else the reference would be unclear. The fact is, however, that *al-ʾilāh* was not used in these passages, the term *aɫɫâh* was used, and the context demands nothing beyond its usual meaning as an epithet for God. There is nothing that demonstrates it is a contraction of *al-ʾilāh.*

The superlative usage is common in biblical Hebrew, where one of the most common epithets for God is *hâ-ʾelohîm* "the god" or "the deity," meaning "the one, true, most high god."[113] There are equivalent epithets in biblical Aramaic and biblical Greek, namely the terms *alâh-â* and *ho theos*, respectively. These expressions are usually translated into English as a proper noun: "God," and similarly in many other European languages, but the original terms are more like epithets, using the "article of uniqueness." One finds this usage in Arabic as well, among both Christians and Muslims, ancient and modern, in their use of the term *al-ʾilāh*. This usage is uncommon but one can find it, especially in lines of poetry where the metrical structure of *al-ʾilāh* fits the meter better than does *aɫɫâh*. A pre-Islamic example of this is a verse cited by Zwemer[114] from the poet Nābigha al-Dhubyānī, in which both terms are found: "Allah has given them a kindness and grace which others have not. Their abode is the God (Al-ilah) himself and their religion is strong."[115]

---

113 The uniqueness comes from having the article of uniqueness. Although the word resembles a plural in form, it is not construed grammatically as plural. The form is better understood as signifying the essence, as in "the Deity." The Hebrew word for virginity, for example, looks the same as the word for virgins, but it is abstract rather than plural. See Joel S. Burnett, *A Reassessment of Biblical Elohim* (Atlanta: Society of Biblical Literature, 2001).

114 Samuel M. Zwemer, *The Moslem Doctrine of God: An Essay on the Character and Attributes of Allah according to the Koran and Orthodox Tradition* (New York: American Tract Society, 1905), 25.

115 Zwemer notes that the poets Nābigha and Labīd use the term *allâh*, but he does an injustice in calling them "pagan." As Zwemer himself notes, some Christian scholars have recognized the Christian motifs in their poems. Zwemer, however, follows the custom of Muslim historians in calling all of the pre-Islamic Arabs *jāhilī* "ignorant, pagan," rarely mentioning that large numbers of them were Christians. Both Nābigha (535–604) and Labīd (560–661), for example, lived in the Arab Christian Lakhmid kingdom, and Nābigha also spent part of his life in the Arab Christian Ghassanid kingdom in southern Syria. While lamenting the humanistic themes of their surviving poems, Trimingham in *Christianity among the Arabs*, 247, nevertheless notes that "the poems of Nābigha adh-Dhubyānī (c. 535–c. 603) show him to be well-acquainted with Christian rites and festivals." Nābigha's famous poem uses *al-ʾilāh* once, in reference to God speaking to Solomon, and it is evident that this three-syllable term maintains the poetic meter.

Zwemer cites this passage as the sole evidence for his claim that *ałłâh* is derived from *al-ʾilāh*, but all this passage demonstrates is that *al-ʾilāh* could be used to refer back to God, who had just been mentioned, and this fact has no bearing on the question of derivation.

In conclusion, there is no clear evidence of *ałłâh* being used as a contraction of the articular common-noun phrase *al-ʾilāh*, not even in its superlative sense. While both terms can be used to refer to God, they nevertheless differ slightly in grammar, in sense, in phonological sound, and in etymology. With regard to grammar, *ałłâh* is a unique epithet for God and hence functions like a name, whereas *al-ʾilāh* is a common noun phrase. In suitable contexts *al-ʾilāh* can be used to describe any supposed god, as in the Arabic translation of Acts 7:43: *al-ʾilāh ramfān* "the god Rompha," whereas there is no clear evidence that the epithet *ałłâh* was ever used in reference to a pagan god. In regard to phonology, the last syllable of *ałłâh* is pronounced with velarization (i.e., as a dark el and back vowel) whereas *al-ʾilāh* is pronounced without velarization. In regard to etymology, *ałłâh* is a loanword from Aramaic, whereas *al-ʾilāh* is native to Arabic. We can conclude, then, that *ałłâh* is a loanword derived from the Aramaic religious language that was used by Arab Jews and Christians and is not a contraction of *al-ʾilāh* (the god).

4. Several Dubious Claims about the Term "Allah"

Dudley Woodberry urged Christians who talk with Muslims to respect the names and terms with which Muslims are familiar.[116] He noted that most of these terms, including the Arabic name for God, have their origin in the faith communities of pre-Islamic Jewish and Christian Arabs. Woodberry was seeking to dispel the mistaken notions that (1) pre-Islamic Arab Jews and Christians did not use the term "Allah" for God prior to Islam but were somehow compromised into doing so, and (2) the term "Allah" originates as the name of a pagan Arab deity rather than as a name for the Most High God. In the previous sections, I presented historical and linguistic evidence in support of Woodberry's statements about the Jewish and Christian origins of the name, in hopes of clearing these myths from the air, so that Muslims and Christians can dialogue with integrity and mutual respect (1 Peter 3:15). In this section I will provide evidence against the second mistaken notion, namely that "Allah" originates as a term for one or more pagan deities and that this makes it unsuitable as a name for God.

Contrary to claims, the fact that a pagan goddess was called *al-lāt* does not imply that *ałłâh* was a pagan god

The Syriac and Arabic epithet *ałâh(â)/ałłâh* is found in Arabia in conjunction with the spread of Jewish and Christian influences in the region, beginning with the Nabataeans in Sinai and the East Bank of the Jordan.[117] The earliest surviving attestation of the term in true Arabic

116 Woodberry, "Contextualization among Muslims," 173.

117 There are thousands of pre-Islamic Nabataean Aramaic inscriptions in Sinai and the East Bank of the Jordan. These are written in the Aramaic/Syriac language using the Nabataean script, but since the Nabataeans were

script is the Christian Zebed inscription of AD 512, while the earliest manuscript evidence is the Arabic translation of Psalm 78 in Greek script. The goddess *al-lāt*, on the other hand, is attested across the ancient Near East and from two thousand years earlier. The oldest surviving mention is evidently an Ugaritic document from about 1200 BC[118] in which the Canaanite goddess Asherah, the wife of El, is referred to as *elat*, meaning "goddess" or perhaps meaning "wife of El."[119] Fahd[120] notes that forms of the name *elat* are mentioned in the Greek works of Herodotus, in Akkadian texts, Safaitic texts, Palmyran texts, Nabataean texts, and ancient Aramaic texts. He writes that "The Arabic form of her name dates back, at least, to the time of the Khuzāʾī ʿAmr b. Luhayy, the reformer of the idolatrous cult in Mecca at the beginning of the third century AD, a period for which there is evidence of the cult of al-Lāt in Nabataea, in Safā, and in Palmyra."[121] Macdonald[122] makes a similar observation and notes that the name is found in some ancient Aramaic inscriptions in Egypt. So it is not the case that *al-lāt* is derived from *ałłâh* or vice versa, or that they originated as a mythological pair.

They are not a semantic pair either. Fahd[123] notes that "Arab lexicographers are unanimous in considering that *al-lāt* is derived from the verb *latta*," which means to knead barley meal. They do not perceive *al-lāt* as a feminine form of *ałłâh*. The feminine form of *ałłâh* would be *ałłâha*, not *al-lāt*. Nor do they perceive *al-lāt* as derived from *al-ʾilāh* "the god."

These names are not an acoustic pair. Although the consonant and vowel of the second syllables are commonly transcribed into English the same way, as *la*, they sound different in Arabic. The word for God has a dark el and a back vowel, whereas the name of *al-lāt* does not. The names do not sound related in Arabic. So in spite of what some people have imagined, the fact that the pagan goddess of North Arabia had the name *al-lāt* has no bearing at all on the derivation, sense, or referential meaning of *ałłâh*.

For the sake of argument, however, let us suppose there were some polytheistic Arabs who supposed that *al-lāt* was God's wife or daughter.[124] That would not prove that *ałłâh* did

---

Arabs, many of the inscribed names are Arabic words, and some names include the Arabic definite article *al-*. One finds many names composed with theophoric elements using *al(l)âh(â)*, indicating a recognition of the Jewish-Christian God. But with time, as the Nabataeans assimilated to the Byzantine Empire and to Greek Orthodoxy, they began to use Greek names more and more. Biblical names occur as well, such as *dnyʾl* (Daniel) and *ywsf* (Joseph). See J. Cantineau, *Le Nabatéen* (Osnabruck, Germany: Otto Zeller, 1978 [1932]); Avraham Negev, *Personal Names in the Nabatean Realm* (Jerusalem: Hebrew University of Jerusalem, 1991); and Macdonald, "Personal Names," 251–90. (Note that MacDonald is quite critical of Negev's work.)

118 Ugaritic texts date from the period 1300–1190 BC, mostly from the latter part of that period.

119 See W. G. Dever, *Did God Have a Wife? Archaeology and Folk Religion in Ancient Israel* (Grand Rapids: Eerdmans, 2005), 226; and Judith M. Hadley, *The Cult of Asherah in Ancient Israel and Judah: Evidence for a Hebrew Goddess* (Cambridge: Cambridge University Press, 2000). Hadley (206) notes that "She [Athirat in the Ugaritic literature] is identified as the consort of the chief god El; the creatress of the gods; and the nursemaid of the gods. Her epithets include *ilt* 'goddess,' and *qdš* 'holy.'"

120 T. Fahd, "Al-Lāt," in *The Encyclopaedia of Islam*, vol. 5, ed. P. J. Bearman (Leiden: Brill, 1999), 693.

121 Ibid., 692.

122 Macdonald, "Ancient North Arabian."

123 Fahd, "Al-Lāt," 693.

124 The medieval Muslim historian Hishām ibn al-Kalbī relates in *The Book of Idols* (*Kitāb al-Asnām*), (Princeton: Princeton University Press, 1952), that some of the ancient pagan devotees of the goddesses *al-lāt*, *al-ʾuzzā*,

not designate the creator; it would only show that those individuals had an unbiblical concept of God. Passages in the Bible and in ancient Hebrew inscriptions indicate that some of the Hebrews thought YHWH had a wife named Asherah.[125] This does not imply that YHWH was a pagan deity; it just indicates that some of the Hebrews had an unbiblical concept of YHWH. As for the New Testament term for God, *ho theos* "the god," ancient Greek philosophers used this same term to refer to the Supreme Being, Creator, Father, and King of all things, yet they attributed to him thousands of sons who ruled with him as gods.[126] Mormons have a similar view today, namely that God has spirit wives, through whom he begets millions of spirit offspring. These unbiblical views of God do not, however, oblige Nicene Christians to quit using the words YHWH, *ho theos*, and "God."

Contrary to claims, there is no evidence that *ałłâh* was a pagan idol in the Kaᶜba

The merchants of Mecca made their town a center of pilgrimage by placing in and around their shrine, the Kaᶜba, an image or emblem of every deity that was worshiped by people anywhere in Arabia.[127] Foremost among these was Hubal, their chief deity. The Meccans, however, were also in competition with the cathedral in Sanᶜa, which drew many Christian pilgrims and which would have had icons or statues of Jesus, Mary, and others. So they included in the Kaᶜba paintings of Jesus, Mary, Abraham, and other prophets, and they included a wooden dove, which might have represented the Holy Spirit.[128] Curiously, there is no evidence that there was an idol of *ałłâh* in the Kaᶜba. But for the sake of argument, suppose there were. If the presence of an emblem of *ałłâh* in the Kaᶜba would indicate that *ałłâh* a pagan deity, then would not the presence of images of Jesus, Mary, and Abraham identify them as pagan deities as well? But in spite of modern claims to the contrary, there seems to be no evidence that there was an image of *ałłâh* in the Kaᶜba or anywhere else in Mecca.

The chief god of Mecca was Hubal. Wellhausen[129] speculated that Hubal was called *ałłâh*, and that Muhammad had proclaimed Hubal to be the Lord and Creator of the uni-

---

and *manāt* called them the "daughters of *al-lâh*." This claim appears to be reflected and ridiculed in the Qurᵓan at al-ᵓIsraᵓ [17]:40 and an-Najm [53]:21ff, where the Meccans are derided for inventing female angels for God.

125 Raphael Patai, *The Hebrew Goddess*, with an introduction by Merlin Stone (New York: Ktav, 1968); and Hadley, *Cult of Asherah*.

126 See in particular the ancient work *What God Is According to Plato* by Maximus Tyrius, in which he affirms that "God is one" (θεος εις) and is the "Father," "King," and "Creator" of all things, and yet goes on to say that God rules with his "sons" (παιδες), who are "gods," of whom there are "thirty thousand." See The *Dissertations of Maximus Tyrius*, Translated from the Greek by Thomas Taylor (Vol. I; London: Whittingham, 1804), 16.

127 The Kaᶜba of that time was not a temple. It was a roofless enclosure around a well, but valued objects were hung on its walls, such as poetry, paintings, icons, and the like. Idols, mostly stone slabs with emblems of gods, were placed near it. Inside the enclosure was a well in which "treasure" was kept. A. J. Wensinck and J. Jomier, "Kaᶜba," in *The Encyclopaedia of Islam*, vol. 4, ed. P. J. Bearman (Leiden: Brill, 1999), 317–322; Guillaume and Ibn Ishaq, *Life of Muhammad*, 84.

128 Wensinck and Jomier, "Kaᶜba," 317–322.

129 Wellhausen, *Reste Arabischen heidentums*, 75–76.

verse. Wellhausen, however, provided no substantiating evidence. Against his claim is the historical fact that the Meccans persecuted Muhammad for opposing their religion. If he had proclaimed Hubal to be the Lord and Creator of the universe, then the Meccans would have tolerated him instead of hating him and trying to kill him. Hubal had chief place among the idols of the Kaᶜba, but when Muhammad conquered Mecca, he is said to have destroyed all of the idols, saving only the pictures of Jesus and Mary.[130] If Hubal had been Muhammad's God, he might have saved his image as well instead of destroying it.

Contrary to Wellhausen's claim, there is no evidence that each Arab tribe called its own tribal god *ałłâh*

Wellhausen[131] conjectured that each Arab tribe called its chief tribal god *al-ᵓilāh*, and that they each abbreviated this to *ałłâh*. Wellhausen based these conjectures on the erroneous assumption that pre-Islamic Arab tribes were almost entirely polytheistic, rather than henotheistic, and so he wrongly assumed they would have had no term for the Supreme Being. While this could have been the case in the prehistoric past, it was not the case for the historical period, when the terms *ałłâh* and *ar-raḥmān* were in use for the Most High God. Wellhausen made the additional assumption that each tribe called its chief deity *al-ᵓilāh*, a claim that is doubtful. Thirdly, he assumed that each tribe contracted *al-ᵓilāh* to *ałłâh*, still in reference to their chief tribal deity. There is no evidence at all for the use of *ałłâh* for tribal deities, and we have already seen the lack of evidence for the claim that *ałłâh* is a contraction of *al-ᵓilāh*. Nevertheless, Wellhausen's claims continue to influence discussions of this topic, even though they are mere conjectures unsupported by the evidence. For a critique of Wellhausen's premises and methodology, see Andræ.[132]

Contrary to some claims, the use of *ałłâh* for God is not in conflict with the use of the name YHWH in the Bible

A website called "ArabBible" has put the Van Dyck Arabic translation onto the Internet,[133] but with one exception: they replaced every instance of *ałłâh* "God" with *al-ᵓilāh* "the god." They did this without the consent of the Bible Societies and in spite of the millions of Arab Christians who call God *ałłâh*. The website provides a rationale that may be summarized as follows

- God has only one name, *YHWH*.
- No other name should be used for God except *YHWH*.
- The Arabic word *ałłâh* is a proper noun rather than a common noun.

130 Guillaume and Ibn Ishaq, *Life of Muhammad*, 552.
131 Ibid., 218–20.
132 Tor Andræ, *Mohammed: The Man and His Faith*, trans. T. Menzel (New York: Dover, 2000 [1936]), 25.
133 http://www.arabbible.com.

- The name *aḷḷâh* applies only to "Islam's deity."

- Hence *aḷḷâh* should be expunged from the Bible.

Let me list some objections to these claims:

1. McLaughlin and Eisenstein[134] write that, according to Jewish reckoning, "The number of divine names that require the scribe's special care is seven: El, Elohim, Adonai, Yhwh, Ehyeh-Asher-Ehyeh, Shaddai, and Ẓeba'ot." Except for *Ehyeh*, *YHWH*, and *Shaddai*, all of these terms are epithets derived from Hebrew common nouns. *Ehyeh* and *YHWH* are forms of the same verb. Of these seven, *Ehyeh* "I am" is regarded by some as the most holy name, followed by *YHWH* "he is," and then the others. The meaning of *Shaddai* is not known, but it is assumed from its form to have been an epithet in origin. So it is not true, as the website claims, that God has only one name, and the names he has in Hebrew seem to be epithets.

2. There is no Scripture that says one must not use any other names for God. There are over six thousand languages in the world, and most of them have a name for the Supreme Being. This is what one would expect in the light of Psalm 19 and Romans 1:19–21. In most of those languages into which the Bible has been translated, the local name for the Supreme Being has been used to refer to God. In English the word "God" is a proper noun that is used as the name of God. The authors of the website, however, deny that "God" is a proper noun, and they argue that one should use no names for God at all in a Bible translation. They justify this on the precedent that the translators of the Septuagint used *Kurios* in place of *YHWH*, and that *Kurios* is a common noun.[135] It should be noted, however, that *Kurios* is treated

134 J. F. McLaughlin and Judah David Eisenstein, "Names of God," in *The Jewish Encyclopedia*, eds. I. Singer and C. Adler (New York: Funk and Wagnalls, 1901–1906).

135 In actual fact, the earliest surviving manuscripts of the Septuagint did not translate *YHWH* at all but just wrote it in Hebrew characters. In manuscripts LXX pOx3522, LXX Nahal Hever Habakkuk, and LXX Nahal Hever Zachariah, *YHWH* is written in paleo-Hebraic characters, while in LXX pFouad 266b the name *YHWH* is written in neo-Hebraic characters. Manuscript LXX pOxy1007 uses an abbreviation of the paleo-Hebraic name. In a later manuscript, LXX 4QLevB, the name *YHWH* is transliterated into Greek as IAΩ (*iaō*). Until the fourth century, Christian scribes transcribed the Hebrew name *YHWH* using Greek characters that resembled the Hebrew characters, namely ΠΙΠΙ (pi iota pi iota) instead of יהוה (yod he waw he). In the third century Origen criticized this use of ΠΙΠΙ in place of the Hebrew characters, but by the sixth century scribes were using ΠΙΠΙ in copies of Origen's own Hexapla edition of the LXX. In the fourth century, however, it became common to use an abbreviation of the Greek term *Kurios* as the name of God in the Septuagint, as seen in the codices Vaticanus and Sinaiticus and in the fifth-century codex Alexandrinus. This is also the practice in

in the Septuagint and in quotations from it in the New Testament as a proper noun rather than as a common noun. It can often be distinguished from the use of *kurios* as a common noun by the lack of an article.[136] It is in English, not Greek, that YHWH is regularly translated as an epithet: "the LORD." In Greek it is a proper noun, Κύριος.[137] So the statement on the website lacks the biblical justification that it claims.

3. As we have shown previously, the Arabic word *ałłâh* is related to the common noun for God and is interpreted by many as a special epithet signifying God in his divine essence.

4. Contrary to the implication on the website, the epithet *ałłâh* is not the name of some being who is different from God; on the contrary, it is the name that Arabic-speaking Jews and Christians used for the God of the Bible. Muslims also identify *ałłâh* as the God of the Bible, the one who created the world, chose Abraham, sent the prophets, sent the Messiah, and will judge the nations on the last day. This description narrows the possible reference of *ałłâh* down to just one person: God.

5. In conclusion, there is actually no justification for omitting *ałłâh* from the Arabic Bible or other materials as an inappropriate term for God. In fact, rejecting the term *ałłâh* is something of an insult to the many millions of Arabic-speaking Christians who have worshiped God as *ałłâh* since pre-Islamic times, and to the millions of Christians in other languages who use Allah as their name for God.

---

all extant manuscripts of the Greek New Testament. In other words, the translators of the Septuagint initially retained the Hebrew form of the name YHWH but translated the other divine names, while the authors of the New Testament used Greek terms for all of them, including use of the proper noun *Kurios*. Similar practices can be seen in translations around the world, including Arabic and languages with Arabic loanwords.

136 The article is absent except where it was needed to correspond to a Hebrew preposition such as *l-* or *et* or to disambiguate the case; this is the practice with all proper nouns in the Septuagint.

137 There are grammatical contexts in Greek where proper nouns require a definite article, especially if they are indeclinable foreign names (as YHWH originally was in the LXX), and there are also grammatical contexts where definite common noun phrases shed their article. That is beyond the scope of a footnote, except to mention that these variations can confuse an investigator who does not understand the Greek linguistic conventions that pertain to this matter.

Conclusion

Jews spread both Judaism and their Aramaic term for God among the Arabs. In Jerusalem on the day of Pentecost, Judaic pilgrims from Arabia heard the name of God being praised in Arabic by the power of the Holy Spirit (Acts 2:11). Jewish Christianity subsequently spread to Arabia, with other Christian sects coming later. The Aramaic name of God became well assimilated into the Arabic language, taking the form *ałłâh*. Meanwhile Nestorian Christians spread their faith eastwards across Asia, using the Syriac Bible and spreading the Syriac term for God: *ałâh-â*. When Islam spread across the same region, it popularized the Arabic form of this same term, *ałłâh*. As a result, forms of this word have been borrowed into many languages as the name of the Supreme Being. Thus a term which our Lord Jesus Christ used to refer to God has been disseminated across much of the world.

Among Arabs *ałłâh* remains the name by which Jews, Christians, and Muslims worship God, and they use it frequently in their speech to praise and acknowledge him. In a poignant article entitled "Allah and the Christian Arab," an evangelical Middle Eastern Christian tries to explain to Western Christians the significance of the name *ałłâh* to Christians in the Arab world. It might be appropriate to close with his concluding remark, which is in the form of a plea:

> PLEASE never never [speak] against the glorious name of Allah, a name that has been loved and revered by millions of God's children down through the centuries.[138]

138 Rafique, "Allah and the Christian Arab," *Seedbed*, 13/1 (1998), 7.

9 Folk Elements in Muslim Expressions of African Religion

BY DEAN S. GILLILAND

Islam and Local Religions

Islam is always shaped to greater and lesser degrees by the local beliefs and practices of the people it encounters. Local expression of any religion means that while a second religion may become the more visible, even official system, the "habits of the heart," so to speak, are fundamentally unchanged. The extent of the influence of African traditional religion on Islam is pervasive, with precedents in the origins of Islam reaching back to Arabia and the prophet Muhammad.

The impact made by Muhammad on his own society was both condemnation of and accommodation to "pagan" Arabian practices. At his birthplace, Mecca, Muhammad's stand against the local gods was eloquent. There is evidence for this in the language of the Meccan suras.

When he was met with fierce resistance from his own people, he may have attempted a compromise with polytheism. There is some idea for this generated in the Hadith. *Sūrat* an-Najm [53] of the Qur᾿an carries what may be some of the remnants of this miscarried attempt. In any case, there was no good result.[1] It is axiomatic that traditional systems which have a strong cultic center will resist change.

Muhammad fared much better in Medina where paganism gave way more easily (perhaps due to the influence of Jews and Christians). With the power and prestige he had gained at Medina, the Prophet returned to Mecca in 630 and overwhelmed the city almost without a struggle. Yet his two-sided attitude toward paganism showed even more clearly once he was back on home ground. On one hand, the Kaᶜba was purged of its ancestral relics, and the destruction of all idols became a condition for joining the new faith. On the other hand,

---

1 Richard Bell, *Introduction to the Qur᾿an* (Edinburgh: Edinburgh University Press, 1963), 22.

loyalty to Arab tradition was honored when the Ka^cba was adopted as the center of the new religion and the *qibla* (direction faced in prayer), though modified somewhat, was retained.

Borrowing from and accommodating to traditional religion is a characteristic of Islam. This was recognized by Islamic scholars from the very beginning. Early in the encounter between Muslims and Christians, al-Kindī said he would not permit certain stories from Arab paganism in the debate, even though they were already fully adopted into Islam. Al-Kindī said at one point, "If thou mentionest the tale of Ad and Thamud and the Camel … we say to thee, 'These are senseless stories and the nonsensical fables of old women of the Arabs, who kept reciting them night and day.'"[2]

Christiaan Snouck Hurgronje, in 1906, was convinced that "each nation adopts that portion of Islam which harmonizes most with its character, its customs and its past history, and in doing so seeks involuntarily to preserve under the new regime as much as possible of its ancient lore."[3]

Samuel M. Zwemer was a prolific observer of the animistic aspects of Islam. While some of Zwemer's terminology may seem somewhat intolerant to the modern reader, no one can question his firsthand observations as coming from one who lived close to Muslim people. His book, *The Influence of Animism on Islam*, is a prolific source for information on the topic.[4] He shows how many observances from Arab religion were taken, with little or no change, into Islamic rituals. Practices such as ceremonial washings after certain kinds of defilement, cleansing the teeth and inner spaces of the body, paring the nails, and even parting the hair were already customary in Arabian animism.

William St. Clair Tisdall's, *The Sources of Islam*, influenced Zwemer and was made available in several translations through William Muir.[5] Tisdall writes about "certain doctrines and practices of the Arabs in the 'days of ignorance' which were maintained in Islam." His contention was that when Muhammad considered the beliefs and practices of their Abrahamic forefathers, he was "unwilling to force abandonment of them all, but desired rather to purify their faith, and to maintain such ancient practices as he thought good and reasonable."[6]

Where resistance to change arises from the cultic center, the secondary religion must find ways to legitimize and accommodate the primary system. The development of Islam in West Africa shows this was, in fact, the case.

Folk Encounters in Early West African Islam (Nigeria and Niger)

The way in which Islam entered West Africa allowed for a process by which African religion and a Moroccan version of Islam could interact. Each system affected the other in a pattern

2 Samuel Marinus Zwemer, *The Influence of Animism on Islam: An Account of Popular Superstitions* (New York: Macmillan, 1920), 4–5.

3 Christiaan Snouck Hurgronje, *The Achehnese*, vol. 2 (Leyden: Brill, 1906), 280.

4 Zwemer, *Influence of Animism*.

5 William St. Clair Tisdall, *The Sources of Islam*, trans./ed. William Muir (Edinburgh: Clark, 1901).

6 Ibid., 3.

of conflict, compromise, and reformation which touched every aspect of life over many years. These cycles were repeated over and over again, with the African forms dominating, especially in the early stages.

The influence of African ancestral religion on the more Arabic-oriented structures is recorded in a semihistorical document called the *Kano Chronicle*.[7] We cannot deal with this history in detail, but we do want to illustrate how pervasive the influence of Hausa religion has been on the Islam of a massive West African territory.

While it is widely accepted that Islam in some form was present in what is now northern Nigeria and southern Niger by the year 1000, the more reliable start-up traditions are between 1300 and 1500. The *Kano Chronicle* is a series of narratives, based chronologically on the various kings of Kano. Even the casual reader gets the feeling that there was massive conflict between African practice and the alien system. While the ancient kingdoms of Ghana, Mali, and finally Songhai form a background, it is with the "coming of the Warangawa from Mali" in 1350 that the long story begins.[8]

There is considerable ambiguity about the status of Islam until the Fulani immigrate "with their books" in 1450. Islam from this period continued to be syncretized with local practices. It was in the early nineteenth[9] century that the jihad of Uthman dan Fodio swept the land. He claimed that the purging of pagan practices from Islam was one of the objectives of the jihad. Obviously, African traditional forms were having a powerful effect on the quality of Islam around 1800. The idealism of dan Fodio led him to write his *Nur al-Albab*, in which he listed "sins" of the unbelievers.[10] Several of the sins show areas of influence that traditional religion was having on Islam. For example:

Veneration of rocks and trees
Divination by stars, sand spirits and movements of birds
Throwing down stones
Consulting diviners and soothsayers
Placing cotton on rocks, trees and paths
Placing of food and clothes on burial places of ancestors
Reciting the Qur'an while beating drums.[11]

7 H. R. Palmer, "The Kano Chronicle," *Journal of the Royal Anthropological Institute of Great Britain and Ireland* 38 (1908): 58–98.

8 Dean S. Gilliland, "Religious Change among the Hausa, 1000–1800: A Hermeneutic of the Kano Chronicle," *Journal of Asian and African Studies* 14, no. 3–4 (July 1979): 245ff.

9 According to J. Spencer Trimingham, the spontaneity of the text, while its author is unknown, shows that the author "had not followed normal scholastic training, for the Arabic is strange and notably free from the usual pious terminology." *Islam in West Africa* (London: Oxford University Press, 1959), 110 footnote.

10 Ismael Hamet, *Nour-el-Eulbab*, Arabic Text with French Translation and an Introduction (Algiers: Libraire Adolphe Jourdan, 1988).

11 Ibid., 248.

Folk influence through cultic practices

The list gives some idea of the strength which traditional religion held in the period before Uthman dan Fodio. From many illustrations of the predominance of African structures, I refer again to the *Kano Chronicle*, where a syncretized practice centered on what was known as the *dirki.*

The dates for Mohamma Zaki are given as 1582–1618. It is stated that the practice of *tchakuna* and *dirki* commenced during the reign of Mohamma Zaki. Of the *tchakuna* nothing more is said, but the *dirki* is shown to have had much influence with the king. The *dirki* was actually a copy of the Qur'an covered with layers of goatskin. The secret contents were not revealed until Mohamma Alwali's reign (1781–1807), just prior to the jihad. By this time Islam had become so apostatized that most of the followers were not aware of its Qur'anic origin. A royal copy of the Qur'an, covered with goatskins and later with cowhide, had become a center of cultic power. Sacrifice was expected on behalf of *dirki.* It had wide sanction with the people. The people said to Alwali, "'If you stop this practice God will bring evil fortune upon you.' Alwali replied, 'Dirki is nothing but the Koran swear I will open it and expose its contents.' When the angry Alwali had axes laid to the *dirki*, a beautiful Qur'an fell out."[12]

Above we noted several of the practices that were widespread among the Hausas who claimed to be Muslims. All of them have to do with magic and divination. The *malamai* (ulamas) were probably more familiar with the rituals of animism than with Islam. In fact, one of the most objectionable things to Uthman dan Fodio was the way the faith and practices of the faithful were being ridiculed.[13]

Though Mohamma Zaki is reported to have been a Muslim, the *Chronicle* shows how much traditional influence extended to the clerical class. On one occasion Mohamma was at a loss as to what he could do to win in a battle with Katsina. The problem was compounded by a famine which had weakened his forces. When Mohamma brought his advisers together for consultation, he was offered a pagan Hausa charm which had special powers for war. Accepting it, he won the battle and was so grateful that he rewarded his counselors with many gifts. Similarly, when the much-feared Kworarafa were menacing the king who professed Islam, he asked the non-Muslim Maguzawa priests to come and perform a dance with their *hauiyas* to protect him.[14] In a similar instance, Yandoya, a non-Muslim practitioner, provided the king with a charm and a verbal formula for his protection.

A certain red snake was a cultic symbol of the pre-Islamic Hausa. This information is contained in the famous legends of Bayajidda. Whenever the snake is introduced into the narrative, it always has to do with power over an enemy. According to the *Chronicle*, the Kano king Kanajeji (ruled 1390–1410) was angry with Islam because he had been defeated

---

12 Palmer, "Kano Chronicle," 93.

13 Palmer notes that at first the Qur'an was covered with goatskins, but afterwards cowhides were used, as many as ten and even forty at a time. The ridiculous practice was stopped by Alwali. See ibid., 82.

14 Ibid.

in war. In desperation Kanajeji turned to the priest of a new "pagan" cult, Tchibiri, for help. Kanajeji promised to do whatever he was required to do. The pagan priest told him to break off a branch from the cultic tree, Shamuz. When he did so, a red snake appeared. This third dramatic appearance of the red snake, and the Muslim king's acceptance of it, symbolized capitulation to ancient, hard-core institutions by an ostensibly Muslim king.[15]

Folk influence in myth and the spirit world

The stories and myths of any people reveal the essence of the world in which they live. These deep-level narratives are most resistant to change because they represent the values that cause people to act and think as they do. The interaction between Arabic and African concepts and terms is a valuable source for understanding the ways of folk influence on Islam.

The German anthropologist Leo Frobenius (1873–1938), while a controversial figure, was famous for his collections of primitive African art and his anthology of Hausa tales.[16] His stories reflect the intense struggle between traditional religion and Islam. The value of these stories is that they show how a serious bifurcation in the ideas of spirit and spirits was introduced when Islam came. This is due to the differences in Muslims and traditional worldviews. The tales are built around Sarkin Aljannu (chief of the Muslim jinn spirits) and Sarkin Iskoki (chief of the traditional spirits). The two systems are in conflict, and the legends play on various themes of tensions and anxiety which arise in the community.

One story between Pati (traditional) and Kundare (Muslim) has to do with a sickness which occurred every Friday (the Muslim holy day). Pati is accused of causing it because of his friendship with Kundare. Because Pati is held responsible for the plague, he finds himself in a dilemma with his own people. He concludes, "What shall I do? When Kundare, my friend, comes to me I cannot prevent him." The story is symbolic interaction between members of the ancestral spirit world and the Muslim spirit world. It suggests the inevitability of the Muslim presence as it overtakes the traditional system. Before the Muslims came, there was one set of spirits (*iskoki*).[17] Since the Muslim arrival, there is a second set of spirits (*aljannu*, jinn).[18] The basic question is whether harm or evil caused by indigenous spirits (*'iskoki*) requires the same ritual as the ills brought on by Muslim jinn (*aljannu*). It works out that the traditional rites were more effective for certain of the traditional spirits, while Islam would have to intervene for the new problems caused by jinn.[19]

---

15 Kanajeji, chief of Kano, was angry because of defeat in war, so he returned to the pre-Islamic practices through a revitalization cult (Tchibiri). See Gilliland, "Religious Change," 246.

16 Leo Frobenius, *The Voice of Africa*, 2 vols., trans. R. Blind (London: Hutchinson, 1913), 539. Frobenius drew his conclusions by attempting to reconstruct the original cultural situation. See discussion in Adolf Jensen, *Myth and Cult among Primitive Peoples* (Chicago: University of Chicago Press, 1963), 3–4.

17 Ibid., 253.

18 Joseph H. Greenberg, *The Influence of Islam on a Sudanese Religion* (Seattle: University of Washington Press, 1946), 68–70.

19 Ibid., 70.

Folk Practices in Contemporary West African Islam

From all of this we now look at present-day folk Islam, using Nigeria as the primary context. This is because there is no place in Africa where Islam exists among such a variety of ethnic groups as in Nigeria. Brief reference will also be made to practices in French-speaking regions, particularly to well-known *tariqas* [sufi orders] in Senegal and Mali.

We noted briefly how from its own history Islam was shaped by indigenous practices. Accordingly, throughout the history of Islam's interaction with African cultures it has been a religion of accommodation and pragmatism. The *Kano Chronicle* showed that distinctives of the ancient African worldview made demands on Islam that resulted in distortions. Similar phenomena continue to be repeated over and over in local situations. I should like to review three aspects of the influence African religion has in shaping folk Islam: (1) the dominance of African worldview, (2) reciprocity with African culture, and (3) traditional impact on rulers and politics.

Dominance of African worldview

Folk elements in West African Islam arise from the assumptions of African worldview. Certain of these worldview features figure strongly in the way Islam adapts itself to the African context. Three factors that Islam must confront are immediacy, compatibility, and continuity.

Immediacy

The African walks a well-worn path. Tradition is pervasive, promising quick and concrete results. In contrast to the immediacy of ancestral practices, Islam is more belief oriented and can seem irrelevant, even powerless. A Bachema man says, "Only my fathers know the reason for my sickness." The Kutep say, "God is not in the ground where Muslims pray." The Kilba believe, "Only the ancestors can tell us why the children are sick."

Day-to-day needs are provided for through traditional practices and in such comprehensive ways that Islam is forced to adapt to local methods. Dangemu, a Kilba Muslim claims he spoke for his whole village when he said that absolute needs are as follows: (1) how to find a wife, (2) how to get money, (3) where to get protection from harmful magic, and (4) how to secure good health. Dangemu went on to say that practices his father taught him are more powerful than Islam in some areas, especially in providing protection against harmful magic. But he was quite sure that Muslim "doctors" could give better medicine because, in addition to the Muslim medicine, they used herbs and poultices which the Kilba have always used.

The nomadic Fulani, while Muslim, have always been highly syncretized with African practices. In this area of need for immediacy they are highly pragmatic. Fulani are known to be dispensers of power and prophetic oracles, and they are willing to share this *baraka* (blessing) with non-Muslims. The *luguji* is a highly specialized oracle. It is accomplished through the unrolling of a long scroll, which gives the client information concerning health, money, children, and personal power. Besides bringing seven gowns, the client must agree to perform the *ṣalāt* (canonical prayer) and to say that he or she is willing to accept the oracle's prophecy concerning his or her death.

Muslim clerics become very useful to the community as traditional rites begin to lose their power. The ambivalence created by the loss of customary ritual is a common source of anxiety. Therefore, when results are not forthcoming in the indigenous way, a person often turns to Muslim practitioners who keep very close contact with community institutions. This points to a second aspect of African worldview that affects Islam.

Compatibility

For the African everything must "hold together." Alien practices are difficult to deal with because all of life turns as a wheel, with strength and unity coming from the hub. Therefore, it is required of Islam that a certain level of compatibility be worked out from community to community. The question is, therefore, "How well does Islam fit into the traditional ethos?" Compatibility, as we speak of it here, is more at the visible level, and may not touch the very heart of the people or culture. But appearance is extremely important in religious change.

Ancestral practices have remarkable visibility in West African Islam. The highly Islamized Pabir kept a ritual of ancestor veneration in connection with the harvest. The "firstfruits" of corn were used in making ritual food for the dead. Four lumps of cornmeal were eaten by the father and four by the mother. With this the ancestors were said to have "finished the food." Prayer was then offered, asking for help in problems that had arisen in the family. The old man who gave me this information was a practicing Muslim. He saw no need of giving it up because, "It was done by the head of the house and the prayer to the ancestor was taught to them by the Muslim imam."

In the area of magic, a Mwaghavul man showed me "medicine" that was prepared especially to render him invisible to certain devils (*aljannu*) which an enemy had put upon him. A magic verse had been written by a Hausa *malam* (teacher) and was kept in a leather phylactery made by his own "pagan" brother. *Aljannu* (jinn) are Islamic spirits and, therefore, he felt that his tribal medicine could not protect him. But the talisman he wore had to have family origins, even though it contained the Muslim medicine.

Continuity

By continuity we are emphasizing the core values of a community (i.e., tribe) which are most resistant to change. Continuity, as we use it here, refers to archaic structures which survive at the deep level even while modernity and social change is taking place on the surface. Continuity means there are strong educational attachments to the past which are expressed ritually. In order for Islam to attract loyalty, it will not only have to accommodate at the superficial level, but must integrate or absorb these features that are of the essence of a people. Communities that have a strong central cultus and well-developed ritual have been able to shape Islam in dramatic ways. The motifs of these expressions, while unmistakably Muslim, are still traditional.

The Maguzawa are an example of the need for continuity. While most demonstrate Islam in a superficial way, the Maguzawa are tenacious about their pre-Islamic belief and practice. In addition to their strong cultus, they have resisted Islam from the days when they were chased from Kano city due to pressure to convert. Today it is an academic question whether the Maguzawa are Muslim or not. If they are, as some would argue, they are a real case for continuity in folk Islam. Imams circumcise the infant boys, and most Maguzawa prefer to be buried with Muslim sanctions. At Tsanyawa, a Maguzawa village, I witnessed a wedding which was performed by the *liman* (imam). The actual ceremony was private and was the only Muslim feature. Afterward there was much dancing and drinking out of a huge beer pot which was sacred to the clan. The *liman* departed following the ceremony because he said he could not control the partying. There is a saying among the Maguzawa: "As a man is born and buried, so he is." This being the case, Islam has the official sanction, but daily life follows almost totally Maguzawa tradition.

The Nupe present an open, visible Islam to even the most casual observer. In this aspect the Nupe are a different case altogether from the Maguzawa. Still, the continuity factor, the traditional core, is extremely important. The ancient Nupe festival, *navu*, is a pre-Islamic ancestor ceremony which was reintroduced into the new religion, Islam.

It may have a parallel to the Muslim Muharram, but it carries specifically Nupe features and is practiced by all as a symbol of Nupe unity. Even Friday services have the imprint of Nupe life. There are Nupe prayers which are said in addition to those in Arabic. These prayers, spoken in the Nupe language, reveal dynamic worldview features with surprising references to Nupe cosmology. They even invoke Soko, not Allah, and in this way retain the content and style of the pre-Islamic prayers.[20]

Reciprocity with African Culture

The influence of African religion on Islam is so pervasive that it is often difficult to see the boundaries between the two systems. Interacting one with the other, African and Muslim beliefs are played out almost simultaneously. Not only does one tolerate the other but, ultimately, it requires the other. As we have been showing from the beginning, the open door to African practices lies within Islam itself. I. M. Lewis contests that magic (*siḥr*), witchcraft, oracles, etc., are all approved in Islam, "as long as they derive their validity from an Islamic source."[21] However, this latter requirement is extremely ambiguous. Reciprocity enlarges the field of available power to both the Muslim and the non-Muslim.

20 S. F. Nadel, *Nupe Religion* (Glencoe, IL: Free Press, 1954), 257–58.

21 I. M. Lewis, "Islam and traditional belief and ritual," in *Islam in Tropical Africa*, ed. I.M Lewis (Oxford: Oxford University Press, 1959), 58–75.

Practitioners and personal needs

The Muslim practitioner (*malam*) renders services to both believers and *arna* (unbelievers) and is extremely lenient when it comes to "orthodoxy." An unofficial relationship of consent exists between the *malamai* (teachers) and the "pagan" priests. The capacity within Islam to accept all forms of spirit, both good and evil, provides a base for African influence. The Islamic source from which methods are shaped is not important, as long as it is agreed that the results are beneficial. The *malam* quite openly gives consent to and employs variations of traditional forms.

Malam Sule in the village of Mutum Daya (Taraba State) said openly that unbelievers came to him especially for help in finding a mate and to get money. The non-Muslim person felt that Malam Sule could give help with these needs because they lie outside the traditional prescriptions. There is much ambiguity in the area of spirits affecting good fortune and good health. Muslims are, in turn, plagued by spirits that have their origin in the traditional cosmology, and for these they need the help of traditional "doctors." The same is true for the traditional African who feels that his or her problem has to do with the jinn (*aljannu*).

This reciprocity leaves open many areas where a so-called folk Islam can flourish. It allows freedom for practitioners to borrow forms from each other. This is permissible with the Muslim as long as traditional beliefs can be adjusted so that the absoluteness of Allah is not questioned. Islam does not require the African person to abandon his or her belief in forces which have always controlled their lives. There is plenty of room in the Muslim system for angels, jinn, and the exorcism of devils.

The ability of Muslim doctors to merge traditional practice with African belief was demonstrated in Gongola State (Nigeria). A non-Muslim man had to leave the school where I was teaching because of an abdominal disorder. He walked twelve miles to a Hausa *malam* who had a wide reputation for healing. The Muslim doctor told him that a certain "evil wind" (*mugun iska*) had blown in from the town of Bauchi. To treat this, the *malam* prescribed drinking a certain "blessing water" (*ruwan albarka*). The *malam* tied various charms around the client's arms and waist. The patient also had to listen to readings from the Qurʾan at appointed times. The patient improved enough to go back to school. When I asked how this treatment would help an "unbeliever," the *malam* only said, "God is no respector of persons."

Social and community interventions

There is such unity in African life that to treat any dimension apart from the totality is almost impossible. Nothing is more cohesive in African society than rituals which hold together family and the extended community. African life forcibly resists anything that brings conflict into the community or endangers the norms that have held the society together.

Over thirty years ago Spencer Trimingham wrote about the process of religious change as the African traditional society becomes Islamized. He spoke of three stages, which we might call preparation, adjustment, and assimilation.[22] Trimingham did recognize many differences and gradations. His analysis showed that Islam will be shaped by traditional belief and practice more significantly than it (Islam) will influence local practices. Trimingham, however, failed to see that the Islamization process is not inevitable with all groups. Many societies never open up to Islam. The subtleties of the "preparation stage" may occur among some groups. But the process is arrested at that point, or perhaps, at the second stage.

These varieties of resistance and acceptance to Islam can be accounted for by looking at the makeup of the given society at its deep level. The ability of the society to have massive influence on the shaping of Islam or to resist Islam altogether, is determined by the degree of relevance between the two systems. Another determining factor is the historical image that Islam had in the society, whether negative or positive. There are three types of change. One is where Islam has been modified but becomes the dominating form. In a second type, Islam maintains its identity but becomes highly syncretized with the traditional structure. In a third type, traditional structures prevail, and Islam becomes decadent and almost lost. Let us develop these three changes further.

First, a changed form of Islam which reflects the social makeup of the society has been dramatically illustrated by several brotherhoods in French-speaking West Africa. The best known are Bakka'iyya, Fadiliyya, and Muridiyya (Senegal). This latter sect developed into saint worship with the belief that the sanctity of the leader redeems the sins of the followers. The Murids hold great sanctity for the land which they have ritualized through labor and production. Visits to the tomb of their founder, Ahmed Bamba, at Touba, is a substitute for the *ḥajj*.

Similarly, a fourth group, the HamaPiyya championed the cause for the poor. This *tariqa* was a social protest against the privileged classes. They went so far as to change the *shahāda* to "There is no God but God, and Hamallah is our sheikh." This group faces west to Nioro during their *ṣalāt*, which was the home of their prophet (Hamallah), and which also became their "Mecca" for purposes of *ḥajj*. But in all of these, Islam is intact. There is no question to the outside observer what the religion is.[23]

Second, an Islam which retains its identity but is highly integrated into society is illustrated by the Jukun Amgbakpariga. The Jukun are related to the Kwororafa who pillaged Hausa towns, as recorded in the *Kano Chronicle*.[24] The Amgbakpariga, however, are Muslims who have lived with the Jukun so long that they have very high acceptance among the Jukun. The word *amgbakpariga* actually means "long-folding gowns," going back to the days when these Muslims were so noticeable because their dress was much different from

22 Triminghan, *Islam in West Africa*, 34–40.

23 Jean-Claude Froelich, *Les Mususlmans d'Afrique Noire* (Paris: Editions l'Orante, 1964), 239-48.

24 Palmer, "Kano Chronicle," 87.

the traditional Jukun. While retaining features of Islam, the Amgbakpariga have almost completely merged with Jukun society.[25]

The Jukun have always resisted Islam, so the Amgbakpariga have made notable concessions in order to live among them. They adopted the matrilineal marriage customs of the Jukun. The visible ritualizing of this adaptation was the removal of the long-folding gown by a husband and the donning of a Jukun garb in the presence of his wife's mother. The Amgbakpariga have much more communication with the non-Jukun Muslims than with other Muslims. While they are not allowed to serve on the Jukun council of elders, they participate fully in almost every other aspect of Jukun life.[26]

Third, an extreme example of the influence of African society on Islam can be found among the Mshelia people at Subwong Hill in Gongola State (Nigeria). Here the Muslim forms have been so distorted that what has resulted is almost complete syncretism into the local practices. The problem began when Muslim immigrants had to travel long distances to their place of origin (Song) in order to get Muslim wives. The third generation met this handicap by agreeing to certain changes to accommodate the Mshelia religion. A new version of the ᶜId al-Fitr was introduced at the site of the original mosque, which is now a ring of cottonwood trees. This celebration is a homogenous mixture of Muslim and traditional Mshelia elements. Eventually, even the *ṣalāt* was abandoned as the marriage demands increased. Even though there is now almost total dysfunction of Islamic forms, the Mshelia Muslims will not give up circumcision, even though it is despised by traditional Mshelia.[27]

Traditional Impact on Rulers and Politics

When looking at the role of chiefs and kings in the formation of religion, we are in touch with the very core of a people's worldview. In traditional Africa, kingship was rarely, if ever, separated from the ritualistic aspects of life. The king (or chief) was the most powerful symbol of the self-consciousness of his people, as well as a mediator who connected them with the ancestor spirits of the community.

The *Kano Chronicle* proves that the king was the catalyst in the transition from ancestral to Muslim practices. As he goes, so go the people. When power was needed, the *sarki* (king) was open to either the traditional way or the Muslim way, or both. Straightforward pragmatism determined which system would prevail in a given situation.

During the colonial years it was common to find two chiefs in a region. One was the natural chief with the indigenous functions and rites, while a second more political chief was selected to handle the secular aspects of governance. This meant the "ritual chief" was shielded from secular affairs while the "administrative chief" was free to represent the

25 Dean S. Gilliland, *African Religions Meets Islam: Religious Change in Northern Nigeria* (Latham, MD: University Press of America, 1986), 88–90.

26 Ibid.

27 Ibid., 71.

people as a kind of civil head. The reason for this was that maintaining the "tribal" cultus was so important that the role of the ritual chief would not be compromised by mixing it with the Muslim system. This need to maintain custom and tradition at all costs put pressure on Islam to accommodate these historical practices centering around the "pagan" chief. We will now look at the two types of influence of indigenous religion on Islam at the level of the chief and his councilors.

Muslim rule with a traditional base

Many of the districts and villages where the chief is a Muslim have the appearance of a Muslim community. However, just below the visible surface of Islam are the strong practices of a pre-Islamic time. To illustrate, one needs to visit the town of Biu, headquarters of the Pabir people and seat of the Muslim emir. The first Muslim king of the Pabir was Ali Pasukur, who ruled as a "divine king" about 130 years ago. It is never said that the Pabir king dies. Rather, he has "gone away" for a time. Tilla Lake, near Biu, was sacred to the kings of Biu. The spirit of the king lived in the crocodiles in this lake. At the king's departure, the head crocodile would leave the water to inaugurate transition rites.

There is still a conflict as to whether the newly installed king should submit to Pabir initiation ceremonies while being head of Pabir Islam. This symbolic Pabir rite requires that the new king disrobe and wash in the river after benniseed and beer have been thrown into the water. This royal initiation was still being followed in 1967 at the installation of the emir. Such concession to "pagan" rites is totally out of line with Islam. An elder told me that this was not a problem because customs (*al'ada*) should not be confused with religion (*addini*). Loyalty to tribal custom, he said, would not be looked upon as contradictory to the practices of Islam.[28]

Traditional rule with a Muslim veneer

It is politically expedient for chiefs and village heads to give the impression of Islam when the government is officially Muslim. Generally, it is acceptable to Muslim hierarchy if a village head gives little more than superficial allegiance to Islam. Traditional chiefs who are under Muslim emirs can effectively steer a course between traditional and Muslim practices. A Muslim chief often rules non-Muslim people, but he will cater to his non-Muslim subjects in policy and attitude without any reprisals from Muslim superiors.

For example, the town of Zing in Gongola State is the headquarters of the Mumuye people. The Mumuye have held closely to a conservative model of traditional religion. Christianity has recently flourished among the Mumuye, but they have never been open to Islam. Yet for years the chief of Zing was a Muslim. He never showed intolerance toward the completely non-Islamic practices of his subjects. He kept favor with the Muslim hierarchy while participating in the life of the people in many ways. He averted conflict since, as a Mumuye, he knows well the areas where religion has final authority.

---

28 Ibid., 23.

Gelo, the chief of the Maguzawa at Madaurare, showed me the sacred burial plot of his father who was chief before him. The grave was but five steps from the door of his house. Across the compound, less than forty feet away, a granary was built over the grave of his grandfather. Gelo had performed the *ṣalāt* for a number of years. But he openly admits that the real sanctions for his right to rule are the rituals connected with these two graves.

During the 1960s and 1970s tremendous pressure was put on chiefs to Islamize, especially in rural areas. There were gratuities attached to converting to Islam which increased power and prestige. Yet many of these conversions were superficial and temporary. In one of the well-known cases, the chief acceded to pressure to "do *ṣalāt*" and even accepted funds from the Muslim head of state to go on the *ḥajj*. But except for a few councilors, no one in the community followed him into Islam. The chief's claim to be a Muslim was bitterly disputed upon his death when his own family refused to have him buried as a Muslim. They said he never was a Muslim at heart, but was given promises of prestige if only he would give the appearance and attend to the minimum observances.[29]

Conclusion

To summarize, these areas of interaction between African religion and Islam have a common phenomenology. Whatever the dimension of expression, the most visible common features are pragmatism and utility. There is little real concern in Islam about formal orthodoxy or what is historically correct. While the Shari^ca is still the social and political code, first considerations have to do with results rather than with piety or conformance to creed for its own sake.

Before launching into this chapter, it would have been helpful to have looked at the *tariqas* that have formed Nigerian Islam. I refer to the earliest domination by the Qadiriyya, which gave way later to the more Sufi-oriented Tijaniyya. In the last two decades both of these orders have been shocked by two expressions of Islamic fundamentalism.

One (Mai Tatsini), which had its origins outside of Nigeria, was a kind of Mahdiism. This movement flared up in several centers in Nigeria, resulting in destruction of property and loss of life. The relentless demands for "reform" were based on African radicalism. That is to say, the features of these reforms would have had little in common with realities outside of the regional African context. A further attempt at reform was the Izala movement of the early 1990s.

Considered as a sect within Islam, Izala Muslims claim rigid adherence to legalistic practices while taking aggressive action against non-Muslims with political implications. Again, the rationale was "purification" of Nigerian Islam from its contamination by secularism and "paganism."

Yet even Izala revisionism supports the observation that the end is always more important than the means. Nigeria has demonstrated in the past thirty years how utilitarian African Islam is. In a state where Christians now outnumber Muslims and where both religions can

29 Ibid., 161.

claim over 50 million adherents, the situation is unique among African nations. Policies taken by civilian government still bear out the contention of this essay—that the forms and practices of West African Islam are highly contextualized into the primary culture and are shaped through the deep-level ethnic assumptions by which ordinary people live.

While conversions to Islam have slowed when compared to the past, an appeal of Islam is still its claim as "the African religion" (when compared to Christianity). One reason for this is that it can be practiced in continuity with ancestral beliefs. "Mission Christianity" needs to evaluate both the limitations and the opportunities this reality represents for Christian-Muslim relations in a country where both religions are seeking for allegiance.

10

The Kaya "Shrine" and the Mosque: Religious Bifurcation among Miji-Kenda Muslims in Kenya

BY STEPHEN MUTUKU SESI

The average Muslim in sub-Saharan Africa maintains double allegiance to Allah and to the local tribal deity. The Muslim in this context sees no contradiction with attending *ṣalāt* in the mosque at least once a week and visiting the local medicine man or woman to address immediate needs or sickness in his family. Some of the old mosques like remains of The Great Mosque within the Gedi remains in Malindi, Kenya, are now traditional shrines. African men and women visit the mosque and face the *miḥrāb*, not to perform prayers to Allah, but to offer sacrifices in order to receive *baraka* (blessing) in form of healing or solve family dispute, from tribal spirit or the tribal Supreme Being, Mlungu. The direction of prayer has been Africanized to bring blessings to the community as a local shrine rather than the point of contact with Allah.

In Africa, shrines are channels of communication between the human and the spirit world. Shrines are usually natural phenomena like big trees, forests, mountains, large rocks, groves, natural caves, waterfalls, and water springs; some shrines, though, are man-made. Among the Digo, these may be small huts made of grass, cleared space in the forest, a stake of wood that is partially buried into the ground, or bottles containing medicinal substance buried completely under the ground, or on the surface. In this chapter I will look at the case of Digo religious experience as an Islamic tribe in East Africa and at the same time a true African tribe in matters of worship in their traditional shrines.

There are at least four kinds of shrines among the Digo called *fingo* (family shrine situated within the homestead), *mzimuni* (village shrine situated somewhere within the village community land), *mizukani* (community shrine situated within the larger community land), and *kaya* (community shrine situated in what used to be traditional homesteads before Islam came). As Benjamin Ray explains, "Whatever its form, the shape and design of the shrine indicates its function as a symbolic crossroads between two worlds and instruments of social unification. The ritual and social focal point of the shrine is often an altar where offerings are placed."[1]

In these traditional shrines, not everyone is allowed to enter. Shrines are sacred space reserved for those who are spiritually fit to perform the rituals. Only the traditional priests and healers are allowed to go there for special sacrificial ceremonies. Among the Digo, the hereditary guardian in charge is called *mwana-ti* (the lord of the land). He is usually a traditional healer or the descendant of a former prominent traditional priest, who is usually buried somewhere within the shrine.

Kayas (traditional shrines) are also known to be places of refuge. When an enemy is chasing a person, she or he can run into the *kaya* to flee from the pursuer's wrath. The person or people seeking revenge are forced to forgive the offender as soon as she or he runs into the *kaya*. Fighting or even quarreling in the *kaya* angers the ancestors and causes a calamity.[2] The ancestors express their anger either by causing drought or by bringing an epidemic upon the community. Prayers and sacrifice (*kafara*) are the only remedy for such a situation. There are at least eighteen possible *kayas* where the Digo can go to offer their sacrifice and prayers in order to deal with a community problem. These *kayas* include: Dzombo, Mrima, Muhaka, Longo ya Mwagadi, Galaani, Magaoni, Tiwi, Ukunda, Diani, Kwale, Shonda, Silimani, Waa, Ganzoni, Bombo, Shimba Hills, Kiteje, and Mivumoni.

---

1 Benjamin Ray, "African Shrines as Channels of Communication," in *African Spirituality: Forms, Meanings, and Expressions*, ed. Jacob K. Olupona (New York: The Crossroad Publishing Company, 2000), 26.

2 In 1997 during a tribal clash between the Digo and other Kenyan up-country groups, the Digo hid in one of these shrines, *Kaya Bombo*, to avoid retaliation from other tribes who were involved in the bloody clash.

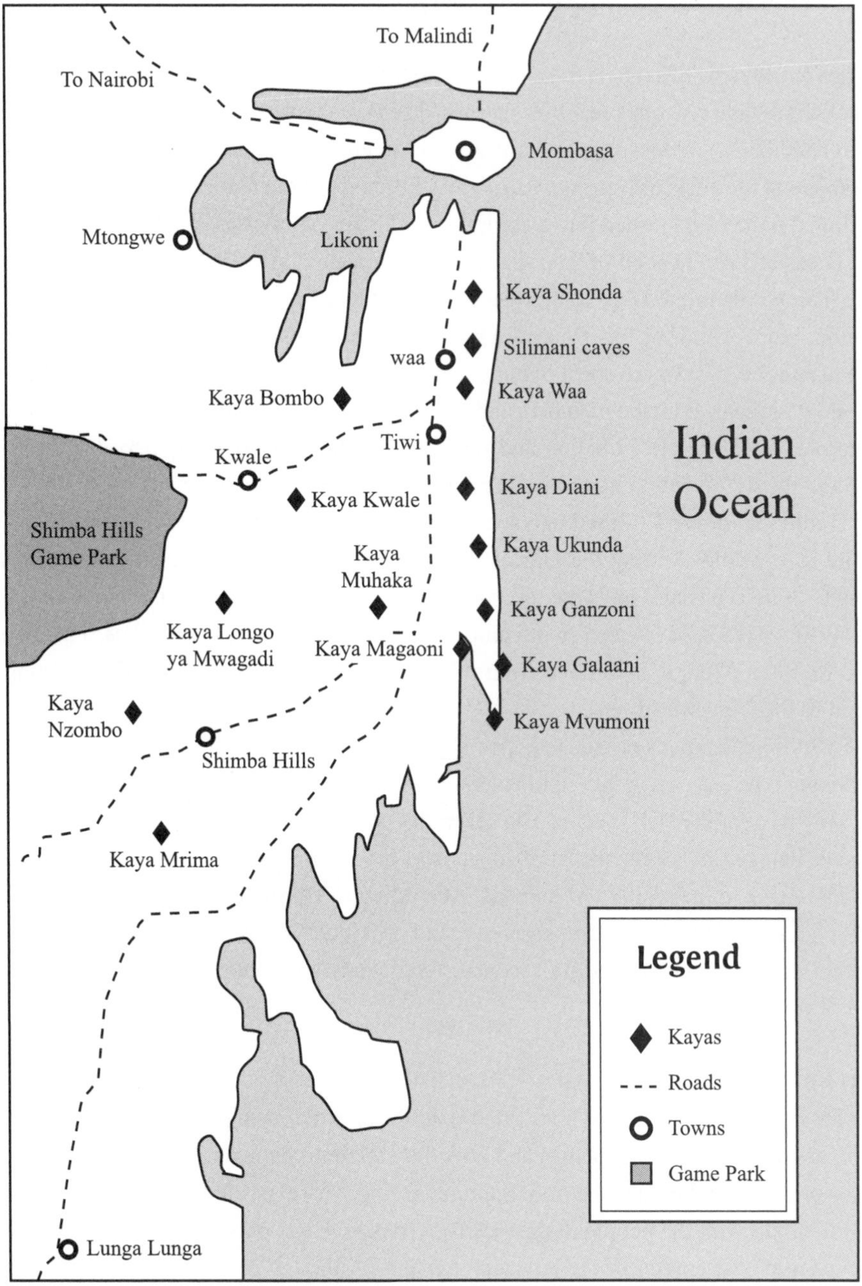

Figure 3: Locations of Community Shrines (kayas) in Digoland[3]

3 Stephen Mutuku Sesi, "Prayer Among the Digo Muslims of Kenya and its Implications for Christian Witness," Unpublished Dissertation, Fuller Theological Seminary, 2003, 55.

God and Spirits in Kaya Worship

In Digo worldview, Mlungu is the highest of all the spiritual beings. He created the universe plus all things and creatures that live on earth. The Digo approach Mlungu through their sacrifices and libation in their shrines, both at home and in designated areas known as *Mizimuni* (the abode of the ancestral spirits), *Mizukani* (the abode of the nature spirits), and *Kaya* (the traditional homestead turned into a community shrine). Mlungu is capable of supplying all their needs and can heal all of their diseases if approached in the right way. Prayer is much more than words in the Digo traditional culture. Prayer includes proper leadership, proper location, proper timing, proper sacrifice or offering, and finally proper words. Although the *mizimu* and the *mizuka* are spirit beings, they are nevertheless a part of their families, and they are guardians of all the members and properties of the living members of their families. Therefore, the Digo offer libation and sacrifices to maintain harmony between the living dead and the living and to gain favor from Mlungu through the *mizimu*.

Traditional prayers of the Digo society are a key element of the Digo worldview and culture as a whole. Among the Digo, all prayers are ultimately directed to the Supreme Being (Mlungu) because he is the ultimate source of the spiritual power or force needed to control life. This name is also found among other East African Bantu tribes. The Swahili name for God, Mungu, is derived from this Bantu name for the Creator God. Mlungu is central to the Digo worldview.

Everything happens or fails to happen by the will of Mlungu. For every prayer offered, the diviners, priests, or traditional healers clearly admit that without the will of Mlungu, they pray or treat the sick in vain. The centrality of Mlungu in their worldview means that all other beings, including ancestral spirits and other spirits (*mizimu* and *mizuka*), play a secondary role in the welfare of humans. According to Dominique Zahan, God in African traditional religion is the creator, sustainer, and provider. God is primary and central while all other divinities and spirits are secondary assistants and intermediaries through whom prayers are offered.[4]

Digo Spirits

In order to illustrate the power associated with the spiritual beings in the Digo cosmology, let me describe the spiritual beings and how they relate to humans according to traditional Digo worldview. Mlungu is the only Supreme Being who exists in the sky (*Mlunguni*). He has little to do with the people in their daily activities. He is only significant because he is believed to be the creator of the physical universe. Although Mlungu exists in the sky, he intervenes in human affairs, especially when he is invoked through prayers.

Mizuka are nature spirits, which inhabit the traditional shrines like the *kaya*, *mizukani*, and *mizimuni*. They can bring calamity to humans by causing natural disasters like drought,

4 Dominique Zahan, "Some Reflections on African Spirituality," in *African Spirituality: Forms, Meanings, and Expressions*, ed. Jacob K. Olupona (New York: The Crossroad Publishing Company, 2000), 3–8.

epidemic, sickness, and other malicious deeds. When invoked in prayer and when participating in a sacrificial fellowship with humans, they can represent humans before Mlungu to heal their bodies or their land. The *koma* are ancestral spirits, which may live within the homestead and are involved in the worship in the *mizimuni* and *mizukani*. Their main functions are to assist the living and protect them. Sometimes when they are unhappy, they may cause sickness in the family to draw attention.

The *phepho* are nature spirits, which possess people. They are associated with many psychological sicknesses and disorders, as well as all kinds of fits when they possess a person. This term is used in the Swahili Bible to translate demons. The *phepho* are closely associated with the Islamic jinn. Unlike the *phepho*, the jinn are created spirits, which are possessed by people and kept at home in order to protect or help the owner to get more wealth. Those who possess good jinn are blessed while those who possess evil jinn end up suffering through demands for human blood offerings. The day they do not get blood, the evil jinn normally kills the host.

Although Islam has been present among the Digo for more than six centuries,[5] the traditional way of life and the traditional prayers are still active and coexist with Islamic teaching. Trimingham observed that, "in established Islamic-African societies there is no conflict between the faith professed and the practices observed. The two elements run parallel, both are an integral part of Swahili culture."[6] This traditional way of life may be branded primitive by modernists, but it is the main way in which most Digo Muslims view the world around them.

Integration of Primal and Islamic Worldviews

The Digo conduct their affairs within two worldviews—the traditional worldview, which is controlled mostly by spiritual beings acting as intermediaries of a Supreme Being (Mlungu), and the Islamic worldview, where Allah is the sole God without associates or intermediaries. Figure 4 shows this integration between primal and Islamic worldviews. Mlungu is at the center of the primal worldview, while Allah is at the core of Islamic worldview. The concepts of Mlungu and Allah have been integrated in a limited way. Digo cultural healers appeal to both Mlungu and Allah for power to heal diseases and to do miracles. The jinn are found in the lists of spirits of both systems of belief. Digo Islamic leaders, imams, sheikhs, and Qurʾanic teachers appeal to ancestral spirits, nature spirits, and Mlungu for protection from witches and sorcerers while upholding the teaching of the Qurʾan and the Hadith.

---

5 The expansion of Islam in East Africa probably dates back to about the year 950, when a new population settled in the East Coast of Africa. This new population came to East Africa from the Arabian Peninsula and settled in Manda, Kilwa, and Old Kipini. James De Vere Allen, *Swahili Origins* (Athens, OH: Ohio University Press, 1993), 24.

6 J. Spencer Trimingham, *Islam in East Africa* (London: Oxford University Press, 1964), 113.

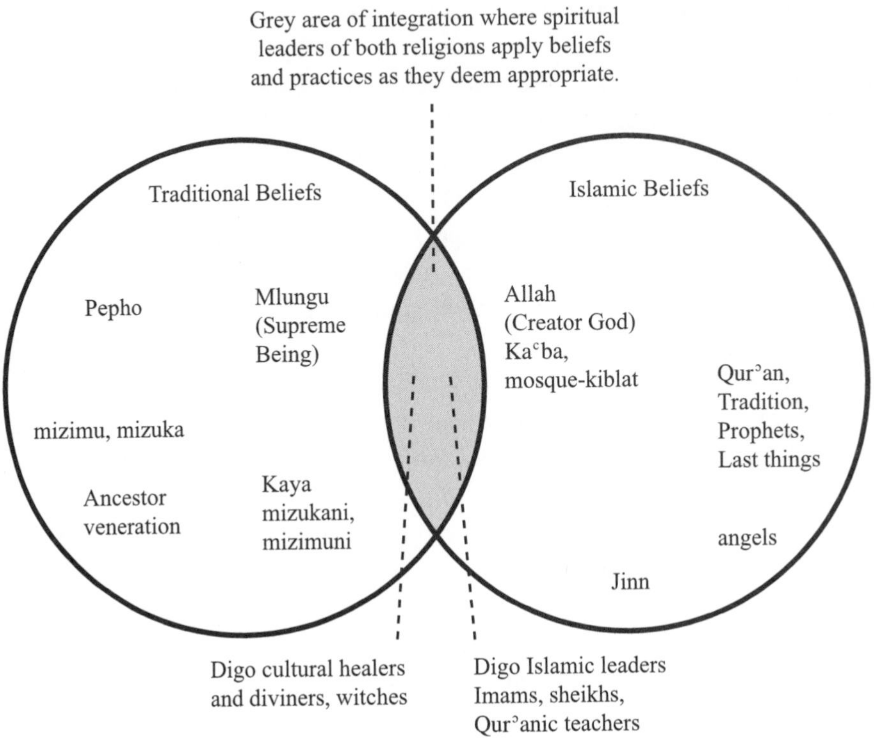

Figure 4: Integration of Primal and Islamic Worldview

Contextual Implications

In relevance theory "the most important type of cognitive effect achieved by processing an input in a context is a contextual implication, a conclusion deducible from the input and the context together, but from neither input nor context alone."[7] In the case of the Digo or Giriama the input is Islamic teaching and the context is their primal worldview. The two brought together by the spread of Islam led to the contextual implication where as the figure above demonstrates there is gray area overlap in their cognitive level. In this way the concept of shrine forms the basis for contextual assumptions about worship. Thus divinity is connected to a shrine, whether that divinity is Mlungu or Allah or Yahweh. Where believers go to offer prayers is therefore a shrine. Churches and mosques are therefore shrines and are points of communication between humans and deities.

7 Deirdre Wilson and Dan Sperber, "Relevance Theory" at http://people.bu.edu/bfraser/Relevance%20Theory%20Oriented/Sperber%20&%20Wilson%20-%20RT%20Revisited.pdf, 2002, 251.

Folk Practices in Digo Islam

Digo culture tolerates the different rules of Islam, and the Digo are willing to adapt Islamic forms into their traditional culture. The result is a marriage between the traditional Digo culture and the orthodox Arabian Islamic culture. These two elements of the current Digo way of life are not in opposition to each other and do not represent any of the original cultural norms of either Digo culture or orthodox Islam.

Two religious systems have been integrated to form the way of life for majority Muslims in Kwale County. Orthodox Islam, which includes all the teaching of the Qur'an and the traditions of Muhammad, which is organized around the mosque and the Islamic schools (*Madarasa*). Traditional Digo religion, which includes the veneration of ancestors, spirits and worship of the traditional Supreme Being Mlungu and the practice of traditional medicine and magic, which is organized around the leadership of *waganga* (traditional healers) and *Wazee* (senior elders). About 75 percent of Digo people are more comfortable with the gray area type of religious beliefs than with pure Islamic worship.

Digo primal worldview is more complex and sophisticated than ordinary observers can deduce. At first glance it seems as if Islamic worldview is dominant until one starts talking to diviners, cultural healers and Muslim leaders. The Digo do not simply go back to try their traditional prayer forms after Islamic and Christian prayers fail; rather, they engage their spirits first and, when they fail to deliver, try other avenues like Islam and Christianity. Digo primal worldview is a present and dominant phenomenon in every area of Digo life cycles.

What we are faced with is not merely an involved past, but mainly an intricate present. The traditional worldviews are in a state of dynamic change characterized by a very high degree of flexibility leading to the creation of ever new forms. Contrary to the over simple conviction of many, the old religious certainties do not yield so easily to modern technological civilization.[8]

8 Anastasios Yannoulatos, "Growing into an Awareness of Primal World-views," in *Primal World-Views: Christian Involvement in Dialogue with Traditional Thought Forms*, ed. John B. Taylor (Ibadan, Nigeria: Daystar Press, 1976), 72–78.

Organic Analogy (Living Beings)			**Mechanical Analogy (Impersonal)**	
Categories	Digo Religion	Islam	Digo Religion	Islam
Unseen supernatural	Mlungu	Allah angels	Mlunguni (abode of God/ Mlungu)	heaven, hell
Unseen natural (may be humanly experienced through dreams and visions)	Mizuka, Mizimu, Koma, Phepho	jinn shaytan saints Zar spirits	kuzimuni (abode of the dead) uganga (magic) utsai (witchcraft) dzongo (evil eye) chirapo (oath) mzizo (curses) baraka (blessings) fingo (fertility)	baraka (blessings) laʿana (curse)
Seen or Empirical	cultural healers, witches, shrine guardians, rain makers, prophets	imams, sheikhs, teachers of law (holy men)	cultural healers' paraphernalia (kituku, kivunga, kayamba, kiruu, kivele, kititi, phe'ngu, ndonga, panga), rocks (Jiwe Kongo), caves, charms (hirizi)	Qurʾan rosary amulets talisman mosque Kaʿba black stone
	animals, plants, forests, shrines			

Figure 5: Paradigms of Spiritual Beings and Forces in the Contemporary Digo Religion (Adapted from Hiebert)[9]

Spiritual Beings and Forces in the Contemporary Digo Religion

Following an analytical framework from Paul G. Hiebert, I would place the spiritual beings and objects of power used by the Digo in their traditional and Islamic religions into six categories.[10] For the Digo primal religion in the seen organic category, the living beings include animals, plants, forests, and shrines. The Islamic religion would not associate spiritual power with any object since it would amount to idolatry. Other categories are seen and mechanical (impersonal), unseen natural organic, unseen natural mechanical, unseen supernatural organic and unseen supernatural mechanical.

As noted in Figure 5, in the visible realm of the world, spiritual force can be found in organic things like plants, shrines (*kayas, Mizimuni, Mizukani*), and houses that are built for healing activities (*chumba cha* Mlungu). It is also found in impersonal objects used as cultural healers' paraphernalia like *kituku, kivunga, kayamba, kiruu, kivele, kititi, phe'ngu, ndonga, panga,* rocks (*Jiwe Kongo*), and caves. Islamic objects that contain power include

9 Paul G. Hiebert, "The Flaw of the Excluded Middle," *Missiology* 10(1), 1982, 40.

10 Hiebert, "The Flaw"; see also Paul G. Hiebert, Daniel Shaw, and Tite Tiénou, *Understanding Folk Religion: A Christian Response to Popular Beliefs and Practices* (Grand Rapids: Baker Books, 1999).

the Qurʾan, rosary, amulets like the hand of Fatima, talisman, Kaʿba, black stone, and mosques. In Digo primal religion, humans control spiritual force through the art of traditional healing, witchcraft, sorcery, and physical phenomena, like evil eye, evil tongue, and evil mouth. Islam offers imams, sheikhs, and teachers of the law (holy men) as the persons of power and spiritual authority, alongside the traditional healers. Islamic prayers and amulets are used to ward off evil or to protect people from sickness and death.

Sometimes there is a competition between the Muslim holy men and the traditional practitioners. Sometimes the Muslim holy men win the power contests. For example, the sorcerers and the priests failed to redress the calamities of drought in the early Malinke kingdom of Malal in western Sudan, through their sacrifices and ritual prayers. The ruler asked the visiting Muslim holy man to pray for rain. "The dramatic effectiveness of the Muslim remedy over that performed by 'sorcerers' led to the destruction of palace shrines and to the monarch's house accepting Islam as an alternative religious practice."[11] In Digo land, traditional practitioners are usually more experienced than the Muslim holy men in control of power and the imams who have been bewitched in the past, forcing them to learn the skills of divination and cultural healing.

In the invisible world, spiritual force is associated with spiritual beings. In the table above, these beings are placed in the middle realm[12] between the Supreme Being (Mlungu) and the visible realm. These spiritual beings (*Mizuka, Mizimu, Koma,* Jinn, *Phepho*) are controlled through divination to be servants of humans, but they are also harmful when they feel offended by human behavior. Mlungu is not associated with any impersonal objects of spiritual force, except his abode, *Mlunguni*. For Islam, Allah is the Supreme Being who exists in his own supernatural state with his angels. In addition to the spirits of the traditional Digo belief, the Digo also use the Islamic jinn, which are used to bring blessings (*barakāt*) of wealth and sometimes to protect their possessors from any form of evil or curse. However, the jinn has to receive human sacrifice to bless his possessor. The jinn only accept human sacrifices of close relatives of the owner, like a mother, father, son, or daughter. Usually the one seeking the blessing names one of his relatives and within a short period the person offered disappears or dies a mysterious death. Therefore, Islam makes a desired addition of power control through its jinn, prayers, and amulets.

Conclusion

How could religious traditions like those of the Digo with a strong belief in a Supreme Being not get the worship of Allah or Yahweh right? With so many similarities in the belief system of the traditional African and Islamic beliefs one would assume that Africans would make

11 David Owusu-Ansah, "Prayer, Amulets, and Healing," in *The History of Islam in Africa*, eds. Nehemia Levtzion and Randall L. Pouwels (Athens, OH: Ohio University Press, 2000), 477.

12 As noted earlier, except for the Islamic solid line between the jinn, shaytan, saints, and Allah and between paradise and the spiritual experiences of *baraka*, the compartments are divided with dotted lines, which means that the divisions between the different realms are fluid and can be crossed.

the best Muslims or best Christians. On the contrary a syncretistic belief system runs deep in the hearts of faithful Muslims. In an attempt to address the problem Muslim missionaries spend more money in the construction of more mosques and *madrassas* (Qurʾanic schools) to teach the religious beliefs and pillars. Apparently in the case of the Digo where the oldest mosque is situated, Tiwi, is also the location of the most famous shrine (Kaya Tiwi), as practical evidence of this bifurcation of faith among Digo Muslims.

The problem lies with the traditional belief about the Supreme Being, Mlungu, who exists alongside other deities and spirits as his mediators between him and humans. The paradox of believing in one Creator of all things and at the same time recognizing the existence and spiritual power of other deities and spirits venerated as gods in worship is explained by the fact that these other deities and spirits enhance the importance and supremacy of the Supreme Being. As Emefie Ikenga Metuh[13] argues, "for the Igbo … this paradox presents no problem … *Chukwu* [Igbo Supreme Being] is not a jealous God."[14] On the contrary Allah is one and exists as simple unity (*tawḥid*) without associates or assistants. However it takes more than teaching to divorce the mind from the concept of a Creator God who is assisted and associated with other deities and spirits.

13 Emefie Ikenga Metuh, *God and Man in African Religion: A Case Study of the Igbo of Nigeria* (London: Geoffrey Chapman, 1981), 61.

14 In Christianity Yahweh is "a jealous God" (Ex 20:5). He cannot permit the worship of other deities or spirits alongside His worship.

SECTION 3

Christian Witness

INTRODUCTION BY DEAN S. GILLILAND

No volume that honors Dudley Woodberry would be complete without obvious attention to the means of Christian witness among Muslims. How to achieve the most respectful and appropriate paths to follow for Christian witness among Muslims has always been of highest importance in Dudley's life. These five chapters deal with the nuances of contextual witness to Muslims, the need for understanding the complex life of Muslim background believers as well as a call to Christian witness through seeking biblical *shalom* within the Islamic world.

Greenlee takes seriously the "bottom line," so to speak, when he asks the question as to what factors motivate a Muslim to change his/her faith, The corollary to this inquiry is that making the right approach in evangelism depends on first understanding what factors lead to conversion. Greenlee calls for research in this area of conversion. He makes his own helpful contribution in this by citing the intricate variety of factors (lenses) that influence Muslims to follow Jesus. While all of these "lenses," or dimensions, of conversion are important—some to a lesser and some to a greater degree—they all interact in complex ways to bring about change. These "lenses" would be factors in conversion from any religion to another, but they carry special relevance for Muslims at this critical time when, unfortunately, Christianity is so closely identified with the West.

In the past forty years much new ground has been broken in how to utilize Islamic forms in order to connect Muslim people to the Christian message. From the beginning of this period, while there was still much resistance, Phil Parshall showed how the selective use of Muslim belief and practice can help in minimizing conflict with Islam. Parshall's published thinking began with his *New Paths in Muslim Evangelism*.[1] As contextual paradigms developed further through the 1980s and 1990s, Parshall also pointed out the risks

1 Phil Parshall, *New Paths in Muslim Evangelism* (Grand Rapids: Baker, 1980).

involved when careful boundaries are not respected. Parshall's contribution in this section is to give an overall summary of development in the evangelization of peoples with a Muslim background. He reviews the approaches that have been most helpful, as well as the problems and questions that still need to be answered.

John Travis, an authoritative practitioner in the Asian Muslim world, begins by recalling John Wilder's 1977 vision of "people movements." The hope of finding ways for Muslims to embrace ʿIsa al-Masih, with minimum disruption from the cultures of their birth, is now being fulfilled in gracious and often miraculous ways. The reality of differences in how Muslims follow Jesus and grow in their faith led Travis to develop what is known as the C–1 through C–6 models. These models deal with the extent of identity and interaction with Muslim practice among Muslim background believers. Besides an overview and critique of the "Jesus movements," Travis interprets several case studies and concludes with ten characteristics of what he calls Asian "ecclesiae." He concludes that "there is no one single ministry or methodology that can account for these breakthroughs."

A chapter by Caleb Chul-Soo Kim, a Korean scholar living and working in Kenya, applies anthropological insights to help us understand the role of jinn and evil spirits in the daily experience and religious worldview of East African Muslims. Kim notes that the Western-influenced worldview of many Christian workers in East Africa fails to take seriously this dimension of their Muslim neighbors' concerns, and Kim offers practical proposals for how to redress this through affective sensitivity and building on common ground.

Following the discussion on understanding the daily experience and worldview of Muslims, Christine Mallouhi takes up the responsibility given to Christians for making peace and working for reconciliation. The essence of Christian witness is "to help people experience life as we understand God intends it to be lived." This is the broader, deep-level peace, not described by cessation of war but by a "third way," found in the simplicity of being with and standing alongside another while taking responsibility for the other's good. Mallouhi finds her stories for this all-embracing peace in Mary's song and, especially, in Simeon. Simeon speaks of peace in recognition of hope and salvation for the Gentiles through Jesus' birth. This, coming from a Jew, is a reversal of what is usually expected. He demonstrates that "this peace does not exclude contraries but includes them."

With these essays we recognize that the fullness of *shalom* must support the invitation to Muslim people to follow Jesus.

11
How Is the Gospel Good News for Muslims?[1]

BY DAVID H. GREENLEE

From the time of Ubaidallah ibn Jahiz, who in Ethiopia became "the first Muslim … to discover and embrace the truth," Muslims in increasing numbers have found that the good news is indeed *good*.[2] Until recently, though, witness among Muslims was often characterized by the title of Charles Marsh's book, *Too Hard for God?*[3] or Bilquis Sheikh's individual journey, *I Dared to Call Him Father*,[4] rather than the large numbers of the 1960s Indonesian revival.[5]

That Muslims in significant numbers are coming to faith in Jesus Christ—in a biblical sense—is no secret. Global news media in 2006 headlined the plight of the "Afghan convert to Christianity." Italy's *Corriere della sera* covered the dangers of being a Christian in Algeria.[6] Meanwhile, the stories of dozens of Muslims who have come to faith in Jesus

---

1 An abbreviated version of this paper was provided to the Edinburgh 2010 "Christian Mission among other Faiths" study group, and was published as "New Faith, Renewed Identity: How Some Muslims Are Becoming Followers of Jesus," in *Witnessing to Christ in a Pluralistic Age: Christian Mission Among Other Faiths*, Edinburgh 2010 series, *Witnessing to Christ in a Pluralistic World*, Lalsangkima Pachuau and Knud Jørgensen, ed. (Oxford: Regnum Books, 2011), 139–48.

2 Yurij Maximov, "A History of Orthodox Missions among the Muslims," 2004, http://www.orthodoxytoday.org/articles4/MaximovMuslims.php.

3 Charles Marsh, *Too Hard for God?* (Carlisle, UK: Authentic Media, 2000).

4 Bilquis Sheikh, *I Dared to Call Him Father*, with Richard H. Schneider (Lincoln, VA: Chosen, 1978).

5 See Avery Willis, *Indonesian Revival: Why Two Million Came to Christ* (Pasadena: William Carey Library, 1977); and Robert W. Hefner, "Of Faith and Commitment: Christian Conversion in Muslim Java," in *Conversion to Christianity: Historical and Anthropological Perspectives on a Great Transformation*, ed. Robert W. Hefner (Berkeley: University of California Press, 1993), 99–125.

6 Agostino Gramigna, "Algeria: Com'è pericoloso oggi essere cristiani a Oran [How Difficult It is to Be a Christian in Oran]," *Corriere della sera* (January 17, 2007): 51–56; and Agostino Gramigna, "Difficile essere cristiani in Algeria," *Corriere della sera* (2007), http://video.corriere.it/media/35df5110-a615-11db-bf0d-0003ba99c53b.

Christ are posted on YouTube's "Muslims4Jesus" channel along with links to numerous websites of "former Muslims who embraced Jesus Christ as their Lord and Saviour."[7]

As I have noted elsewhere, relatively little research has been published describing the processes by which Muslims are coming to faith in Jesus Christ.[8] Fortunately, that situation is changing. A key contributor to this development has been J. Dudley Woodberry, both with his ongoing global study and through those he has inspired.[9] In appreciation for his ministry and personal encouragement, it is a privilege to offer this essay in Dr. Woodberry's honor.

Why Research Is Needed

Research into the conversion processes among Muslims who have become believers in Jesus Christ is needed because, as Richard Peace observed, "How we conceive of conversion determines how we do evangelism."[10] A better understanding of conversion may make us more fruitful in our witness. Colin Edwards discovered that South Asian Muslims "see themselves as linked to others in a deep way, particularly with leaders. As Muslims they had considered linkage with the prophet Muhammad as the means to salvation."[11] This understanding is central in understanding how people here are now coming to faith in ᶜIsa al-Masih and impacts Edwards' witness.

We also need to do research because it can challenge our assumptions and uncover surprises. Counter to his expectations, in Denmark Mogens Mogensen found that most baptisms of converts from other religions to Christianity take place in the folk church and migrant congregations, not in the free churches.[12] Elsewhere he found that "the vast majority of those involved in the mission projects [among Nigerian Fulbe] attached no importance to the use of the *Qur'an* [in witness], but thirty percent of the converts stated that it had much influence on their conversion."[13] In my own research, the relative absence of eldest

---

7 http://www.youtube.com/user/Muslims4Jesus.

8 David Greenlee, "Coming to Faith in Christ: Highlights from Recent Research," *Missionalia* 34, no. 1 (2006): 46–61.

9 J. Dudley Woodberry, Russell G. Shubin, and G. Marks. "Why Muslims Follow Jesus," *Christianity Today* 51, no. 10 (October 2007): 80–85; J. Dudley Woodberry, "A Global Perspective on Muslims Coming to Faith in Christ," in *From the Straight Path to the Narrow Way: Journeys of Faith*, ed. David H. Greenlee (Downers Grove, IL: InterVarsity Press, 2006): 11–22.

10 Richard Peace, *Conversion in the New Testament: Paul and the Twelve* (Grand Rapids: Eerdmans, 1999), 286.

11 Colin Edwards, "Patronage, Salvation, and Being Joined with Jesus: Socio-anthropological Insights from South Asia," in David Greenlee, *Longing for Community: Church,* Ummah, *or Somewhere in Between?* (Pasadena: William Carey Library, forthcoming 2012).

12 Mogens S. Mogensen, "Migration and Conversion: The Conversion of Immigrants to Christianity in a Danish Context," in *Mission to the World: Communicating the Gospel in the 21st Century: Essays in Honour of Knud Jørgensen,* eds. Tormod Engelsviken and Thor Strandenæs (Oxford: Regnum, 2008), 67–84.

13 Mogens S. Mogensen, "Contextual Communication of the Gospel to Pastoral Fulbe in Northern Nigeria" (PhD diss., Fuller Theological Seminary, 2000), 238, http://www.intercultural.dk/component/content/article/11-inenglish/184-literature-on-fulanis.

sons among the new believers was unexpected and surprising both to missionaries and to leaders among the Moroccan believers.[14]

Because God *is* at work, research will help us apply lessons learned in one area to other settings, being sensitive to God's sovereign initiative as well as the distinctives of human societies. This includes study of our current setting as well as learning from history and from ecclesiastical traditions different from our own. Yurij Maximov, for example, refers to the conversion of entire tribes and to St. Pachomy, a nephew of the caliph and martyred about 820, as among "the greatest evidence and fruit of the Orthodox Church's missionary labors and its great spiritual (if not statistical) triumph."[15] I, for one, need to learn more from this history.[16]

Filtered Views of Conversion

Just as conceptions of conversion affect evangelism, *pre*conceptions and *mis*conceptions of conversion affect the way people respond to religious change. Not long ago the world press covered the story of Lina Joy, born a Malaysian Muslim but baptized a Roman Catholic. Denying her appeal to have "Islam" removed from her identity card, Malaysian chief justice Ahmad Fairuz Abdul Halim ruled that "she cannot at her own whim simply enter or leave her religion. She must follow rules." Dissenting justice Richard Malunjam said that Joy's "fundamental constitutional right of freedom of religion" had been violated. Meanwhile, the journalist cited notes that the court "refused to recognize the conversion of a Muslim-born woman to Christianity."[17] These three view conversion through different filters: denial of its possibility, affirmation as a constitutional right, and recognition as a fact linked to actions and beliefs.

We researchers must be aware of our own biases as well as those of the sources and stories we analyze. Mohammad Hassan Khalil and Mucahit Bilici of the University of Michigan write that "the ways in which conversion narratives are deployed in each of the sources we analyzed significantly vary and reflect the religious or ideological orientations of the sources as much as they reflect individual accounts of what really happened."[18]

Their paper recognizes the fact of conversion out of Islam. It is an effort to fill a gap in the "literature [that] does not tell us much about the overall landscape of conversion out of

---

14 David Greenlee, "Christian Conversion from Islam: Social, Cultural, Communication, and Supernatural Factors in the Process of Conversion and Faithful Church Participation" (PhD diss., Trinity Evangelical Divinity School, 1996), 223.

15 Maximov, "History of Orthodox Missions."

16 See Jean-Marie Gaudeul, *Called from Islam to Christ: Why Muslims Become Christians* (Crowborough, UK: Monarch, 1999), both for helpful findings and for reference to numerous Roman Catholic and French-language sources.

17 Thomas Fuller, "Malaysian Court Refuses to Recognize Muslim's Conversion to Christianity," *New York Times* (May 30, 2007), http://www.iht.com/articles/2007/05/30/news/malaysia.php.

18 Mohammad Hassan Khalil and Mucahit Bilici, "Conversion Out of Islam: A Study of Conversion Narratives of Former Muslims," *The Muslim World* 97, no.1 (January 2007), 121.

Islam. It fails to address such questions as: By what processes and under what conditions do people leave Islam? How do former Muslims or those who speak on their behalf represent their departure?"[19]

Khalil and Bilici's findings are limited to negative perceptions of Islam and Muslims with the conclusion that "the status of women in Islam" and "Muslims [perceived] as cruel, oppressive, and backward" are the two primary factors.[20] Although their sources include 128 testimonies posted on the "Answering Islam" website,[21] these researchers evidently do not see—with one exception referred to below—any attractive factors about Jesus Christ, the Bible, or Christians, so frequently reported by Christian researchers.

Lenses to Clarify Our Vision

Conversion is a complex phenomenon. We will never be able to describe it fully. However, as Paul Hiebert often said, "We see in part, but we do see" (cf. 1 Cor 13:12).

To help clarify our understanding of how Muslims are coming to faith in Jesus Christ, Rick Love and I suggest seven lenses—categories—that are useful in research and reflection.[22] Like filters that pass only certain colors of light, observing conversion through these lenses draws out aspects lost in the glare of other factors. Valuable as individual images, we should also attempt to recombine them into an enhanced, multidimensional whole.

The psychological lens

Andreas Maurer[23] builds on the psychological framework of such writers as Abraham Maslow[24] and Lewis R. Rambo.[25] Rather than looking at humans from a simplistic, spiritual framework, we should see them "holistically as [people] with different needs, all of which play a role in the movement to conversion."[26] Misused, psychology can be a tool of manipulation; used properly, it can help us in the task of understanding people and their complex inner responses to the gospel and thus "prepare the way for communicating Jesus Christ as God's Son and the unique Savior."[27]

Hannes Wiher, drawing on experience in Guinea, links psychology and missiology in a helpful analysis of shame and guilt orientations and how God convicts us of sin. He observes

---

19 Ibid., 111.

20 Ibid., 118, 120.

21 See http://www.answering-islam.de.

22 David Greenlee and Rick Love, "Conversion through the Looking Glass: Muslims and the Multiple Facets of Conversion," in Greenlee, *From the Straight Path*, 35–50.

23 Andreas Maurer, "In Search of a New Life: Conversion Motives of Christians and Muslims" (ThD diss., University of South Africa, 1999); and Andreas Maurer, "In Search of a New Life: Conversion Motives of Christians and Muslims," in Greenlee, *From the Straight Path*, 93–106.

24 A. H. Maslow, *Motivation and Personality* (New York: Harper & Row, 1970).

25 Lewis R. Rambo, *Understanding Religious Conversion* (New Haven: Yale University Press, 1993).

26 Maurer, "In Search" (2006), 106.

27 George J. Jennings, "Psychocultural Study in Missiology: Middle Eastern Insecurity," *Missiology* 15, no. 1 (January 1987): 96.

that "the content of every conscience is close enough to God's norms in order to be an initial reference point (Rom 2:1–16). In initial evangelism, the missionary should therefore speak of sin with reference to the indigenous conscience, particularly [the aspect] … in agreement with Scripture." If our message is based on issues irrelevant to the local conscience, it may cause "misunderstanding in the audience and [represent] a call to accept the culture of the missionary," leading to refusal, or a merely opportunistic, outward change. "Conversion [that] bypasses the indigenous conscience," Wiher warns, "may lead to superficial conformity or to compartmentalized conformity, that is, syncretism."[28]

The role of dreams in drawing Muslims to faith in Jesus Christ has been frequently reported. Seppo Syrjänen,[29] though, is among the few to move beyond phenomenology and consider psychological aspects of how God works in this way. Analyzing conversion in the framework of a search for meaning and identity, he discusses the role of many dreams as the culmination of an inner struggle granting license to do that which is otherwise prohibited.

Richard Kronk disagrees with Sigmund Freud who considered dreams to be "purely a psychological phenomena [that] were the outward manifestation of an internalized conflict." Kronk instead builds on the thought of Carl Jung who "upholds the possibility that some dreams have an outside source both in their content and in the occasion of their occurrence … that there is more to dreams and their interpretations than a collective consideration of internal conflict." Dreams, Kronk says, are significant because they are "sources of religious significance for the Muslim … [who] relies heavily upon such to define reality, answer ultimate questions and guide his day-to-day activities."[30]

Syrjänen and Kronk both point to cases of God's special initiative in granting dreams as part of the process of conversion. Their findings, though, are consistent with those of Jean-Marie Gaudeul who writes that we should not "overlook the fact that the obscure mechanisms of the human psyche are also subject to divine action … [God] speaks to us in the kind of language we can understand, and it is not surprising if he uses dreams and visions and healings to people who believe in them."[31]

The behavioral lens

Paul Hiebert reminds us that conversion must involve all levels of culture, including the outer layer of behavior. There is a danger of deceptive actions or that we misinterpret the actions of those who indeed have turned to God through Jesus Christ. But "transformed behavior is … a sign of inner transformation and a testimony to the world of that transformation."[32]

---

28 Hannes Wiher, *Shame and Guilt: A Key to Cross-Cultural Ministry* (Bonn: Edition IWG, Mission Academics, Band 10, Verlag für Kultur und Wissenschaft, 2003), 367.

29 Seppo Syrjänen, "In Search of Meaning and Identity: Conversion to Christianity in Pakistani Muslim Culture," *Annals of the Finnish Society for Missiology and Ecumenics* 45 (1984): 132, 137.

30 Richard Kronk, "Non-Literary Personal Revelation: The Role of Dreams and Visions in Muslim Conversion" (MA thesis, Dallas Theological Seminary, 1993), 14, 22, 25–26.

31 Gaudeul, *Called from Islam*, 225.

32 Paul Hiebert, "Worldview Transformation," in Greenlee, *From the Straight Path*, 29.

Observed behavior in itself attracts others to faith in Christ. Khalil and Bilici's only reference to a positive, attractive factor of the new faith has to do with Christian behavior.[33] They quote S. V. Bhajjan who never observed a Muslim "who confessed that he accepted Jesus Christ as his Lord and Saviour" because of theological arguments. Instead, "it is always through a small deed of brotherly love done by a Christian that the heart of a Muslim is moved."[34]

Participation is a third part of the behavioral aspect of conversion. Mary McVicker observes that "while physical and cognitive experiences of Jesus tend to differ according to social, economic, or educational backgrounds of the women, behavioral experience is a significant aspect for most Muslim women growing in relationship to God." Her point has to do with moving beyond the logical, cognitive level in order to communicate with Asian Muslim women who "taste *behavioral experience* that impacts their journey of coming to faith."[35]

The sociological lens

The sociological lens is broad, and can help us consider groups such as migrants. Hasan Abdulahugli finds that those most open to the gospel are "those who have tasted hard economic conditions in traditional villages and have moved to the city, away from the social pressures of family, neighbors, and the mosque and into the freedom and love of Christian communities located in urban areas."[36] Mogensen finds "a pattern that links the conversion of immigrants to Christianity closely to their integration into the Danish society."[37] Perhaps a negative confirmation of this, Gabriël Jansen, reporting only a handful of Moroccans in the Netherlands who have become believers in Jesus Christ, finds that "integration [into Dutch churches] … has turned out to be a disappointment for many."[38]

Evelyne Reisacher describes important differences between North African male and female followers of Jesus. The women she interviewed perceive that, once having come to faith, they are more resilient and likely to persevere than are the men. Women's social status, limitations on freedom, and the impact of rejection by family set women apart from men in coming to and growing in faith.[39]

---

33 Khalil and Bilici, "Conversion Out of Islam," 118.

34 S. V. Bhajjan, "Identifying Barriers in the Church's Reception of Muslim Converts." *The Bulletin of Christian Institutes of Islamic Studies* 3, no. 3 (1982): 94. Cited in Khalil and Bilici, "Conversion Out of Islam," 118.

35 Mary McVicker, "Experiencing Jesus: Reflections of South Asian Women," in Greenlee, *From the Straight Path*, 133–34.

36 Hasan Abdulahugli, "Factors Leading to Conversion among Central Asian Muslims," in Greenlee, *From the Straight Path*, 162.

37 Mogensen, "Migration and Conversion," 74.

38 Gabriël Jansen, "Reaching Moroccans in Amsterdam (the Netherlands) with the Gospel" (MA thesis, Tyndale Theological Seminary, 2000), 133.

39 Evelyne Reisacher, "North African Women and Conversion: Specifics of Female Faith and Experience," in Greenlee, *From the Straight Path*, 109–23.

A common accusation, even if we engage in "worthy witness" is that Christians promote conversion through economic incentives.[40] Tobias Rink recognizes this economic factor, and concludes from his study among Sudanese that "social needs and political pressure are for many converts the only reason why they open up to the Christian faith. These motives should not disqualify them as 'rice Christians' because they mark only the beginning phase of the faith development process" (translation mine).[41]

Robert L. Montgomery observes that "the religions that have spread often seem to have offered a resource to leaders or to people as a whole in resisting threats to continued existence," while conversion is less likely when no advantage is perceived.[42] Complementing this thesis, Robert Hefner found that "with Christianity [Javanese Muslim youth of the 1960s] declared their independence from a village social order that, in their eyes, had brought their families pain and humiliation."[43] In Pakistan, Seppo Syrjänen[44] writes that although "awareness of Christianity might very well be present," few Muslims have become Christians because one main source of witness, foreign missionaries, is perceived of as "enemy" while Pakistani Christians are seen as "inferior."

Such political factors are significant in the former Soviet republics of Central Asia. A young man born a Muslim citizen of the U.S.S.R. is currently researching evangelized but "not-yet-believing" youth in the Caucasus. Their "minds have been blinded to understand the true personality and work of Christ," he writes, "because this knowledge has been limited and distorted over the years and the person of Jesus Christ still remains as [the] 'God of Russians.'"[45]

In comparison, Anthony Greenham was surprised that political instability played only a contributory role, and that, only in a minority of Palestinian MBBs' stories. "For most of the Palestinians, political instability may be too common a factor in their lives to suggest itself as an avenue for the transforming encounter of conversion."[46]

Persecution is another sociological factor affecting conversion. In my study of urban Moroccan young men,[47] those who had come to faith and had passed through a period of

---

40 David Greenlee, *One Cross, One Way, Many Journeys: Thinking Again about Conversion* (Tyrone, GA: Authentic, 2007), 85–95.

41 Tobias Rink, "Eine multidimensionale methodik zur analyse von bekehrungsmotiven" (MTh thesis, University of South Africa, 2006), 131. Also available online at http://uir.unisa.ac.za/bitstream/handle/10500/723/dissertation.pdf?sequence=1.

42 Robert Montgomery, "The Spread of Religions and Macrosocial Relations," *Sociological Analysis* 52, no. 1 (1991): 50.

43 Robert W. Hefner, "Of Faith and Commitment: Christian Conversion in Muslim Java," in *Conversion to Christianity: Historical and Anthropological Perspectives on a Great Transformation*, ed. Robert W. Hefner (Berkeley: University of California Press, 1993), 116.

44 Syrjänen, "In Search of Meaning," 120.

45 Russell Eleazar, "Knowing but Not Confessing: Attitudes of Youth in Baku who have Heard the Good News," in Greenlee, *Longing for Community* (forthcoming).

46 Anthony Greenham, "Muslim Conversions to Christ: An Investigation of Palestinian Converts Living in the Holy Land" (PhD diss., Southeastern Baptist Theological Seminary, 2004), 190–91.

47 Greenlee, "Christian Conversion," 203.

persecution tended to be more faithful evangelists than others, but less likely to be known for "bearing one another's burdens" (Gal 6:1,2).

Prakash Gupta focused on areas of significant persecution. He finds that few severely persecuted believers in Jesus were passing on their faith to others. Where faith *does* move into the second generation, it springs from the lives of believers who share many of the following:

- A personal relationship with Jesus Christ
- Prayer central to their lives
- Knowledge of how to talk with God
- Memorization of large portions of the Bible
- Indigenous hymns, choruses, and songs central to daily life and worship
- Those incarcerated know they are supported by the believing community
- Knowledge that persecution is normal and is for Jesus' sake
- Have claimed their freedom and lost their fear
- Have a genealogy of faith[48]

Finally, under the sociological lens we can look at the question of group conversions and movements. We learn with Lowell DeJong of the need for patience, avoiding the pressure to quickly plant a church that almost certainly will be marked by the outside messenger's culture rather than leading to a culturally imbedded church.[49] This approach may help to avoid the problems Mogensen found in a related setting where "almost all the [approximately five hundred] *Fulbe* converts still had a strong identity as *Fulbe* and as Christian *Fulbe*, but the majority of them had serious problems being accepted by their *Fulbe* community." He concludes that this is evidently because "the primary method of evangelism used among *Fulbe* has been 'extraction evangelism.'"[50]

48 Prakash Gupta, "Servants in the Crucible: Findings from a Global Study on Persecution and the Implications for Sending Agencies and Sending Churches" (unpublished manuscript, 2004).

49 Lowell DeJong, "An Insider Movement among Fulbe Muslims," in Greenlee, *From the Straight Path*, 217, 224–28.

50 Mogensen, "Contextual Communication," 273, 275.

John Kim suggests that in fostering a church planting movement an early priority is to understand the "social, political, ethnic, and economic backgrounds" of the people that constrain them from change. In the setting he analyzed, outside Christians' loving response after a destructive storm opened a cluster of villagers to consider change from the traditional beliefs.[51] The movement spread through further collective decisions as the outside missionaries—aware of the sociological issues involved—remained in the background while the new believers themselves assumed leadership of the new movement.[52]

In a tribal setting in West Africa, Dan McVey asked why, after an initial period of significant growth, a movement reached a plateau. Beyond the theological question of God's timing, McVey notes the limited population of hearers, some of them pausing and observing the new believers and their response to persecution. The group nature of society limited access and opportunity to engage in meaningful religious dialogue. However, "the single greatest obstacle to church growth among the Jijimba has been communicating the concept that one can be a follower of Jesus while maintaining identity as a Jijimba." Faithfulness in persecution and lived-out, biblical contextualization have won the confidence of many, McVey writes, and give hope that the community of believers will grow beyond the current plateau in numbers.[53]

The cultural lens

McVey's comment leads us into consideration of the cultural lens. At a very basic level, this lens helps us to see common-sense issues that will help us avoid giving offense in our witness to people of other cultures. At a deeper level, the lens of culture is important in moving beneath surface issues of behavior to understand underlying values and worldview. True contextualization, and not just a contextualized approach to witness, requires the leading input of believers who are insiders to the culture. Well-informed outsiders—or "inbetweeners" as some have called them[54]—can help, but the cultural lens should be used by outsiders with caution and humility.

Lewis Rambo notes that "the more consonant the cultural systems [of messenger and receiver] the more likely it is that conversion will transpire. The more dissonant, the less likely it is that conversion will occur."[55] Manfred Schmid confirms this point, noting that the reason only a small number of Turks in Germany have "committed their lives to Jesus Christ" may be the German Christians' lack of awareness of "the multicultural character of the Body of Christ," their conventional forms and traditions "creating barriers between

51 John Kim, "Muslim Villages Coming to Faith in Christ: A Case Study and Model of Group Dynamics," in Greenlee, *From the Straight Path*, 239–53.

52 See also John Kim, "The Anotoc Story Continued: The Role of Group Dynamics in Insider Movements," *International Journal of Frontier Missiology* 27, no. 2 (2010): 97–104.

53 Dan McVey, "Hindrances to Evangelistic Growth among Muslim Background Believer Churches of the 'Jijimba' People of West Africa," in Greenlee, *From the Straight Path*, 208–13.

54 Kim, "The Anotoc Story Continued," 99.

55 Rambo, *Understanding Religious Conversion*, 42.

Germans and foreigners."[56] A similar barrier appears to be present in northern Nigeria where Mogensen reports that "a significant percentage of the *Fulbe* converts complained that they felt that the Christians did not welcome them in the church during the decision and incorporation phases."[57]

Schmid further observes that "conversion to the Christian faith does not end in betrayal of the oriental culture [nor] threaten Turkish identity" but, in fact, it holds a high chance for the development of a healthy Turkish or Kurdish identity.[58] This reaffirmed my own finding that a byproduct of coming to faith for young Moroccan men was a heightened, positive sense of national identity.[59]

This, however, will not always be the case. William Clark[60] compares the ethnic identity responses of new believers from neighboring ethnic groups of Central Asia.

For many Turkic urbanites, whose first language is Russian, a participation in Kazakh- or Uighur-language Christian worship is an overwhelmingly ethnic experience. Many of the new converts reported experiencing a renaissance of their own ethnicity as they explored the language and culture in ways that are new to them through cell groups and Sunday gatherings. There are local-language songs during worship with strong national themes. A popular song, "Kazakhstan," asks for God's blessing of the nation. As a contrast there is a recently written Uighur worship song entitled "*Vatan*" (Homeland), a semantically powerful word for Uighurs who do not have an independent state. The song encourages worshipers to think of heaven as their true home.

The two songs highlight a key difference between Kazakh and Uighur believers: the lack of a nation-building project among Uighurs, and its impact on the culturally rooted expressions of faith of these neighboring communities of believers.

The Question of Identity

This complex question of identity has been increasingly explored in recent research. "Does one have to go through Christianity to enter God's family?" asks Rebecca Lewis.[61] Far from suggesting religious inclusivism, she along with others such as John and Anna Travis[62] are exploring ways that believers in Christ may remain completely faithful to Jesus and to

56 Manfred Schmid, "Identitätsentwicklung von Christen aus islamischem hintergrund in Deutschland: Eine qualitative untersuchung [Identity Development among Muslim Background Believers in Germany: A Qualitative Study]" (MA thesis, Columbia International University, 1999), vi.

57 Mogensen, "Contextual Communication," 270.

58 Schmid, "Identitätsentwicklung," vii.

59 Greenlee, "Christian Conversion," 125–27.

60 William Clark, "Networks of Faith in Kazakhstan," in *Conversion after Socialism: Disruptions, Modernisms, and Technologies of Faith in the Former Soviet Union*, ed. Mathijs Pelmans (Oxford: Berghahn, 2010), 134.

61 Rebecca Lewis, "Insider Movements: Honoring God-given Identity and Community," *International Journal of Frontier Missiology* 26, no. 1 (2009): 16–19.

62 John Travis and Anna Travis, "Factors Affecting the Identity that Jesus-Followers Choose," in *From Seed to Fruit: Global Trends, Fruitful Practices, and Emerging Issues among Muslims*, ed. J. Dudley Woodberry (Pasadena: William Carey Library, 2008), 193–205.

the Bible, yet without unnecessarily rejecting (or giving the perception of rejecting) their families and culture.[63]

Instructive for us from the broader field of religious conversion, Mark R. J. Faulkner[64] explores the multiple layers of identity in the conversion to Islam by the animist Boni of Kenya. Such analysis is "messy," he says, and evades the application of distinct boundaries that outside observers might desire to apply. The collective memory of the Boni remains strong, and as demonstrated in this ethnography, those memories are revived and applied in times of crisis and in daily life in traditional domains such as by men in the hunting fields and by women around the homestead, while the new religious practices are applied where they are advantageous. Faulkner's study reminds us that conversion involves transformation at multiple levels, both in the individual, and in society. Outside observers may see only the change at the surface, perhaps in some ritual behavior, but not recognize the absence (or presence) of deep change.

Approaching the subject from the combined perspectives of history of religions, cultural anthropology, and Christian theology, Jonas Adelin Jørgensen studied followers of Jesus in Dhaka and Chennai who have not openly become part of the existing churches. Jørgensen supports the authenticity of the faith of these groups, for whom Jesus Christ is central, arguing that "the practice of the *imandars* (faithful to Jesus) and *bhaktas* (devotees of Christ) could be viewed as new and creative manifestations of Christianity in a global age." He concludes that "the resemblance with the larger Christian tradition and community ensures Christian identity. At the same time, the differences enlarge our understanding of what actual and lived Christian life and Christian theology might include in globalized Christianity."[65]

Kathryn Kraft explores the question of identity among Middle Eastern Muslims who have become followers of Jesus, including many who encountered difficulties in integrating into and being identified with the existing churches. She notes that "for most Muslims, leaving Islam cannot even be conceived of as a possibility. While choosing to follow Christ involves for most … consciously rejecting the Muslim creed, they do not want this to entail rejecting their strong cultural heritage, which is identified as Islamic. The biggest challenge they face in developing a new identity is determining how to continue to be culturally Muslim while following a Christian faith."[66] How do these followers of Jesus find this new identity?

---

63 See also Woodberry, "Global Perspective," 17–22; and from non-Muslim settings: Dasan Jeyaraj, *Followers of Christ outside the Church in Chennai, India: A Socio-historical Study of a Non-church Movement* (Zoetermeer, Netherlands: Boekencentrum, 2010); and Greenlee, *One Cross*, 67–84.

64 Mark R. J. Faulkner, "Overtly Muslim, Covertly Boni: Competing Calls of Religious Allegiance on the Kenyan Coast," in *Studies of Religion in Africa*, supplements to the *Journal of Religion in Africa* 29 (Leiden: Brill, 2006).

65 Jonas Adelin Jørgensen, "Global Christianity, Contextual Religious Identity and Local Theologies: Īsā Imandars and Khrist Bhaktas in South Asia," *Lausanne World Pulse*, February 2008, http://www.lausanneworldpulse.com/themedarticles.php/895/02-2008; see also Jonas Adelin Jørgensen, *Jesus Imandars and Christ Bhaktas: Two Case Studies of Interreligious Hermeneutics and Identity in Global Christianity* (Frankfurt: Peter Lang, 2008); and Jeyaraj, *Followers of Christ*.

66 Kathryn Ann Kraft and Abu Atallah, "The Lives of Arab Muslims Who Choose the Christian Faith," *Mishkan* 54: 16–24.

Kraft summarizes that while they … generally recognize and feel a sense of commonality with each other, they approach their identity negotiation in a variety of ways. Some reject everything about their past and choose to become fully "Christian." These are the individuals who are most likely to break off relations with their former communities. Others consider their faith and their ethnicity to be completely separate and consider themselves to be both Muslim and followers of Christ; some of these sought to be socially indistinguishable from their Muslim neighbours. If pressed, most participants admitted to being Muslim in culture, and Christian in creed, although the historical animosity between the world's two largest religions would preclude them from ever calling themselves "Muslim Christians." The participants who demonstrated the greatest degree of comfort with a well-developed identity were those who had successfully adhered a Christian religious identity onto a preexisting Muslim ethnic identity. Nonetheless, each participant worked through this process in his/her own way, usually using careful analysis and critique of his/her own beliefs and circumstances. They expressed a great deal of identity frustration but also agency to negotiate a new identity for themselves.[67]

The spiritual warfare lens

The spiritual warfare lens is especially relevant in ministry among Muslims because of the prevalence of folk Islam.[68] We must discern not just the dazzling "angel of light" (2 Cor 11:14), sorcerers (Acts 8:9–24), and fortunetellers (Acts 16:16), but also the subtle deceptions of false teachers who slip into the church (2 Pet 2:1; Jude 4).

Interested in issues of power, Bård Løkken Knapstad focuses on the role of miracles as a factor among Indonesian MBBs coming to faith. His findings included the following summary points:

- Miracles provide clear answers to a genuine need in the life of the convert.
- Miracles often serve as punctual events leading into the following period of the conversion process.
- Miracles have the ability to trigger an interest in Christianity.
- Certain miracles exhibit such a "power of change" that the influence of social bonds is reduced to a minimum up until the period of discipleship.

67 Kathryn Ann Kraft, "Community and Identity among Arabs of a Muslim Background Who Choose to Follow a Christian Faith" (PhD diss., University of Bristol, 2007), 204.

68 Rick Love, *Muslims, Magic, and the Kingdom of God.*

- Miracles, particularly dreams, visions, and "inner voices," are seen to reveal the will of the Divine, and are therefore decisive in the conversion process. However, they can also be a seduction by Satan.

- Healings, deliverances, and exorcisms display the power of Jesus Christ over the spirit world and strike an inner cord in the power-oriented folk Islamic worldview.

- Assurance of salvation remains the most significant reason for the conversions, even among those informants who fervently exalt the power aspects of the gospel.[69]

The human communicator lens

The process of conversion is intimately linked with divinely enabled human witness (Acts 1:8). In a study of MBBs in Bulgaria and Turkey, Richard Hibbert found it "clear that personal relationship with a Christian is a vital factor for nearly all Muslims" who had come to faith in Jesus Christ.[70] Gabriël Jansen writes that among Moroccan MBBs in Amsterdam "the most prominent shared factor [in witness] appears to be the continued personal friendly contact with one or more individual Christians, and most often with a living, loving Christian group."[71]

Reinhold Straehler reminds us that "holistic ministries or nonverbal ministries alone will not communicate to the Muslim that an alternative worldview is possible for him or her." Since "there needs to be some verbal communication or communication via media (audio, visual or print)," his ongoing research is done with the hope of providing "suggestions as to which subjects are appropriate for discussion at each stage [of the conversion process] and what kind of activities can be done in order to stimulate the contact person to experience a change in the cognitive direction or in the affective direction."[72]

The role of media and the methods of our witness vary and should not be seen in isolation from other factors in the process of conversion.[73] However, as Tobias Rink observes, "The way in which the gospel is communicated, from the convert's viewpoint, is as meaningful as the content of the presentation."[74] It may also affect the ability of the new believers to become fruitful witnesses themselves, especially where issues of literacy and orality are involved.[75]

---

69 Bård Løkken Knapstad, "Show Us the Power: A Study of the Influence of Miracles on the Conversion Process from Islam to Christianity an Indonesian Context" (MA thesis, Norwegian Lutheran School of Theology, 2005), 154–55.

70 Richard Hibbert, "Insights from Research and Interviews with Missionaries among Muslims Elsewhere, in Turkey, and with Turkish Believers in Bulgaria" (unpublished manuscript, n.d.), 2.

71 Jansen, "Reaching Moroccans in Amsterdam," 80.

72 Reinhold Straehler, "Conversion from Islam to Christianity in the Sudan" (MTh thesis, University of South Africa, 2005), 103–4.

73 Greenham, "Muslim Conversions to Christ," 193.

74 Rink, "Eine multidimensionale methodik," 126.

75 David Greenlee, "Coming to Faith in Christ: Insights from the Conversion Stories of MBB Women" (paper presented at the "Seeking Answers" consultation, Southwestern Baptist Theological Seminary, Fort Worth, TX, 2003), 27; and Gupta, "Servants in the Crucible," 17.

The lens of God's divine role

True Christian conversion is an act initiated and enabled by God. All of the other factors we have considered are the ways and means by which he draws us to himself (2 Cor 5:18). I limit my comments here to two factors frequently referred to in research among MBBs: the role of the Bible and the person of Jesus.

Numerous studies refer to the importance of Bible study as a factor in drawing Muslims to faith in Jesus Christ. David Maranz analyzed published testimonies of MBBs and found several motivations for Muslims to read the Bible:

- Searching for truth
- Setting out to attack, refute, or oppose Christianity
- Attempts to relieve inner conflict or a spiritual void
- Superficial motivations (for example, the color of the book)
- The claims of Jesus or the Bible
- Obeying or following up a dream
- Doubts about Islam, Muhammad, or the Qurʾan[76]

Not all who read the Bible come to faith in Jesus Christ. However, for those who do, personal Bible reading, Bible correspondence courses, observing Luke's Gospel in the form of the *Jesus* film, and chronological Bible storying are reported in many studies as significant factors in the process of conversion.[77]

Finally, Abraham Durán speaks of the "beauty of Jesus" as a vital factor in conversion. Describing how a significant number from an ethnic minority came to faith in Jesus Christ, Durán notes that we must follow Jesus' own example: "a gradual approach that will lead people to discern the truth and beauty of Jesus' personality, teachings, and life motivating them to be his followers."[78] In the words of Jean-Marie Gaudeul, "The formulas of faith only begin to make sense, either suddenly or little by little, when Jesus has been recognized as one who loves us and saves us."[79]

---

76 David Maranz, "The Role of the Scriptures in Muslims Coming to Faith in Jesus," in Greenlee, *From the Straight Path*, 54–56.

77 See for example: Greenham, "Muslim Conversions to Christ"; Greenlee, "Christian Conversion"; Greenlee, "Coming to Faith in Christ"; Gupta, "Servants in the Crucible"; Hibbert, "Insights from Research"; and McVicker, "Experiencing Jesus."

78 Abraham Durán, "The Beauty of Jesus as an Evangelistic Factor," in Greenlee, *From the Straight Path*, 274.

79 Gaudeul, *Called from Islam*, 52–53.

Anthony Greenham agrees. He writes:

> The most significant conversion factor is the person of Jesus … This is not surprising, given the nature of conversion. He is the one to whom individuals turn in humble surrender and encounter by the power of God. Without the person of Jesus, there is no conversion … The converts are drawn to him through differing means. These are God's miraculous involvement, the truth of his message, believers' roles, Bible reading and an array of other factors. However, Jesus is always central.[80]

Three Summary Factors

Dudley Woodberry[81] refers to the hand of God in the glove of circumstances. Distinguishing between God causing and God working through tragedies, from his ongoing, global research project Woodberry points to five trends and their significant relation to the increasing numbers of Muslims coming to faith in Jesus Christ:

- Politics: Islamic resurgence coupled with attractive Christian witness leads to receptivity and persecution
- Catastrophes: An opportunity to give a cup of water in Christ's name
- Migration: Receptivity within a window of opportunity
- The desire for blessing and power: Ministering in healing and power
- Ethnic and cultural resurgence: The gospel translated into various cultural forms

How is God at work in drawing Muslims to faith in Jesus Christ through these diverse circumstances? Each person is unique; God's grace is creative. Those Muslims who now follow Jesus came to and live out their faith in many different ways. Prediction and prescription are to be avoided. However, three summary factors are independently referred to by several researchers.[82] Muslims who have come to faith in Jesus Christ usually have:

80 Greenham, "Muslim Conversions to Christ," 211, 215.

81 Woodberry, "Global Perspective," 12–13; with reference to Willis, *Indonesian Revival*.

82 Greenham, "Muslim Conversions to Christ," 193; Gupta, "Servants in the Crucible," 13; David Smith, "Looking Ahead," in Greenlee, *From the Straight Path*, 287–88; and Syrjänen, "In Search of Meaning," 171–72.

- Encountered the truth of God's word
- Received a touch of God's love through his people
- Seen a sign of the power of Jesus Christ

God's mercy is deep; his love is wide. The gospel is good news—for all people! To God be all the glory!

12
Contextualization

BY PHIL PARSHALL

The subject before us in this essay has been besieged by widespread controversy. Intense scrutiny of contextual methodology as a means to evangelize Muslims has often led to divisiveness within the evangelical camp. The heart of the issue focuses on where each individual or group draws the line between proper contextualization and unacceptable syncretism. The exegesis of where that line is drawn is precisely the point at which well-entrenched positions collide.

To better understand this controversy, it is prudent to commence with a historical overview. In 1975, I was part of a team that pioneered contextualization in a certain South Asian country (which will be designated as *Quristan* throughout this chapter). Only twenty-five years later did we learn that we were not the real "pioneer." Enter Sadrach.

Sadrach

A friend asked me if I had ever heard of Sadrach, the Indonesian Muslim background believer (hereafter MBB) who broke new ground with his culturally sensitive church. I confessed my ignorance; which led to my being given a copy of a PhD dissertation authored by Indonesian, Sutarman Soediman Partonadi. The title of this University of Amsterdam book is *Sadrach's Community and Its Contextual Roots: A Nineteenth Century Javanese Expression of Christianity.*[1] What a tremendous help it would have been for our Quristan team back in 1975 if we had learned about Sadrach's ministry.

Sadrach was born in Central Java in 1835, and died in 1928 at age ninety-three. He was raised in a Muslim home under the influence of folk Islam. He was thirty-two when he became a Christian. Over the next sixty years Sadrach worked tirelessly to establish a

1 Sutarman Soediman Partodani, *Sadrach's Community and Its Contextual Roots: A Nineteenth Century Javanese Expression of Christianity* (Amsterdam: Rodopi, 1990).

church that would be faithful to Scripture, while also maximally incorporating Javanese expression of culture and rituals.

The established colonial Dutch Reformed Church regarded Sadrach's creation as "a new sect of Islam with a Christian color." Some leaders even went so far as to call his work "the rock of sin." Meanwhile Muslims were beginning to take notice of a message clothed in a garb very different from that of the Dutch church which they designated as "the religion of pig manure."

Sadrach ended up with 7,500 MBBs in church membership at the time of his death. Some scholars of Indonesian history have postulated that Sadrach is the real father of the present church in Java. To what degree did Sadrach engage in contextual innovation? A brief overview will have to suffice:

- Sadrach was the undisputed leader, much like a bishop. He remained humble and lived in simplicity. "Great Shepherd" was the title his flock gave to him.

- Church leaders were referred to as imams. They were self-supporting farmers for the most part.

- Sadrach adopted a Christian name upon conversion. It does not appear that others followed his example.

- *Zakāt* (offerings) were regularly received from members. No outside financial assistance was accepted.

- Annual three-day "great gatherings" were held. These were similar to a Muslim *ᶜīd* (festival).

- Evangelical doctrine was taught. High moral standards were mandated, and church discipline was practiced.

- Buildings were made of local material with a design similar to a mosque. In fact, they were called mosques. No crosses were displayed. A three-tier roof symbolized the Trinity. On the top of the roof was a disk with several protruding arrows which was said to represent the unity of the community. These "mosques" became the functional substitute of the Islamic mosque, which the believers no longer frequented.

- A drum was used to call believers to worship, as was done in the mosque.

- The names *ᶜIsa* and *Allah* were used in both Scripture and worship.

- The following *shahāda* (creed) was recited in Javanese musical form:

  I believe that God is One.
  There is no God but God.
  Jesus Christ is the Spirit of God
  whose power is over everything.
  There is no God but God.
  Jesus Christ is the Spirit of God.

This creed was recited with a soft voice, gradually getting louder, accompanied by hand clapping and head movements from side to side and up and down alternately. Emotion became intense until a worshiper experienced a sort of mystical union with Allah.

- The Apostle's Creed was quoted with reference to Jesus as "Beloved Son, my Lord." It was stated that he ascended to the "quite flowery heaven."

- MBBs did not divorce their multiple wives, but polygamy was opposed with respect to acquiring additional wives.

- Cows were prayed over at the time of their slaughter in Muslim fashion.

- Modified Islamic rituals were followed:

  - Women's first pregnancies

  - Fortieth day infancy celebrations

  - Male circumcision

  - Festival at time of planting crops

  - New Year celebrations

  - Funeral ceremonies

Sadrach did not follow the Islamic rituals of honoring dead spirits, did not observe Muharram (a Shiᶜite ceremony), or celebrate the birth and death anniversary of Muhammad. No mention was made of the two Muslim *ᶜĪd* festivals. More noteworthy, the believers did not affirm Muhammad as a prophet of God, but rather, spoke openly of the superiority of Jesus over Muhammad.

And so what happened to this movement after Sadrach died? It seems that the believers split into three groups and gradually became assimilated into the Dutch Reformed Church. Reportedly, none returned to the Islamic faith.

How do we, in this present day, evaluate Sadrach's church? Is this an early example of contextualization that is true to biblical faith as well as relevant to local culture and religion? The reader perhaps can pause and ponder these questions. Most likely our own experiences, presuppositions, and theological understandings will color our response.

How interesting it would be to have a perspective on this from the deceased "apostle to Islam," Samuel Zwemer, whose lifespan (1867–1952) overlapped with Sadrach. Most likely these two missionary giants never heard of each other. At least there is no such reference in Zwemer's biography as authored by J. Christy Wilson, Sr.[2] But the possibility exists as both were interacting with the Dutch Reformed Church. Also, it should be noted that there are no references to Zwemer engaging in serious contextual ministry to Muslims, at least not in the Sadrach style.

One last word of comparison. In Wilson's book there is no mention of Zwemer actually leading Muslims to Christ. I do not state this to denigrate his efforts, but it does stand in contrast to Sadrach's success. Also, it should be said that other records may exist that indicate conversions from Zwemer's ministry. And lastly, the disparity between the Middle East and Indonesia is well understood in regard to relative openness to the gospel.

Quristan

This country of 120 million Muslims had proved resistant to the gospel and that in spite of the best efforts of scores of dedicated missionaries and tentmakers. My research indicated that there were less than one hundred conversions from Islam in the fifty years between 1925 and 1975. After thirteen years as a missionary in Quristan, I was ready to try something new, as was our team of twenty-three who came from six different countries.

In 1975 we commenced a process of experimentation. Team members would go out into rural areas with a mandate to try out some particular new type of evangelistic methodology. They would then return and report success or failure. Group dynamics would develop and, after discussion, the strategy would either be rejected or approved. This process led on to acceptance of a methodology which today would be termed C4.[3] In its day, it was

2 J. Christy Wilson, Sr., *Apostle to Islam: A Biography of Samuel M. Zwemer* (Grand Rapids: Baker, 1952).

3 For a definition of C4, see the "Church Planting Spectrum" borrowed from John Travis and discussed in Phil Parshall, *Muslim Evangelism: Contemporary Approaches to Contextualization* (Waynesboro, GA: Gabriel,

revolutionary. Today it is considered conservative. In 1980 I documented this case study in my book *New Paths in Muslim Evangelism*.[4] The basics of this strategy have been adapted and used in numerous Muslim-majority countries. Significant features of our work with MBBs are as follows:

- Biblical fidelity. A pressing desire to see conversions must not override an unmovable commitment to an evangelical understanding of the truth of God's word. Put another way, syncretism—and even pragmatism—are not to be the engines which drive the contextual approach to Muslim evangelism.

- Our effort was tremendously assisted through the Muslimized translation of the New Testament. This monumental work was accomplished by the diligent efforts of Association of Baptists for World Evangelism missionaries, surgeon Vic Olsen and his wife, Joan. The *Kitab Injil* was bound in a green color with Islamic design on the cover. Operation Mobilization teams went throughout the country selling this attractive book at a reasonable price. It soon became the best-selling book in all of Quristan. Without doubt, this was the foundation to the movement that was soon to take place. To date, over fifty such Muslimized translations have been produced throughout the Islamic world.

- Our team agreed on a target group for our evangelistic efforts. We would aim for the rural farmer or fisherman who was a married male, preferably literate, and a reasonably well-respected member of Muslim society. We felt such a group of men would present the best possible opportunity for the networking of the gospel to the MBB's circle of friends and relatives. In our context, young persons, or women of any age, would not be appropriate as an initial direction for evangelism. It was hoped that they would follow into the faith of their husband/father.

- As this strategy was rural-oriented, it was necessary for our missionaries to take up residence in small towns. From there, village forays could be easily undertaken. An important decision was reached. We would seek to be low profile in our lifestyle. We did not allow the

---

2003), 62: "C4—Contextualized Christ-centered communities using insider language and biblically permissible cultural and Islamic forms. Similar to C3, however biblically permissible Islamic forms and practices are also utilized (i.e., praying with raised hands; keeping the Fast; avoiding pork, alcohol, and dogs as pets; using Islamic terms, garb, etc.) … C4 believers identify themselves as 'Followers of ʿIsa the Messiah' (or something similar)."

4 Now revised as Parshall, *Muslim Evangelism.*

purchasing of any kind of property. Basic rented houses allowed for mobility in case of any change in direction of strategy. To the present, this decision has been followed.

- Other alterations were made; such as our men and women on the team wearing national dress. It was preferable for the men to grow beards, as this was common among the religious males. Hospitality was extremely important in Quristan, so the wives learned how to cook and present food in a lavish manner to guests. Eating schedules were altered in order to be free for visitation that usually took place in the early evening.

- Priority was given to language acquisition. No team member was allowed to minister in English.

- There was flexibility regarding the missionary children's education. Local schools, boarding schools in an adjacent country, and home-schooling were all valid options left to the preference of the parents.

- Initially, outreach centered around "Reading Rooms" in large villages. These rented rooms served as a place to meet inquirers. Literature and correspondence courses were given out freely. Out of these contacts came the first MBBs, often within just a few months after the room was opened. This even occurred in areas where there had never before been an MBB.

- From the start, MBBs were taught how to witness and were encouraged to share their faith within their circle of influence. But we insisted that this be done with sensitivity and tact.

- Believers were not called "Christians." This designation carried too much negative baggage among Muslims in Quristan. "Followers of ᶜIsa" was the preferred identity.

- Prayer was a key emphasis during worship. At other times we prayed with Muslims for their felt needs.

- After significant discussion, we decided to provide a large container of water for inquirers and new believers so that they could wash before they prayed. We made it very clear in our teaching that such ablutions are not a meritorious requirement in Christianity. However, we recognized that these men would feel very uncomfortable praying with dirty hands and feet. Within a short time after conversion, believers ceased doing the ablutions in the strict Islamic mandated form, but they continued to wash their hands and feet prior to prayer.

- Fasting during the month of Ramadan was a difficult issue to deal with. This Fast is not only a spiritual exercise, it is also a pervasive sociological experience. Muslims all over the world enter into this physical deprivation. It matters not if they are nominal or actively spiritual. In some ways, Ramadan can be compared to Christmas celebrations. One doesn't need any real spiritual credentials to engage in either festival. But if a new believer refuses to keep the Muslim Fast, then severe persecution can follow. After much research, our team decided to simply allow freedom of conscience to be the guide for each believer, whether he or she was a national or an expatriate missionary. Biblical teaching on fasting was emphasized, especially in the area of works versus grace. I personally kept the Fast three different years. It is a harsh discipline. Refraining from eating for fourteen daylight hours is quite manageable. However, the abstaining from all liquids is excruciating, particularly in countries where temperatures can exceed 100° F for each of the thirty days of Ramadan. My Muslim friends were uniformly appreciative that I was willing to enter into their ritual, even though they were aware of differences in the content of my prayers and Scripture reading.

- Bible verses were chanted. Christian words were sung to Islamic tunes that Muslims appreciated.

- Days and times for worship were pragmatically suggested according to the convenience of the MBBs.

- The prototype MBB church was not part of a denomination. It was hoped that each cell would meet in homes. This would be cost-effective and also give the church a low profile within the Muslim community. Over the years, various denominations and groups have commenced work in Quristan among Muslims. So at present there are a number of ecclesiastical traditions being followed. Overall, it can be said that the believers meet separately from the traditional Hindu-background church. I believe this has facilitated their growth, but it has also caused misunderstandings and, in some cases, alienation. There has been an ongoing effort to heal this rift.

- A recent gathering of 1,100 MBBs for four days of spiritual instruction was a great encouragement to all who attended. Believers could get a sense of the new *umma* (community) to which they now belonged. A significant achievement in that meeting was that 450 women and two hundred children attended. It appears that the efforts of the past decades to reach these two segments of Muslim community are finally being realized. Marriages are now taking place between the children of MBB families.

- In a minority of instances, Muslims with multiple wives have come to faith in Christ. It was decided to counsel the new MBB husbands to continue to live with their wives as in the past, but not to marry again. Single men were exhorted to have only one wife.

- Baptism is performed by immersion. A great problem is that the Muslim perception of baptism is that this is the point when the believer leaves his family and community and takes on a Christian name. To counter this problem, baptism is often performed in the early morning at a nearby river or pond. No videos, singing, or white faces are present. Also, the believer retains his or her family name. All of this is done to seek to reduce alienation from the Muslim community.

- Direct financial aid or loans were discouraged. Over the years, a number of Christian development organizations have commenced work in Quristan. They have provided employment, particularly for the leadership level of MBBs. The good news is that there are now so many believers that it is impossible for all of them to obtain foreign-funded employment. Many MBBs have received training from these groups that has resulted in their financial well-being.

- Christmas and Easter have a distinctly Christian content. Christmas trees, Santa Claus, Easter bunnies, and colored eggs have yet to make their debut into the believers' community!

What are the results of these contextualization efforts over the past three decades? The numbers of MBBs in Quristan vary greatly. Patrick Johnstone, in *Operation World*, put the figure at over four hundred thousand total within all groups. Until recently, one ministry was claiming between five hundred thousand and six hundred thousand. This claim was discredited after a team went in and surveyed the outreach areas. I personally feel comfortable with saying there are tens of thousands of MBBs in Quristan. This estimate is based upon interviews, as well as a survey trip in which I participated. It was exciting to personally interact with seventy-two believers, many of them leaders in their congregations.

It is apparent that God is at work in Quristan in a way unparalleled in its history. Muslims around the world have taken note of these conversions. Articles in the print media and on the Web have called for regulations to be imposed on all foreign Christian activity in the country. Visas are more difficult to obtain. But the number of believers has reached a critical mass, and I am confident that the movement will not only continue, but will also become more spiritually mature.

Controversies

It was almost inevitable that the contextualization movement would create a missiological atmosphere wherein certain individuals and groups would push the boundaries of experimentation, and even practice, into uncharted territory. This has been done with the result that, to some, the entire contextualization strategy has become suspect. A few of these practices should be noted.

Most contextualists make room for an MBB to have a time of transition from the old to the new. Often it is prudent to not immediately withdraw from the mosque. A gradual decline in attendance may generate less controversy and attendant persecution.

But there are those who identify their strategy as "insider" who teach that MBBs should remain permanently in the mosque as a witness for Christ. This raises the question of integrity. If other Muslims view the believer as one of themselves religiously, then where is the distinction of belief in Jesus as God? Can an MBB recite the *shahāda* ("There is no God but God, and Muhammad is his Prophet") with good conscience? Is agreement not implied if one is present in the *ṣalāt* (canonical prayer)?

There are those who feel they can affirm Muhammad as a prophet of God similar to the way David is considered an Old Testament prophet. They see Muhammad as more BC than AD. Emphasis is laid upon his deeds and words that are compatible with biblical teaching.

This brings up the question of the Qurʾan. Should believers continue to regard the Qurʾan as authoritative and as a guide for behavior? I have attended an evangelical meeting where the Qurʾan was quoted in Arabic during prayer and worship. Where is the line to be drawn? It is not uncommon for the Qurʾan to be used selectively in witness. This is particularly utilized in regard to passages about Jesus. A popular example of this usage is spelled out in Kevin Greeson's *The Camel*.[5]

---

5 Kevin Greeson, *The Camel: How Muslims Are Coming to Faith in Christ!* (Bangalore: WIGTake Resources, 2007).

What about religious identity? Some support MBBs continuing to refer to themselves as "Muslim." This is done without a qualifier, such as "Muslim follower of ᶜIsa." The argument is that the meaning of *Muslim* is simply, "one who submits to God." Certainly the MBB qualifies for that understanding of the word. Also, there is the sociological impact of the word. Perhaps *Muslim* carries as much community emphasis as does the word *Christian.* Few would state that all people who call themselves *Christian* are really born again. The counter argument goes that the word *Muslim* cannot be divorced from the worldwide religious *umma* (community) of Islam. It is their word and definitely not a word to be used by those who designate Jesus as divine.

"Son of God" is a biblical term which causes much confusion for Muslims. Their interpretation is strictly biological. As much as Christians seek to introduce the metaphysical into the discussion, Muslims refer back to the Qurʾan where it says, "Say not 'three,'—Cease! (it is) better for you!—Allah is only One God. Far is it removed from His transcendent majesty that he should have a son" (an-Nisāʾ [4]:171 Pickthall).

A partial solution to this dilemma is postulated by some Bible translators. They advocate deleting *Son of God* in vernacular translations of the New Testament. Their replacement is *God's beloved* or *only beloved* or *Messiah.* There may be other substitutions of which I am unaware. They argue that *Son of God* and *Messiah* were similarly understood by first-century hearers. Messiah is a word referring to Jesus that is found in the Qurʾan, but few Muslims have any idea of its meaning. Therefore, in light of these realities, some feel a substitution for *Son of God* is appropriate. Others are extremely vocal in their denunciation of any attempt to change the actual words of the original Scriptures.

A final word on this subject. I agree that even careful contextualization can spill over into improper syncretism. As the proponents of various strategies listed above are (1) evangelicals, and (2) all dedicated to the task of seeing Muslims come to Christ, I feel we must be slow to be overly denunciatory. Let us be open to dialogue and critique, and especially seek to be understanding of unique contexts in which the gospel is being preached. Saudi Arabia and Bangladesh are distinct in regard to how their Muslim citizens view Christianity. A good "contextualist" will take this into account while at the same time strive to be faithful to the teaching of the word of God.

Other Issues of Relevance

I have purposefully refrained from giving an exposition of C1 through C6. I have published extensively on this subject, as have other competent missiologists. I refer the interested reader to back issues of both the *Evangelical Missions Quarterly* and the *International Journal of Frontier Missions* (IJFM); IJFM, in particular, which has had thorough and thoughtful articles on these topics.

Any consideration of Islamic contexts must take into account the history of Muslim-Christian relations. Western missionaries are prone to overlook or downplay past violations of Muslims by nominal Christian individuals and nations. I have visited the largest existing Crusader fortress, the Krak des Chevaliers, which is located in western Syria near the Mediterranean Sea. As I surveyed the interior of this massive structure, I could visualize the hundreds of white "Christian" crusaders with the cross emblazoned in red paint covering their breastplates of armor. I could hear the hoofs of the horses pounding on the packed dirt. I could see the men laying down their spears at the chapel door and then going in reverently to kneel and pray fervently that God would allow them to destroy the Jews and Muslims in the holy city of Jerusalem. This, so that once again the name of Jesus could be freely proclaimed and worshiped in the land of his incarnation.

At the same moment, my imagination moved south into Palestine where Muslims were preparing to defend with their blood the land where the Prophet was said to have ascended into heaven on his "Night Journey." No sacrifice would be too great to preserve the honor of Allah and his messenger in the soil where they had lived and toiled for the previous six hundred years. "*Allāhu akbar* (God is most Great)" was their battle cry of defense.

This 200-year conflict is often relegated to a few pages in Western world-history books. For the Muslim, this violation is kept vibrantly alive through writings and oral traditions. Can the Christian humbly apologize for his ancestors' part in committing a "Christian jihad"?

Next came colonialism. It is my estimate that 90 percent of the majority-Muslim nations were ruled by Western colonial powers at some time during the period between 1700 and 1962. This occupation by foreign troops, considered to be Christians, was deeply resented by the nationals of these countries. Much blood was spilled as Muslims fought to gain their independence.

In the more recent past, American soldiers have resided in or occupied parts of Somalia, Saudi Arabia, Afghanistan, Kuwait, and Iraq. In addition to these nations, US troops are stationed in a number of other Muslim countries. All of this creates a backlash of anger, which leads to violence. The missionary who comes from an "occupier" nation must deal with these issues with great care.

Support of Israel by the West is deeply resented by Muslims. Little has been accomplished to resolve this longstanding disagreement.

Western standards of morality shock Muslims. Many say they would prefer their daughters to be clothed in burqas rather than in bikinis. A mother in Kabul, Afghanistan, recently expressed despair over her son's addiction to pornographic websites, which are so easily accessible in Internet cafés throughout that city.

A contextually sensitive ambassador for Christ is forced to deal with these and many other issues. For the missionary, arrogance and a defensive attitude is counter productive.

A Final Word

At times, the contextualization controversy has become quite polemic. A moderating voice in this discussion has been that of Dudley Woodberry. He has sought to be a peacemaker, a pursuit in which he has been quite successful. He has urged both sides to exercise maximum restraint in attacking differing opinions. Dudley is a Christian gentleman. I have known Dudley for forty-two years, and I commend him as a missionary stateman who is truly a "gentle man."

13

Reflections on Jesus Movements among Muslims with Special Reference to Movements within Asian Muslim Communities

BY JOHN JAY TRAVIS

Thirty years ago, *Missiology* published a thought-provoking article by missionary John Wilder[1] entitled "Some Reflections on Possibilities for People Movements among Muslims."[2] In this largely theoretical work, Wilder drew upon the ideas of Donald McGavran,[3] mission executive John Anderson,[4] the recent experience of the Messianic Jewish movement, and his own long-term observations in the Muslim world. Movements strikingly similar to what he suggested then as possibilities have, in fact, now taken place. In what follows, I first discuss some of what has occurred since 1977 when this article was published. I then turn to the writings of J. Dudley Woodberry, showing how his work has contributed to our understanding of movements to Christ among Muslims. Finally, I close with a recent case study and a description of some dynamics being observed in several Jesus movements within Asian Muslim communities. Before proceeding, I need to make a few comments related to the study of Jesus movements among Muslims.

---

1 John Wilder was a Presbyterian missionary who served for several decades in the non-Arab Muslim world, beginning in the 1950s. He studied Messianic Judaism and saw potential parallels with Muslim ministry.

2 John W. Wilder, "Some Reflections on Possibilities for People Movements among Muslims," *Missiology: An International Review* 5, no. 3 (July 1977).

3 Donald McGavran was the founding dean of the School of World Mission, Fuller Theological Seminary. He was one of the mission world's leading thinkers on the subject of people movements. *The Bridges of God* (London: World Dominion, 1955) is considered one of his seminal works on the dynamics of people movements.

4 John D. C. Anderson, a medical missionary who worked in Muslim lands, wrote an article in 1976 which, to my knowledge, is the first article to suggest a movement of Muslim followers of Jesus: "The Missionary Approach to Islam: Christian or 'Cultic'?" *Missiology: An International Review* 4, no. 3 (July 1976): 258–99.

Studying Movements to Christ

McGavran described a "people movement" as a phenomenon in which large numbers from a particular tribe, clan, or strata of society (i.e., a "people") make decisions at the same time to follow Jesus as Lord, initiating a movement to Christ that sweeps through much of the group. McGavran stated that this generally occurs as the gospel is shared through family networks ("bridges"). Much of the expansion of the church historically has been through such movements. However, relatively few of these have occurred among Muslims.

In recent decades this has begun to change. While it is premature to use the word "people movement" to the full extent that McGavran intended (i.e., impacting the entire people group), at least there are movements to Christ of varying sizes occurring among Muslims.[5] These movements display many of the characteristics McGavran describes, yet on a smaller scale. These characteristics include the forming of biblical *ekklēsiae* (hereafter ecclesiae), rapid multiplication, and the gospel moving through family networks. For security purposes, I do not mention specific locations or numbers, as that information, in the wrong hands, could hurt the very movements over which we rejoice. I do, however, use relative terms such as *large, small,* or *emerging* in describing these movements.[6]

Finally, it is fitting to start our discussion about movements by acknowledging the wondrous variety of ways that God sovereignly reaches human beings with his love. Some of this wonder is expressed in the words of Father Jean-Marie Gaudeul, an expert on the subject of Muslims turning to Christ:

> My first thought is a sense of wonder at God's ways of leading people toward a real, live encounter with Himself. We are treading on holy ground as we examine the extraordinary variety of personal experiences through which God revealed his tenderness and love to so many millions of human beings. Each human conscience is a holy temple where the Lord meets his children and draws them to Himself.[7]

---

5 The largest movement of Muslims to Christ in recent history occurred in Indonesia before Wilder's article was published. Avery Willis reports that, from 1965–1971, 2 million mostly nominal Muslims were baptized during a time of much violence and social unrest in the country following an aborted coup. See Avery Willis, *Indonesian Revival: Why Two Million Came to Christ* (Pasadena: William Carey Library, 1977).

6 Few books are available on the topic of movements among Muslims; in part because so few have occurred. Three books do serve as good resources containing numerous case studies and principles. See David Greenlee, *One Cross, One Way, Many Journeys: Thinking Again about Conversion* (Tyrone, GA: Authentic, 2007; Willis, Indonesian Revival; and J. Dudley Woodberry, *Muslims and Christians on the Emmaus Road* (Monrovia, CA: MARC, 1989).

7 Jean-Marie Gaudeul, "Learning from God's Ways," in *From the Straight Path to the Narrow Way: Journeys of Faith*, ed. David H. Greenlee (Downers Grove, IL: InterVarsity Press, 2006), 81.

Wilder's Article and the Following Thirty Years

In 1977 Wilder postulated that if a movement were to occur in a particular Muslim context, it would most likely take one of two forms: "a people movement to Christ which remains within Islam" or a "people movement constituting a new church of Muslim cultural orientation."[8] In terms of the C1–C6 continuum,[9] Wilder was describing what I have referred to elsewhere as C4 and C5 types of movements. Wilder made it clear that he would prefer "a people movement constituting a new church of Muslim orientation" (i.e., C4), but also felt a movement to Jesus that remained within Islam (i.e., C5) would be valid and might occur quite naturally as the gospel moves through a Muslim community. He astutely pointed out that a genuine movement, settling either within Islam (C5) or outside of it (C4), would likely not be led by outsiders (e.g., missionaries or non-Muslim background church leaders).

Regarding movements to Christ within Islam, Wilder stated that those coming to faith would differ in many ways from Muslims who do not yet follow Jesus. However, by remaining a part of the community, hopefully, they would be considered neither traitors to their people nor "apostates" (*murtaddūn*).[10] He postulated four other features of movements to Christ within Islam: (1) they would engage in self-theologizing,[11] (2) they might have different views of the sacraments,[12] (3) they might emphasize different parts of the Bible from

---

8 Wilder, "Possibilities for People Movements," 310.

9 I developed this continuum to show a range of types of biblical ecclesiae that I refer to as "Christ-centered communities" that exist in the Muslim world today. See John Travis, "The C1–C6 Spectrum," *Evangelical Missions Quarterly* 34, no. 3 (1998), 411–15. C4 is an ecclesia that is Islamic in flavor but seen as outside of Islam. C5 movements have also been called *insider movements or Jesus movements within Muslim communities* due to the fact that believers stay socioreligiously within Islam. For further explanations on Jesus movements within Muslim communities see: Travis, John J. and J. Dudley Woodberry, "When the Gospel Grows Like Yeast: Frequently Asked Questions About Jesus Movements within Muslim Communities" in *Mission Frontiers* (July-August 2010), 24-30; Kevin Higgins, "Acts 15 and Insider Movements among Muslims: Questions, Process, and Conclusions," *International Journal of Frontier Missiology* 2, no. 1 (2007); John Travis, "Must All Muslims Leave Islam to Follow Jesus?" *Evangelical Missions Quarterly* 34, no. 3 (1998); John Travis and Anna Travis, "Appropriate Approaches in Muslim Contexts," in *Appropriate Christianity*, ed. Charles Kraft (Pasadena: William Carey Library, 2005); Joshuah Massey, editorial in *International Journal of Frontier Missions* 17, no. 1 (January–March 2000); J. Dudley Woodberry, "Contextualization among Muslims: Reusing Common Pillars," in *The Word among Us: Contextualizing Theology for Mission Today*, ed. Dean Gilliland (Dallas: Word, 1989); J. Dudley Woodberry, "To the Muslim I Became a Muslim?" *International Journal of Frontier Missiology* 24, no. 1 (January–March 2007). For cautions expressed over C5 or insider movements, see Woodberry, "To the Muslim," 27–28; and Phil Parshall, "Danger! New Directions in Contextualization," *Evangelical Missions Quarterly* 34, no. 3 (1998).

10 There are many sects and spiritual streams within Islam, including millions of Sufis, numerous Asian mystical orders, and Alevis in Turkey. They are seen as different, but are not rejected, because they remain a part of the Muslim community.

11 While creative theologizing is characteristic of many of the movements I have learned of or observed, the basic gospel message, including the true death and resurrection of Jesus Christ, is the very foundation of them all.

12 They may not emphasize Communion or baptism. It is interesting to note that at least two Christian groups, the Salvation Army and the Quakers, do not practice, as outwardly celebrated rites, these two sacraments.

what Christians traditionally emphasize,[13] and (4) they would likely have very little contact, if any, with existing non-Muslim background churches. Wilder stated, however, that "missionaries and concerned nationals might have opportunities through personal contacts, of forming links of fellowship, understanding and dialogue," thus keeping this portion of the body of Christ linked in some ways to other parts of Christ's body.[14]

Regarding movements that settle outside of Islam, Wilder believed that they would likely retain a strong Islamic cultural flavor. He also felt that they may need the broader perspective of cross-cultural workers to assist them in thinking through different issues. Examples were whether to retain circumcision, on which day of the week to worship, the role of clergy, the use of Muslim wedding customs, the need for and/or method of baptism, the place of women in the church, and how the church is to be governed. Whatever the case, Wilder believed that for a movement to occur, a Bible translation for Muslim readers that used familiar Islamic terms such as *ᶜIsa* for Jesus and *Allah* for God would be essential.[15]

Since the publication of Wilder's article, tens of thousands of Muslims worldwide have come to faith in ᶜIsa al-Masih. By current nomenclature, not only have C4 and C5 movements occurred, such as Wilder foresaw, but movements have begun which reflect all points along the C1–C5 continuum.[16] (Thus far, C6 would not describe movements, as it refers only to small, isolated, or secret groupings of believers.) It is especially interesting to note that over the past thirty years, in a number of countries and ethnic groups, the first known believers in history from that people group have come to Christ.

We now turn to the research of J. Dudley Woodberry to better understand some of the dynamics of these movements.

Woodberry's Contributions toward Understanding Movements among Muslims

Dudley Woodberry's writings show a deep love and understanding of Muslim peoples and their cultures, flowing out of his many years spent in the Muslim world. Through courses he has taught, books he has edited, and numerous articles he has written, Woodberry has trained several generations of cross-cultural workers to approach Muslims with respect and humility, while "hold[ing] out the word of life" (Phil 2:16 NIV) that they might be saved.

13 Wilder stated that, due to the Islamic belief in the Taurat (Pentateuch or entire Old Testament), Zabur (Psalms), and Injil (the Gospels or New Testament), it would be possible that Jesus movements inside Muslim communities would emphasize only those parts of the Bible.

14 Wilder, "Possibilities for People Movements," 315.

15 Ibid.

16 This includes a number of significant movements that are C1, C2, or C3 in nature. In another article I have described how different social, cultural, religious and historical factors tend to influence the identity that new Jesus followers embrace in terms of the C1–C6 continuum. See John Travis, Anna Travis with contributions by Phil Pharshall, "Factors Affecting the Identity That Jesus-Followers Choose" in *From Seed to Fruit: Global Trends, Fruitful Practices, and Emerging Issues among Muslims*, ed. Dudley Woodberry (Pasadena: William Carey Library, 2008), 193–205.

Woodberry's work and teaching have covered a wide array of subjects, including folk or popular Islam, Christian-Muslim relations, peace initiatives, Islamic history and theology, contextualization, insider movements, and spiritual warfare. Five of Woodberry's articles in particular are helpful in this discussion of movements among Muslims.[17] The 2006 article contains data that Woodberry collected in surveying 650 Muslims who have come to faith in Christ. In what follows, built largely on Woodberry's work, I mention five circumstances that impact movements among Muslims today, six aspects of ministry that help facilitate movements, and comments on research that Woodberry, Higgins,[18] and others carried out in a large Jesus movement in Asia.

Movements to Christ and the Hand of God in the Glove of Current Events

Woodberry has described five circumstances present in the Muslim world today that God is using to draw Muslims to himself. He speaks of these circumstances as "the hand of God in the glove of current events."[19]

The first finger in the glove is *political factors*, in particular, resurgent Islam, a situation causing many Muslims to reject extremism and search for other spiritual options. The second and third fingers are *natural catastrophes* and *mass migration of refugees due to war and famine*, met with the sacrificial love shown by Christ's people in response. The fourth is the *desire for blessing* (baraka) *or power*, a very real issue for vast numbers of Muslims worldwide. The fifth is *ethnic and cultural resurgence*, sometimes expressing itself in a rejection of an oppressive Muslim regime or a dominant Islamic people group.

Ways that Followers of Jesus Can Facilitate Movements to Christ

Movements to Christ involve the hand of God and the actions of his people. The following six factors can help facilitate movements to Christ among Muslims by properly responding both to world events and spiritual conditions (e.g., dreams, visions, personal spiritual hunger).[20]

17 J. Dudley Woodberry, "Contextualization among Muslims: Reusing Common Pillars," *International Journal of Frontier Missions* 13, no. 4 (1996); Woodberry, *Muslims and Christians*; J. Dudley Woodberry, "The Relevance of Power Ministries for Folk Muslims," in *Wrestling with Dark Angels*, eds. C. Peter Wagner and F. Douglas Pennoyer (Ventura, CA: Regal, 1990), 313–31; J. Dudley Woodberry, "A Global Perspective on Muslims Coming to Faith in Christ," in *From the Straight Path to the Narrow Way: Journeys of Faith*, ed. David H. Greenlee (Downers Grove, IL: InterVarsity Press, 2006): 11–22; and Woodberry, "To the Muslim."

18 Higgins, "Insider Movements."

19 Woodberry, "Global Perspective," 11–13.

20 I am not mentioning general dynamics of movements (e.g., the gospel moving through community networks, the need for group decisions, minimal outsider involvement, etc.), but rather data which pertains more specifically to Muslim contexts.

1. *Prayer with and for Muslims:* This factor is placed first to emphasize the strong correlation between prayer and movements to Christ.[21] In a movement in one Muslim country, the number of followers of Jesus increased tenfold during the year that hundreds of people worldwide joined together to intercede for that nation. Woodberry states that answered prayer in the name of Jesus was one of the most important factors mentioned regarding people coming to Christ in his survey.[22]

2. *An appropriately contextualized message:* A key aspect of contextualization is developing appropriate ways to express the gospel message for specific audiences.[23] When Jesus and his followers proclaimed the gospel to Jews, Samaritans, and Gentiles, people in all three groups received the message as one of hope for them—it spoke to their hearts and met their needs.[24] When sharing the gospel with Muslims, our message must convey, and they must understand, that Jesus really is for them and not just for others (like Westerners and Christians).[25] He is the healing Prophet and Savior who is on the side of all peoples. In addition, for the gospel to take root and spread through an unreached people group, following Jesus must be understood as a viable or feasible life option for them right now, just as they are. Jesus and his followers not only preached truth but also shared the next appropriate step that people could take to demonstrate allegiance to Christ.[26]

3. *An appropriate messenger:* For movements to take place, it is important to consider not only what is shared and how it is shared, but who shares it. In Woodberry's survey regarding why Muslims came to Christ, the lifestyle and life message of a follower of Jesus that the respondent had known personally, ranked number one.[27] Who that

---

21 Of course prayer is essential in any move of God, but perhaps even greater prayer—"extraordinary prayer"—is needed where resistance to the gospel is particularly great. David Garrison has stated that "extraordinary prayer" was the number one factor he identified in seeing church planting movements happen in *Church Planting Movements: How God is Redeeming a Lost World* (Virginia: WIGTake, 2004), 172.

22 Woodberry, "A Global Perspective," 15.

23 On the contextualization of the gospel message, see Rick Love, *Muslims, Magic, and the Kingdom of God*; Parshall (1985); and Woodberry (1989b).

24 The good news of the kingdom has many facets. Jesus and his followers ministered differently in their words and actions depending upon the ethnicity, felt needs, and social standing of the audience (e.g., Matt 4:23–25; 8:5–13; Mark 1:21–27; John 4:7–42).

25 In the movement that I describe in the case study below, a key dynamic has been a clear sense that Jesus loves Muslims and is *for* them.

26 For some examples of steps given to show allegiance, see Mark 1:17; 5:19; Luke 19:5; John 8:11; Acts 2:38; 26:29.

27 J. Dudley Woodberry, Russell G. Shubin, and G. Marks, "Why Muslims Follow Jesus: The Results of a Recent Survey of Converts from Islam," *Christianity Today* (October 24, 2007), http://www.christianitytoday.com/

appropriate messenger of the gospel might be, in order to see movements begin in a given context, depends upon a cluster of political, historical, religious, and social factors in that context. Generally, however, people tend to come to faith and the message tends to spread more readily when the people see the messenger as being one of them. Sinclair notes the importance of the spiritual gifting of the messenger as well.[28]

4. *Contextualized Bible translations:* In order for a movement to occur, it is crucial to have an appropriately contextualized Bible (or Bible portions) that a Muslim will read and then want to pass on to fellow Muslims. Terminology is a vital part of appropriate translation.[29] Typically, although an existing non-Muslim background Christian population may not use the words Muslims use, it is still essential to depart from "churchy" language and tradition for the sake of the Muslims and use vocabulary that is affectively and cognitively meaningful for them.[30]

5. *The use of "power ministries":* Woodberry points out that today "the major movements to Christ in the Muslim world are among folk Muslims," with "power ministries" (e.g., prayer for healing, inner healing, deliverance) being an important part of all these movements.[31] Woodberry states that cross-cultural workers can pray more effectively for Muslims by understanding first the effect that power objects, power rituals, power times, power places, and power people exert over many Islamic people groups. Woodberry's survey indicates that prayer for healing and deliverance was highly ranked as a reason associated with people coming to faith.[32]

---

ct/2007/october/42.80.html.

28 Daniel Sinclair, *A Vision of the Possible: Pioneer Church Planting in Teams* (Waynesboro, GA: Authentic, 2006), 1–13, 251–59.

29 Woodberry, "Contextualization among Muslims"; Wilder, "Possibilities for People Movements"; and John Travis, "Producing and Using Meaningful Translations of the Taurat, Zabur and Injil," *International Journal of Frontier Missiology* 23, no. 2 (2006): 73–77.

30 At the very least, the words Taurat, Zabur, and Injil, and personal names such as ᶜIsa al-Masih, Yahya (John), and Maryam (Mary) should be used; Allah should be considered for YHWH, Elohim, or both; and culturally appropriate ways to translate Holy Spirit, Son of God, Lord, Christian, and church need to be discovered.

31 Woodberry, "Relevance of Power Ministries," 321.

32 Woodberry, Russell, and Marks, "Why Muslims Follow Jesus." For a model integrating power ministries and evangelism, see Charles H. Kraft, "What Kind of Encounters Do We Need in Our Christian Witness?" *Evangelical Missions Quarterly* 27, no. 3 (1991): 258–65. For models of healing, inner healing, and deliverance among Muslims, see Anna Travis, *The Undivided Heart Prayer Manual* (2002), available by email request (annajtravis@gmail.com); and Stacey, "Exorcism and Healing."

6. *Compassionate responses to natural, economic, and political crisis:* Woodberry states that from the Sahara to South Asia, a "cup of cold water or milk in Christ's name" has met people's physical needs and helped open the way for the meeting of spiritual needs as well.[33] While assistance from Christians has at times aroused suspicion on the part of Muslims, the sincerity and selflessness of many Christian relief and development workers, especially those living in close proximity to the community, has afforded many opportunities to share and exemplify the good news of the kingdom.

Key Findings from Research Done on a Movement in South Asia

Higgins reports on research that he, Woodberry, and others carried out in a large Jesus movement in South Asia.[34] Research questions were grouped into three categories—affective, cognitive, and behavioral—in order to reflect these three dimensions of the new believers' faith in Christ. In response to questions dealing with the affective (feeling/emotions) and behavioral (actions/habits) dimensions, the Muslim followers of Christ reflected a very biblical, Jesus-centered life. In response to some of the cognitive (propositional) dimension questions, however, some interviewees gave answers differing from typical Christian understandings. Higgins points out that in this movement, behaviors and allegiance to Jesus have preceded the ability to express some aspects of belief in the cognitive, propositional categories that theologians often emphasize. Three important points are brought out by this study: First, the allegiance of one's heart and subsequent demonstrated behavior may be a very valid way to understand the direction and maturity of a movement to Christ. Second, in Christward movements, people may come to faith and wholeheartedly follow Jesus with only a minimal amount of biblical knowledge at first. Third, the ability to state propositional, theological truths may not be a good indicator of a movement's true spiritual condition. We now turn to one such emerging Asian movement.

A Recent Case Study of an Emerging Movement in Asia

For more than twenty years my family and I have had the privilege of living in two different Asian Muslim neighborhoods. In the last number of years we have watched the emergence of a small yet growing Jesus movement that began in the community where we lived and has spread to several surrounding towns and villages.

33 Woodberry, "Global Perspective," 12–13.
34 Higgins, "Insider Movements."

This movement began with just a handful of men and women. The human agent most active in the initial stages is a jovial Muslim woman whom we will call "Anisa." Previously, over a ten-year period of time, she read the New Testament weekly with a Christian and privately on her own. During this time, God miraculously healed one of her relatives when Christians prayed for him. She felt drawn to Jesus but thought this was improper for her as a Muslim. One day a Christian she happened to meet told her that salvation comes through faith in Jesus alone and not through religious affiliation. That very day, as a Muslim, she felt free to pledge her allegiance to Christ without an added requirement of leaving the religious community of her birth.[35] During the five years following her decision, she regularly attended a small gathering of Muslims who also had found Christ (the group was started by an expatriate Asian). Then came a change in jobs and a new circle of acquaintances; Anisa sensed God was going to do something new. In a matter of months, her new acquaintances became dear friends and fellow Muslim followers of Christ. Shortly thereafter, her husband, children, extended family, and finally some neighbors came to faith. Simple fellowships like the one Anisa had attended were started, and the gospel spread to several outlying areas, continuing on to other towns.

The home fellowships in this small movement include men, women, and children. Most are from a lower middle-class background. The gospel is spreading through family networks, similar to what McGavran referred to as "bridges." Some members of these groups had been previously witnessed to and prayed for by Christians, but it seems their final decision to make Jesus their Lord and join an ecclesia[36] came about only after a fellow Muslim shared the gospel with them. The group meetings, which I do not attend but hear about regularly, are quite simple. They meet weekly at a set time and are led by a group leader. They pray for the guidance of the Holy Spirit to help them understand the Scriptures, then study at least one chapter from the Injil. They use a translation produced specifically for Muslim readers. After the passage is read and discussed, they decide as a group how to apply it in their lives. They then pray for each other, have a simple snack, and go home. Among the believers that my wife and I know personally, we observe that they admit sin to each other and turn from it, forgive each other, pray for the sick in Jesus' name, read Scripture regularly with their families, and routinely share Christ with their neighbors and relatives. Out of their own meager salaries, they help each other and the poor in their neighborhoods as well. As new groups develop, they are led by the believer who started the group, who then later appoints an assistant. The evidence of the grace of God is obvious.

---

35 For Anisa, her ethnicity, culture, and religion are fused, reflecting what Martin Goldsmith observed while working in Muslim lands: "Islam is within the whole warp and woof of society—in the family, in politics, in social relationships. To leave the Muslim faith is to break with one's society. Many a modern, educated Muslim is not all that religiously minded; but he must, nevertheless, remain a Muslim for social reasons … This makes it almost unthinkable for most Muslims even to consider the possibility of becoming a follower of some other religion." "Community and Controversy: Key Causes of Muslim Resistance," *Missiology* 4, no. 3 (1976): 318.

36 When I use the word *ecclesia* I am referring to a local body of believers in Christ. I refrain from using the word "church" because of the foreign or Western traditions often associated with this term.

Not many years after the movement began, Anisa's husband shared his new faith in Jesus with a Muslim teacher who works in their neighborhood. That teacher is now sharing Christ with his students in his small Islamic boarding school, and gives copies of the Injil to his older students.

They, in turn, have started to share what they are learning with families in their hometowns. A second Muslim teacher has come to faith as well.

The Muslim followers of Christ in these groups are bold in their witness. Most witnessing and forming of new groups occurs through family networks, yet many neighbors and nonfamily members are also hearing the good news. The new followers of Jesus, like Jesus followers anywhere, experience the normal challenges of living out their new faith—forgiving enemies, dealing with "crucifixion of the flesh," taking on the disciplines of Bible study and personal prayer—yet up to this point, this emerging movement has not faced any serious threat to its existence. A major challenge, however, has been in seeing members set free from some entrenched occult folk practices. In spite of challenges, by the grace of God, this movement is consistently growing in size and spiritual maturity.

Some General Dynamics of Asian Religious Jesus Movements

Movements similar to the one I have just described are happening in a number of Asian settings. I have studied the dynamics of several of these Jesus movements. Dynamics vary from place to place depending upon nationality, ethnicity, and culture. Some movements involve primarily men, others primarily women; some are rural, some have good leaders, some have suffered through poor leadership. Some have gone through times of intense persecution from Muslims while others have faced interference from local Christians. In spite of the differences, however, I have seen a number of dynamics which seem to hold true in most of these Asian ecclesiae of Muslim followers of Christ:

1. Muslim followers of Christ have a strong desire to share Jesus with family and other fellow Muslims who do not yet know Christ.

2. Muslim followers of Jesus see themselves as a unique type of Muslim due to their relationship with Jesus Christ as Lord and Savior. This does not mean, however, that they use a label other than simply "Muslim" to refer to themselves.

3. Muslim followers of Christ reinterpret or give new biblical meaning to some Muslim practices. For example, some say, "I used to fast during Ramadan in hopes of my sins being forgiven; now I fast dur-

ing Ramadan to draw near to God, to intercede for family members yet outside of Christ, and to pray about special needs."

4. The first believers in a Jesus movement were often led to Christ and discipled by non-Muslim believers in Jesus (either expatriate or national), but the movement did not happen until the believers in the Jesus movement took the lead in sharing their faith with other Muslims, usually within preexisting family or community networks.

5. Muslim followers of Jesus gather regularly as biblical ecclesiae for prayer, Bible study, and Christ-centered fellowship in ways that are appropriate and natural in their communities. Typically, those who do not yet follow Jesus (prefollowers) also attend the gatherings.

6. When the Muslim followers of Jesus study the Bible (reading it or listening to it read), they pray for wisdom and understanding, discuss the passage together, and decide how to apply it in their lives. While some senior members of the groups do teach, most theological understanding comes about over time, primarily through this group inductive process. The words of Gilliland emphasize how important it is that these groups remain centered on God's word: "If believers in any fellowship, anywhere on the face of the earth, stay centered on the Word of God, over time they will get it right. If believers in any fellowship, anywhere on the face of the earth, do not stay centered on the Word of God, over time they will get it wrong! This applies to my Methodist church here in Pasadena, in the same way it applies to the gatherings of Muslim followers of ᶜIsā in South Asia."[37]

7. These biblical ecclesiae experience the grace of God through transformed lives, restored relationships, and a deep inner peace. Like the early church, they also practice and experience, with varying degrees of frequency, miraculous healings, divine dreams, and deliverance from demons.

8. Muslim followers of Christ generally continue to worship with Muslim family and friends as they always have. At the same time, they are a part of a biblical ecclesia, which typically includes their own family.

---

37 Dean S. Gilliland, "Doing Theology in Context" (lecture notes, Fuller Theological Seminary, Pasadena, CA, 2000).

9. Muslim followers of Christ have learned to explain their biblical faith to fellow Muslims through the use of Islamic categories, forms, and themes.

10. The Muslim followers of Christ seem to have an understanding of a spiritual unity between themselves and others who call on ^{c}Isa al-Masih as Lord, regardless of race, ethnicity, or religious affiliation.

Summary

Over the past few decades the Lord has ushered many tens of thousands of Muslims into his kingdom. In some places, these believers are the first known followers of Jesus in history from their particular people group. These movements have happened in a variety of ways involving divine intervention, the actions of the body of Christ, and certain world events. There is no one single ministry or methodology that can account for these breakthroughs. Ecclesiae and movements of every type represented on the C1–C6 continuum are emerging in the Muslim world in our day. Some have gone through intense persecution—even martyrdom; others have enjoyed relative peace. We rejoice that many Muslims are finding salvation and new life in Jesus, often times with very little socioreligious dislocation. Yet we must bear in mind the big picture: the task of sharing the love and message of ^{c}Isa al-Masih in the Muslim world on a large scale is just beginning. These reflections, at this juncture in history, are simply one researcher/practitioner's best attempt to understand what God is doing through his people to bring the gospel to Muslims. As we continue to listen intently to the voice of God's Spirit, as well as to the heart cry of Muslims, may the Lord further clarify our vision, methods, and models of ministry as we live among them.

14

Afflictions by Jinn among the Swahili and an Appropriate Christian Approach

BY CALEB CHUL-SOO KIM

Introduction

My first personal interactions with Muslims in East Africa, particularly Kenya, date back to 1989. As a newcomer to the Africa Inland Church (AIC), I served with one of their local churches in the town of Isiolo, 300 kilometers north of Nairobi. From 1990 to 1993, part of my ministry in Isiolo included meeting and talking with many local Muslims as I shared the good news of Jesus with them. We became friends, and after exchanging different religious views over a period of time, I and some of my friends realized that neither of us was bad or harmful; we were both eager to share our different faiths with the spirit of hospitality and without animosity. One of my Muslim friends even invited me to pray for his sick baby.

In those early days I was not aware of Muslim life apart from aspects of the "official" Islamic lifestyle, such as the five Muslim duties and the six articles of Islamic belief. This was true even though the local Muslims I knew—most of whom were Borana and Somali people—seemed syncretistic and not orthodox to me. It was only when I ministered to a young convert named Hussein—who had been a Qur᾿anic teacher (sheikh) for Muslim children at the town mosque—that I began to know about the complicated spiritual world of Muslims. Hussein helped me learn much about this spiritual world in which many Muslims live and struggle with evil powers.[1] He also puzzled me with odd stories, including his personal experiences of jinn, which were the most captivating and troubling. I also discovered that Muslims' "folk" belief in jinn was not just a popular idea of spiritual beings but was part of their official teachings based on the canonical traditions of the Qur᾿an and the Hadith.

---

1 In fact, Hussein suffered from attacks by his father's jinn every night since he came to the Lord. He complained that his Muslim father kept sending his jinn to bother his son so that he could come back to Islam.

Later in 1991 when I came across the book *Muslims and Christians on the Emmaus Road*, edited by Dudley Woodberry,[2] I gained further exposure to the dynamic features of Islam, including the idea of folk Islam and Muslim supernaturalism.

Thanks to my engagement in Hussein's life during my ministry and to my studies with Woodberry later on, which greatly stimulated my interest in folk Islam, I was privileged to spend a few years researching the phenomenon of jinn among Swahili Muslims in East Africa. The following discussions are based partly on my field research conducted from 1997 to 1998 and in 2010.

The Swahili Experience of the Jinn Spirits

Swahilis are both African and Muslim.[3] This identity generally makes them conversant with the supernatural world. They also tend to take the existence of jinn for granted and presuppose the possibility of experiencing jinn in ordinary life.[4] Their encounters with jinn usually entail unpleasant and even painful results, both physically and psychologically. In many cases psychological depression follows an encounter with jinn.[5] Even so, while anthropologists attend to sociocultural issues relating to spirit possession, they fail to address the deeply seated spiritual or psychological need that influences many lives of the Swahili on a daily basis.[6] In other words, anthropologists have not dealt adequately with the Swahili's spiritual need for overcoming the uncanny world of spirits or their struggle with spirits. Thus, in this paper I will attempt to look closely at Swahili experiences of jinn from a Christian anthropological perspective, so as to further develop a missiological approach to the same issue.

---

2 J. Dudley Woodberry, *Muslims and Christians on the Emmaus Road* (Monrovia, CA: MARC, 1989).

3 For detailed discussions of the Swahili identity, see the second through fourth chapters of Caleb Chul-Soo Kim, *Islam among the Swahili in East Africa* (Nairobi: Actons, 2004).

4 For the Islamic teaching on jinn, see the fifth chapter of Kim, *Islam among the Swahili*; Ahmed H. Sakr, *Al-Jinn* (Lombard, IL: Foundation for Islamic Knowledge, 1994); Abu Ameenah Bilal Philips, *The Exorcist Tradition in Islam* (Shariah, UAE: Dar el Fatah, 1997); and Umar Sulaiman al-Ashqar, *The World of the Jinn and Devils* (Boulder, CO: Al-Basheer, 1998).

5 See Kim, *Islam among the Swahili*, 180–88.

6 My view is that those anthropologists dealing with the phenomenon of spirit possession among "folk Muslims" fail to see more important needs than sociocultural issues. I. M. Lewis views spirit possession as an oblique strategy for socially downtrodden people (mostly women) to gain social attention, power, and status. *Ecstatic Religion: A Study of Shamanism and Spirit Possession*, 2nd ed. (New York: Routledge, 1989). Linda L. Giles views it as an ideal medium for the creation of cultural texts with the symbolism approach to the ritualistic spirit possession. "Spirit Possession on the Swahili Coast: Peripheral Cults or Primary Texts?" (PhD diss., University of Texas at Austin, 1989), 143. For other similar cultural-sociological views, see John G. Kennedy, "Nubian Zar Ceremonies as Psychotherapy," *Human Organization* 26 (1967): 185–89; Vincent Crapanzano, *The Hamadsha: A Study in Moroccan Ethnopsychiatry* (Berkeley: University of California Press, 1973); idem, "Mohammed and Dawia: Possession in Morocco," in *Case Studies in Spirit Possession* (New York: John Wiley and Sons, 1977), 141–76; and Janice Patricia Boddy, *Wombs and Alien Spirits: Women, Men, and the Zār Cult in Northern Sudan* (Madison: University of Wisconsin Press, 1989). See also John Janzen's article for anthropologists' varied views of the therapeutic ritual in sub-Saharan Africa. "Drums of Affliction: Real Phenomenon or Scholarly Chimaera?" in *Religion in Africa: Experience and Expression*, eds. Thomas Blakely, Walter van Beek, and Dennis L. Thomson (London: James Currey, 1994), 161–81.

Jinn as a supernatural causality[7]

The struggle with the unseen world (Arabic *ghayb*) by the Swahili is plainly expressed in their desperate search for the causes of human misfortune. More important than knowing "how" something happened is knowing "why" something happened; answering "how" is not enough to satisfy the Swahili mind.[8] Regarding "why" humans experience misfortune, most Swahilis generally believe in two sources of causality: impersonal spiritual forces—such as *laana* (curse), *baraka* (blessing), and *jicho* (evil eye)—and personal beings—such as God, jinn, and ancestors. Among these, jinn seem to be involved in most misfortunes in ordinary Swahili life. This section of my discussion will focus on the causality of jinn.

Jinn afflict people with various illnesses through mysterious incidents. They also lurk everywhere and cause people all kinds of misfortunes. Swahilis believe that some jinn carry the power of the evil eye, and they often attribute sudden death to the *laana* (curse) of jinn. By inflicting an incurable illness upon them, jinn often call people to their services. In 1997 Said (pseudonym), one of my Swahili informants who had been a shamanic practitioner for many years on the Tanzanian coast, told me an interesting story about his shamanic vocation. A jinni had caused him a physical illness, but the illness had not been cured in any local clinic or hospital. It had eventually disappeared only when the jinni was satisfied through a spirit-possession ritual that was prepared for Said's dedication to his shamanic service.

Power struggle: Muslim spiritual warfare

The causal relationship between people and spirits in the Swahili society can be depicted as a power struggle. A critical issue in that relationship is whether humans can control the power of the spirits that are believed to be the main cause of most human afflictions, such as illnesses (*maradhi*) and misfortunes (*bahati mbaya*). In this context, "power" can be defined as the force that helps either humans (individuals or groups) or spirits gain control over the other party and earn what they desire from the other. Then, the therapeutic séance that is performed to heal the patient under attack by jinn may also be considered a kind of human performance of warfare against the spirit world. Each side strives for power to control the other. However, in all cases of this spiritual competition, spirits seem to be intruders, and humans are fugitives; people always take the defense when dealing with the force of harmful spirits. This kind of warfare looks unfair because the spirits are always superior, and their superiority is the fundamental assumption that most Swahilis hold as Muslims. As a result, the Swahili keep experiencing spirits as the intruders based on that assumption.

---

7 Michael Kearney's definition of the term "causality" is helpful for my discussion here. He defines "causality" as "effective power," as he borrows Emile Durkheim's definition of "cause," which is "the force before it has shown the power which is in it; the effect is this same power, only actualized." *World View* (Novato, CA: Chandler and Sharp, 1984), 85. Thus, the term "causality" is synonymous with the concept of "power" in his discussion. I also use the term "causality" in this tone.

8 Cf. David Nyamwaya, *African Indigenous Medicine: An Anthropological Perspective for Policy Makers and Primary Health Care Managers* (Nairobi: African Medical and Research Foundation, 1992), 5–6.

In consequence of such a folk-Islamic view of the spirit world,[9] interestingly enough, when it comes to the spiritual contest, humans hardly ever perform offensive activities. Although some Swahili practitioners often assume ostensibly aggressive attitudes toward possessing spirits, they tend to show them little animosity, as is seen in the Christian deliverance ministry (or exorcism). Even the successful séance does not mean that they have expelled the possessing spirits from the patient entirely. Rather, a successful ritual means a skillful method of pacifying the spirits so that their power over the patient may be reduced. Thus, the spirits always win; humans always become subject to them and, even worse, may become slaves under their power. Once occupied by spirits, both the body and the mind of the patient become their playground.

Dealing with jinn–Swahili *Uganga*

The only way to counteract or thwart malevolent jinn-spirits seems to be to reduce their power and domesticate them so that they may not continue to harm afflicted patients. In this case, the spiritual warfare is not to cast out the jinn-spirits with force and hostility but to control and reduce their power by pacifying them through satisfying their wishes.[10] Traditionally, Swahilis have developed various kinds of ritualistic strategies and tactics for this purpose, and most therapeutic rituals of spirit possession are thus designed to manipulate and domesticate jinn. Unless they control the spirits, they do not expect the effect of *uganga* (healing). Or, put differently, the primary concept of *uganga* in the Swahili therapeutic setting is to maintain a good relationship with the spirits in order to cure the patient. Thus the healing or *uganga* expected of the therapeutic ritual always heals more than pathological symptoms; it is also very concerned with a peaceful relationship between people and spirits. In fact, Swahilis perceive physio-psychological problems as a result of the breakdown between the two species.

One of the prominent strategies that reflect the Swahili understanding of illness (*maradhi*, or symptoms) in terms of relationship is to reveal the identities of jinn that possess a patient undergoing therapy. This strategy operates based on the shamanic belief that "knowledge" of the spirit world overpowers spirits. A Swahili therapeutic ritual that I observed in Dar es Salaam, Tanzania, from 1997 to 1998 illustrates this belief. At a set point in time during that healing ritual, the practitioner (one of my informants) spent considerable time verbally communicating with the spirits that were allegedly possessing the patient. At that moment, the primary concern of the practitioner was to know their origins and names. He assumed

9 See Caleb Chul-Soo Kim, John Travis, and Anna Travis, "Relevant Responses to Folk Muslims," in *From Seed to Fruit: Global Trends, Fruitful Practices, and Emerging Issues among Muslims*, ed. J. Dudley Woodberry (Pasadena: William Carey Library, 2008), 267–70, for a detailed discussion on the Swahili folk-Islamic worldview.

10 Luc de Heusch calls this type of approach to the spirit world "adorcism," as opposed to the concept of "exorcism," in which people expel spirits from the possessed person with hostility. *Why Marry Her? Society and Symbolic Structures* (Cambridge: Cambridge University Press, 1981), 156. For more details on this, see Kim, *Islam among the Swahili*, 192–93.

that identifying their names and origins would give him, the shaman, the ability to overpower and control the spirits. Once the practitioner exposed the names of the jinn, both he and the other participants were happy. The rest of the ritual then seemed to go efficiently. By contrast, however, the next ritual was disastrous, because the allegedly possessing jinn refused to reveal their names. Though the practitioners struggled to extract the names, they had no success.[11] Eventually, they gave up the ritual, and the patient became extremely exhausted, both physically and psychologically. While this second ritual demonstrated the shamanic nature of the jinn-possession ritual, which is aimed at healing, the spiritual warfare ended with great frustration for the Swahili.

Different from the shamanic approach, another method of healing exists that is favored by those Swahili practitioners who claim to be more Islamic than traditionally African. According to Abdala (pseudonym), who had been involved in Islamic or Qur'anic therapy for the past five years when I interviewed him in Zanzibar, *uganga* is an avenue through which the practitioner looks into the matters of the *ghaib*, or the unseen world, referring to the world of jinn. To Abdala, *uganga* is a spiritual skill of removing all kinds of human problems (*kuondosha matatizo aina yo yote*), although he admits it does not cure every *maradhi* (symptom or illness).

The main feature that differentiates the type of healing Abdala uses from other African traditional ones is his Islamic approach that does not allow the practitioner to communicate with jinn. There should be no *siri* (meaning "secret," but here referring to the names of jinn) shared between people and spirits. So he would not try to know the names of possessing jinn.[12] Unlike African traditional practitioners (called *waganga*), Islamic healers like him perform only the ritual of the Qur'anic recitation, similar to exorcism; they "punish" (*adhabu* in Kiswahili) jinn by reciting the Qur'an. Obviously, Islamic healers lean on the authority of their sacred scripture when dealing with evil spirits. Abdala also said that the traditional healing method (referring to *ngoma*, which is a traditional African ritual that includes traditional music accompanied by drum and dance) is not Islamic. However, he

11 Surprisingly, Swahili practitioners whom I interviewed demonstrated great knowledge of the jinn world in Swahili society. I was able to identify at least five categories based on the information that they provided. They are as follows: (1) Muslim jinn (e.g., Ruhani, Maiti, Sharif Hhaibu, Kisomali) who come across oceans from Arabia, (2) pagan Arabic jinn (e.g., Subiani, Bedui, Makata, Merkhe, Machinja, Maanga, Samsui, Jabali, Fahari, Jafari) who come from Arabia or from the Swahili coast, (3) African traditional pagan spirits (e.g., Umundi, Sharifu, Maua, Ufunfuo, Nyoka, Joto, Kinyamkera, Zuhura) who come from African inland and Swahili hinterland, (4) African spirits from neighboring countries (e.g., Kibuki from Madagascar, Kihebeshia from Ethiopia, Kisomali from Somalia, Kipemba from Pemba Island, Tanzania), and (5) European spirits (e.g., Kizungu spirits with many Western names). This classification also shows how Swahilis project their understanding of surrounding societies onto the spirit world.

12 However, Abdala admitted that knowing the names of jinn would empower the practitioner more than not. According to him, jinn also know this fact, and this is why jinn usually resist giving away their names to the practitioner. If they did, the practitioner would control them easily. So *uganga* has to do much with the knowledge of the unseen world; the knowledge such as what jinn like and what they do not. This interview as well as participant observations were conducted in June 2010.

admitted that Swahilis are socially, if not religiously, allowed to practice the traditional rituals despite their pagan nature.[13]

Even in this type of Islamic *uganga* method, extreme hostility against jinn as seen in Christian exorcism is hardly detected; instead, *uganga* is a form of "punishment" inflicted on social members who behave like malicious rascals or rogues against their neighbors. In both traditional and Islamic types of *uganga*, jinn are not objects to be driven out completely from the Swahili society; rather, they are perceived to be invisible neighbors with whom people ought to continually wrestle in order to maintain peace in their personal lives. The following story of Fatima may present a real picture of how dreadful the Swahili feel about jinn, their constantly harassing neighbors.

A case of healing[14]

Fatima (pseudonym) is a single Swahili woman who claims to have been delivered from harassment by five jinn through the healing of the Qur᾿anic recitation. She is now an apprentice under Sheikh Abdala. Fatima used to suffer from attacks by a male jinni called Subiani that caused her headaches, moodiness, compressed feelings (*uzito*), and visual decrease (*giza cha macho*). She also suffered from other symptoms such as chest pressure (*kifua*) and sneezing, and she was diagnosed with an attack by a male jinni called *jini ya bahari* (jinni from the ocean). Fatima told me an interesting story about her experiences of the ocean-jinni's attack. She said that her legs moved like the ocean waves and even her stomach sounded like them when she was struck by the jinni.

More interestingly, among those five kinds of jinn that harassed Fatima, both male and female jinn called *majini ya mahaba* (jinn of love) seem extremely dangerous. When these jinn possess people, they make their victims have sex with them. According to Fatima, jinn of love usually attempt to keep their victims from having sexual relationships with their human spouses. They often make women hate their husbands and then get sick. If the victim is not married, the jinn make him or her hate marriage. Fatima further explained that the only way to survive their stalking and harassment is to make friends with them. If, however, the jinn are *jini ya kutumwa*, the "jinn sent by enemies," people cannot make friends with them; they must be expelled through treatment. Fatima had occasionally seen a male jinni of love who looked handsome but very angry with her. He was a sent-jinni, thus Fatima eventually had to consult a local practitioner.

The healer recited the Qur᾿an over Fatima's head for a long period of time. This therapeutic session was held for a couple of hours almost every weekend for several months. Besides the Qur᾿anic recitation, the practitioner also used herbal fumigation and *kombe*, which refers to drinking the water into which written Qur᾿anic verses were washed. The

13 Abdala mentioned some examples of the traditional *ngoma* rituals, such as Umundi and Kumbwaya originated from Pemba Island, and Kibukim from Comoro Island.

14 The description in this section is based on my ethnographic interviews with Swahili informants in Zanzibar in June 2010. I was able to interview some Swahili women with kind assistance from the practitioners in their healing place.

assumption underlying these two methods is that jinn can dwell in the human body through its parts, such as the blood or stomach. Thanks to the sheikh's persistent endeavor, Fatima no longer has those symptoms, and she wishes to become like him as an *mganga* (healer) to help her fellow women that suffer from jinn harassment.[15]

Swahili self-perception

To what extent the evil spirits contributed to the symptoms that the Swahili informant described is not easy to figure out. This topic deserves extensive research with tools from psychology and other medical sciences, but what interests me more here is how Swahilis view themselves in terms of their relationship with jinn or in light of their experiences with jinn. It is apparent that Swahilis consider spirits to be superior to humans as they ascribe the cause of most illnesses to jinn. In the Swahili worldview, jinn are more powerful than people. This is evident in the Swahili myth about people's relationships with jinn. According to the myth, Allah predestined the Swahili to live with jinn on this earth. As a result of the jinn's failure to win the battle against the angels, the jinn fled to earth and began to reside in oceans and caves on beaches, or on dry land. However, Allah kindly granted the request of the defeated jinn that he provide what they needed to live; Allah allowed the jinn to feed on human beings, particularly on human blood, as their primary source of food.[16]

This legend reflects well how ordinary Swahilis view themselves as inferior to jinn in terms of power. It explains the inevitable interruption of human life by jinn. The myth may be an attempt by Swahilis to justify, though unwillingly, the defeat and frustration in their struggle with evil spirits. It could also be a cultural tool used to rationalize human predicaments caused by spirits. By being internalized within the deep structure of their worldview, this Swahili myth seems to provide for Swahilis "a way to externalize, comprehend, and hopefully transform an otherwise inarticulate" psychological suffering.[17] Consequently, Swahilis take the phenomenon of jinn to be normal, and thus take for granted their

15 There are many other stories similar to Fatima's experiences. Some of them show that the Swahili Islamic treatment is not always successful, unlike Fatima's case.

16 The following is the myth that Kjersti Larsen collected: When God had created the earth, the spirits were the first to live there; they lived on earth before human beings but were created after the angels. Then God set the rules that the spirits should go away and leave the earth to human beings. He made this decision because he had given the spirits the ability to pass through the air and to understand every language, and because he created them as more knowledgeable and educated than human beings. God did not give human beings the same abilities as spirits to do everything and to live everywhere, so they must live on earth. Most of the spirits did not agree to leave the earth, and then God sent the angels to earth to fight the spirits. A war broke out between the spirits and the angels. The spirits were beaten by the angels and fled into the ocean, to the caves on the beaches, and to dry land. However, some of the spirits had agreed to leave the earth. They were forgiven and were told that they could return to earth and live together with human beings. After this war, the spirits asked God how they could live in this world when God has given human beings everything necessary to live on earth. They asked, "Where are we going to eat?" God answered, "Take hold of the human beings. They will provide you with what you need. You shall drink the blood of human beings." "Where Humans and Spirits Meet: Incorporating Difference and Experiencing Otherness in Zanzibar Town," (Doctor Politicarum diss., University of Oslo, 1995), 88–89.

17 Bradd Shore, *Culture in Mind: Cognition, Culture, and the Problem of Meaning* (New York: Oxford University Press, 1996), 254.

inferiority to spirits and continue to suffer from that assumption. For this reason, most ordinary Swahilis are desperately obliged to hinge on the power and skill of Swahili practitioners (*waganga*) in order to avoid being completely overpowered and devastated by jinn. Thus, emotions such as powerlessness, confusion, and fear usually characterize the minds and hearts of ordinary Swahilis in wrestling with the spirit world, known as *ghaib*.

An Appropriate Approach to Swahilis Afflicted by Jinn

Above, I attempted to describe the Swahili experience of jinn in a phenomenological way. A number of anthropologists have already endeavored to provide varied scholarly explanations about the phenomenon of spirit possession and its related cults in Africa. Although holding many contrasting views, most of them concurrently start their discussions from the fact that various therapeutic rituals dealing with possession and sicknesses caused by spirits are the rituals of *affliction*.[18] Simply put, most of the rituals of spirit possession are designed to help humans cope with their afflictions. Inspired by the anthropologists, I have also attempted to grapple with the same issue, particularly in Swahili society, from a missiological perspective. From my anthropological fieldwork as well as my ministry experiences, one of my conclusions is that Swahilis experience spirits in a very painful way.

Oftentimes those who strive to share the good news of Jesus with Muslims overlook the dimension of affliction and the profound need it creates in their spiritual life. Before encountering "real" people like Hussein in Muslim societies, I, too, had been carried away with the passion to "convert" them to my belief system. Contrary to my wish, however, I realized that some of them had become more resistant and even hostile to the gospel than they were before meeting with me. Learning from Hussein innumerable life challenges that ordinary Muslims experience in everyday life, I underwent a great shift of my perspective of people, especially the people of Islam. As a fellow human being and co-monotheist, we must continually strive to develop an appropriate way of helping those afflicted by jinn to overcome all evil hindrances and eventually come to Christ through his victorious power.[19] The remainder of this paper is thus concerned with Christian approaches to afflicted Swahilis.

---

18 It is Victor Turner who has begun to use the term "drums of affliction" in anthropological circles since the 1960s. *The Drums of Affliction: A Study of Religious Processes among the Ndembu of Zambia* (London: Oxford University Press, 1968). Turner and his followers have attempted to interpret Africans' misfortunes and afflictions in terms of the dominant role played by spirits (ancestors or other nonhuman spirits) in society. In their observations, afflicted individuals try to come to terms with their suffering by joining the healing ritual whereby they venerate the afflicting agent (either ancestors or nonhuman spirits) that has inflicted sufferings on them. See Janzen, "Drums of Affliction," for various views on this topic.

19 In this chapter, the "appropriate way" refers to a Christian approach in the cross-cultural context that is "appropriate both to a given social context and to the Scriptures," following Charles Kraft's definition. *Appropriate Christianity* (Pasadena: William Carey Library, 2005), 4.

Approaching more affectionally than doctrinally

Focusing solely on doctrinal issues in evangelistic efforts does not seem to follow the ministerial philosophy of Paul, who encourages us to speak the truth in love (Eph 4:15). If we share only the doctrines of the gospel, we will probably prove our faithfulness to the truth; however, we may not demonstrate fully the quintessence of the gospel unless we willingly make efforts to understand the heart of our audience and become appropriate to them, as Jesus did for us.[20] Sharing the gospel is more than preaching the doctrine of salvation. Reinhold Strähler has evidenced in his doctoral thesis that conversion to Christ in Kenya entails both cognitive and affective changes in the convert's life, and these changes occur dynamically in sociological, psychological, anthropological, and theological milieus as influencing factors.[21] In all these factors, it is obvious that the "people" element is the most important human key to the authentic change or transformation of a soul. In order to be effective in communicating the gospel, the communicator needs to interact with Muslims within their life situations more personally and empathetically than dutifully.

Unfortunately, most Westerners and even non-Westerners who are influenced by Western views tend to understand conversion to faith in Christ mostly in terms of intellectual comprehension of the gospel. More often than not, the emotive dimension is overlooked, if not neglected, when the communicator of the gospel invites people to faith in Christ.[22] People are often told not to lean on an emotional response; rather, they must use the intellectual faculty to understand the logic of the gospel. Emotion should follow understanding and will. It seems, then, that people have treated emotion as secondary to human reason or intellect. However, emotion is a very important, integral part of the mind. It is not appropriate to think of intellect and emotion as two separate entities. Dallas Willard affirms, "The connection between thought and feeling is so intimate that the 'mind' is usually treated as consisting of thought and feeling *together*" (italics in the original).[23] Regarding the importance of emotions, I reiterate the words of Robert Solomon that Anna Wierzbicka quotes:

> Emotions are not just disruptions of our otherwise calm and reasonable experience; they are at the very heart of that experience, determining our focus, influencing our interests, defining the dimensions of our world …

---

20 For a comprehensive discussion on various issues of contextualization in terms of faithfulness to truth and appropriateness to people or culture, see Kraft, *Appropriate Christianity*. The first and the nineteenth chapters of his book are helpful for our discussion of the contextualization of the relationship with Swahili Muslims.

21 Reinhold Strähler, "Coming to Faith in Christ: Case Studies of Muslims in Kenya" (Doctor of Theology thesis, University of South Africa, 2009).

22 Anna Wierzbicka points out, "There is a tradition within Anglo academic psychology which tends to be hostile to 'emotion.'" *Emotions across Languages and Cultures: Diversity and Universals* (Cambridge: Cambridge University Press, 1999), 17. It is not just Western psychologists that tend to view emotion less importantly; from daily experiences it is quite common that emotion is being treated as less significant than intelligence.

23 Dallas Willard, *Renovation of the Heart: Putting on the Character of Christ* (Colorado Springs: NavPress, 2002), 33.

> Emotions … lie at the very heart of ethics, determining our values, focusing our vision, influencing our every judgment, giving meaning to our lives.[24]

Therefore, the aspect of emotion should not be overlooked in sharing the gospel. As Swahilis are harassed by jinn in everyday life, the gospel must be presented as truly "good" news to them as a gracious gift from the perfect Comforter and Healer. Even the communicator should be able to touch the hearts of his or her audiences by evoking good emotions that are culturally appropriate to them. As often observed, it is when people see the goodness and kindness of the communicator that they begin to respond positively to the message being delivered.

Emotions also seem to be the locus at which possession by evil spirits can occur. Willard points out the vulnerability of the ruined soul, or the corrupt mind, which "becomes a fearful wilderness and a wild intermixture of thought and feeling, manifested in willful stupidities, blatant inconsistencies, and confusions, often to the point of obsession, madness, or possession."[25] Especially damaged emotions can become the so-called emotional "garbage" on which evil spirits tend to feed in order to harass and ruin people.[26] This seems to be very true of Swahilis. Since many Swahilis suffer from conflicts in various relationships, such as marriage and friendship, they carry negative emotions on a daily basis; they even fear the possible attack by the evil eye of their own family members. Moreover, Swahilis also fear the possible loss of their benefits. As a peasant society, they sense the limit of their good, based on a common cultural assumption in peasant society that "one person's gain with respect to any good must be another's loss."[27] They know that some people may employ the power of jinn to punish others for their individual success. One of my informants in Zanzibar in June 2010 told me that one of the reasons for the rampant practice of *sihiri*[28] is people's wish to thwart others' success *(kuzuia fanyiko ya wengine)*.[29] As a result, Swahilis carry such heavy, negative emotions as pressure, tension, suspicion, bitterness, fear, worry, anxiety, and apprehension, on top of the fear of spirits. Burdened with this kind of emotive condition, they can easily succumb to the overpowering force of jinn whenever the jinn attack.[30] This may be one of the major reasons why many Swahilis experience jinn possession so frequently.

---

24 Wierzbicka, *Emotions*, 18.

25 Willard, *Renovation of the Heart*, 33.

26 Charles Kraft, *Deep Wounds, Deep Healing: Discovering the Vital Link between Spiritual Warfare and Inner Healing* (Ann Arbor, MI: Vine, 1993), 65.

27 George Foster, *Traditional Societies and Technological Change*, 2nd ed. (New York: Harper and Row, 1973), 35.

28 The word *sihiri* has been mistakenly translated as "witchcraft" or "magic," but it is difficult to find an English word that conveys its concept.

29 Some people also employ the power of jinn to protect themselves from such thwarting or punishing attacks.

30 Jinn seem to be involved in almost every affair of ordinary Swahili life. To borrow the words of Patricia Caplan, who did her anthropological research among Swahilis in Mafia Island for several decades: "Because spirits [referring to jinn] are everywhere, it would be impossible to ignore them, and because of their amoral

Sihiri is the Swahili traditional practice of dealing with the jinn's power. Interestingly, this practice always has something to do with the psychological alleviation of the heavy sense of fear and anxiety. From my observations, many people feel greatly relieved when they buy the practitioner's prescriptions, such as talisman, charm, amulet, and the like, which are believed to protect them from malicious jinn. In Zanzibar, as one of my informants said,[31] *sihiri* is so popular that approximately 80 percent of the Zanzibari population is currently involved in the practice. This statistic shows how desperately Swahilis look for a solution to their life predicaments. However, the spiritual medicines they seek from the *waganga* are always temporary. The Swahili need to know that a permanent solution exists in ᶜIsa al-Masih (Jesus Christ), God's perfect Prophet whom even Muslims recognize as the great healer (Āl ᶜImrān [3]:49; al-Māᵓida [5]:110). As fellow sojourners on such a perilous earth, the communicators of the gospel should humbly become instruments that God can use to touch the heavily laden hearts of the Swahili (cf. Matt 11:28); they must present the gospel in a way that both touches the wounded hearts of the Swahili and opens their intellectual eyes, which have been blinded by the god of this age (2 Cor 4:4).

Friendship: Beyond differences toward common ground

In order to present the gospel as the solution to the Swahili suffering from jinn, we also need to discuss an appropriate avenue for the delivery of the gospel. I suggest that a culturally relevant, genuine friendship is an apt channel for the love and power of the gospel to be appropriately communicated to Swahilis.

Certainly the Christian communicator would have problems with Swahilis regarding many theological differences. For example, Christians assert that the evil spirit (Greek *daimon*) is another label for the fallen angel,[32] whereas Muslims believe that the evil spirit (Arabic *shayṭān*) refers to a jinni that is rebellious toward God and malicious toward people.[33] Despite these different theological views, however, both Christians and Muslims would agree

---

and capricious nature, it is difficult always to know how to avoid offending them." *African Voices, African Lives: Personal Narratives from a Swahili Village* (London: Routledge, 1997), 195.

31 Aisha (pseudonym) is a highly educated person who is studying for the master's degree in Arabic linguistics at a university in Zanzibar.

32 For the biblical evidence for the identity of the evil spirit with the fallen angel, see Merrill Unger, *Biblical Demonology: A Study of Spiritual Forces at Work Today* (Grand Rapids: Kregel, 1994), 52–55; C. Fred Dickason, *Demon Possession and the Christian* (Westchester, IL: Crossway, 1987), 24–25; and Wayne Grudem, *Systematic Theology: An Introduction to Biblical Doctrine* (Grand Rapids: Zondervan, 1994), 412–15.

33 For some Qurᵓanic references, see al-ᵓAnᶜām [6]:112; Fāṭir [35]:6; Ṣād [38]:37; az-Zukhruf [43]:62; etc. For extensive discussions on Islamic teachings on jinn, see al-Ashqar, *World of the Jinn;* and Abu'l-Mundhir Khaleel ibn Ibrahim Ameen, *The Jinn and Human Sickness: Remedies in the Light of the Qurᵓaan and Sunnah,* 1st ed., trans. Nasiruddin Al-Kattab (Riyadh: Darussalam, 2005). Abdullah Yusuf Ali refuses to be dogmatic about the definition of jinn. He states, "Some people say that jinn therefore means the hidden qualities or capacities in man; others that it means wild or jungle folk hidden in the hills or forests. I do not wish to be dogmatic, but I think, from a collation and study of the Qurᵓanic passages, that the meaning is simply 'a spirit,' or an invisible or hidden force." Footnote 929 to al-Māᵓida [6]:100 in *The Holy Qur'an: Text, Translation and Commentary* (Brentwood, MD: Amana, 1983), 319. For more discussions on the meanings and the usage of the words "jinn" and *shayṭān* in Swahili society, see the fifth chapter of Kim, *Islam among the Swahili*.

that evil spirits not only exist but also intend to harm people. In the past, missionaries used to focus on correcting wrong views held by people whom they intended to serve. In spite of their many efforts, however, the recipients did not respond positively to their doctrinal correction. This historical fact actually enlightens us to see the mistake or deficiency in the conventional missionary approach. Missionaries should not have focused mainly on doctrinal issues; rather, they should have adequately taken into account the recipient's heart condition and its receptivity. In most majority-world societies, people respond positively to doctrinal issues when they "feel" good about the person who addresses them. Thus a doctrinal discussion or correction is more likely to happen smoothly when both parties first come to good terms.

Indeed, it is difficult to convince Swahilis that the intent of a communicator is good, even when he or she has something to offer. They may cast suspicious eyes and even direct hateful attitudes toward Christians, as they often do in many Muslim societies. Furthermore, due to theological disparities and different perspectives on the spirit world, even a friendly conversation regarding spiritual life can result in mutual frustration. What is worse, the communicator of the gospel may lose his or her positive attitude and become impatient with his or her listeners. Therefore, it is highly recommended that the communicator should build a meaningful friendship first.

Friendship is the initial point of contact and foundation for any further relationships. Here I do not discuss ways to build friendships in the cross-cultural situation, but I can at least affirm that people can always find common ground on which to build a meaningful friendship. Considering the Swahili worldview, we can list the following important denominators that both Christians and Swahili Muslims believe: the morally deficient human nature,[34] the human quandary that is full of spiritual afflictions caused by evil spirits, the incessant need for God's grace in daily life, and so forth. Essentially, both Muslims and Christians recognize this human condition; hence they both recognize humanity's need for God's mercy.

We can initiate a relationship with Muslims on the basis of these shared concerns by telling them our personal stories. Many times various people (including Swahilis) have really appreciated my stories, including my testimony of faith in Christ, which I shared in private settings. My experience is an example of how sharing our personal lives with humility can help us move beyond theological and cultural disparities and can even help Muslims listen to us. Responding to our openness, they may also invite us into their lives, where we would eventually be able to lovingly offer Christ's solution to their spiritual struggles.

---

34 Dudley Woodberry has extensively discussed an extremely important common ground that is found between Christian and Muslim diagnoses of the human condition; that is, the critical human predicament or corruption. See his articles: "Different Diagnoses of the Human Condition," in Woodberry, *Muslims and Christians*, 149–60; and "Toward Common Ground in Understanding the Human Condition," in Woodberry, Zümrüt, and Köylü, *Muslim and Christian Reflections*, 23–31.

Conclusion

Envisioning effective ministries among Swahilis, I would like to recommend an excellent ministry that has been carried out by Anwar Berhe in a neighboring country, Ethiopia.[35] Berhe has witnessed many cases of Ethiopian Muslims coming to Christ through the ministry of "power encounter,"[36] as well as what he calls the Christian "life-example ministry." He works for a local denomination called the Ethiopian Kale Heywet Church, where he is in charge of the missions department. Under the department's very active Muslim Outreach Program, Berhe and his team members have worked diligently among Ethiopian Muslims throughout the country to win twenty-four to twenty-five thousand of them to Christ in the past eleven years. His ministry program runs two types of approaches to Muslim neighbors: what Berhe calls the "C3–4" and "C4–5" approaches, adopted from the C1–C6 continuum by John and Anna Travis.[37]

Many of the Muslim societies in Ethiopia are rather open to the gospel and are peace-loving, and so the program invites converts as well as their Muslim neighbors to what Berhe calls the "house church" (Amharic *Yebet Bete Christian*). In house churches, attendees hear the word of God and receive deliverance ministry, inner healing, and physical healing, together with material provisions; leaders carry out discipleship, prayer ministry, and rudimentary education for converts. It is through these ministries that even nonconverted Muslims experience God's power and love. These Muslims usually join the faith in Jesus some time later. Berhe says that the genuine love and concern for the people as well as the passion for God is the key to such good fruits.

Christians of Berhe's house churches are always eager to demonstrate the love of Jesus in every possible way for their new converts, as a result of which very few go back to their former religion. In other words, the house churches are being presented as sincere communities of friendship to their Muslim neighbors. Greatly inspired by Berhe's sharing, I want to recommend this kind of holistic approach even to those intending to minister among Swahilis, as I have recently seen Swahili communities begin to open their minds to the Christians present in Zanzibar Island.

---

35 Anwar Berhe was once a Muslim. After his conversion to Christ, he has been involved in a very effective ministry of evangelism and discipleship for Ethiopian Muslims, and is currently studying for a master's degree at Nairobi Evangelical Graduate School of Theology in Africa International University.

36 Among many materials on power encounter, the following articles are helpful for discussing the ministry of power encounter among Muslims: Bill Musk, *The Unseen Face of Islam: Sharing the Gospel with Ordinary Muslims* (Speldhurst, UK: MARC, 1989), 239–56; Paul Hiebert, "Power Encounter and Folk Islam," in Woodberry, *Muslims and Christians*, 45–61; Vivienne Stacey, "The Practice of Exorcism and Healing," in Woodberry, *Muslims and Christians*, 292–303; J. Dudley Woodberry, "The Relevance of Power Ministries for Folk Muslims," in *Wrestling with Dark Angels*, eds. C. Peter Wagner and F. Douglas Pennoyer (Ventura, CA: Regal, 1990), 313–31; Rick Love, *Muslims, Magic, and the Kingdom of God* (Pasadena: William Carey Library, 2000), 111–64; and Kim, Travis, and Travis, "Relevant Responses," 272–78.

37 John and Anna Travis, "Appropriate Approaches in Muslim Contexts" in *Appropriate Christianity*, ed. Charles Kraft (Pasadena: William Carey Library, 2005), 397–414. Also "Factors Affecting the Identity That Jesus-Followers Choose" in *From Seed To Fruit*, ed. Dudley Woodberry (Pasadena: William Carey Library, 2008), 193–205.

15
Peacemaking as a Witness

BY CHRISTINE AMAL MALLOUHI

At first reading this title suggests an activity in which most of us are rarely engaged or expect to be engaged, that of peacemaking at an organizational level, or between high-ranking individuals who it is expected have enough power to influence a positive outcome. We would all agree that peacemaking is vitally important, but most of us do not see ourselves as having enough clout or importance to be influential in making significant change. Moreover, peacemaking is so broad and diverse a topic that it raises the question of what peacemaking entails. There are numerous groups engaged in peacemaking as a Christian witness, giving evidence to a wide range of practices and understanding of what the gospel means to society and ways in which to engage.[1]

Peacemaking as a Calling

Among the forefront groups engaging in peacemaking as a calling is the Christian Peacemaker Teams (CPT), a Chicago and Toronto-based organization working to reduce violence in areas of armed conflict. Originally a violence-reduction initiative of the historic peace churches (Mennonite, Church of the Brethren, and Quaker), it now enjoys support and membership from a wide range of Christian denominations. CPT seeks to enlist the whole church in organized, nonviolent alternatives to war and places teams of trained peacemakers in regions of lethal conflict. They believe that they must devote the same discipline and self-sacrifice to peacemaking and nonviolence that the military devotes to war. Rich Meyer who is an American farmer has been involved in the Hebron project in West Bank Palestine for nine years. He has deliberately placed himself in one of the hottest spots of the world between the parties in conflict trying to protect the powerless. He says this work is "a calling,' and

1 Special thanks to Paul-Gordon Chandler for his thoughts on "Communicating Peace" which he delivered to the Arab Media Convention in Beirut, March 2004.

adds, "We really need people to get involved in peacemaking at the conflict zone level … I deeply believe that God is in the business of reconciliation."[2]

The ecumenical organization Christian Peace Witness is another group believing that to actively pursue peacemaking at personal cost is integral to putting Jesus' teachings into practice. Their vision statement clarifies why they believe they must engage in nonviolent anti-war demonstrations and civil disobedience which has resulted in arrest. The group organized an ecumenical peace march against the US war on Iraq in March 2007 when three thousand protesters, mainly Christians, marched on the White House resulting in one hundred arrests.[3]

"Our purpose is to share a vision of how all of God's people—of all faiths—can live in peace. As Christians, we are keenly aware of the way that Jesus consistently surprised his friends and his enemies by responding in love to those who attacked him. Further, the gospel makes clear that there is a direct connection between the work of doing justice and being peacemakers. Therefore:

We remind ourselves of the life and teachings of Jesus as the Prince of Peace, the lover of enemies, and the reconciler of the world.

We ask God to work a change of heart in our elected leaders who have carried out this war in all of our names, and we ask for God's forgiveness for the suffering of so many in Iraq and the United States during the course of the war.

We accept responsibility to witness to our faith, especially Jesus' hard teachings that secure communities are built on the foundation of living in right relationship with one another.

We look forward to the day when all people know that the word "Christian" means a movement that yearns and aches for the Kingdom of God to come here on Earth with people of all faiths."[4]

Many Facets to Peacemaking

A bouquet of vision statements from various Christian groups describe peacemaking has many dimensions. These include the study of peacemaking strategies, involvement in mediation and conflict resolution, making peace by developing partnerships, building a culture of peace, calling for disarmament and refusing to participate in warfare, Christians as catalysts for conflict transformation, overcoming racism, sexism, and militarism, advocacy and challenge around God's call to work for economic justice, and local and international efforts to overcome poverty.

There is a multifaceted "third way" of responding to violence which is love of enemy, peacemaking as a journey of truth-telling, reconciliation, and memory work, storytelling

---

2 BBC World News, Online Edition, "In Pictures, Christian Peacemakers, Hebron." http://news.bbc.co.uk/2/shared/spl/hi/picture_gallery/07/middle_east_christian_peacemakers0_hebron/html/4.stm.

3 http://www.umc.org news archives March 2007.

4 "Questions of faith," http://christianpeacewitness.org/why.

as peacemaking, ecumenical dialogue and redeeming the fractured Christian community, peace education inside and outside the church, naming the power of prayer and song in peacemaking, and Christian involvement in solidarity and the refugee sanctuary movement.

One of the most unusual innovations is "eating the way Jesus lived—the food system as an arena for peacemaking."[5] Some groups listed various activities of evangelizing as witness, but "peacemaking" was not a word used as part of their agenda, although probably all would see their efforts as peacemaking between individuals and God. After reading this rather overwhelming list of things in which we apparently need to be involved we might be ready to give up even before we begin. So I was glad to find this had been anticipated and a class was offered "Having (Christian) faith in the future."[6]

What Is Real Peace?

It is clear from the above that most would agree that real peace is not simply a cessation of hostilities, but reconciliation. Reconciliation is a special word for Christians, and we have definite ideas of how and with whom it should take place. Evangelical Christians usually hope that evangelism and witness will result in someone being reconciled with God through Christ. Although Christians may disagree about which term best describes their activity of peacemaking, evangelism, or witness all three activities actually have the common goal of reconciliation.

Most Christians are engaged in peacemaking, although some may not have thought of it in those terms, but in terms of personal witness. Christian peacemaking is attempting to help people experience life as we understand God intends it to be lived. It is coming alongside people to stand with them in hard places by giving our presence to shelter them while we work towards reconciliation. Some groups do this by standing between combatants to protect the weaker party while they work towards reconciliation. Others view this happening as part of the conversion process, where they cover someone with prayer while they encourage reconciliation with God. It is involvement with people that empowers them to make life-giving choices of peace in place of unrest and violence, love in place of hate, forgiveness in place of retaliation, hope and courage in place of fear, joy in place of despair, life not death, and freedom not bondage.

At the heart of the gospel message is God's desire to bring all creation—people and nature—into life-giving participation with God. Jesus' life ministry was centered on bringing people into this renewal with the Father, or more succinctly, participation in the relationship of love between the Father, Jesus, and Spirit. When we participate in the life of Jesus by sharing his life with others, we in fact become peacemakers. This is usually taking place in our families and with our friends and neighbors by our life and our explanation of the

5 Matthew Bailey-Dick, "Christian Approaches to Peacemaking." University of Waterloo. Course Syllabus (Winter, 2008), 3.

6 Ibid.

meaning of what they see us being and doing. When we intentionally live among those of other faiths, the same model for being a witness holds true. So peacemaking is not the complicated global matter it first appears to be. It actually can also be something very simple and feasible for everyone.

Judging the Success of Peacemaking

Peacemaking in the secular arena can be judged as achieving or failing, and success is visible and can be measured, whether war or peace. But true reconciliation may not be happening. In our goal of peacemaking as a witness, how can we judge success? To whom are we witnessing? Is the witness to God, to ourselves, or to the other? Is it successful because we are engaged in what is an integral part of our faith and therefore does not need any further judgment as a success or failure, or should it be judged as secular efforts are judged and, therefore, requiring identifiable results? Can the witness and the peacemaking be judged with different criteria with different outcomes? I am not attempting to answer these questions, as the answers will vary from person to person according to their theology, and the way witness is conducted will be different in each case. Individuals may move through different stages of how they do this and do it differently at different times along their faith journey, or differently in different circumstances.

Let's return to the model of peacemaking by "eating the way Jesus ate." At first I had no clue as to what it could mean, but upon reflection I realized this is the way I most often peace-make, although I had not thought of it in those terms before. In our case, it means having an open home and inviting strangers into our family and sharing our lives and our bread with them. Sharing bread in the Arab tradition means to enter into relationship with the other and carry a mutual responsibility for the others' good. Bringing people together to share bread is a way to break down walls of hostility and foster true community. We can intentionally invite guests to share our sacred space along with those of whom they would normally be suspicious, or those whom they intentionally keep at arm's length. We intentionally bring Christians and Muslims together in our home for meals and specially invite those who have no friendships with the "other" group. This face-to-face brokered involvement usually breaks down walls and suspicious strangers leave as friends. These interactions of sharing life and thought have contributed to all of us moving more deeply into the life of God. Muslims have much to teach us of sacred hospitality and are great at embracing strangers as part of their family.

Witness and Suffering

Witness is central to the Christian faith. There have been some catastrophic interpretations of what witness means throughout history when the Christian faith was spread in arrogance and domination and forced on others by violence. In recent years Christian groups conducted walks of repentance asking Muslims for forgiveness for wars conducted centuries ago in the Crusades. While this activity seems to easily fit both categories of witness and peacemaking, it still may fail to bring about reconciliation. The peacemaker cannot orchestrate reconciliation. He or she can only try to make the way easy.

Voluntary suffering is one of the building blocks in the vocation of Christian peacemaking. When peacemaking takes place between Muslims and Christians in these days that have been labeled as a clash of civilizations or religions, the task is often fraught with difficulties and danger. Christian peacemakers and missionaries have been murdered for their activities, or died because they put themselves into dangerous situations in order to witness, bring peace, and protect others. In March 2006 Tom Fox was abducted and murdered in Baghdad while he was working with the Christian Peacemaker Teams (CPT).

In another incident in Yemen a gunman invaded the Baptist missionary hospital at Jibla, on December 30, 2002, and gunned down three American medical workers and critically wounded an American pharmacist. The gunman, an Islamist militant, believed he was serving God by killing them. In the aftermath of the deaths, many people asked why missionaries serve in dangerous places. The mission spokesman responded:

> The answer is love. Love is the reason these three left. Love is the reason their colleagues are still there. Love is the reason Jesus came. It is God's reconciling love that purchased us and gave us this wonderful gift of the gospel. That love compels us to share it with those who have never heard. We go and live the gospel among them so they might know God's love and grace themselves.[7]

The person who leads the work in the region said, "Since the murders, many people in Jibla have talked about the love they saw in the hospital workers' lives … As we walked through the city, people all along the way kept grabbing our hands and telling us, 'They … are with God. This is sure.'"[8]

> Jesus warned his disciples that some would meet violent death at the hands of religious extremists, but did not rescind his call to go out and make peace, "Indeed an hour is coming when those who kill you will think that by doing so they are offering worship to God. And they will do this because they have not known the Father or me." (John 16:1-3 NRSV)

Among the dangers Christian peacemakers face is not so much being the victim of militants, but the more subtle danger of carrying out witness in ways that Jesus expressly

7 Mark Kelly, "Murdered Workers Victorious Even in Death, Rankin Says," *International Mission Board*, http://www.imb.org/yemen/stories/story14.asp.

8 Ibid.

forbade or did not engage. Western Christianity is in a position of dominance today, linked with political exploits of the superpowers. A culture of fear encourages retaliation, and coalitions of preemptive strikes (kill them in case they think of trying to kill us) react quickly to strike at the enemy. An Australian daily paper insightfully asked, "At what point did Jesus change from being the Prince of Peace to being the Prince of the Pre-emptive strike?"[9] Peacemakers need to go into the tense no-man's land between two camps going like Jesus did on the cross with arms outstretched to each side inviting them to reconcile through his/her body in the middle. This is not limited to going into a war zone. It can be trying to reconcile two hostile camps of beliefs within the church and paying the price of being in the middle with both sides against you. Going out to a perceived enemy who is suspicious of you and maybe too ready to assign base motives to your behavior makes one vulnerable. The human reaction to vulnerability is fear and anxiety. Add to this the possible scenario of civil unrest and random violence in the country, or a war, or an unjust violent regime that makes life feel like a roulette wheel with a loaded gun hidden on one of the numbers, and there is plenty of reason to feel afraid and act aggressively without thinking.

Jesus' Peace

Peacemaking, witness, and fear are not new to our era, as the following event illustrates:

> When it was evening on that day, the first day of the week, and the doors of the house where the disciples had met were locked for fear of the Jews, Jesus came and stood among them and said, "Peace be with you!" After he said this he showed them his hands and his side. Then the disciples rejoiced when they saw the Lord. Jesus said to them again, "Peace be with you! As the Father has sent me, so send I you." When he had said this, he breathed on them and said, "Receive the Holy Spirit." (John 20:19–22 NRSV)

The disciples were in a complex situation; they were a minority group cowering behind locked doors and due to their connection with Christ, who had just been executed as a common criminal, they were also implicated. They were hiding from the very people whom Jesus intended to send them to. The last thing that could have described them was "peaceful," and the last place they wanted to go was outside, and the very last thing they wanted to do was to talk to anyone about Jesus and his teachings.

Then Jesus presented himself to them, in this most confusing and difficult of times, blessed them with peace and said, "As the Father has sent me, I am sending you." The meaning of that short word *as* is critical. I see this as the link between the various ways in which Christians engage as peacemakers as a witness to Christ. While there are many different

9 Cheryl Lawrie, "With God on Side," *The Age* (May 27, 2007), http://www.theage.com.au/news/opinion/with-god-on-side/2007/05/26/1179601730254.html?page=fullpage.

ways to do it, there is really only one manner in which to do it. Jesus is saying that the way, the method, the strategy, the approach God the Father used in sending him, we should use in presenting him to the world. Jesus gives a special gift for the task which is peace.

The primary and basic idea of the biblical word *peace* is completeness, soundness, and wholeness. It is not just absence of conflict. *Peace* has reference to health, well-being, security, an internal settled-ness, restfulness. It was a favorite biblical greeting found at the beginning or end of most of the New Testament epistles and the archangel's greeting to Mary. To this day it is still the traditional greeting used in the Arab world by Muslims and Christians. It is on this foundation—an internal restfulness, an inner peace, a calmness of heart—that Jesus gives them the task of communicating him to the world and taking this peace out to others. According to Jesus' own words, true peace comes from and with him. The essence of the gospel is peace. If anything about Christianity brings peace, it brings peace because of Christ, not because of Christianity.

Muslims often have many true reasons to refuse to look at Christianity, but they are fascinated with Jesus as he really was and is. We first and foremost need to see ourselves as individuals loyal to a Person we have found to be our peace and truth, and we are simply presenting him more than anything else. At the heart of our communication of our faith, especially in thinking about peace, must be the deepest and yet simplest conviction about the singular importance of presenting the Jesus of the Gospels. Christ fully earns the title, the Prince of Peace. Faith in Christ brings peace to the heart, and his teachings, when applied, will bring peace between individuals. And if he can bring peace to each heart, he can bring peace throughout the earth.

Preparing the Way

John the Baptist exemplifies an important aspect of being a peacemaker and a witness to Jesus. John saw himself as "preparing the way," and our primary responsibility is simply a role of preparation for the increased coming of the Lord. John prepared the way by "making straight paths for him." The challenge at that time was that the king's entourage couldn't turn on the roads easily when traveling. Roads needed to be as straight as possible. In other words, make Christ's coming as easy and as smooth as possible. This is the essence of the decision of the first Jerusalem council in Acts 15, in a nutshell in verse 19: to make the way easy for those coming to Christ.

So while we think of communication approaches and methodology as ways of making the road easier, first and foremost it has much more to do with us and with our lives. The messenger embodying the message of peace is more important than relying on the latest communication techniques, or using the study of psychology, or planning that, by using certain stories or images, people will respond more significantly. This is the significance of why Jesus says those powerful words, "My peace be with you," to the disciples twice before he sends them out with the words, "As the Father has sent me, I am sending you"

(John 20:21 NIV). Only in this sense can peace be demonstrated. St. Francis of Assisi understood this and when sending his brothers to Muslim lands is reported as saying, "Preach the gospel all the time, and if necessary use words." So often witnesses focus on getting the words right in verbal communication in order that others may change. But Jesus' commission to the disciples starts with the peacemaker fully experiencing peace. First Jesus breathes his life into them in order for them to change and live their experience of him out in the world.

There is another example of peace linked with the ministry of Jesus in the story of Simeon in the temple and the song he sang (Luke 2:25–35 NRSV). When the baby Jesus was put into his arms, he sang, "Master, now you are dismissing your servant in peace." What he saw provided a new sense of release, of peace. But what exactly did this aged saint see when he said, "For my eyes have seen your salvation"? The best word here is probably *revelation*, which illuminated his own experience and life as well as new vistas into God's character. What was revealed to him at that moment released him to a new understanding and experience and dimension of living at peace, of being at rest.

Simeon was one of the Hasidim conservatives, who were strict in their worship and who kept all the Jewish religious law. Their whole existence was reserved for and devoted to one thing: looking for the "consolation of Israel," a phrase used to signify the coming of the Messiah, the Savior of the Jewish people. His whole life had one purpose and focus, to help prepare the way. It had been revealed to Simeon, by the Holy Spirit, that he would not die before he had seen the Messiah. For the elderly Simeon time was running out. All of his life existed for the future possibilities, and he could have been consumed and driven by this intensity of purpose. This intensity of purpose can become a servitude or enslavement for those who have great vision. We first need to be released ourselves.

Living Now in the Eternal Moment

The Apostle Paul says, "Let the peace of God rule in your hearts" (Col 3:15 NRSV). He is also saying that it is necessary to have peace in the heart and life in order to be about properly serving God. Only when we find peace within ourselves can we be about bringing peace to others. This peace must be experienced now in the present, not a hope for the future, because the present moment is all that we have. We are cautioned with, "Come now you who say, 'Today or tomorrow we will go to such and such a town and spend a year there'" (Jas 4:13–17 NSRV). In other words, do not miss today's opportunity by living in your future plans.

When we learn to live in the present moment, and not in the future, we recognize that the result of our living is out of our hands and the future is left to God. We then recognize God coming to us in the person in front of us *now*, in the situation we are in right *now*, even if we planned something different. Living mindfully in the eternal moment of life now, as it is in its sacred ordinariness and accepting that God is in it, brings a release from worrying about finding and doing the strategic program to serve God.

We tend to have more grandiose plans for God's will than the little daily things that occupy us and that we view as keeping us from getting into the big plan. For example, in the first week after we purchased a newer car, the windshield wiper stopped working. We had appointments that we considered more important than fixing a small car part and kept postponing it. Finally my husband listened to my pleas to fix it and decided to go the next day. When he made the troublesome trip down to the spare parts quarters of our North African city, our mechanic exclaimed, "I have been waiting for you. Last night God told me that you would come today and answer my questions about Christ."

Simeon was guided by God to come into the temple at the right moment to see Jesus and sang, "Master, now you are dismissing your servant in peace, according to your word, for my eyes have seen." It seems that what he saw was a fresh and even wholly other and new perspective on God. What is amazing is that what Simeon says in his song contradicts all he lived, hoped, and prayed for in one way. He says God's salvation is "a light for revelation for the Gentiles." For as devout in Jewish religious law as Simeon was, it is amazing that he is so open to salvation coming to the Gentiles. He is given a new and fuller perspective on God and his purposes. And this new revelation of God's character brought him tremendous security and calm.

Knowing that God is about God's own purposes brings a cessation to the enslavement to living in the future and the driven-ness that accompanies it. Simeon says, "For I have seen your salvation." All throughout his Gospel, Luke closely connects the concept of peace with salvation and God's preference for those on the margins or judged to be outside God's grace. And this requires, as Simeon experienced, a bigger view of God. God works in unorthodox ways. God works paradoxically. At the heart of Christian ministry there must be a place for mystery.

We so long to neatly package God up with systems as to how God works or is not allowed to work. Often it appears that God reminds us that our strategy, theory, and approaches are just that, and God seems to purposely go around them to accomplish the divine purpose in ways that prove it is God's work not ours. We are reminded that Jesus said the Spirit blows where it pleases (John 3:8). The kingdom of God is bigger than our own experience of it, and we are encouraged toward a view of God that allows dialectical thinking, that does not exclude contraries but includes them. It keeps us in awe of the mystery instead of trying to gain control of it. Jesus told the disciples to first experience his peace and then take it out to the world in the same way he did.

Powerlessness and Vulnerability

A. W. Tozer said:

> Every age has its own characteristics. Right now we are in an age of religious complexity. The simplicity which is in Christ is rarely found among us. In its stead are programs, methods, organizations, and a world of nervous activities, which occupy time and attention … That servile imitation of the world which marks our promotional methods all testify that we, in this day, know God only imperfectly, and the peace of God scarcely at all.[10]

Perhaps in some ways the greatest temptation for Christians is to use a form of power as an apt instrument for proclaiming the Christian faith. However, we note that God sent Jesus as a baby. The messianic ideas which were in the minds of the Jews when Jesus came were of a Messiah of power who would overthrow their enemies. It is against these dreams that we have Jesus' coming as a little baby. Therefore Jesus' coming as a child is not an example of humility, but an example of coming with no influence, with no power. For it is via the small, or through powerlessness, that God chooses to communicate Godself more often than not in our world. This whole account demonstrates Jesus' choice of powerlessness as his *modus operandi*.

What marked the life of Jesus was in every situation the choice not to use power but to be vulnerable. He preaches his Sermon on the Mount, which in all ways contradicts the contemporary understanding of power. He sometimes refused to work miracles that people wanted as proof that he was the Messiah to gain a following. He poured scorn on all requests to give them a sign from heaven, even when it came from his disciples. He never performed miracles to gather crowds or showed his power to gain credibility. He only performed miracles as a sign of his love. He washed his followers' dusty feet, a chore reserved for the lowliest servant in first-century Palestine. When Peter tried to defend him with a sword, Jesus stopped him and said, "Do you think that I cannot appeal to my Father, and he will at once send me more than twelve legions of angels?" (Matt 26:53 NRSV). He was able to mobilize celestial forces, but did not choose to do so.

When confronted by violent enemies, Jesus chose nonviolent resistance along with doing good. He told Peter to put his sword away and healed the person Peter injured. Jesus sought out those of no account and power with whom no one spoke; he dined with the lowest members of society; he touched the untouchables; he had no throne, no crown, no bevy of servants, no armored guards. He said, "My kingdom is not of this world," and on the cross he refused to come down in response to their challenge (John 18:36 NIV; Matt 27:40–42).

---

10 A. W. Tozer, *The Pursuit of God* (Radford, VA: Wilder, 2008), 15.

The whole time the extraordinary choice was operative not to take the way of power as Messiah. He refused to take the way of power to get people to see who he was, to get them to follow him, in order to save them.

And the account of Simeon and the Christ child illustrates that God's way is going the path of weakness as opposed to power. The consideration that the all-powerful, omnipotent God, in coming among us decides not to use power is revolutionary. And this orientation of Jesus, this express choice not to use power, places us Christians in a very delicate situation. Because we are set in a society where the main orientation is power. One of the greatest ironies of Christian history is that its leaders constantly gave in to the temptation of power—political power, military power, economic power, moral power, and spiritual power. Even though they continued to speak in the name of Jesus, they forgot that Jesus did not cling to his divine power but emptied himself.

Sacrificial Love and Unorthodox Ways

Jesus declared he would save the world through sacrificial love and refused to meet violence with violence. It is a challenge to believe sacrificial love is more powerful than anything else to change the world. Since 9/11 our culture of fear has pushed many Christians into condoning retaliation to militant Islamic extremists. By their silence or their vote, they agreed that the way to deal with them is to wipe them out and humiliate them. We face a great challenge today to practice our faith. One example of God's paradoxical ways of working is that the best-known world leader who openly followed Christ's teaching and changed his nation in his days was a Hindu, Mahatma Ghandi. He also refused violent retaliation and gave his life for his message.

The first reference in the Gospel to Christ and suffering is in Simeon's revelation of the Messiah bringing salvation for all. *"A sword will pierce through your soul"*—a sword through Mary's heart and one through Christ's side. Not many will be martyrs, but most will feel the sword of Mary as they live with Christ wanting him to do his stuff in the world, often perplexed that it just doesn't happen easily and go to plan. But the paradox of salvation is that of suffering. In times of perplexity and *swords through us*, Christ is revealed as the Spirit of Jesus and, living in our darkness, touches others at their place of darkness. Simeon's release entails a revelation into seeing suffering. Yet it seems to be a contradiction to what he was living and looking for all his life, which was the comfort brought by the Messiah to his people.

We notice again the paradox of God's ways, the paradox of suffering. In his statement to Mary, Simeon is saying that the greatest event or circumstance of suffering in this world brought about the greatest miracle of peace that has ever taken place and keeps on taking place in your life and my life and in lives all over the world. A holy God dying a criminal's death on the cross is, of course, the ultimate example of God using irregular channels to communicate Godself. God seems to often work in reverse—the opposite of our carefully and prayerfully calculated ways. John the Baptist, in prison, sends his followers to ask Jesus, "Are you the one?" (Luke 7:19 NRSV). Things were not working the way he expected. In Luke 7:22, Christ's answer to John's disciples, "Go and tell John what you have seen and heard: the blind receive their sight, the lame walk, the lepers are cleansed, the deaf hear, the dead are raised, and the poor have good news brought to them," told John, I am working in *my* way. John the Baptist also lost his life preparing the way. One sees throughout Scripture that God communicates the divine self in ways totally other than what people expected. God's tremendous generosity shows God using every angle to communicate divine peace. The most common theme one finds is that God works in unorthodox ways.

There is a sense that all of this is impossible for us to truly grasp, understand, or embody. However, we are promised supernatural aid. When Christ gave them his peace, he breathed on them and said, "Receive the Holy Spirit" (John 20:22 NRSV). At the end of John the Baptist's call, we are told God was to "give knowledge of salvation to his people" (Luke 1:76,77 NRSV). And in Simeon's song he says, "My eyes have seen your salvation, which you have prepared in the presence of all peoples" (Luke 2:30–31 NRSV).

God's peace is made known to the world as we go about communicating God in the same way that Christ demonstrated for us. It is not about doing it perfectly, or powerfully, but prayerfully. It is about doing it, in whatever way we feel called while knowing it is God's work not ours. It is about living mindfully while trusting that God is working out divine purposes in history. It did not begin with us and never ends with us.

The story of Peter and Cornelius reminds us not to put God in any box and be especially wary if it looks very religious and pious (Acts 10). There are modern day numerous stories from all over the Muslim world of God speaking with and guiding Muslims. These stories from the biblical accounts and current life warn us not to make assumptions that people labeled as "unbelievers" are unable to know God and hear from God. This realization should give us peace. God allows us to be involved in the process of reconciliation but is not dependent on us. We remind ourselves that the story is bigger than individuals and personal peace. Beginning in the Genesis stories and throughout world history, there is a chain of witnesses who have witnessed to God and tried to be peacemakers in their generation. These stories remind us that it is not our cleverness, nor diligence, but our trust in the historical God who never changes and continues to intervene in the lives of men and women to bring peace to the world. God is saving history and has been and will continue to do so. Witness as peacemaking is ones life offered or laid down as an act of love and worship, trusting that the glory of God will be revealed as God reconciles all through Christ.

Conclusion

BY JOSEPH L. CUMMING

As a young man twenty-five years ago, when I began living and working in a Muslim country in North Africa, I looked around for role models of godly Christians who had lived long-term among Muslims and consistently conducted themselves in a Christlike manner toward their Muslim neighbors. At that time, I noticed something about the people who stood out for me as outstanding role models, of whom Dudley Woodberry was one. They all seemed to combine a certain loving and gentle quality with a deep trust in divine sovereignty. I concluded that either people like me who did *not* possess that kind of character and faith were not going to be effective in authentically following Jesus among Muslims, or else the experience of living and working daily with Muslim friends and neighbors would change us and sanctify us over time, so that eventually we would *take on* the loving, gentle character and trust in God's sovereignty which I saw in Dudley and other role models. Of course, I'm still working on sorting out whether I will have those beautiful qualities by the time I go to be with the Lord! But I feel that Dudley embodies in his person his own philosophy of ministry. This is a man whom it is impossible not to like. He is such a lovable human being, and so humble for such an accomplished man. This is evident in his hilarious, self-deprecating humor and the uproarious stories he frequently tells at his own expense. But beyond his humor, anyone who spends time with Dudley will note that his whole demeanor is humble and gracious, and he is always seeking others' well-being. After rubbing shoulders with Dudley, you quickly notice these characteristics, and you know that Muslims who interact with him swiftly perceive these same qualities.

What is the legacy of Dudley Woodberry? The pages of this book are only a humble offering to highlight what we believe to be the qualities and contributions that Dudley has made and continues to make. And the sections of the book were not chosen randomly: Dudley has both modeled and inspired others to emulate the kind of genuine hospitality toward both Muslims and Christians that encourages friendly conversations, and the kind of rigorous, excellent scholarship on Islam that illuminates and instructs us toward truth, and the kind of respect and love and humility that should be the hallmarks of Christian witness.

First, he has modeled and inspired others to emulate a lifestyle and attitude that encourages friendly conversations between Muslims and Christians. Quite simply, Dudley Woodberry helps Christians and Muslims love each other in ways that honor Jesus. Dudley has had cordial conversations with Muslims of all kinds of backgrounds—from princes in the Saudi royal family, to poor Afghan villagers, to cosmopolitan Muslim American businessmen. In these conversations, Dudley has been consistently respectful of his Muslim friends and their convictions while faithfully expressing his own Christian convictions. You can see the cordiality and respect in the way he conducts himself in every relationship, regardless of the faith background of the other person.

The beautiful hospitality shown by him and his wife, Roberta, and their three sons toward both Muslims and Christians in their various homes in Pakistan, Afghanistan, Lebanon, Saudi Arabia, and America is well-known by many. How many Muslims, Christians, and those of other faith backgrounds have experienced the Woodberry family's warm and caring hospitality and have been touched by this expression of love? The biblical virtue of hospitality, which is often forgotten in the West and about which I have learned so much from my Muslim neighbors and friends, is a virtue which I have also learned from observing and receiving the Woodberrys' exceptional hospitality. The authors of the chapters in Section 1 of this book are just a small sampling of people who have learned from Dudley's example and are influencing Christians to engage in a different kind of conversation with their Muslim neighbors, namely one marked by cordiality and respect.

Dudley Woodberry has also modeled and inspired others to emulate excellent Christian scholarship on Islam. Throughout the years, too many Christian writers on Islam have been sloppy in their research, jumping quickly to spurious conclusions, and painting a picture of Islam that Muslims feel is an inaccurate and distorted caricature of what they actually believe and live. In contrast, Dudley has modeled what a faithful Christian can do in undertaking serious scholarship on Islam with integrity—beginning with his doctoral research on medieval Islamic law and on the twentieth-century theology of Hasan al-Banna, and continuing with his analysis of contemporary South- and Central-Asian Sufi piety. Dudley's example inspires us to avoid jumping to oversimplified conclusions, but instead challenges us to engage in rigorous study of relevant primary sources in order to understand in a nuanced way Muslim beliefs and practices and Islamic theology, Islamic philosophy, and Islamic law. Not only does Dudley provide an excellent model for credible research on Islamic primary texts that shed light on important beliefs and practices, but he has promoted the application of social sciences like cultural anthropology and sociology to understanding with greater integrity the dynamics of Muslim-Christian relations, helping us communicate more effectively on matters of faith. Dudley Woodberry's academic legacy is evident through his own writings, through his deanship at the Fuller School of Intercultural Studies, and through his influence on countless other Christian scholars of Islam, such as the authors represented in Section 2 of this volume.

Finally, Dudley Woodberry has modeled and inspired others to emulate the kind of Christian witness that is irenic, respectful, humble, and loving while at the same time deeply faithful to the historic Christian faith. Dudley's convictions as an evangelical believer in Jesus Christ are evident to all who meet him, not just by the fact that he talks about Jesus, but by the manner in which he goes about talking about Jesus. Every Muslim who has known Dudley would say that Dudley Woodberry is a gracious, loving, and respectful person, and that Dudley Woodberry is a man of deep faith in Jesus Christ. And every Christian who has known Dudley would say that Dudley influenced us in that direction.

Muslims frequently try to "evangelize" Christians. I have been the "evangelized" as often as the "evangelist." And I have rarely felt violated by Muslim friends' efforts to evangelize me; in fact, I have understood that often they were honoring me as a person, because they cared enough about me to be concerned that I understand something they consider to have eternal consequence. Dudley likewise taught me about honoring people as we demonstrate and bear witness to our faith in the Lord Jesus. Dudley has always stood unambiguously for faithful witness that does not engage in coercion, inducement, exploitation, disrespect, or demeaning of the other. Every Muslim who meets Dudley—indeed every human being who meets Dudley—quickly knows what he believes and that he stands firmly in the mainstream of the historic Christian faith, but finds this to be refreshing and winsome even if they disagree with those convictions, because of the demonstrable respect shown in the manner in which Dudley interacts with others and expresses his own convictions. The various authors of this volume's third section have followed Dudley's example in encouraging Christians toward respectful witness.

Thus we hope that the various chapters in this book have reflected what we believe to be the theme of Dudley Woodberry's life: cordial, respectful witness to Jesus Christ. In each of the areas covered, from encouraging friendly conversations, to dedicating ourselves to excellent scholarship, to engaging in respectful Christian witness, he has modeled these qualities and inspired others to emulate him.

This is the legacy of Dudley Woodberry.

Complete Works of J. Dudley Woodberry

COMPILED BY JARED HOLTON

This bibliography includes all published books, articles, forewords, electronic sources, reviews, and lectures. The following list does not include visual media publications or the numerous theses and dissertations produced under the guidance of J. Dudley Woodberry.

1953 "South of the Equator and Back." *Stony Brook Bulletin* 21, no. 7: 3–4.

1954 "Thumbing through Latin America: Dudley Woodberry tells the fascinating story of his trip through eight missionary countries." *His Magazine of Campus Christian Living* 14, no. 9 (June): 1–4, 19–21.

1955 "A Faculty Profile—James W. Morley." *The Idol: A Quarterly Magazine of Union College* 31, no. 3: 19, 21.

1958 "Lebanon Today: A Baffling Picture." *Faith at Work* (April): 22–24, 62.

1960 "Adapting Missions to Our Day." *Bulletin of Fuller Theological Seminary* (Summer): 4, 9, 12.

1963 "Toward the Understanding of the Qur'anic Concept of Sin: A Preliminary Study in Semantics." M.A. unpublished thesis, American University of Beirut, Lebanon.

1967 Review: *City of Wrong: A Friday in Jerusalem*, by M. Kamel Hussein. Translated from the Arabic with an Introduction by Kenneth Cragg. New York: Seabury Press, 1966. In *Evangelical Missions Quarterly* 3, no. 4 (Summer): 251–252.

1968a "Hasan al-Banna's *Articles of Belief*." Ph.D. unpublished dissertation, Harvard University.

1968b "Summary of Doctoral Dissertation: Hasan Al-Banna's *Articles of Belief*." *Harvard Theological Review* 61: 652.

1970a "Christmas in the Quran." *Al-Mushir* 12, no. 11/12 (November–December): 20–22.

1970b "Three Days of Sacrifice: Eid al-Azha, Ashura, and Good Friday." *Al-Mushir* 12, no. 3/4 (March-April): 5–7.

1971 "Sin in the Quran and the Bible." *Al-Mushir* 13, no. 3/4 (March–April): 1–4.

1972a “Divine Love in the Quran and the Bible.” *Al-Mushir* 14, no. 5/6 (May–June): 130–131.

1972b *Al-Mushir*. Editor. Rawalpindi, Pakistan: The Christian Study Centre. 1972–1973.

1972c “Quran awr Baibal may gunah ka tasawwur” (“The Concept of Sin in the Qur’an and the Bible”). *Al-Mushir* 14, no. 5/6 (May–June): 139–45.

1979 “What Jesus Would Say to A Muslim.” *Trinity World Forum* 5 (Fall): 1–4; reprinted in *Muslim World Pulse* 9, no. 1 (April, 1980): 2–5; reprinted in North Africa Mission’s *Church Growth Bulletin* and *Manual for Candidate School*, n.d.

1981a “The Assassination of President Sadat.” *Reflector* (October 16): 1, 6.

1981b “Muslim and Christian Perspectives on Iran.” *The Banner* 116, no. 10 (March 9): 8–9.

1981c Review: *Islam: A Survey of the Muslim Faith*, C. George Fry and James R. King. Grand Rapids, MI: Baker Book House, 1980. In *Banner* 116, no. 44 (November 16): 18.

1981d Review: *Sharing Your Faith with a Muslim*, by Abdiyah Akbar Abdul-Haqq. Minneapolis: Bethany Fellowship Inc., 1980. In *Banner* 116, no. 49 (December 21): 27.

1981e “Three Perspectives on Palestine.” *The Church Herald* (May 15): 14–15, 29; Braille trans., in *John Milton Magazine*, n.d.

1981f “Understanding Muslims.” *RBC Newsletter*. Reformed Bible College 17, no. 1 (Winter): 10–11.

1982a “Our Lives a Thank Offering.” *Reflector* (Fall): 4, 7.

1982b Review: *New Paths in Muslim Evangelism: Evangelical Approaches to Contextualization*, by Phil Parshall. Grand Rapids, MI: Baker Book House, 1980. In *Banner* 117, no. 1 (January 4): 20.

1983a “Consultant Finds Communication Techniques Crucial.” Interview. *Saudi Introspect* 7, no. 7 (July): 4–5.

1983b “The Great Cop Out.” *Insight* 64, no. 6 (July–August): 18–19.

1983c “My Son, My Son.” *Insight* 64, no. 5 (May–June): 12–13.

1983d Review: *New Paths in Muslim Evangelism: Evangelical Approaches to Contextualization*, by Phil Parshall. Grand Rapids, MI: Baker Book House, 1980; *Blessing in Mosque and Mission*, by Larry G. Lenning. Pasadena, CA: William Carey Library, 1980. In *International Bulletin of Missionary Research* 7, no. 1 (January): 42–43.

1983e “Successful Negotiation in Saudi Culture.” *Saudi Introspect* 7, no. 10 (October): 3–4.

1984a “Iran vs. Iraq: The Bloody War Between Islamic Brothers.” *Eternity* 35, no. 11 (November): 31–33, 35–38.

1984b "New Means of Reaching the Unreached." In *Reaching the Unreached*. Edited by Harvie M. Conn, 120–34. Phillipsburg, NJ: Presbyterian and Reformed Publishing Co.

1984c "Saudi Justice Different but Swift and Fair." *Saudi Introspect* (February).

1984d "16 Tips That Make a Difference." *Saudi Introspect* 8, no. 8 (August): 5–7.

1985a "Current Trends in Islam." With Denis J. Green. Unpublished syllabus and reader. MR556: Fuller Theological Seminary, Pasadena, CA; revised annually (1985–2006); republished in "The World of Islam: Resources for Understanding." Edited by J. Dudley Woodberry. CD-ROM. Global Mapping International (2000), and the second edition, Global Mapping International (2006).

1985b "Folk Islam." With Denis J. Green. Unpublished syllabus and reader. MR555: Fuller Theological Seminary, Pasadena, CA; republished in "The World of Islam: Resources for Understanding." Edited by J. Dudley Woodberry. CD-ROM. Global Mapping International (2000), and the second edition, Global Mapping International (2006); revised annually (1985–2009); revised with J. Travis as "Islamic Popular Piety" (2010–present).

1985c "Introduction to Islam." With Denis J. Green. Unpublished syllabus and reader. MR550: Fuller Theological Seminary, Pasadena, CA; revised annually (1985–1999); revised and enlarged for Individualized Distance Learning Course. Edited by Elizabeth Glanville and Sharon Carlson. Pasadena, CA: Fuller Theological Seminary (2000); republished in "The World of Islam: Resources for Understanding." Edited by J. Dudley Woodberry. CD-ROM. Global Mapping International (2000), and the second edition, Global Mapping International (2006).

1985d "The Muslim Neighbors We Cannot Ignore." *Voices of Trinity Evangelical Divinity School* 11, no. 4: 3–6.

1986a "The Bombing of Libya and Christian Witness." *Sharing God's Love with Muslims: The Zwemer Institute Newsletter* (Summer): 3.

1986b "Folk Islam Requires New Understanding and Approaches: An Interview with Dr. J. Dudley Woodberry." Edited by Gail C. Bennett. *Pulse* 21, no. 6 (March 21): 2–4.

1986c "Islam and Its Relationship with Christianity in the United States." *New Age Dawning* 2, no. 1 (Spring): 11–12.

1986d "Militant Islam: Root and Response." *Sharing God's Love with Muslims: The Zwemer Institute Newsletter* (Fall): 6.

1987a "Pulse Commentary: We Need Deeper Understanding of Fundamentalist Islam." *Pulse* 22, no. 14 (July 24): 5.

1987b "Studies of Four Countries: Nigeria, Indonesia, Egypt, The United States of America." With Donald G. Dawe, et al. In *Christians and Muslims Together: An Exploration by Presbyterians*. Edited by Byron L. Haines and Frank L. Cooley, 66–99. Philadelphia: The Geneva Press.

1988a "The Church in Egypt." With J. K. Hoffmeier, T. C. Muck, and R. R. Clapp. *Christianity Today* 32, no. 9 (June 17): 25–39.

1988b "The Cross within the Crescent." *Christianity Today* 32, no. 9 (June 17): 32–33.

1988c "Introduction: Islam and Stones." *Theology News and Notes* 35, no. 4 (December): 3–5, 26.

1989a "A House Divided: The Philippines." *Sharing God's Love with Muslims: The Zwemer Institute Newsletter* (Summer): 1, 5.

1989b "Contextualizing Among Muslims: Reusing Common Pillars." In *The Word Among Us*. Edited by Dean Gilliland, 282–312. Dallas, TX: Word Books; reprinted for the Summer Institute of Linguistics in *Interconnect* 6 (January, 1992): 9–42; revised and reprinted in *International Journal of Frontier Missions* 13, no. 4 (October–December, 1996): 171–186; reprinted in *The Last Great Frontier: Essays on Muslim Evangelism*. Edited by Phil Parshall, 127–153. Quezon City, Philippines: Open Doors with Brother Andrew (2000); reprinted in *Intensive Study of Integrated Global History and Theology (INSIGHT) Module 3 Reader*, 7th edition. Pasadena, CA: U.S. Center for World Mission (2007).

1989c "Different Diagnoses of the Human Condition." In *Muslims and Christians on the Emmaus Road.* Edited by J. D. Woodberry, 163–176. Monrovia, CA: MARC; republished in "The World of Islam: Resources for Understanding." Edited by J. Dudley Woodberry. CD-ROM. Global Mapping International (2000), and the second edition, Global Mapping International (2006); Korean trans., n.d.

1989d "Influences II." *Theology News and Notes* 36, no. 4 (December): 6.

1989e "The March of Islam Across the Centuries: Historical Development of Islam." In *Target Earth.* Edited by Frank Kaleb Jansen, 124–125. Pasadena, CA: Global Mapping Inc.

1989f "The Muslim World." In *Target Earth.* Edited by Frank Kaleb Jansen, 126–127. Pasadena, CA: Global Mapping Inc.

1989g *Muslims and Christians on the Emmaus Road.* Editor. Monrovia, CA: MARC; republished in "The World of Islam: Resources for Understanding." Edited by J. Dudley Woodberry. CD-ROM. Global Mapping International (2000), and the second edition, Global Mapping International (2006); reprinted by World Vision Resources (2006).

1989h Review: *African Religion Meets Islam: Religious Change in Northern Nigeria*, by Dean Gilliland. Lanham, NY: University Press of America, 1986. In *Missions Tomorrow* 2, no. 1 (Spring/Summer): 53–54.

1989i Review: *Islam in Revolution: Fundamentalism in the Arab World*, by R. Hrair Dekmejian. Syracuse, NY: Syracuse University Press, 1985. In *Missions Tomorrow* 2, no. 1 (Spring/Summer): 52.

1989j *Where Muslims and Christians Meet: Area Studies*. Editor. Pasadena, CA: Zwemer Institute; reprinted in *Intensive Study of Integrated Global History and Theology*

(INSIGHT) Module 3 Reader, 7th edition. Pasadena, CA: United States Center for World Mission (2007).

1990a "Faith and Iman: The Human Response." In *My Neighbour is Muslim: A Handbook for Reformed Churches*, 69–79. Geneva: John Knox International Reformed Center; French translation by Claude Molla, in *Quand nos voisins sont musulmans* (*When Our Neighbors are Muslims*). Edited by Jean-Claude Basset, 93–105. Lausanne: Éditions du Soc, 1993; republished in "The World of Islam: Resources for Understanding." Edited by J. Dudley Woodberry. CD-ROM. Global Mapping International (2000), and the second edition, Global Mapping International (2006).

1990b "Reaching Muslims." In *Proclaiming Christ Until He Comes.* Edited by J. D. Douglas, 418–420. Minneapolis, MN: World Wide Publications.

1990c "The Relevance of Power Ministries for Folk Muslims." In *Wrestling with Dark Angels: Toward a Deeper Understanding of the Supernatural Forces in Spiritual Warfare.* Edited by Peter Wagner and F. Douglas Pennoyer, 313–331. Ventura, CA: Regal Press; Korean trans., n.d.

1990d Review: *Frontiers in Muslim-Christian Encounter*, by Michael Nazir-Ali. Oxford: Regnum Books, 1987. In *International Bulletin of Missionary Research* 14, no. 2 (April): 91.

1991a "After the Gulf War: Islam and the Church." *Impact* 48, no. 2 (May): 4.

1991b "Can Muslims Be Evangelized?" *Equipping the Saints* 5, no. 3 (Summer): 21–25.

1991c "Has the Gulf War Been a 'Just War'?" *Bulletin of Fuller Theological Seminary* (Winter): 5.

1991d "Muslims, Mission to." In *The New Twentieth Century Encyclopedia of Religious Knowledge*. Edited by J. D. Douglas, 579–581. 2nd edition. Grand Rapids: Baker Book House.

1991e "Our Turn in Babylon." *Christianity Today* 34, no. 3 (March 11): 24.

1991f "Searching for Footprints of Mission Life in China." *Sketches* 4 (Fall): 3.

1992a "A Case for Religious Freedom From the Earliest Muslim Sources." In *Rights of Muslims*. Edited by David Bentley, 28–32. Pasadena, CA: Zwemer Institute of Muslim Studies; reprinted in *Interconnect* 7 (June): 35–41 (1992/3); reprinted in *Seedbed* 8, no. 1 (1993): 1–7; reprinted in *Intensive Study of Integrated Global History and Theology (INSIGHT) Module 3 Reader*, 7th edition. Pasadena, CA: United States Center for World Mission (2007).

1992b "The Church in Iraq Today." *The Banner* 127, no. 2 (January 20): 4–6.

1992c "Conversion in Islam." In *Handbook of Religious Conversion*. Edited by H. Newton Malony and Samuel Southard, 22–40. Birmingham, AL: Religious Education Press.

1992d "How Muslims Are and Can Be Evangelized." *Missionary Monthly* 99-A (November), 12–15.

1992e "Introduction: Muslim-Christian Encounter." *Theology News and Notes* 38, no. 3 (March): 2–3.

1992f "The Middle East: Crescent, Cross, and Plowshare." *Theology News and Notes* 38, no. 3 (March): 4–5, 14–19.

1992g "Pasadena Arab Fellowship Installs Egyptian Pastor from Iraq." *Keeping in Touch*. Presbytery of San Gabriel (September–October): 3.

1992h "Reaching Muslims from Beijing to Los Angeles." *Chinese in North America*. Chinese Coordination Centre for World Evangelism (September–October): 2–5.

1992i Review: *The Gospel of Barnabas: Its True Value*, by William Campbell. Rawalpindi, Punjab: Christian Study Centre, 1989. In *Evangelical Missions Quarterly* 28, no. 1 (January): 98–99.

1992j Review: *The Salmon Rushdie Controversy in Interreligious Perspective*, edited by Dan Cohn-Sherbok. Lewiston, NY: The Edwin Mellen Press, 1990. In *The Christian Librarian* 35, no. 4 (August): 120–121.

1992k Review: *Judaism, Christianity, and Islam: The Classical Texts and Their Interpretation*. 3 vols. Edited by F. E. Peters. Princeton, NJ: Princeton University Press, 1990. In *Journal of Church and State* 34, no. 1 (Winter): 159–160.

1992l "Selected Annotated Bibliography on Missiology: Islamic Studies." *Missiology* 20, no. 3 (July): 419–422.

1992m "South Asia: Vegetables, Fish, and Messianic Mosques." With Shah Ali. *Theology News and Notes* 38, no. 3 (March): 12–13; Korean trans., 1999; reprinted in *Perspectives on the World Christian Movement*. Edited by Ralph D. Winter and Steven C. Hawthorne, 141–144. 3rd ed. Pasadena, CA: William Carey Library (1999); Russian trans. (Lewis World Mission Manuals), 2001; reprinted in *Encountering the World of Islam*. Edited by Keith Swartley, 423–426. Waynesboro, GA: Authentic (2005); French, Telegu, Hindi, Gujarati, and Tamil trans., n.d.

1993a "The Art of Remembering and the Remembering of Art." *Forwarding the Missionary Task* 15, no.3 (Summer): 1.

1993b "Foreword." In *Japan Diary of Cross-Cultural Mission*. By J. Lawrence Driskill, xi. Pasadena, CA: Hope Publishing House.

1993c "If Christ Met a Muslim: Biblical Foundations for Islamic Approaches." With Borge Schantz. *Advent-Muslim Review* 1, no.1 (Spring): 14–15.

1993d "Lessons from Christian-Muslim Dialogue for Jewish-Muslim Dialogue." In *Shalom/Salaam: A Resource for Jewish-Muslim Dialogue*. Edited by Gary M. Bretton-Granatoor and Andrea L. Weiss, 15–20. New York: Union of Hebrew Congregations Press.

1993e "New Curriculum at SWM." With Edgar Elliston. *Forwarding the Missionary Task* 15, no. 2 (Spring): 1, 4.

1993f "What's Behind the Handshake? Religious Dimensions of the Peace Accord." *The Semi* (September 20–25): 1, 3.

1994a "Like Restless Thoroughbreds." *Theology News and Notes* 41, no.1 (March): 22–26.

1994b "The Middle East Puzzle: Introduction." *Theology News and Notes* 41, no. 4 (December): 2–3.

1994c "Religious Dimensions of Islam." *Theology News and Notes* 41, no. 4 (December): 12, 23.

1994d "Where Three is not a Crowd: Urban Studies at Fuller." *Forwarding the Missionary Task* 16, no.1 (Winter): 3.

1995a "Creativity in Theological Education." *The Semi* (February 13–17): 1, 5.

1995b *Missiological Education for the 21st Century: The Book, the Circle, and the Sandals: Essays in Honor of Paul E. Pierson*. Edited by J. D. Woodberry, C. E. Van Engen, and E. Elliston. Maryknoll, NY: Orbis; reprinted by Wipf & Stock Publishers (2005).

1995c "Past Symbols of Interacting Theory, Reflection, and Experience." In *Missiological Education for the 21st Century*. Edited by J. D. Woodberry, C. E. Van Engen, and E. J. Elliston, 3–8. Maryknoll, NY: Orbis.

1995d "Reaching Muslims." *World Mission* (March): 4–5.

1995e "Till the Final Book Is Opened in the Final Circle." In *Missiological Education for the 21st Century.* Edited by J. D. Woodberry, C. E. Van Engen, and E. J. Elliston, 271–276. Maryknoll, NY: Orbis.

1995f "The View from a Refurbished Chair." In *Missiological Education for the 21st Century.* Edited by J. D. Woodberry, C. E. Van Engen, and E. J. Elliston, 189–197. Maryknoll, NY: Orbis; first given as the inaugural address for installation as Dean of the School of World Mission at Fuller Theological Seminary, November 2, 1992.

1995g "Western Perceptions of Islam." *World Evangelization* 69. Lausanne Committee for World Evangelization: 18–19.

1996a "The Church in West and Central Asia." In *Church in Asia Today: Challenges and Opportunities.* Edited by Saphir Athyal, 479–509. Singapore: The Asia Lausanne Committee for World Evangelization.

1996b "Contextualization among Muslims." Rev. ed. *International Journal of Frontier Mission* 13, no. 4: 171–186; Korean trans., n.d.

1996c "Foreword." In *Worldwide Mission Stories for Young People*. By J. Lawrence Driskill, ix. Pasadena, CA: Hope Publishing House.

1996d "The Muslim Understanding of Jesus." *Word & World: Theology for Christian Ministry* 16, no.2 (Spring): 173–178; republished in "The World of Islam: Resources for Understanding." Edited by J. Dudley Woodberry. CD-ROM. Global Mapping International (2000), and the second edition, Global Mapping International (2006).

1996e "Scholar Sees 'Hand of God' Nudge Muslims to Christ." Interview by Stan Guthrie in *World Pulse* 31, no. 8 (April 19): 1–2.

1996f "When Failure is Our Teacher: Lessons from Mission to Muslims." *Great Commission Quarterly* (August): 8–11; reprinted in *International Journal of Frontier Missions* 13, no. 3: 121–124; reprinted in the *Intensive Study of Integrated Global History and Theology (INSIGHT) Module 3 Reader*, 7th edition. Pasadena, CA: U.S. Center for World Mission (2007); Korean trans., n.d.

1997a *Dimensions of Witness Among Muslims* [in English and Korean]. Seoul: Chongshin University; republished in "The World of Islam: Resources for Understanding." Edited by J. Dudley Woodberry. CD-ROM. Global Mapping International (2000), and the second edition, Global Mapping International (2006).

1997b "How a Religious Muslim Lives." In *Through Muslim Eyes: Understanding How Muslims Think and Feel*. Edited by R. S. Peck, 43–54. Springfield, MO: Center for Ministry to Muslims.

1998a "Foreword." In *Islamic Ideology and Fundamentalism in Pakistan: Climate for Conversion to Christianity?* By Warren F. Larson, xv–xvi. Lanham, MD: University Press of America.

1998b "History in the Making and Writing at Fuller." *The Semi* (May 4–8): 3.

1998c "Muslim Cities." Guest Editorial. *Urban Mission* 15, no. 3 (March): 3–7.

1998d *Reaching the Resistant: Barriers and Bridges for Mission*. Editor. Evangelical Missiological Society Series, No.6. Pasadena, CA: William Carey Library.

1998e "The School of World Mission: A New School for a New Movement." *Fuller's First Fifty*, no. 3 (Spring): 1–2.

1999a "My Last View From the Bridge." *Fuller Focus* 7, no. 2 (Summer): 8–10.

1999b Review: *The Call to Retrieval: Kenneth Cragg's Christian Vocation to Islam*, by Christopher Lamb. London: Grey Seal, 1997. In *International Bulletin of Missionary Research* 23, no. 2 (April): 84–85.

1999c "Toward the 21st Century: Educating People for God's Mission." In *Mission at the Dawn of the 21st Century*. Edited by Paul Varo Martinson, 315–322. Minneapolis, MN: Kirk House Publishers.

1999d "The View from a Fraying Chair: Perspectives on World Trends and the School of World Mission's Future." *Forwarding the Missionary Task* 21, no.2 (Spring): 1–5.

2000a "Annotated Bibliography." In "The World of Islam: Resources for Understanding." Edited by J. Dudley Woodberry. CD-ROM. Global Mapping International; second ed., 2006.

2000b "Islam, Muslim." In *Evangelical Dictionary of World Missions*. Edited by A. S. Moreau, H. Netland, and C. E. Van Engen, 504–506. Grand Rapids, MI: Baker Books.

2000c "Missiological Issues in the Encounter with Emerging Islam." *Missiology* 28, no. 1: 19–34; Korean trans., in *Mission Journal* 30 (Summer): 76–93; republished in "The World of Islam: Resources for Understanding." Second edition. Edited by J. Dudley Woodberry. CD-ROM. Global Mapping International (2006).

2000d Review: *Muslim-Christian Relations: Past, Present and Future*, by Ovey N. Mohammed, SJ. Maryknoll, NY: Orbis Books, 1999. In *Missiology* 28, no. 4 (October): 510–511.

2000e Review: *Understanding Folk Religion: A Christian Response to Popular Beliefs and Practices*, by Paul G. Hiebert, R. Daniel Shaw, and Tite Tiénou. Grand Rapids, MI: Baker Book House, 1999. In *Evangelical Missions Quarterly* 36, no. 4 (October): 522.

2000f "Why go to all the trouble of creating a CD-ROM on the World of Islam?" *GMI World* (Summer/Fall): 1.

2000g "The World of Islam: Resources for Understanding." Editor. CD-ROM. Global Mapping International; revised and enlarged second edition, Global Mapping International (2006).

2001a "Is Islam Peaceful or Militant?" *Canadian Christianity* (Winter).

2001b "Muslims Tell: Why I Chose Jesus." With Russell G. Shubin. *Mission Frontiers* 23, no. 1 (March): 28–33; republished in *Encountering the World of Islam* [Online]. Edited by Keith Swartley. Available at http://encounteringislam.org.

2001c Review: *Peaceable Witness among Muslims*, by Gordon D. Nickel. Scottsdale, PA: Herald Press, 1999. In *Evangelical Missions Quarterly* 37, no. 1 (January): 102–103.

2002a "Back at the Taliban Recruiting Center on Sept. 11, 2002." *The Semi* (September 11): 3.

2002b "The Fullness of Time for the Muslim World: 9/11 as its Herald." In *Islam and Grantmaking in the Middle East*, 2–15. Naples, FL: The Gathering.

2002c "Islam and Christian Mission After 9/11." *Theology News and Notes* 49, no. 2 (Fall): 6–9.

2002d "Justice and Peace: A Conversation with J. Dudley Woodberry." *Christian History* 21, no. 2, Issue 74: 43–45; republished as "Christians & Muslims: Christian History Interview with J. Dudley Woodberry." *Christian History* [Online]. Posted on April 1, 2002. Available at http://www.christianitytoday.com/ch/2002/issue74/12.43.html.

2002e "Muslim Missions after September 11." *Evangelical Missions Quarterly* 38, no. 1: 66–75; reprinted in *Envisioning Effective Ministry: Evangelism in a Muslim Context*. Edited by Laurie Fortunak Nichols and Gary R. Corwin, 40–48. Wheaton, IL: EMIS (2010).

2002f "My Pilgrimage in Mission." *International Bulletin of Missionary Research* 26, no. 1: 24–28.

2002g "The Palestinian-Israeli Question: Reflections of a Guest of the Participants." *The Semi* (May 20–24): 4–5.

2002h "Post-September 11 Muslim Ministry—Reflections and Concerns" [parallel Korean trans.]. *First Evangelical Church Association Bulletin* 14 (June): 18–21.

2002i "Reflections on Islamist Terrorism." *Fuller Focus* 10, no. 1 (Spring): 4–6.

2002j Review: *Christians and Muslims: The Dialogue Activities of the World Council of Churches and Their Theological Foundation*, by Jutta Sperber. Berlin and New

York: Walter de Gruyter, 2000. In *International Bulletin of Missionary Research* 26, no. 1 (January): 36.

2002k "Terrorism, Islam, and Mission: Reflections of a Guest in Muslim Lands." *International Bulletin of Missionary Research* 26, no. 1 (January): 2–7; reprinted in *Islam and Christianity: Contemporary Mission Insights*. Edited by Jonathan J. Bonk, 29–33. New Haven, CT: Overseas Ministries Study Center (2004).

2002l "The War on Terrorism." *Stimulus* 10, no. 1 (February): 38–41.

2003a "Biblical Faith and Islam." In *Biblical Faith and Other Religions: An Evangelical Assessment*. Edited by David Baker, 148–161. Grand Rapids, MI: Kregel Publications.

2003b "Evangelicals, Stereotypes, and Diversities." *Mission Frontiers* 25, no. 5 (September-October): 10–11; *Mission Frontiers* [Online]. Posted on October 1, 2003. Available at http://www.missionfrontiers.org/issue/article/evangelicals-stereotypes-and-diversities.

2003c "Foreword." In *Christianity and Islam*. By Chae Ok Chun, 10–11. Seoul, South Korea: Ewha Women's University Press.

2003d "Al-na'ama wa al-rahma muqābil al-šarī'a" [Grace and Mercy Against Law]. In *Qirā'a Sūfia li-Injīl Yuhannā* [A Sufi Reading on the Gospel of John]. Pp. 87–89. Beirut: Dār al-Jīl.

2003e "Muslim Month of Fasting Begins." *The Semi* (October 27–31): 3.

2003f Review: *Islam, Christianity and the West: A Troubled History*, by Rollin Armour, Sr. Maryknoll, NY: Orbis Books, 2002. In *Evangelical Missions Quarterly* 39, no. 3 (July): 382–383.

2004a "The Christian Response to Islam." In *Christian Witness in Pluralistic Contexts in the 21st Century*. Edited by Enoch Wan, 31–47. Evangelical Missiological Society Series, no. 11. Pasadena, CA: William Carey Library.

2004b "Do Christians and Muslims Worship the Same God?" *Christian Century* (May 18): 36–37.

2004c "Lessons from an Afghan Carpet." In *Fuller Voices: Then and Now*. Edited by Russell P. Spittler, 165–170. Pasadena, CA: Fuller Seminary Press.

2004d Review: *A Faithful Presence: Essays for Kenneth Cragg*, edited by David Thomas with Clare Amos. London: Melisende, 2003. In *International Bulletin of Missionary Research* 28, no. 4 (October): 180–181.

2004e Review: *Understanding Other Religious Worlds: A Guide for Interreligious Education*, by Judith A. Berling. Marknoll, NY: Orbis Books, 2004. In *Missiology* 32, no. 4 (October): 514.

2005a "A Global Perspective on Muslims Coming to Faith in Christ." In *From the Straight Path to the Narrow Way: Journeys of Faith*. Edited by David H. Greenlee with associate editors J. D. Woodberry, et al., 11–22. Waynesboro, GA: Authentic.

2005b "A Global Perspective on the Current Status of Christian-Muslim Relations." In *Anabaptists Meeting Muslims: A Calling for Presence in the Way of Christ*. Edited by J. R. Kraybill, D. W. Shenk, and L. Stutzman, 63–75. Scottdale, PA: Herald Press.

2005c "Counsel to the Anabaptist Community." In *Anabaptists Meeting Muslims: A Calling for Presence in the Way of Christ*. Edited by J. R. Kraybill, D. W. Shenk, and L. Stutzman, 467–68. Scottdale, PA: Herald Press.

2005d "The Encounter of Christ and the Crescent Today: Receptivity as Well as Resistance." *The Covenant Quarterly* 63, no. 3 (August): 12–29.

2005e "Forms of Witness: Here is how I share Christ." *Encountering the World of Islam* [Online]. Edited by Keith Swartley. Available at http://encounteringislam.org.

2005f "Foreword." In *Encountering the World of Islam*. Edited by Keith Swartley, xxi-xxii. Waynesboro, GA: Authentic.

2005g "Foreword." In *Unveiling God: Contextualizing Christology for Islamic Culture*. By Martin D. Parsons, xix–xx. Pasadena, CA: William Carey Library.

2005h *From the Straight Path to the Narrow Way: Journeys of Faith*. Edited by David H. Greenlee with associate editors J. Dudley Woodberry, et al. Waynesboro, GA: Authentic.

2005i "The Kingdom of God in Islam and in the Gospel." In *Anabaptists Meeting Muslims: A Calling for Presence in the Way of Christ*. Edited by J. R. Kraybill, D. W. Shenk, and L. Stutzman, 48–58. Scottdale, PA: Herald Press.

2005j *Muslim and Christian Reflections on Peace: Divine and Human Dimensions*. Edited by J. D. Woodberry, O. Zümrüt, and M. Köylü. Lanham, VA: University Press of America; Turkish ed., *Dünya Barişina bir Katki Olarak: Dinler Arasi Diyalog*. Istanbul: Din ve Bilim Kitaplari (2005).

2005k "Power Ministry in Folk Islam." In *Encountering the World of Islam*. Edited by Keith Swartley, 201–208. Waynesboro, GA: Authentic.

2005l "Preface." In *Muslim and Christian Reflections on Peace: Divine and Human Dimensions*. Edited by J. D. Woodberry, O. Zümrüt, and M. Köylü, v–ix. Lanham, VA: University Press of America.

2005m Review: *Occidentalism: The West in the Eyes of Its Enemies*, by Ian Buruma and Avishai Margalit. New York: The Penguin Press, 2004. In *International Bulletin of Missionary Research* 29, no. 2 (April): 109.

2005n Review: *The West and the Rest: Globalization and the Terrorist Threat*, by Roger Scruton. Wilmington, DE: Intercollegiate Studies Institute, 2002. In *International Bulletin of Missionary Research* 29, no. 1 (January): 42–43.

2005o Review: *Why the Rest Hates the West: Understanding the Roots of Global Rage*, by Meic Pearse. Downer's Grove, IL: InterVarsity Press, 2004. In *Christianity Today* 49, no. 3 (March): 83–84; republished as "Islam's Culture War." *Christianity Today* [Online]. Posted on March 8, 2005. Available at http://www.christianitytoday.com/ct/2005/march/28.83.html.

2005p "Toward Common Ground in Understanding the Human Condition." In *Muslim and Christian Reflections on Peace: Divine and Human Dimensions*. Edited by J. D. Woodberry, O. Zümrüt, and M. Köylü, 23–31. Lanham, VA: University Press of America.

2006a "Introduction: Resources for Bridges." In *Resources for Peacemaking in Muslim-Christian Relations: Contributions from the Conflict Transformation Project*. Edited by J. Dudley Woodberry and Robin Basselin, vii–ix. Pasadena, CA: Fuller Seminary Press.

2006b "The Palestinian-Israeli Question: Reflections of a Guest of the Participants." In *Resources for Peacemaking in Muslim-Christian Relations: Contributions from the Conflict Transformation Project*. Edited by J. Dudley Woodberry and Robin Basselin, 3–5. Pasadena, CA: Fuller Seminary Press.

2006c *Resources for Peacemaking in Muslim-Christian Relations: Contributions from the Conflict Transformation Project*. Edited by J. Dudley Woodberry and Robin Basselin. Pasadena, CA: Fuller Seminary Press.

2006d "To the Muslim I Became A Muslim?" In *Contextualization and Syncretism: Navigating Cultural Currents*. Edited by Gailyn van Rheenen, 143–157. *Evangelical Missiological Society* Series, no. 13. Pasadena, CA: William Carey Library; reprinted in *International Journal of Frontier Missiology* 24, no. 1 (January–March 2007): 23–28; reprinted in *Intensive Study of Integrated Global History and Theology (INSIGHT) Module 3 Reader*, 7th edition. Pasadena, CA: United States Center for World Mission (2007).

2007a "Can We Dialogue with Islam?" *Christianity Today* 51, no. 2 (February): 108–9; *Christianity Today* [Online]. Posted on January 31, 2007. Available at http://www.christianitytoday.com/ct/2007/february/26.108.html.

2007b "Foreword." In *A Worldview Approach to Ministry Among Muslim Women*. Edited by Cynthia A. Strong and Meg Page, xi. Pasadena, CA: William Carey Library.

2007c "The Great Purpose, Crossing Boundaries: Reflections on the Life of the School of Intercultural Studies and How One of its Students has Fulfilled Fuller's Statement of Purpose." *Fuller Focus* 15, no. 3 (Fall): 15–17.

2007d "Islam." In *Encyclopedia of Missions and Missionaries*. Edited by Jonathan Bonk, 202–206. Religion and Society Series, vol. 9. New York: Routledge; reprinted by New York: Berkshire Publishing Group (2010).

2007e "The Peacemaking Process: A Call to Evangelicals to Respond to a Significant Muslim Overture." *Christianity Today* [Online]. Posted on October 25. Available at http://www.christianitytoday.com/ct/2007/octoberweb-only/143-42.0.html.

2007f "Why Muslims Follow Jesus." With Russell G. Shubin and G. Marks. *Christianity Today* 51, no. 10 (October): 80–85; *Christianity Today* [Online]. Posted on October 24, 2007. Available at http://www.christianitytoday.com/ct/2007/october/42.80.html.

2008a *From Seed to Fruit: Global Trends, Fruitful Practices, and Emerging Issues among Muslims*. Editor. Pasadena, CA: William Carey Library; revised and enlarged second edition (2011); Portuguese trans., *Da Semente ao Fruto*, 2011.

2008b "Introduction to Part III: Spiritual Power." In *Paradigm Shifts in Christian Cultures: Insights from Anthropology, Communication, and Spiritual Power.* Edited by J. D. Woodberry, C. E. Van Engen, and D. Whiteman, 87–89. Maryknoll, NY: Orbis.

2008c "Islam." In *Global Dictionary of Theology*. Edited by W. A. Dyrness and V. Karkkainen with associate editors J. F. Martinez and S. Chan, 425–431. Downers Grove, IL: IVP Academic.

2008d *Paradigm Shifts in Christian Cultures: Insights from Anthropology, Communication, and Spiritual Power.* Edited with Charles E. Van Engen and Darrell Whiteman. Maryknoll, NY: Orbis.

2008e "Power and Blessing: Keys for Relevance to a Religion as Lived." In *Paradigm Shifts in Christian Cultures: Insights from Anthropology, Communication, and Spiritual Power.* Edited by J. D. Woodberry, C. E. Van Engen, and D. Whiteman, 98–105. Maryknoll, NY: Orbis.

2009a "A Christian Response to Chapters on Interfaith Dialogue." In *Peace-Building By, Between, and Beyond Muslims and Evangelical Christians.* Edited by Mohammed Abu-Nimer and David Augsburger, 203–211. Lanham, MD: Lexington Books.

2009b "Comparative Witness: Christian Mission and Islamic *Da'wah*." *The Review of Faith and International Affairs* 7, no. 1 (Spring): 67–72.

2009c "Toward Mutual Respectful Witness." In *Peace-Building By, Between, and Beyond Muslims and Evangelical Christians.* Edited by Mohammed Abu-Nimer and David Augsburger, 171–177. Lanham, MD: Lexington Books; reprinted in *Muslim-Christian Conversations for Peace: A Manual for Effective Interfaith Dialogue*. Edited by Fuller Theological Seminary and Salam Institute of Peace and Justice, 30–35. Pasadena, CA: Fuller Theological Seminary, n.d.

2010a "Reflections on Christian-Muslim Dialogue." *Theology News and Notes* 57, no. 2 (Fall): 16–18.

2010b "When God's Kingdom Grows Like Yeast: Frequently-Asked Questions about Jesus Movements within Muslim Communities." With John J. Travis. *Mission Frontiers* 32, no. 4 (July–August): 24–30; *Mission Frontiers* [Online]. Posted on July 1, 2010. Available at http://www.missionfrontiers.org/issue/article/when-gods-kingdom-grows-like-yeast.

2011a "Afghanistan." In *Oxford Encyclopedia of South Asian Christianity*. 2 vols. Edited by Roger E. Hedlund, s.v. Oxford, New Delhi: Oxford University Press.

2011b "Flames of Love: How a Terrorist Attack Reshaped Efforts to Reach Muslims." *Christianity Today* 55, no. 9 (September): 32–36.

2011c "Foreword." In *Jesus and the Incarnation: Reflections of Christians from Islamic Contexts*. Edited by David Emmanuel Singh, vii–x. Oxford: Regnum Books International.

2011d "Foreword." In *Teatime in Mogadishu: My Journey as a Peace Ambassador in the World of Islam*. By Ahmed Ali Haile, as told to David W. Shenk, 9–10. Harrisonburg, VA: Herald Press.

2011e "The Fullness of Time for Muslims." In *A Man of Passionate Reflection: A* Festschrift *honoring Jerald Whitehouse*. Edited by Bruce L. Bauer, 47–52. Berrien Springs, MI: Andrews University.

2011f "Muslim Missions: Then and Now." *Christianity Today*. Posted on September 8. Online at http://www.christianitytoday.com/ct/2011/september/muslim-missions.html.

2011g "Muslim Spirituality." In *Dictionary of Christian Spirituality*. Edited by Glen G. Scorgie, 629–630. Grand Rapids, MI: Zondervan.

2011h Review: *Dreaming in Christianity and Islam: Culture, Conflict, and Creativity*, edited by Kelly Bulkeley, Kate Adams, and Patricia M. Davis. New Brunswick, NJ: Rutgers University Press, 2009. In *International Bulletin of Missionary Research* 35, no. 1 (January): 53.

2011i Review: *The Price of Freedom Denied: Religious Persecution and Conflict in the Twenty-first Century*, by Brian J. Grim and Roger Finke. Cambridge: Cambridge University Press, 2011. In *International Bulletin of Missionary Research* 35, no. 4 (October): 227.

2011j "Sufism." In *Dictionary of Christian Spirituality*. Edited by Glen G. Scorgie, 775–76. Grand Rapids, MI: Zondervan.

Forthcoming

From Seed to Fruit: Global Trends, Fruitful Practices, and Emerging Issues among Muslims. Editor. Korean, Spanish trans.

"Fruitfulness from the Perspective of the Fruit and the Farmer." In *Longing for Community: Church,* Ummah, *or Somewhere in Between?* Edited by D. Greenlee with associate editors B. Fish, et al. Pasadena, CA: William Carey Library.

"Missions in the Muslim World: A Decade After 9/11." *Asian Society of Missiology.*

"Muslim Responses to Plurality in the Last 100 Years." In *Christianity and Religious Plurality in Historical and Global Perspective.* Edited by Wilbert Shenk and Rick Plantinga.

Longing for Community: Church, Ummah, *or Somewhere in Between?* Edited by D. Greenlee with associate editors B. Fish, T. Green, M. McVicker, N. Ravelo-Hoerson, F. Saidi, and J. D. Woodberry. Pasadena, CA: William Carey Library.

Selected Bibliography

This selected bibliography will serve as a convenience for those who intend to further explore the ideas and arguments presented in this Festschrift. This list does not include all the sources cited or consulted in the book. Please refer to the footnotes in the chapters for complete citations of works consulted/cited.

Accad, Martin. "Corruption and/or Misinterpretation of the Bible: The Story of the Islamic Usage of Taḥrīf." *The Near East School of Theology Theological Review* 24, no. 2 (2003).

———. "The Gospels in the Muslim Discourse of the Ninth to the Fourteenth Century: An Exegetical Inventorial Table (Parts I–IV)." *Islam and Christian-Muslim Relations* 14, no. 1 (2003).

———. "The Interpretation of John 20:17 in Muslim-Christian Dialogue (8th–14th Centuries): The Ultimate Proof-Text." In *Christians at the Heart of Islamic Rule*, by ed. David Thomas, 199–214. Leiden: Brill, 2003.

Adeney, Miriam. *Daughters of Islam: Building Bridges with Muslim Women.* Downers Grove, IL: InterVarsity, 2002.

Ahmed, S. Akbar. "Women and the Household in Baluchistan and Frontier Society." In *Family and Gender in Pakistan*, edited by Hastings Donnan and Frits Seller, 64–87. New Delhi: Hindustan, 1997.

al-Ashqar, Umar Sulaiman. *The World of the Jinn and Devils.* Boulder, CO: Al-Basheer, 1998.

al-Hudaybi, Hasan. *Duᶜat la Qudat* [Summoners, Not Judges]. Cairo: Dār al-Tabaᶜa wa-l-Nashr al-Islamiyya, 1977.

Ali, Ayaan Hirsi. *The Caged Virgin: An Emancipation Proclamation for Women and Islam.* New York: Free Press, 2006.

———. *Infidel.* New York: Free Press, 2007.

Allard, Michel. *Le problème des attributs divins dans la doctrine d'al-Ashᶜarī et de ses premiers grands disciples.* Beirut: Imprimerie Catholique, 1965.

Allen, James De Vere. *Swahili Origins.* Athens, OH: Ohio University Press, 1993.

Ameen, Abu'l-Mundhir Khaleel ibn Ibrahim. *The Jinn and Human Sickness: Remedies in the Light of the Qur'an and Sunnah.* 1st. Translated by Nasiruddin Al-Kattab. Riyadh: Darussalam, 2005.

Anderson, J. N. D. *Islam in the Modern World.* Leicester: Apollos, 1990.

Anderson, John D. C. "The Missionary Approach to Islam: Christian or 'Cultic'?" *Missiology: An International Review* 4, no. 3 (July 1976): 258–99.

Andræ, Tor. *Mohammed: The Man and His Faith.* Translated by T. Menzel. New York: Dover, 2000 [1936].

Arkoun, Mohammed. *Rethinking Islam: Common Questions, Uncommon Answers.* Edited by Robert D. Lee. Boulder, CO: Westview, 1994.

Aslan, Reza. *No god but God: The Origins, Evolution, and Future of Islam.* New York: Random House, 2005.

Bailey, Kenneth E. *Finding the Lost: Cultural Keys to Luke 15.* St. Louis: Concordia, 1989.

Bailey, Kenneth E., and Harvey Staal. "The Arabic Versions of the Bible: Reflections on Their History and Significance." *Reformed Review* 36 (1982): 3–11.

Barazangi, Nimat Hafez. *Woman's Identity and the Qur'an: A New Reading.* Gainesville: University Press of Florida, 2004.

Barlas, Asma. *"Believing Women" in Islam: Unreading Patriarchal Interpretations of the Qur'an.* Austin: University of Texas Press, 2002.

Bartlett, John R. "From Edomites to Nabataeans: A Study in Continuity." *Palestine Exploration Quarterly* 111 (1979): 53–66.

Bawer, Bruce. *While Europe Slept: How Radical Islam Is Destroying the West From Within.* New York: Random House, 2006.

Baylor Institute for Studies of Religion. *American Piety in the 21st Century: New Insights to the Depths and Complexity of Religion in the U.S.* Waco, TX: Baylor University, 2006.

Beeston, Alfred F. "Background Topics." In *Arabic Literature to the End of the Ummayad Period* edited by A. F. Beeston, T. M. Johnstone, R. B. Serjeant and G. R. Smith, 1–22. Cambridge: Cambridge University Press, 1983.

Bellamy, James A. "The Arabic Alphabet." In *The Origins of Writing*, edited by W. M. Senner, 91–102. Lincoln: University of Nebraska Press, 1990.

Berlinski, Claire. *Menace in Europe: Why the Continent's Crisis Is America's Too.* New York: Three Rivers, 2006.

Bhajjan, S. V. "Identifying Barriers in the Church's Reception of Muslim Converts." *The Bulletin of Christian Institutes of Islamic Studies* 3, no. 3 (1982): 92–101.

Bilal Phillips, Abu Ameenah. *The Exorcist Tradition in Islam.* Shariah, UAE: Dar el Fatah, 1997.

Boddy, Janice Patricia. *Wombs and Alien Spirits: Women, Men, and the Zār Cult in Northern Sudan.* Madison: University of Wisconsin Press, 1989.

Bodman, Herbert L., and Nayereh Esfahlani Tohid, eds. *Muslim Societies: Diversity Within Unity.* Boulder, CO: Lynne Rienner, 1998.

Brock, Sebastian P., and Susan Ashbrook Harvey. *Holy Women of the Syrian Orient.* Vol. 13. Los Angeles: University of California Press, 1998.

Brown, Rick. "Who Is 'Allah'?" *International Journal of Frontier Missions* 23, no. 2 (2006): 79–82.

Burnett, Joel S. *A Reassessment of Biblical Elohim.* Atlanta: Society of Biblical Literature, 2001.

Caner, Ergun Mehmet, and Emir Fethi Cane. *Unveiling Islam: An Insider's Look at Muslim Life and Beliefs.* Grand Rapids: Kregel, 2002.

Caplan, Patricia. *African Voices, African Lives: Personal Narratives from a Swahili Village.* London: Routledge, 1997.

Caspar, Robert. *Traité de théologie musulmane.* Rome: Pontificio Istituto di Studi Arabi e d'Islamistica, 1987.

Cate, Mary Ann, and Karol Downey, eds. *From Fear to Faith: Muslim and Christian Women.* Pasadena: William Carey Library, 2002.

Chapman, Colin. "Second Thoughts about the Ishmael Theme." *Seedbed* 4, no. 4 (1989).

———. *Cross and Crescent: Responding to the Challenge of Islam.* Leicester: InterVarsity, 1995.

Charles Herbermann, ed. *Catholic Encyclopedia.* New York: Robert Appleton, 1913.

Cox, Bob. "The Etymology of the Word 'Allah.'" *Seedbed* 20, no. 2 (2006): 14–17.

Cragg, Kenneth. *The Arab Christian: A History in the Middle East.* Louisville: Westminster John Knox, 1991.

Crapanzano, Vincent. "Mohammed and Dawia: Possession in Morocco." In *Case Studies in Spirit Possession*, edited by V. Crapanzano and V. Garrisson, 141–76. New York: John Wiley and Sons, 1977.

———. *The Hamadsha: A Study in Moroccan Ethnopsychiatry.* Berkeley: University of California Press, 1973.

Cross, Frank M. "Geshem the Arabian, Enemy of Nehemiah." *The Biblical Archaeologist* 18, no. 2 (1955).

Culver, Jonathan. "The Ishmael Promises: A Bridge for Mutual Respect." In *Muslim and Christian Reflections on Peace: Divine and Human Dimensions*, by J. Dudley Woodberry, Osman Zümrüt and Mustafa Kö, 67–80. Lanham, MD: University Press of America, 2005.

———. "The Ishmael Promise and Contextualization among Muslims." *International Journal of Frontier Missions* 17, no. 1 (January–March 2000): 61–70.

———. "The Ishmael Promises in the Light of God's Mission: Christian and Muslim Reflections." PhD diss., Fuller Theological Seminary, 2001.

Dever, W. G. *Did God Have a Wife? Archaeology and Folk Religion in Ancient Israel.* Grand Rapids: Eerdmans, 205.

Dickason, C. Fred. *Demon Possession and the Christian.* Westchester, IL: Crossway, 1987.

Donaldson, Terence L. *Paul and the Gentiles: Remapping the Apostle's Convictional World.* Minneapolis: Fortress, 1997.

Dumbrell, William J. "The Tell El-Maskhuta Bowls and the 'Kingdom' of Qedar in the Persian Period." *Bulletin of the American Schools of Oriental Research* 203 (1971).

Eisenstein, Judah David, and J. F. McLaughlin. "Names of God." In *The Jewish Encyclopedia*, edited by I. Singer and C. Adler. New York: Funk and Wagnalls, 1901–1906.

El Fadl, Khaled M. Abou. "The Ugly Modern and the Modern Ugly." In *Progressive Muslims: On Gender, Justice, and Pluralism*, edited by Omid Safi, 33–77. Oxford: Oneworld, 2003.

———. *The Great Theft: Wrestling Islam from the Extremists.* New York: HarperCollins, 2005.

Esposito, John L. *The Islamic Threat: Myth or Reality?* Oxford: Oxford University Press, 1992.

———. *Unholy War: Terror in the Name of Islam.* New York: Oxford University Press, 2002.

Esposito, John L., and Dalia Mogahed. *Who Speaks for Islam? What a Billion Muslims Really Think.* New York: Gallup, 2007.

Esposito, John, and Natana J. Delong-Bas. *Women in Muslim Family Law.* New York: Syracuse University Press, 1982.

Ess, Joseph Van. *Theologie und gesellschaft im 2. und 3. jahrhundert Hidschra,* vol. 4. Berlin: Walter de Gruyter, 1991–1997.

Forster, Charles. "Is Isaac Without Ishmael Complete? A Nineteenth-Century Debate Re-visited." *Islam and Christian-Muslim Relations* 2, no. 1 (1991): 42–55.

Foster, George. *Traditional Societies and Technological Change.* 2nd. New York: Harper & Row, 1973.

Frank, Richard. *Beings and Their Attributes: The Teaching of the Basrian School of the Muᶜtazila in the Classical Period.* Albany: State University of New York Press, 1978.

———. "Al-Maᶜnā: Some Reflections on the Technical Meanings of the Term in the Kalām and Its Use in the Physics of Muᶜammar." *Journal of the American Oriental Society* 87 (1967): 248–59.

———. "The Ash^c arite Ontology: I Primary Entities." In *Arabic Sciences and Philosophy*, vol. 9, 163–231. Cambridge: Cambridge University Press, 1999.

Friedrich, Gerhard, and Gerhard Kittel. *Theological Dictionary of the New Testament.* Translated by Geoffrey W. Bromiley. Grand Rapids: Eerdmans, 1966.

Frobenius, Leo. *The Voice of Africa.* Translated by R. Blind. 2 vols. London: Hutchinson, 1913.

Froelich, Jean-Claude. *Les Musulmans d'Afrique Noire.* Paris: Editions l'Orante, 1964.

Fuller, Thomas. "Malaysian Court Refuses to Recognize Muslim's Conversion to Christianity." *New York Times.* May 30, 2007. http://www.iht.com/articles/2007/05/30/news/malaysia.php.

Garrison, David. *Church Planting Movements: How God is Redeeming a Lost World.* Virginia: WIGTake, 2004.

Gerges, Fawaz A. *The Far Enemy: Why Jihad Went Global.* Cambridge: Cambridge University Press, 2005.

———. *Journey of the Jihadist: Inside Muslim Militancy.* Orlando: Harcourt, 2006.

Gibson, Margaret Dunlop. *An Arabic Version of the Acts of the Apostles and the Seven Catholic Epistles: With a Treatise on the Triune Nature of God.* London: Clay and Sons, 1899.

Gilliland, Dean S. "Religious Change among the Hausa, 1000–1800: A Hermeneutic of the Kano Chronicle." *Journal of Asian and African Studies* 14, no. 3 (July 1979): 245ff.

———. *African Religion Meets Islam: Religious Change in Northern Nigeria.* Lanham, MD: University Press of America, 1986.

Gimaret, Daniel. *La doctrine d'al-Ash^c arī.* Paris: Cerf, 1990.

Goldziher, Ignaz. *Introduction to Islamic Theology and Law.* Translated by Andras Hamori and Ruth Hamori. Princeton: Princeton University Press, 1981 [1910].

Graf, David. "Arabia During Achaemenid Times." In *Achaemenid History IV: Centre and Periphery*, by H. Sancisi-Weerdenburg and A. Kuhrt, 139–40. Leiden: Brill, 1990.

Graf, Georg. *Die Christlich-arabische literatur bis zur fränkischen zeit (ende des 11. jahrhunderts): Eine literarhistorische skizz.* Freiburg im Breisgau: Hercer, 1905.

Gramigna, Agostino. "Algeria: Com'è pericoloso oggi essere cristiani a Oran [How Difficult It is to Be a Christian in Oran]." *Corriere della sera*, January 17, 2007: 51–56.

———. "Difficile essere cristiani in Algeria." *Corriere della sera.* 2007. http://video.corriere.it/media/35df5110-a615-11db-bf0d-0003ba99c53b.

Grant, Michael. *The Roman Emperors: A Biographical Guide to the Rulers of Imperial Rome, 31 BC–AD 476.* New York: Scribner's, 1985.

Greenberg, Joseph H. *The Influence of Islam on a Sudanese Religion.* Seattle: University of Washington Press, 1946.

Greenlee, David H. "Coming to Faith in Christ: Highlights from Recent Research." *Missionalia* 34, no. 1 (2006): 46–61.

———. *From the Straight Path to the Narrow Way: Journeys of Faith.* Downers Grove, IL: InterVarsity Press, 2006.

———. *One Cross, One Way, Many Journeys: Thinking Again about Conversion.* Tyrone, GA: Authentic, 2007.

———. "New Faith, Renewed Identity: How Some Muslims Are Becoming Followers of Jesus." In *Witnessing to Christ in a Pluralistic World*, edited by Pachuau Lalsangkima and Knud Jørgensen, 139–48. Oxford: Regnum Books, 2011.

Greeson, Kevin. *The Camel: How Muslims Are Coming to Faith in Christ!* Bangalore: WIGTake Resources, 2007.

Griffith, Sydney H. "The Gospel in Arabic." *Oriens Cristianus*, 1985: 126–67.

Grohmann, Adolf. *Arabische paläographie II: Das schriftwesen und die lapidarschrift.* Vienna: Hermann Böhlaus Nochfolger, 1971.

Grudem, Wayne. *Systematic Theology: An Introduction to Biblical Doctrine.* Grand Rapids: Zondervan, 1994.

Gruendler, Beatrice. *The Development of the Arabic Scripts: From the Nabatean Era to the First Islamic Century according to Dated Texts.* Atlanta: Scholars, 1993.

Guillaume, Alfred, and Muhammad Ibn Ishaq. *The Life of Muhammad: A Translation of Isḥaq's* "Sīrat Rasūl Allāh" with Introduction and Notes. New York: Oxford University Press, 2002 [1955].

Guthrie, Stan. *Missions in the Third Millennium: 21 Key Trends for the 21st Century.* Waynesboro, GA: Paternoster, 2002.

Haddad, Yvonne Yazbeck, Jane I. Smith, and Kathleen M. Moore. *Muslim Women in America: The Challenge of Islamic Identity Today.* Oxford: Oxford University Press, 2005.

Hadley, Judith M. *The Cult of Asherah in Ancient Israel and Judah: Evidence for a Hebrew Goddess.* Cambridge: Cambridge University Press, 2000.

Hallaq, Wael B. *A History of Islamic Legal Theories: An Introduction to Sunni Uṣūl al-Fiqh.* Cambridge: Cambridge University Press, 1997.

Hamid, Tawfik. *The Roots of Jihad.* Newton, PA: Top Executive Media, 2006.

———."The Development of a Jihadi's Mind." In *Current Trends in Islamic Ideology*, Vol. 5, edited by Hillel Fradkin, Husain Haqqani and Eric Brown. Washington, DC: Hudson Institute, 2007.

Hanna, Mark. *The True Path: Seven Muslims Make Their Greatest Discovery.* Colorado Springs: International Doorways, 1975.

Harding, G. Lankester. *An Index and Concordance of Pre-Islamic Names and Inscriptions.* Toronto: University of Toronto Press, 1971.

Hassan, Riffat. "Equal before Allah: Woman-Man Equality in the Islamic Tradition." *Harvard Divinity Bulletin* 17 (January–May 1987 1987): 2–4.

———. "Challenging the Stereotypes of Fundamentalism: An Islamic Feminist Perspective." *The Muslim World*, Spring 2001: 55–70.

Hefner, Robert W. "Of Faith and Commitment: Christian Conversion in Muslim Java." In *Conversion to Christianity: Historical and Anthropological Perspectives on a Great Transformation*, edited by Robert W. Hefner, 99–125. Berkeley: University of California Press, 1993.

Hengel, Martin, and Anna Maria Schwemer. *Paul Between Damascus and Antioch: The Unknown Years.* Translated by John Bowden. Louisville: Westminster John Knox, 1997.

Heusch, Luc de. *Why Marry Her? Society and Symbolic Structures.* Cambridge: Cambridge University Press, 1981.

Hick, John, and Brian Hebblethwaite, eds. *Christianity and Other Religions: Selected Readings.* Philadelphia: Fortress, 1980.

Hiebert, Paul G. "The Flaw of the Excluded Middle." *Missiology* 10, no. 1 (1982): 35–47.

Hiebert, Paul G., Daniel Shaw, and Tite Tiénou. *Understanding Folk Religion: A Christian Response to Popular Beliefs and Practices.* Grand Rapids: Baker Books, 1999.

Higgins, Kevin. "Acts 15 and Insider Movements among Muslims: Questions, Process, and Conclusions." *International Journal of Frontier Missiology* 2, no. 1 (2007).

Hikmat Kachouh, "Sinai Ar. N.F. Parchment 8 and 28: Its Contribution to Textual Criticism of the Gospel of Luke." *Novum Testamentum* 50/1 (2008): 28–57.

Hughes, Thomas Patrick. *A Dictionary of Islam.* New Delhi: Asian Educational Services, 2001 [1885].

Huntington, Samuel P. *The Clash of Civilizations and the Remaking of World Order.* New York: Touchstone, 1996.

Hurgronje, Christiaan Snouck. *The Achehnese.* Vol. 2. Leiden: Brill, 1906.

Janzen, John. "Drums of Affliction: Real Phenomenon or Scholarly Chimaera?" In *Religion in Africa: Experience and Expression*, edited by Thomas Blakely, Walter van Beek and Dennis L. Thomson, 161–81. London: James Currey, 1994.

Jeffery, Arthur. *The Foreign Vocabulary of the Qur'an.* Baroda, India: Oriental Institute, 1938.

Jennings, George J. "Psychocultural Study in Missiology: Middle Eastern Insecurity." *Missiology* 15, no. 1 (January 1987): 91–111.

Jensen, Adolf. *Myth and Cult among Primitive Peoples.* Chicago: University of Chicago Press, 1963.

Johnston, David L. "A Turn in the Epistemology and Hermeneutics of Twentieth-Century *Uṣūl al-Fiqh.*" *Islamic Law and Society* 11, no. 2 (2004): 233–82.

———. "Hassan al-Hudaybi and the Muslim Brotherhood: Can Islamic Fundamentalism Eschew the Islamic State?" *Comparative Islamic Studies* 3, no. 1 (June 2007): 39–56.

———. "*Maqāsid al-Sharī'a*: Epistemology and Hermeneutics of Muslim Theologies of Human Rights." *Die Welt des Islams* 47, no. 2 (2007): 149–87.

Johnstone, Patrick. *Projected Growth of Islam.* London: Paternoster, 2001.

Joseph, Suad. *Encyclopedia of Women and Islamic Cultures*. 6 vols. Leiden: Brill Academic, 2003–2008.

Kachouh, Hikmat. *Arabic Gospels: A Classification, Description, and Textual Examination of the Arabic Gospel MSS of a Continuous Text.* Birmingham: University of Birmingham, 2007.

Kasem, Abul. *Who Authored the Qur'an?* 2005. http://www.islam-watch.org/AbulKasem/WhoAuthoredQuran/who_authored_the_quran.htm.

Kennedy, John G. "Nubian Zar Ceremonies as Psychotherapy." *Human Organization* 26 (1967): 185–89.

Khalil, Mohammad Hassan, and Mucahit Bilici. "Conversion Out of Islam: A Study of Conversion Narratives of Former Muslims." *The Muslim World* 97, no. 1 (January 2007): 111–24.

Kim, Seyoon. *Paul and the New Perspective: Second Thoughts on the Origin of Paul's Gospel.* Grand Rapids: Eerdmans, 2002.

Kitchen, K. A. *Documentation for Ancient Arabia, Part I: Chronological Framework and Historical Sources.* Liverpool: Liverpool University Press, 1994.

Knauf, Ernst. *Ismael: Untersuchungen zur Geschichte Palästinas und Nordarabiens Im 1. Jahrtausend V. Chr (Ishmael: Investigations on the History of Palestine and North Arabia in the First Millennium B.C.).* Wiesbaden: Harrassowitz, 1985.

———. "Nabataean Origins." In *Arabian Studies in Memory of Mohamed Ghul: Symposium at Yarmuk University December 8–11, 1984*, edited by Moawiyah Ibrahim, 56–61. Wiesbaden: Harrassowitz, 1989.

Kraft, Charles. *Deep Wounds, Deep Healing: Discovering the Vital Link between Spiritual Warfare and Inner Healing.* Ann Arbor, MI: Vine, 1993.

———. "What Kind of Encounters Do We Need in Our Christian Witness?" *Evangelical Missions Quarterly* 27, no. 3 (1991): 258–65.

———. *SWM/SIS at Forty: A Participant/Observer's View of Our History.* Pasadena: William Carey Library, 2005.

Kurzman, Charles. *Modernist Islam, 1840–1940: A Source-Book.* New York: Oxford University Press, 2002.

Langfeldt, John A. "Recently Discovered Early Christian Monuments in Northeastern Arabia." *Arabian Archaelogy and Epigraphy* 5, no. 1 (1994): 32–60.

Laqueur, Walter. *The Last Days of Europe: Epitaph for an Old Continent.* New York: St. Martin's, 2007.

Larson, Warren F. *Islamic Ideology and Fundamentalism in Pakistan.* Lanham, MD: University Press of America, 1998.

Lewis, Bernard. *Crisis of Islam: Holy War and Unholy Terror.* New York: Random House, 2004.

Lewis, I. M. "Islam and Traditional Belief and Ritual." In *Islam in Tropical Africa*, edited by I. M. Lewis, 58–75. Oxford: Oxford University Press, 1959.

———. *Ecstatic Religion: A Study of Shamanism and Spirit Possession.* 2nd. New York: Routledge, 1989.

Lewis, Rebecca. "Insider Movements: Honoring God-given Identity and Community." *International Journal of Frontier Missiology* 26, no. 1 (2009): 16–19.

Loewen, Joy. *Woman to Woman: Sharing Jesus with a Muslim Friend.* Grand Rapids: Chosen, 2010.

Love, Fran, and Jeleta Eckhart, eds. *Longing to Call Them Sisters: Ministry to Muslim Women.* Pasadena: William Carey Library, 2004.

Love, Rick. *Muslims, Magic, and the Kingdom of God.* Pasadena: William Carey Library, 2000.

Lüling, Günter. *A Challenge to Islam for Reformation: The Rediscovery and Reliable Reconstruction of a Comprehensive Pre-Islamic Christian Hymnal Hidden in the Koran under Earliest Islamic Reinterpretations.* Delhi: Motilal Banarsidass, 2003.

Luxenberg, Christoph. *Die syro-aramäische lesart des Koran: Ein beitrag zur entschlüsselung der Koransprache.* 2nd. Berlin: Verlag Hans Schiler, 2004.

———. *The Syro-Aramaic Reading of the Koran: A Contribution to the Decoding of the Language of the Koran.* Berlin: Hans Schiler, 2007.

Maalouf, Tony. *Arabs in the Shadow of Israel: The Unfolding of God's Prophetic Plan for Ishmael's Line.* Grand Rapids: Kregel, 2003.

MacDonald, D. B. "Ilāh." Vol. 3, in *The Encyclopaedia of Islam*, edited by P. J. Bearman, 1093–94. Leiden: Brill, 1999.

Macdonald, Michael C. A. "Personal Names in the Nabataean Realm." *Journal of Semitic Studies* 44, no. 2 (1999): 275.

———. "Ancient North Arabian." In *The Cambridge Encyclopedia of the World's Ancient Languages*, edited by R. D. Woodward, 488–533. Cambridge: Cambridge University Press, 2004.

———. "Reflections on the Linguistic Map of Pre-Islamic Arabia." *Arabian Archaelogy and Epigraphy* 11, no. 1 (2000): 28–79.

Mallouhi, Christine. *Miniskirts, Mothers, and Muslims: A Christian Woman in a Muslim Land.* Oxford: Monarch, 2004.

Manji, Irshad. *The Trouble with Islam Today: A Muslim's Call for Reform in Her Faith.* New York: St. Martin's, 2003.

Marsh, Charles. *Too Hard for God?* Carlisle, UK: Authentic Media, 2000.

Maslow, A. H. *Motivation and Personality.* New York: Harper & Row, 1970.

Mathijs Pelmans, ed. *Conversion after Socialism: Disruptions, Modernisms, and Technologies of Faith in the Former Soviet Union.* Oxford: Berghahn, 2010.

Maximov, Yurij. *A History of Orthodox Missions among the Muslims.* 2004. http://www.orthodoxytoday.org/articles4/MaximovMuslims.php.

McGavran, Donald A. *The Bridges of God.* London: World Dominion, 1955.

Mernissi, Fatema. *Beyond the Veil: Male-Female Dynamics in Modern Muslim Society.* Cambridge, MA: Shenkman, 1975.

———. *The Veil and the Male Elite: A Feminist Interpretation of Women's Rights in Islam.* Translated by Mary Jo Lakeland. Jackson, TN: Perseus, 1991.

———. *Scheherazade Goes West: Different Cultures, Different Harems.* New York: Washington Square, 2001.

Metuh, Emefie Ikenga. *God and Man in African Religion: A Case Study of the Igbo of Nigeria.* London: Geoffrey Chapman, 1981.

Metzger, Bruce. "Early Arabic Versions of the New Testament." In *On Language, Culture, and Religion; in honor of Eugene A. Nida*, edited by M. Black and W. A. Smalley, 157–68. The Hague: Mouton, 1974.

Miller, William McElwee. *Ten Muslims Meet Christ.* Grand Rapids: Eerdmans, 1976.

Mingana, Alphonse. *1. Timothy's Apology for Christianity. 2. The Lament of the Virgin. 3. The Martyrdom of Pilate, Woodbrooke Studies* 2. Cambridge: W. Hefer & Sons, 1928.

Mircea Eliade, ed. *The Encyclopedia of Religion.* New York: Macmillan, 1987.

Montgomery, Robert. "The Spread of Religions and Macrosocial Relations." *Sociological Analysis* 52, no. 1 (1991): 37–53.

Musk, Bill. *The Unseen Face of Islam: Sharing the Gospel with Ordinary Muslims.* Speldhurst, UK: MARC, 1989.

Nadel, S. F. *Nupe Religion.* Glencoe, IL: Free Press, 1954.

Nomani, Asra. *Standing Alone: An American Woman's Struggle for the Soul of Islam.* New York: HarperOne, 2005.

Nyamwaya, David. *African Indigenous Medicine: An Anthropological Perspective for Policy Makers and Primary Health Care Managers.* Nairobi: African Medical and Research Foundation, 1992.

Okholm, Dennis L., and Timothy R. Phillips. *Four Views on Salvation in a Pluralistic World.* Grand Rapids: Zondervan, 1996.

Owusu-Ansah, David. "Prayer, Amulets, and Healing." In *The History of Islam in Africa*, edited by Randall L. Pouwels and Nehemia Levtzion, 477–88. Athens, OH: Ohio University Press, 2000.

Palmer, H. R. "The Kano Chronicle." *Journal of the Royal Anthropological Institute of Great Britain and Ireland* 38 (1908): 58–98.

Parshall, Phil. *New Paths in Muslim Evangelism.* Grand Rapids: Baker, 1980.

———. "Danger! New Directions in Contextualization." *Evangelical Missions Quarterly* 34, no. 3 (1998).

———. *Muslim Evangelism: Contemporary Approaches to Contextualization.* Waynesboro, GA: Gabriel, 2003.

Parshall, Phil and Julie Parshall. *Lifting the Veil: The World of Muslim Women.* Waynesboro, GA: Gabriel, 2002.

Partodani, Sutarman Soediman. *Sadrach's Community and Its Contextual Roots: A Nineteenth Century Javanese Expression of Christianity.* Amsterdam: Rodopi, 1990.

Patai, Raphael. *The Hebrew Goddess*, with an introduction by Merlin Stone. New York: Ktav, 1968.

Peace, Richard. *Conversion in the New Testament: Paul and the Twelve.* Grand Rapids: Eerdmans, 1999.

Pearse, Meic. *Why the Rest Hate the West: Understanding the Roots of Global Rage.* Downers Grove, IL: InterVarsity, 2004.

Phillips, Melanie. *Londonistan: How Britain is Creating a Terror State Within.* New York: Encounter, 2006.

Pines, Shlomo. *The Jewish Christians of the Early Centuries.* Jerusalem: Central Press, 1966.

Polliack, Meira. *The Karaite Tradition of Arabic Bible Translation: A Linguistic and Exegetical Study of Karaite Translations of the Pentateuch from the Tenth and Eleventh Centuries C.E.* Leiden: Brill, 1997.

Potts, Daniel T. *The Arabian Gulf in Antiquity.* Vol. 2. Oxford: Clarendon, 1990.

Preuschen, Erwin. "Origen." In *New Schaff-Herzog Encyclopedia of Religious Knowledge*, vol. 8, edited by P. Schaff, 268–73. Grand Rapids: Baker, 1953 [1908].

Pritchard, James B. *Ancient Near Eastern Texts Relating to the Old Testament.* Princeton, NJ: Princeton University Press, 1955.

Qazz, Joseph. *The Priest and the Prophet: The Christian Priest, Waraqa ibn Nawfal's Profound Influence upon Muhammad, The Prophet of Islam.* Edited by David Bentley. Translated by Maurice Saliba. Los Angeles: Pen Publishers, 2005.

Rabinowitz, Isaac. "Aramaic Inscriptions of the Fifth Century B.C.E. From a North-Arab Shrine in Egypt." *Journal of Near Eastern Studies* 15, no. 1 (1956): 1–9.

Ramadan, Tariq. *Western Muslims and the Future of Islam.* Oxford: Oxford University Press, 2004.

———. *Radical Reform: Islamic Ethics and Liberation.* New York: Oxford Univeristy Press, 2008.

Rambo, Lewis R. *Understanding Religious Conversion.* New Haven: Yale University Press, 1993.

Ray, Benjamin. "African Shrines as Channels of Communication." In *African Spirituality: Forms, Meanings, and Expressions*, edited by Jacob K. Olupona, 26–37. New York: The Crossroad Publishing Company, 2000.

Richardson, Don. *Secrets of the Koran: Revealing Insights into Islam's Holy Book.* Ventura, CA: Regal, 2003.

Riddell, Peter G., and Peter Cotterell. *Islam in Context: Past, Present, and Future.* Grand Rapids: Baker Academic, 2003.

Roded, Ruth. *Women in Islamic Biographical Collections: From Ibn Sa'd to Who's Who.* Boulder, CO: Lynne Rienner, 1994.

Safi, Omid ed. *Progressive Muslims: On Justice, Gender, and Pluralism.* Oxford: Oneworld, 2003.

Sahas, Daniel J. *John of Damascus on Islam: The "Heresy of the Ishmaelites."* Leiden: Brill, 1972.

Sakr, Ahmed H. *Al-Jinn.* Lombard, IL: Foundation for Islamic Knowledge, 1994.

Sanneh, Lamin. *Translating the Message: The Missionary Impact on Culture.* Maryknoll, NY: Orbis, 1989.

Savignac, Antonin, and Raphaël Savignac. *Mission archéologique en Arabie.* Vol. 4. Paris: Leroux, 1914.

Schacht, Joseph. *An Introduction to Islamic Law.* Oxford: Oxford University Press, 1982.

Schnabel, Eckhard J. *Early Christian Mission: Paul and the Early Church* . Vol. 2. Downers Grove, IL: InterVarsity, 2004.

Shahid, Irfan. *Byzantium and the Arabs in the Fifth Century.* Cambridge, MA: Harvard University Press, 1989.

Sharkey, Heather J. "Arabic Anti-Missionary Treatises: Muslim Responses to Christian Evangelism in the Modern Middle East." *International Bulletin of Missionary Research* 28, no. 3 (2004): 98–104.

Shehadeh, Imad. "Do Muslims and Christians Believe in the Same God?" *Bibliotheca sacra* 161, no. 641 (2004): 14–26.

Sheikh, Bilquis. *I Dared to Call Him Father.* Lincoln, VA: Chosen, 1978.

Shore, Bradd. *Culture in Mind: Cognition, Culture, and the Problem of Meaning.* New York: Oxford University Press, 1996.

Sinclair, Daniel. *A Vision of the Possible: Pioneer Church Planting in Teams.* Waynesboro, GA: Authentic, 2006.

Soroush, Abdolkarim. *Reason, Freedom, and Democracy in Islam: Essential Writings of Abdolkarim Soroush.* Edited by Mahmoud Sadri. Translated by Mahmoud Sadri. Oxford: Oxford University Press, 2000.

Steyn, Mark. *America Alone: The End of the World as We Know It.* Washington, DC: Regnery, 2006.

Strong, Cynthia A., and Meg Page, eds. *A Worldview Approach to Ministry among Muslim Women.* Pasadena: William Carey Library, 2007.

Sultan, Wafa. *A God Who Hates: The Courageous Woman Who Inflamed the Muslim World Speaks Out Against the Evil of Islam.* New York: St. Martin's, 2009.

Sweetman, J. Windrow. *Islam and Christian Theology*, part 1, vol. 2. London: Lutterworth, 1945–1967.

Syrjänen, Seppo. *In Search of Meaning and Identity: Conversion to Christianity in Pakistani Muslim Culture.* Helsinki: Finnish Society for Missiology and Ecumenics, 1984.

Taber, Shirin. *Muslims Next Door: Uncovering Myths and Creating Friendships.* Grand Rapids: Zondervan, 2004.

Tardy, René. *Najrân: Chrétiens d'Arabie avant l'Islam.* Beirut: Dar el-Mashriq, 1999.

Taylor, Jane. *Petra and the Lost Kingdom of the Nabataeans.* London: Tauris, 2001.

Thomas, David. *The Bible in Arab Christianity.* Leiden: Brill, 2006.

Thomas, Kenneth J. "Allah in the Translation of the Bible." *International Journal of Frontier Missions* 23, no. 4 (2006): 171–74.

Tisdall, William St. Clair. *The Sources of Islam.* Edited by William Muir. Translated by William Muir. Edinburgh: Clark, 1901.

Tozer, A. W. *The Pursuit of God.* Radford, VA: Wilder, 2008.

Travis, John. "Must All Muslims Leave Islam to Follow Jesus?" *Evangelical Missions Quarterly* 34, no. 3 (1998).

———. "The C1–C6 Spectrum." *Evangelical Missions Quarterly* 34, no. 3 (1998): 411–15.

———. "Producing and Using Meaningful Translations of the Taurat, Zabur and Injil." *International Journal of Frontier Missiology* 23, no. 2 (2006): 73–77.

Travis, John, and Anna Travis. "Appropriate Approaches in Muslim Contexts." In *Appropriate Christianity*, edited by Charles Kraft, 397–414. Pasadena: William Carey Library, 2005.

Travis, John J., and J. Dudley Woodberry. "When the Gospel Grows Like Yeast: Frequently Asked Questions About Jesus Movements within Muslim Communities." *Mission Frontiers*, July-August 2010: 24–30.

Trimingham, J. Spencer. *Islam in East Africa.* London: Oxford University Press, 1964.

———. *Christianity among the Arabs in Pre-Islamic Times.* New York: Longman, 1979.

Unger, Merrill. *Biblical Demonology: A Study of Spiritual Forces at Work Today.* Grand Rapids: Kregel, 1994.

Van Sommer, Annie, and Samuel M. Zwemer. *Our Moslem Sisters: A Cry of Need from Lands of Darkness Interpreted by Those Who Heard It.* 4th. New York: Revell, 1907.

Violet, Bruno. "Ein zweisprachiges Psalmfragment aus Damascus (A Bilingual Psalm Fragment from Damascus)." *Orientalistische litteratur zeitung* 4, no. 10 (1901): 384–403.

Wadud, Amina. *Qur'an and Women: Rereading the Sacred Text from a Woman's Perspective.* New York: Oxford University Press, 1999.

Watt, W. Montgomery. *The Formative Period of Islamic Thought.* Edinburgh: Edinburgh University Press, 1973.

———. *Muhammad: Prophet and Statesman.* New York: Oxford University Press, 1974.

———. *Islamic Philosophy and Theology.* 2nd edition. Edinburgh: Edinburgh University Press, 1985.

———. "Women in the Earliest Islam." *Studia Missionalia* 40 (1991): 161.

Wierzbicka, Anna. *Emotions across Languages and Cultures: Diversity and Universals.* Cambridge: Cambridge University Press, 1999.

Wiher, Hannes. *Shame and Guilt: A Key to Cross-Cultural Ministry.* Bonn: Edition IWG, Mission Academics, Band 10, Verlag für Kultur und Wissenschaft, 2003.

Wilder, John W. "Some Reflections on Possibilities for People Movements among Muslims." *Missiology: An International Review* 5, no. 3 (1977): 302–20.

Willard, Dallas. *Renovation of the Heart: Putting on the Character of Christ.* Colorado Springs, CO: NavPress, 2002.

Willis, Avery. *Indonesian Revival: Why Two Million Came to Christ.* Pasadena: William Carey Library, 1977.

Wilson, J. Christy Sr. *Apostle to Islam: A Biography of Samuel M. Zwemer.* Grand Rapids: Baker, 1952.

Winder, R. B. "Al-Madina." In *The Encyclopaedia of Islam*, vol. 5, edited by P. J. Bearman, 999–1007. Leiden: Brill, 1999.

Winnett, Frederick V. "A Study of the Thamudic and Lihyanite Inscriptions." *Oriental Series* (University of Toronto Studies) 3 (1937): 51.

Wolfson, Harry Austryn. *The Philosophy of the Kalam.* Cambridge, MA: Harvard University Press, 1976.

Yannoulatos, Anastasios. "Growing into an Awareness of Primal World-views." In *Primal World-Views: Christian Involvement in Dialogue with Traditional Thought Forms*, edited by John B. Taylor, 72–78. Ibadan, Nigeria: Daystar Press, 1976.

Ye'Or, Bat. *The Dhimmi: Jews and Christians under Islam.* Cranbury, NJ: Fairleigh Dickinson University Press, 1985.

———. *Eurabia: The Euro-Arab Axis.* Cranbury, NJ: Fairleigh Dickinson University Press, 2005.

Zahan, Dominique. "Some Reflections on African Spirituality." In *African Spirituality: Forms, Meanings, and Expressions*, edited by Jacob K. Olupona, 3–8. New York: The Crossroad Publishing Company, 2000.

Zarinebaf-Shahr, Fariba. "Women, Law, and Imperial Justice in Ottoman Istanbul in the Late Seventeenth Century." In *Women, the Family, and Divorce Laws in Islamic History*, edited by Amira El Azhary Sonbol, 81–95. Syracuse, NY: Syracuse University Press, 1996.

Zollner, Barbara. *The Muslim Brotherhood: Hasan al-Hudaybi and Ideology.* New York: Routledge, 2011.

Zwemer, Samuel M. "Hagar and Ishmael." *The Evangelical Quarterly* 22, no. 1 (1950): 32–39.

———. *The Moslem Doctrine of God: An Essay on the Character and Attributes of Allah according to the Koran and Orthodox Tradition.* New York: American Tract Society, 1905.

———. *The Moslem World: A Quarterly Review*, Vol. 1, 1911. New York: Krause Report, 1996.

———. *The Moslem World.* New York: Board of Foreign Missions of the Presbyterian Church in the U. S. A., 1908.

Zwemer, Samuel M., and Amy Zwemer. *Moslem Women.* West Medford, MA: The Central Committee of the United Study of Foreign Missions, 1926.

Index

K

L

M

T

U

V

W

Y

Z